STUDIES ON THE CHINESE ECONOMY

General Editors: Peter Nolan, Lecturer in Economics and Politics, University of Cambridge, and Fellow and Director of Studies in Economics, Jesus College, Cambridge, England; and Dong Fureng, Professor, Chinese Academy of Social Sciences, Beijing, China

This series analyses issues in China's current economic development, and sheds light upon that process by examining China's economic history. It contains a wide range of books on the Chinese economy past and present, and includes not only studies written by leading Western authorities, but also translations of the most important works on the Chinese economy produced within China. It intends to make a major contribution towards understanding this immensely important part of the world economy.

Published titles include:

Derong Chen
CHINESE FIRMS BETWEEN HIERACHY AND MARKET

Dong Fureng
INDUSTRIALIZATION AND CHINA'S RURAL MODERNIZATION

Du Runsheng (*edited by Thomas R. Gottschang*)
REFORM AND DEVELOPMENT IN RURAL CHINA

Qimiao Fan and Peter Nolan (*editors*)
CHINA'S ECONOMIC REFORMS

Christopher Findlay, Andrew Watson and Harry X. Wu (*editors*)
RURAL ENTERPRISES IN CHINA

Hong Wang
CHINA'S EXPORTS SINCE 1979

Michael Korzec
LABOUR AND THE FAILURE OF REFORM IN CHINA

Nicholas K. Menzies
FOREST AND LAND MANAGEMENT IN IMPERIAL CHINA

Ryōshin Minami
THE ECONOMIC DEVELOPMENT OF CHINA

Yuming Sheng
INTERSECTORAL RESOURCE FLOWS AND CHINA'S ECONOMIC
DEVELOPMENT

Wang Xiaoqiang and Bai Nanfeng (*translated by Angela Knox*)
THE POVERTY OF PLENTY

Malcolm Warner
THE MANAGEMENT OF HUMAN RESOURCES IN CHINA

Tim Wright (*editor*)
THE CHINESE ECONOMY IN THE EARLY TWENTIETH CENTURY

Shujie Yao
AGRICULTURAL REFORMS AND GRAIN PRODUCTION IN CHINA

Xun-Hai Zhang
ENTERPRISE REFORMS IN A CENTRALLY PLANNED ECONOMY

Zhu Ling
RURAL REFORM AND PEASANT INCOME IN CHINA

Banking and Financial Control in Reforming Planned Economies

Haiqun Yang

First published in Great Britain 1996 by
MACMILLAN PRESS LTD
Houndmills, Basingstoke, Hampshire RG21 6XS
and London
Companies and representatives
throughout the world

A catalogue record for this book is available
from the British Library.

ISBN 0–333–64557–X

First published in the United States of America 1996 by
ST. MARTIN'S PRESS, INC.,
Scholarly and Reference Division,
175 Fifth Avenue,
New York, N.Y. 10010

ISBN 0–312–12724–3

Library of Congress Cataloging-in-Publication Data
Yang, Haiqun, 1949–
Banking and financial control in reforming planned economies /
Haiqun Yang.
p.   cm.
Includes bibliographical references and index.
ISBN 0–312–12724–3
1. Banks and banking—China.   2. Banks and banking—Government
ownership—China.   3. Finance, Public—China.   4. Economic
stabilization—China.   5. Monetary policy—China.   6. Monetary
policy—Europe, Eastern.
HG3334.Y35   1996
332.1'0951—dc20   95–14399
                                                                CIP

10   9   8   7   6   5   4   3   2   1
05   04   03   02   01   00   99   98   97   96

Printed in Great Britain by
Ipswich Boook Co Ltd, Ipswich, Suffolk

To Eastern Reformers
and Foreign Investors

Contents

Preface

This study of banking system reforms analyses the advantages and disadvantages, with particular reference to costs, of decentralising the banking systems in centrally planned economies (CPEs) that are themselves undergoing decentralisation. The work discusses the functions of the banking system during transition, the direction of reforms, how far decentralisation of banks can actually go, whether a market competitive banking system can be easily copied and whether it is possible to stabilise an economy through the banking system.

The study starts with socialist banking developments and shows that in a CPE the banking system fulfils a control function for the economy. Chapter 2 analyses the economic and financial problems faced by banks after the economic reforms. Chapter 3 comprises a theoretical and critical exposition of models of banking, monitoring and corporate control in relation to the main issues of the work. In Chapter 4 the financial disorders experienced by China following its radical reforms are examined and used to illustrate the necessity of control of and by banks in the present transition. Chapter 5 puts forward full arguments against some established theories on socialist economy and banking. With a new approach, Chapter 6 estimates systematically the demand for and supply of money in China in order to show that control is not only necessary, but possible. Finally, in Chapter 7 some policy conclusions are formulated, together with advice to foreign investors in emerging markets.

The main conclusion of the study is that liberalisation of the banking system should not be attempted as long as the industrial system is not subject to proper financial discipline. Given that the production system of a reforming CPE is decentralised, the banking system should be correspondingly controlled in terms of central bank regulation, credit planning and control, and bank supervision over the production system. Without proper control and a well-designed corporate governance structure, the economic and social costs of reform, such as inflation and/or financial disorders, will be increased. Reformers and (foreign) investors should cooperate closely in narrowing the 'control vacuum' and minimising 'disorder costs'. Even if the industrial system is well disciplined, monetary control is still necessary and important, and long-term financing by banks remains essential.

Vice President and Chief Economist China   HAIQUN YANG
ABN AMRO Bank
Address: 3308 Jing Guang Center, Hu Jia Lou, Beijing 100020, PRC
Telephone: (8610) 5012055/5019697. Fax: (8610) 5015110.

Acknowledgements

This book is based on my two degree theses. The central hypothesis of the research originated from my MPhil thesis, *China's Banking System and Its Reforms*, which was completed under the supervision of Mr M. G. Kuczynski at the University of Cambridge, where I was sent to study by the State Planning Commission of the PRC in 1987. Mr Kuczynski at Pembroke College and Dr P. Nolan at Jesus College recommended that I go on to take a Ph D degree. Mr D. Wall of Sussex University responded to my application and helped me to obtain an Overseas Research Student Award to start the course in the autumn of 1988 in Sussex, England. Shell Hong Kong Ltd kindly sponsored me to the extent of providing my living expenses and part of the tuition fees for four academic years. I transferred to the University of London in April 1989.

R. Portes, a professor at Birkbeck College and director of the Centre for Economic Policy Research, supervised my Ph D thesis, *Costs and Benefits of Decentralising a Banking System in Transition*, from beginning to end, giving much support to my general ideas and arguments, especially those in Chapter 5. Professor C. A. E. Goodhart of the London School of Economics and Politics (LSE) offered me external supervision on the research proposal and the first two chapters. Discussions with Professor D. M. Nuti at his home in Florence in the summer of 1989 and with Professor P. Wiles of the LSE in the same year gave me great encouragement for the research. Professor R. I. McKinnon of Stanford University and Dr J. Corbett of Oxford University kindly sent me their papers in support of my research. Professor C. Mayer of the City Business School also provided constructive comments on my work and discussed the banking system reforms in 1992. Professor L. Harris and Professor M. Fry helped to restructure the thesis and made many extremely valuable comments and suggestions for its improvement. Professor R. Smith made a great contribution to the econometric approach in Chapter 6. From him and Professor Harris I have learnt what the word 'gentleman' means. Useful feedback for the drafts also came from Dr D. Blake, Dr J. Coakley, Dr S. Kapur, Dr A. Timmermann, Dr H. Davis, Professor V. Grilli and Dr Bian Jiang. I also thank the many Chinese overseas students and visiting scholars with whom I had some illuminating discussions.

My research has also benefited from field studies in Eastern and Western Europe and North Africa, including Hungary (1989 and 1990), China (1990), the GDR (1989), the FRG (1989), the USSR (1989 and 1990), Poland (1989), Yugoslavia (1989), Romania (1989 and 1990),

Egypt (1990) and Algeria (1990). Some field work was also conducted in the UK. Officers of the various authorities, especially the central banks, their managers and companies and the intellectuals of the academic institutions of these countries arranged many meetings, discussions and investigations for me. At his home in Budapest in 1990 Professor Szalkai Istvan kindly acquainted me with the situation in Hungary. I thank all those I met in these countries for their friendly welcome.

My greatest debt is due to my mother, Yire Yang, my wife, Li Liu, my son, Maker Yang, the other family members and colleagues in China. All these people contributed to the strong recommendation in the examination report that my Ph D thesis should be considered for the Sayers Prize. Macmillan encouraged me to develop this thesis into a book following strong recommendations by Dr P. Nolan and Professor L. Harris. I am very grateful to the British friends who have contributed to the English editing of this work. The complete manuscript was edited by three very helpful volunteers, Mr S. Fakir, Miss P. Hurley and Dr B. E. Turner, and eventually by Macmillan's professional editors. They are Ms Anne Vickerson and Mr Keith Povey.

List of Abbreviations

ABC	Agricultural Bank of China
ACCs	The Agricultural Credit Corporations of China
ADB	Agricultural Development Bank
ADL	Autoregressive distributed lag
B	government bonds
BB	Budapest Bank of Hungary (or K&H)
BoC	Bank of China
BoK	Bank of Korea
BRJGP	Beijing People's General Machine Plant
C	Consumption
CBC	Communication Bank of China
CFBS	Consolidated National Banking System Credit Funds Balance Sheet
CITIC	China International Trust and Investment Corporation
CIB	China Investment Bank
CPC	Communist Party Committee
CPE	Centrally planned economy
CPI	Consumer price index of social commodity retail sales
CSFR	Czecho-Slovakia Federal Republic
CSY	*China Statistical Yearbook*
D	Dummy variable
DW	Durbin Walson statistics
ECM	Error correction mechanism
ED	Enterprise deposits in banks
FEAC	Foreign exchange adjustment centres
F.F.	Ramsey's RESET test using the square of the fitted values (1 d.f.)
GB	Government borrowing and overdrawing from the banking system
GB & TC	General Banking and Trust Company Ltd, Hungary
GDP	Gross domestic product
GDR	German Democratic Republic
GNP	Gross national product
HCB	Hungarian Credit Bank
Het.	LM Chi-squared test for Heterosdasticity of the residual (1 d. f.)
HFTB	Hungarian Foreign Trade Bank
I	Investments

IBC	Investment Bank of China
IECB	Import and Export Credit Bank
ICBC	Industrial and Commercial Bank of China
IG	Industrial output, including the industries of towns and the countryside
IR	Interest rate
IS-LM	A macroeconomic model showing the equilibrium of investment and savings curve and liquidity and money curve
K&H	National Commercial and Credit Bank of Hungary, or NC & CB
LDC	Less developed country
LR	Likelihood ratio test
M	Money balance
M0	Currency in circulation (cash and notes)
M1	$M0 + ED$
M2	$M1 + RD + UD$
MD	Demand for money
MoF	Ministry of Finance
MS	Money supply
NBH	National Bank of Hungary
NC & CB	National Commercial and Credit Bank, Hungary
NCFS	Consolidated National Cash Flow Statement
NFI	Fixed assets investments of the state sector part of *I*
NIC	Newly industrialised country
NMP	Net material product
Norm.	LM chi-squared test for normality of the residuals (2 d.f.)
OCB	Overseas Credit Bank of Hungary
OLS	Ordinary least squares
PBC	People's Bank of China
PCBC	People's Construction Bank of China
PICC	People's Insurance Company of China
pp	Inflation on a quarterly basis over the previous quarter
PPI	Purchasing power index
PRC	People's Republic of China
r	Real annual household deposit rates
R	Nominal household deposit rates
RC	Per capita rural consumption level, including the population of towns and the countryside; part of *C*
RCPE	Reforming centrally planned economy
RD	Rural household deposits
RNI	Real national income

SC	Serial correlation
SC	Inventories of commercial companies
SDB	State Development Bank
SDI	State Development Institute
SE	Standard error of the regression
SI	Inventories of industrial enterprises that have an independent accounting system
SOE	State owned enterprise
SPC	State Planning Commission
SPP	Social purchasing power
SSB	State Statistical Bureau of China
STAQS	Securities Trading Automatic Quotation System
t	*t* ratio
T	Taxation
TOCB	The Hungarian commercial banks as a whole
UC	Per capita urban consumption level; part of *C*
UD	Deposits of households in cities and towns
V	The velocity of money
VAR	Vector auto regression
Y	Output

Introduction

All that glisters is not gold (W. Shakespeare, 1564–1616)

This work analyses the advantages and disadvantages of decentralising the banking system in centrally planned economies that are themselves undergoing decentralisation. In doing so, it examines the functions of the banking system in the transitional period. The research covers some extremely interesting and important issues, such as the direction of reforms and how far decentralisation of the banking system can actually go. The study also considers whether a competitive market banking system could be easily copied, and whether it is possible or necessary to control the economy through the banks.

The central proposition is that financial liberalisation in the context of transition from central planning to a market economy creates problems of financial control at two levels: the supervision of enterprises by the banking system is eroded without a new system of monitoring and supervision developing endogenously; and problems that lead to macroeconomic instability can arise in the control of the financial system by the monetary authorities.

BACKGROUND

In a textbook model of a centrally planned economy (CPE), the banking system and other financial intermediaries are merely parts of an economic accounting system that is subject to national planning – they have no independence in the allocation of resources. The characteristic feature of the state bank is that it acts as a universal credit institution, carrying out a wide range of functions (with the exception of insurance) that in industrially developed Western countries are conducted by different parts of the credit system. In practice, despite some differences the banking systems in CPEs have followed this classical model, with all its inherent rigidity and its limited ability to raise funds. In the Soviet-type economy, money was supposed to be 'neutral' and 'passive'; the banking system played a derivative and supporting role and there was no independent monetary policy. Under this standard system, interest on bank loans was differentiated neither as a function of the financial position of the enterprises nor by maturity (Garvy, 1974).

1

In a decentralised market economy, financial intermediaries, particularly the banking system, play an active and important role in the allocation of resources. The financial system may determine the entry, expansion and exit of enterprises from particular economic activities. This occurs because the financial system is able to impose control and constraints on a wide range of business enterprises. Enterprises may not, for example, be able to secure loans to finance investment projects or obtain working capital if the banks are not convinced of the viability of the proposed uses of the funds. The costs and benefits of an independent financial system have been analysed from many points of view. If extreme assumptions are made the financial system can diminish in importance (as in the famous Modigliani–Miller result on corporate financial strategy, 1958), or it can become all-important (Schumpeter, 1934).[1] What is clear is that, in practice, enterprises in decentralised market economies seem to be keenly aware of the problems of corporate finance. Their responses to such problems – for example mergers, financial asset acquisitions and retention – have raised important allocational issues (Prais, 1979). Diversification of financial intermediaries together with that of their assets and liabilities reduces risks and secures the portfolio for investors (Lewis and Davis, 1987).

Among the wealthy economies, Japan and West Germany provide rather striking examples of countries that have established a strong banking system that has stimulated their growing economies. They are analysed in some detail by Goldsmith (1969), McKinnon (1973), Suzuki (1980), Corbett (1989, 1990a), Corbett and Mayer (1990) and Harm (1992a, 1992b). In both countries the banking system dominates the capital markets and direct finance is less important than in other advanced countries. Indeed this is the major reason why their capital markets remain fragmented with widely dispersed rates of return.

By introducing market mechanisms, former CPEs are being changed on both the production side and the financial side. Although changes are necessary, many economists inside and outside the CPEs, especially those in the West, underestimate the problems of transition. The period of transition is an historical stage of development in which a CPE is effectively dominated neither by the original planning mechanisms nor by sufficient and effective market mechanisms. It would be unrealistic to expect a sound market model to be realised in a short period of time, as is graphically illustrated by the problems encountered during the radical transformations in Eastern Europe. However I am among those searching for a better way of achieving this goal.

ISSUES

Much of the literature on socialist reforms in China, Eastern Europe and the West in the 1980s stressed the advantages of introducing market mechanisms in the CPEs (for example Brus and Laski, 1989). Very few of these works show a proper understanding the costs of transition, particularly the costs of decentralising the banking system. The experience of some economic reforms suggests that an economy can achieve a certain efficiency when decentralising the production system by introducing appropriate competition, profit incentives and penalties for failure. However it may be an altogether different and difficult matter to decentralise the allocation of savings and funds.

As the economy is being transformed from a so-called 'product economy' to a 'commodity economy'[2] the planning system may reposition itself from a direct to an indirect mode of production management. Decentralisation of decision making effectively leaves a gap for the financial system to fill. The reforms of the financial system in Central and Eastern Europe and China are frequently discussed. One of the main obstacles is the lack of a properly designed and well-functioning financial system. Important issues in this area relate to central banking, monetary and exchange rate policies, convertibility, political pressure on financial institutions (and in particular on banks), involuntary trade credit and arrears, and foreign indebtedness and international finance.

There are a variety of approaches to the problems of the model, such as those of disequilibrium and of shortage from the macro point of view. Of particular interest is the extent to which the costs and benefits associated with an independent financial system will affect the reforming economies, for example by increasing allocation efficiency while decreasing bureaucracy, or increasing fragility while increasing sensitivity to profitable opportunities. Here the experience of both the East and the West is worthy of research.

QUESTIONS

It is important to stress the issues relating to the control of the banking systems in CPEs and reforming centrally planned economies (RCPEs). This study considers four key questions in analysing the decentralisation of the banking system.

What are the costs and benefits of decentralising the banking system during transition?

It is crucially important for RCPEs to understand the two-way relationship between financial organisation and capital accumulation, and also between the production system and the financial system. Otherwise reform will proceed in an undesirable direction: rather than combining the merits of market and planning mechanisms it will combine the defects of the two.

If the banking system is not controlled during the transition, inflation or other financial disorders often occur. Abandoning the old form of monetary control with no substitute method of disciplining the markets in the presence of real disequilibrium may bring about economic chaos.

Although in advanced market economies the interest rate has a key role in market control, the setting up of an effective mechanism of interest rate adjustment in RCPEs is obviously complex. If the banking system is properly controlled by the monetary authority, either through administrative methods and/or by any viable economic levers, the cost of inflation and financial disorder is likely to be reduced.

Can the banking systems of market economies be easily copied?

The banking systems in market economies are varied, and each type has its problems as well as its advantages. The most successful, especially in the early stages of industrialisation, are those in which the central authorities have the highest degree of monetary control. Even if the Western models are easy to copy in a RCPE, there is still debate about which model best suits the economic conditions of the country in question.

It is not, in fact, easy to imitate a Western banking model. Competitive financial systems are thought by many Eastern peoples to serve the West very well, as individuals and as a society. However 'all that glisters is not gold'. The contention here is that constructing a competitive banking system within a RCPE will lead to financial distress and inflation unless there is tight central control.

First, there is a danger that, in a competitive decentralised system in which individual banks are chasing profits, they may end up by advancing fragile loans: in Keynesian terms, 'speculation' will prevail over 'enterprise'.

Second, inflationary forces elsewhere in the economy may be all-too-easily amplified by the actions of banks. This process may even occur with relatively high rates of interest. The monetary authorities may try to reverse the trend by raising interest rates; but in the competitive atmosphere in which banks are allowed to grow, the demand for their expansion may prevail over the higher rates of interest. If rates then rise further, inflation may still not decline, rather the likely result is the stagflation that many CPEs have experienced.

What kind of a banking system is suitable during transition?

It is not difficult to replace planning idealism by market idealism. However markets and market economies do not always perform efficiently, as recessions illustrate. Some older market economies have indeed already experienced decline. Neither do banking systems perform well when their economies are shrinking. Monobanks in CPEs are of course too centralised, but it may be necessary to think of how best to utilise their advantages while introducing reforms to overcome their disadvantages.

The argument here is that the existing basic financial framework, composed of the central bank and the specialised banks, should not necessarily be disposed of wholesale. After certain specific reforms have been applied it may help if the central authority exercises macroeconomic control and structural adjustments, at least in the early stages of transformation. The costs of modifying and regulating could be lower than those of fundamental redesigning and reorganisation.

It may be possible to have a banking system that facilitates the achievement of positive outcomes on both micro and macro levels. In particular, such a system may preferentially finance long-term investments for their social benefits, and it may have an active role in restructuring the corporate governance system in the RCPEs.

Is it possible to exercise control during transition through the banking system?

The banking systems in the CPEs did well in helping the economic authorities to supervise the production system and finance economic growth (see Chapter 1), and they were also effective in controlling inflation through credit planning. A significant effect of the reformed banking system is that the planning institutions are able to influence economic activities – via the additional financial and monetary means at their disposal – more extensively than through purely administrative means. However there is a question of how to control bank lending, given a lack of the timely and accurate information normally supplied by price and interest rate mechanisms. Even in the West, central banks control their financial institutions by various measures, both direct and indirect, traditional and modern, administrative and economic. The urgency of the situation and the relative efficiency of these methods determine which are used.

The argument here is that an RCPE can control demand and supply through the banking system and that banking reform designed with that aim in mind can facilitate the transition to economic decentralisation. It is important to emphasise the rationing of credit that can occur in the banking system: rationing is, of course, a widespread phenomenon.

Grunewald and Pollock (1985) argue that, unlike the stock market in which 'price' risk operates over a continuum, the money market is a rationing market and reacts discontinuously to risk. As a legacy of credit planning, rationing may have a positive role, enabling financial policy to manage economic development in a way that avoids crisis.

The banking system has a responsibility to stabilise the economy. As the decentralisation of the management of enterprises unfolds in the developing commodity-based economy, an ever-more-disciplined banking system can help to overcome a variety of market failures. It may also encourage investment in less profitable areas and projects, including the long-term investments desperately needed by the reforming economies, and assist in overcoming economic bottlenecks in orde cessful reforms and economic stability during the peric

The central argument of this study is that liberalisa system should not be attempted as long as the indu subject to proper financial discipline. Given that the p an RCPE is decentralised, the banking system should controlled via central bank regulation, credit control vision over the production system, including the scrut of clients and project appraisal. Without proper cont control over production borrowers and a well-desig nance structure, the economic and social costs of refc and/or financial disorders, will be higher. Even if tr_ well-disciplined, monetary control is still necessary and important, and banks' long-term financing remains essential.

It is hoped that this study will be informative, explanatory and useful to both academics and businessmen, particularly to investors. However the central thrust of the study is aimed at macroeconomic policy makers.

STRUCTURE

This study begins with an examination of socialist banking system reforms and shows that, in a CPE banking model, the banking system performs a control function for the economy. Chapter 2 assesses the recent economic problems faced by Hungarian and Chinese banks and discusses the financial effects of the banking system reforms in these countries. Chapter 3 presents the main Western financial development and banking theories, focusing on the special role of the banking system in the economy. The implication of these theories in the CPE and RCPE models is examined.

Financial upheavals experienced after radical reforms in China are discussed in Chapter 4. This account supports the need for economic control by banks and control of banks by the monetary authorities. Chapter 5 establishes this contention through theoretical analysis and by means of arguments against published theories, such as those of the 'Shortage School' (Kornai, 1980, 1982) and of Peebles (1991a, 1991b). This paves the way for a discussion, in Chapter 6, of econometric estimates of the demand for and supply of money in China, in order to consider the effectiveness of control of monetary aggregates. The modelling also supplies an econometric approach dealing with a small sample size. Finally, Chapter 7 concludes that banking control via correct policies is both necessary and possible during transition.

It is to be hoped that the arguments and conclusions presented in the study will contribute to the improvement of policy formulation in RCPEs. The main focus here are the experiences of China and Hungary, but the arguments also have a wider relevance and application to other RCPEs.

1 Socialist Banking Systems and their Reforms

> If you want to know what a pear tastes like, you should taste it
> (Chinese idiom).

This chapter presents a background to the traditional socialist banking model applied in certain selected CPEs and describes the changes they have undergone since the banking reforms. The major proposition here is that the traditional banking model was determined by the economic system and played a control function in the system.

INTRODUCTION

Centrally planned economies (CPEs) have been characterised by public ownership of the means of production, centralised bureaucratic management of the economy, a high rate of mobilised savings at the macro level, strict planning of outputs and stock at the micro level, and output-orientated planning based upon priorities. However most CPEs, for reasons of 'operational dissatisfaction' or 'performance dissatisfaction' (Brown and Neuberger, 1989), or even owing to a growing awareness of problems beyond the purely economic, have been reforming their economic systems. They have been abolishing comprehensive control hierarchies and their system of mandatory planning and centralised resource allocation. As an essential component, their banking systems have also been through a process of great change. The conventional goal of the reforms is to decentralise the 'overly centralised' banking system in order to achieve greater competition and efficiency. However there are side effects, and there remain some problems regarding the functions, in particular the control functions, of the banking systems of these economies.

Since 1917 banking systems in socialist countries have followed one of two general models. The first was the banking system of the traditional CPEs prior to the fundamental reforms of the last decade. The Gosbank system in the USSR was the most typical example, but the banking systems in the remainder of the socialist economies were essentially similar. The second model is the partially reformed banking system that

8

was created after certain fundamental economic reforms had been implemented, such as the systems in Hungary, China and former Yugoslavia.

By the winter of 1989 there were three subtypes of banking system within the partially reformed model of the RCPEs:

1. *'Planning biased systems'* were administered mainly by the planning system of the economies. East Germany, Czechoslovakia and Romania operated this model, in which the national banks continued to monopolise banking operations and the entire banking system remained under the supervision of the Ministry of Finance (MoF). Interest rates did not play a significant role in this system.

2. *'Modestly reformed systems'* incorporated some prudent but significant changes. The national banks passed some of their operational business on to other banks, and more specialised banks than had previously existed were established. The formation of commercial banks, even by private enterprises, had begun, although the financial market had not yet been developed. Nevertheless some compulsory planning targets had been rejected and market mechanisms were being introduced step by step. The USSR and Bulgaria used this model.

3. *'Market oriented systems'* had seen significant changes. A new banking system, led by the central bank, had become an important sector of the national economy. The national banks had relinquished most of their control over direct financial transactions in favour of specialised and commercial banks. The central banks had much more influence upon the other banks in the system. Indeed a growing number of banks – both commercial and specialised, plus non-bank financial intermediaries – were under the supervision of the central banks. The latter, however, were not yet independent of their respective governments. Ownership had been rearranged through increasing either autonomy or shareholding, and the banks in some of these economies had been allowed to conduct commercial banking business. However the financial markets were still in their infancy and financial mechanisms were far from perfect. Yugoslavia, Hungary, Poland and China operated this version of the partially reformed model.

Changes within the CPEs have occurred very rapidly, especially since the latter part of 1989, as almost all the Eastern European countries and the former Soviet Union have adopted one or other version of the partially reformed model. The link between the differences in the types of banking system outlined above and economic performance have not been properly established. It may be quite subtle and difficult to ascertain, either theoretically or empirically. It was once held that the degree and extent of general economic reform should be faithfully reflected in reforms of the banking system, and that economic development is commensurate with the depth of reform. In fact it is often the case that the more radical the reform, the higher the inflation. Thus evaluating desirable change in financial systems is rather complex and requires explanation in terms of the functions the banking system 'ought' to adopt.

It is important to stress the control functions of the banking systems in CPEs and RCPEs. By reviewing the typical structures and functions of the above three basic banking models and the institutional and functional changes to the banking systems in a few selected reforming countries, it can be argued that it is the changes in the control functions of a banking system that are crucial.

THE BANKING MODEL OF CPEs

Different banking models are suited to different economic environments. The CPE banking model was a product of an economic system characterised by the quantitative planning of physical allocation throughout all strata of the economy, right down to the very disaggregate levels. This model worked well in the CPE system, and the control function helped the banks to support it.

The structure of the CPE banking model

Socialist banking is subordinate to planning. However the banking system retains a very important role on a par with that of finance in economic planning.

The importance of planning to the financial system and the banking system – socialist banking was centralised

Hilferding (1910) found that monopolies and cartels introduce a degree of regulation and planning into the economy, and that this 'socialisation effected by finance capital has made it enormously easier to overcome capitalism'. He suggested a takeover of the bourgeois state and the extension of its role in planning and controlling socialised production.

Lenin (1917) noted Hilferding's findings. He analysed further the relationship between financial capital and the financial oligarchy by criticising Kautsky's definition of imperialism. He found that 'the concentration of production and capital has developed to such a high stage that it has created monopolies which play a decisive role in economic life'; and also that 'the merging of bank capital with industrial capital, and the creation, on the basis of this "financial capital", of a financial oligarch' (Lenin, 1917, p. 106). This banking system seemed to be the most convenient way for the Soviet state to implement planning. Lenin therefore ordered the Soviet government to take over the banks and structure a state banking monopoly.

The credit system – 'a powerful lever' (Marx, 1887) – was the aggregate of socialist credit institutions. It was composed of state banks, savings banks and pawnshops,[1] which were controlled and managed by the higher central organs of state power and administration. The structure and activities of the credit system were determined and guided by state plans. Centralisation was one of the abiding characteristics of the traditional banking system in the CPEs. This facilitated planning and control.

From a sectoral point of view, Soviet financial planning had a distinctly subordinate role in the overall planning process. However the key role of financial planning was that of policing the execution of non-financial plans. 'Control by the rouble', a phrase that applies primarily to banking operations but also extends to the discipline imposed by financial plans, was an elaborate and extensive system. Financial plans also played a major role in particular areas of economic management. They provided a check on the accuracy of planning in physical terms. Besides the consolidated financial plan and the state budget, the cash and credit plans of Gosbank and Stroybank and the state social insurance budget played an important part in the whole range of financial plans.[2] Thus planning in the USSR followed the procedure shown in Figure 1.1.

Figure 1.1 illustrates the total subordination of the banking system to planned economic objectives. The same arrangement occurred in China, where the system was called 'a big plan and a small budget plus a cashier' (*Da ji wei, xiao cai zheng, jia ge chu na*). Bank planning occupied a sectoral position and was a component of the overall sectoral plan, which included agricultural, industrial and other elements. It was efficient for the state to position the banks thus in order to fulfil planned targets. Planning was also a method of control, whereby banks, together with the budgetary system, were able systematically to allocate funds and supervise the utilisation of those funds. Both finance and credit are reflections of the value movement in its monetary form, a movement that is associated with the

Figure 1.1   Central planning procedure

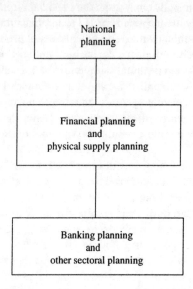

distribution of money incomes and accumulation. The banking system therefore cannot be regarded as passive in a CPE due to its important role in planning.

In fact, even in a market economy '[b]oth economic theory and historical experience demonstrate that the role of banks in either hindering or facilitating industrialisation was not as great as has been believed' (Rudolph, 1976, p. 200). The decisive factors in the industrial development of the Czech lands, as well as Austria, during the period 1880–1913 'are to be sought more in the social and political sphere and more in the "real" sectors of the economy – in the industrial, agricultural and foreign trade sectors – than in the financial sector. Combining profit maximisation and risk sharing, industrial investment was approached with great caution by banks' (ibid.)

Bauer (1919) declared: 'Only by nationalisation of the banks does society obtain the power to regulate its labour according to a plan and to distribute its resources rationally among the various branches of production, so as to adapt them to the nation's needs'. Zwass (1979) is correct in saying that 'A centralised economy requires a centralised banking system that is an integral part of the administrative apparatus and pursues no separate goals'. It should, in addition, have no self-interest over and above the national interest.

In the 1950s China followed a centralisation procedure similar to that of the Soviet Union. It took three years from 1952 to fulfil the socialist restructuring of the private financial sector. The highly centralised banking system was based on public ownership of the means of production. During the First Five-Year Plan period, the centralised system was strengthened through the implementation of three strategies. First, banks based in cross-provincial areas were removed from the system in order to unify the leadership through a vertical management hierarchy and to strengthen the management structure under the headquarters of the People's Bank of China (PBC). Second, joint venture or public–private corporate banks were merged into the PBC between January 1955 and July 1956. Thirdly, the Agricultural Bank of China was transformed into the Bureau of Rural Financial Management inside the PBC. In this way the PBC monopolised currency issuance and banking management, assuming entirely the responsibility for central and commercial banking throughout China (see Liu *et al.*, 1991).

The authority of the fiscal system over the banking system – socialist banks were controlled

Using his analysis of money and credit, Hilferding (1910) explained the increasing concentration and centralisation of capital in large corporations, the formation of cartels and trusts, the role of banks and the economic and political effects of these changes on the structure of the capitalist economy. He showed that formation of joint stock companies and the considerable increase of wealth leads to the centralisation of capital, the growth of giant corporations and eventually to cartels and trusts controlling whole industries. He stated that 'taking possession of six large Berlin banks would mean taking possession of the most important spheres of large scale industry'. He pointed to the emergence of close personal and organisational links between industrial and bank capital, which he described as 'financial capital', and analysed this as well as the general tendency towards an ever greater centralisation of capital.

Centralisation was the easiest way of implementing national planning and control. As noted above, bank planning was directly subordinate to financial planning and indirectly subordinate to national planning. Thus banking was always supervised and even directly organised by the Ministry of Finance (MoF) in the USSR and the other CPEs, where financial control was conducted mainly through budget systems. However both the banks and the MoF worked for the same planned macroeconomic targets. The planners arranged projects, the MoF appropriated the funds to implement the projects and the banking system then granted working capital to assist their implementation as well as maintaining a system of bookkeeping.

There is a material foundation for the control of banks by the budgetary system. The liability structure of the Polish banking system provides one example – at the end of 1961 no one type of bank account accounted for more than 20 per cent of total liabilities. The exceptions were the bank accounts of the state budget, which, when combined with those from the other public funds, made up 35.5 per cent of the total. Other significant sources of liabilities were the units of the so-called 'socialised economy', which were also financed by the state budget. The savings of the ordinary population (just 2.6 per cent)[3] accounted for a very small part of the total liabilities.

In the classical CPE model, state credits – which differed from bank credits – were used to plan and organise monetary contracts between the state and the general public. The socialist state participated as the debtor (the borrower) and the general public was the main creditor (the lender). Funds were gathered from the sale of government bonds and these, combined with savings bank deposits, were used by the state to finance economic, social and cultural programmes.

The principles of bank credit were as follows: (a) credits were planned in line with planned allocations; (b) credits were given by the banks directly to enterprises, being tied to specific projects of the state-owned enterprises (SOEs); (c) credits were to be repaid to the bank within a period set in accordance with the planned turnover of the enterprise's stocks; (d) credits had to be secured by collateral (some portion of working assets) belonging to the enterprises concerned, except in cases of new construction projects; (e) a charge was made for advancing credit, and the rate of interest was determined by the state. However 'interest' was no more than an accounting parameter of banks. It became accepted not as the market price of money, but as an instrument to influence banks' relations with enterprises (Zwass, 1979, p. 112).

Both long-term and short-term credit plans and the measures to ensure the implementation of those plans were drawn up, executed, analysed and supervised by the banks and the higher institutions of economic administration, such as the MoF and the State Planning Commission.

Concentration of the banking structure in the USSR

Concentration means fewer banks, commercial banking being combined with central banking and sectoral specialisation. Until the late 1950s the

Soviet system consisted of the state bank and a few specialised banks, such as Prombank (long-term transactions for industry), Selkhozbank (agriculture), Torgbank (trade) and Tzecombank (credit municipal services). It was natural to have a concentrated banking structure when the economy was so centralised.

The state bank (Gosbank) was the principal banking agency and one of the main financial organs in the USSR. It was responsible for planning and carrying out public financial transactions in the national economy, but not for transactions with foreign countries. It also dealt with the administration of capital investment funds. Again, funds allocated to ventures with foreign countries were not included. The state bank combined the functions of a central bank with those of a commercial bank, namely note issuance, commercial banking, investment, organising savings and deposits, accounting, clearing, fulfilment of the state budget and so on.

The internal structure of the state bank was organised according to specialised industrial sectors administrative levels and regions. Sectoral specialisation was even more obvious in some specialised banks, such as Stroybank in the USSR (Borodin, 1963, pp. 73, 75). Enterprises were grouped into Gosbank accounts and the bank reported about settlement and short-term credit operations. The grouping had two distinct principles of classification – by branch and by agency.[4] This made it easier for the banks to exercise financial supervision and control. The same feature could also be found in China, where the banking system was relatively diversified.

'Passive' money as a means of control

It is argued that money by no means fulfilled the same function in a CPE as in a market economy, despite certain superficial similarities. The planned financial result (profit or loss) was 'a passive reflection of the price structure and the compulsory indices' (Brus, 1972). Thus 'money is not an active instrument, influencing the movement of real factors in the production process' (ibid.) In fact it was the system that made money passive, or more precisely rendered it unnecessary for money to be active: passive money was a means of control. Money transcribed and reinforced directives and prevented enterprises from escaping specified obligations. Furthermore, all payments from one state enterprise to another had to be made by credit transfer from their accounts with the state bank. Enterprises were authorised to hold only very limited reserves of bank notes and they could not grant each other credit. There was a separate budgetary constraint on each type of expenditure (purchase of raw materials, repairs, wages and so on).

Separation of the two monetary circuits – cash and cash-convertible accounts for the payment of incomes to households on the one hand, and money used by enterprises for transactions within the state sector on the other – and the planners' previous attempts at balancing the income and expenditure of the population through wage policy and control, hid inflation in the CPEs. The implementation of planned transactions intensified the compartmentalisation of money flows, which was merely the counterpart of rationing. There was no scope for monetary policy because the quantity of money was automatically adjusted by the monetary authorities to match planned physical flows (given planned prices) with the degree of implementation. Normal monetary measures such as prices and interest rates therefore did not necessarily play a powerful regulatory role.

Banking structures following the 'planning biased model', such as existed in Czechoslovakia, were similar to those of the classic CPE model.

The control functions of the banking system mattered in CPEs

Despite the broad differences between banking systems in CPEs and those in market economies, certain banking function showed notable similarities. With regard to the essential functions of banks to satisfy simultaneously the portfolio preferences of borrowers and lenders and the cautious attitude of banks towards risk and repayment, the two systems were very similar, although they used different methods.

Control functions of CPE banking systems

The functions and rights of Gosbank were defined in the statute of the state bank of the USSR (see Zwass, 1979, pp. 140–54). Financial control was stressed in this statute, along with credit operation and payment services. 'The Gosbank was to ensure effective control by the rouble over the realisation of the national budgets' (Decree of 20 March 1931), that is, it worked as a supervisor and controller of government budgets and agency financial plans approved by the MoF. Gosbank exercised similar control over the current operating expenditures of all institutions maintained on union and republican budgets; as well as capital investment financing and certain outlays of *khozrashet* units (that is, units financed not by the state, but by themselves).

The term 'control by the rouble' was given to the surveillance Gosbank exercised over the financial activities of enterprises and other organisations in order to assure fulfilment of production and financial plans, proper use of funds and maintenance of financial discipline. It had the right to inspect all financial documents and accounting records of enterprises, to demand of directors and higher officials that certain measures be taken to improve financial operations, and to terminate or curtail credit to enterprises that failed to fulfil their obligations. There were, however, practical difficulties in implementing these rights.

The payment system could also be used as a means of supervision. All payments of taxes and other state revenues by enterprises and other organisations, such as the service industry and those of the public institutions, were made to Gosbank, which in turn credited the payments to the appropriate accounts of the all-union, republican or local budgets. The transfer of money between budgets or payments from budget accounts was likewise effected by Gosbank. Enterprises were obliged to make all payments, except payrolls and petty cash disbursement, from their Gosbank accounts. The bank maintained a record of receipts and expenditure and compiled monthly and annual reports on the execution of the union and republican budgets.

The basic functions of banks specialising in different industrial and commercial sectors were similar to those of the national bank, except for some central bank functions of the latter and the sectoral specialities of the former.[5] These features were general among CPEs, including those subscribing to the 'planning biased model'.

Structural differences between a CPE banking system and that of a typical market economy

In a typical market economy banking model, central banks are clearly separated from commercial banks and other financial intermediaries. In the CPEs, central banking and commercial banking were conducted simultaneously by the state bank, although it was not required to play as full a role in central banking as in the West. Another important difference is that socialist banks, including branches of the state bank and the specialised banks, were restricted to certain businesses or sectors while most commercial banks in Western market economies have no such restriction and can engage in wide-ranging banking business, within certain legal limits. The justification for relaxing this restriction lies in the strict legal framework and central bank supervision that operated in the West.

The dual role of the state bank in performing both central and commercial banking functions does not necessarily give rise to any fundamental problems. Istvan Hagelmayer argued that in practice the state bank does not fulfil its central banking tasks, whereas in its credit-granting activity it operates without business risk and quantitative, institutional constraint. He wrote that 'the "central banking seed" of the sole bank has not had – and cannot have – any influence on the volume of credits' (quoted in Suranyi and Antal, 1987, pp. 35–48). However it can be argued that there was no necessity for the banking system in a CPE to perform the same function as that in market economies. In a CPE the volume of credit had already been decided by planners, and risks had been reduced to the minimum.

The relationship between the banking system and the production system – socialist bankers were economic controllers

Lenin (1917) showed great interest in how German bankers controlled the production system by replacing the domination of capital with the domination of financial capital. This must surely have helped him to design the Soviet economic system. Gosbank had to plan and regulate the amount of money and credit in order to stabilise the value of the rouble. Moreover it had to supervise and control the microeconomic and financial activities of the individual economic entities and projects.

The 'secondary master' Corporate governance in the CPEs was characterised by the subjection of economic agents to different levels of administrative principals. The 'primary masters' of enterprises in the CPEs were of course the planners and those in the MoF, simply because the funds they appropriated provided the bulk of investment finance.[6] The expenditure of enterprises was effected through credits on 'budgetary' bank accounts rather than by actual transfers of funds to 'current' bank accounts. However banks should be regarded as secondary controllers or supervisors of enterprises.

Figure 1.2 shows the corporate governance structure of CPEs, which are regimes dominated by plans within the framework of a political economy. The corporate governance structure is a framework within which there are central mechanisms for the effective governance of the corporate activities. The Communist Party and the authorities controlled the production system through a series of institutions. Once the party committee had made a strategic decision and the State Planning Commission had followed with a national plan, the branches of the party and the local administrations would make specific plans and regulations to allow the planning, fiscal and banking systems at the administrative levels to implement them. The penalties and rewards to firms' leaders according to their performance would be arranged by party branches (in accordance with the party's regulations), and by the local authorities (following administrative regulations), sometimes jointly and in most cases contingently. The powerful Communist Party systems effectively guaranteed this administrative control.

Figure 1.2   The corporate governance structure of CPEs

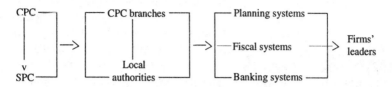

The central importance of the national bank apparatus in the socialist financial system was that it was the chief vehicle for reaching settlements between enterprises and organisations throughout the economy. It was also the only source of short-term credit for the greater part of the economy and the major source of working capital in the productive sphere (for the collective farm sector it was the only source of long-term credit).

Controller and supervisor   Accounts kept in the state bank – basically settlement, budgetary and current accounts,[7] – provided national banks with an excellent means of supervising the production system. This was not only in the case of banks' own lending projects but also in the general financing sense. Surplus-and-deficit accounts recorded the volume of funds received from the budget on the one hand, and the degree to which those funds had been utilised (usually reflected in the costs section of the accounts) on the other. Those accounts recorded the results of the economic activity of the budgetary unit in the fulfilment of its individual financial plans.

According to Kuschpeta (1978, pp. 180–2), supervision was systematically carried out by the Soviet banks whenever they extended credit, executed transfers, made funds available and received cash. This encouraged clients to improve management, minimise expenditure and maximise profitability: 'It is clear that the controlling bank has a complete right of inspection of the activity of the enterprise and is entitled to inquire into the economic and financial activities of its clients'. Banks advised firms on the best way to correct observed deviations from the plans. According to Mitelman (1967), even after the economic reform of 1965 banking control in the USSR was still very comprehensive. Banks made progress reports on the annual plans of enterprises entrusted to their care, particularly on the realisation of production, cost–price, sales, profit and profitability targets. Furthermore, banks enquired into projects for which credit was granted, into whether the supply of raw materials and other necessities conformed to the plans and whether the enterprises met their obligations to

their customers. Additional checks were carried out on financial management, organisation of production, results of investment funds, 'credit discipline', reorganisation of funds, repayment of long-term credits and
realisation of investment projects, as well as the accuracy of reports.
According to Maegd (in Kuschpeta, 1978, p. 322), the bank assured itself
that the funds had indeed been used for the stated purpose. The bank had
to prevent funds destined for repayment of investment credit from being
used to finance liquid assets.

In Poland in the 1960s the banks had the additional task of evaluating
proposed investments and could refuse finance if formal requirements
were not fulfilled and if they disapproved of projects on substantive criteria. These criteria included an assessment of whether the proposal was
economically efficient, had a definite purpose and was planned in a realistic manner.[8]

Financial control over the management of institutions and enterprises
was exercised by the Hungarian National Bank even after certain economic reforms in the late 1960s (Marer and Pall, 1971, pp. 145, 373). This
control could be exercised particularly when individual economic institutions submitted credit applications and applied for loans. The preparation
and submission of development credit applications by local councils, as
well as the system of credit-application investigation and credit granting,
were regulated by the banks. The system was rigid. It set down a strict set
of accounting and bookkeeping procedures for all economic units, with
little scope for variation, in order to provide centrally available standardised quarterly data in the form of balance sheets for all enterprises. A rigorous enterprise reporting system and a procedure for the collection of
reports by the banks guaranteed that the system worked efficiently.

Sanction imposer   Banks were also entitled to impose sanctions on SOEs
and state organisations. According to Kuschpeta (1978), the sanction
could take the form of cash, credit or clearing restrictions. Efficient firms
could be rewarded by financial privileges. 'Other controlling agencies do
not have these rights and this places the banks in a particular position'
(Kuschpeta, 1978, p. 182).

To make control and supervision more effective, according to Maegd
(in ibid., p. 323), sanctions were imposed on the grounds of (a) poor composition of working capital and inefficient conservation of 'owned' liquid
assets; (b) undisciplined payments; (c) inadequate bookkeeping and lack
of punctuality in reporting; and (d) poor execution of certain planned
tasks. A 'good' enterprise was entitled to credit without collateral for a
term of 60 days and also credit for the payment of wages for a term of 30

days, even if other debts had not been repaid on time. A 'bad' enterprise could be sanctioned by (a) raising debit interest by 20 per cent; (b) credit to supplement the means available for financing liquid assets being extended only if the higher managing agency gave a credit guarantee; and (c) an end to the extension of all other credit (with some exceptions). If the enterprise concerned had not improved within six months, the sanctions might be strengthened by (a) cessation of almost all forms of credit; and (b) foreclosure of all outstanding debts and the impounding of cash receipts in order to pay them off (ibid., p. 184).

Thus socialist bankers were controllers of the production system. They helped the state to discipline enterprises and to support and stabilise economic development. However this was only one side of the coin. Enterprises dealt more frequently with the state budgetary system than with banks. Once they had received a 'budget license' they were able to set up a bank account, and as there was no bankruptcy law to sanction financially irresponsible enterprises, bank-held information on their activities was limited to a resume extracted partly from the enterprises' own reports. Thus 'control by the rouble' was fairly difficult. Furthermore sanctions could hardly be imposed if the higher managing agency was acting to protect 'bad' firms. However this was not the fault of the banks.

The main problems of the CPE banking model

CPEs and market economies are, of course, completely different systems. Thus it is senseless to criticise CPEs for problems that arise when part of their foundation is marketised. However it is worth identifying the main problems that forced CPEs to change in this way.

General problems of the system

The planning system of CPEs was highly centralised and organised around a scheme of vertical decision making. While it could serve to overcome problems of coordination between broad sectors of the economy and regulate aggregate consumption in line with supply availability, it suffered from inbuilt organisational problems.

The disadvantages of the system were (a) a lack of distinction between the responsibilities of the central administration and those of enterprises; (b) bureaucratic inflexibility in the management of enterprises and consequent lack of risk-taking and competition at the enterprise level; (c) neglect of price indicators through suppression of market mechanisms; (d) a lack of communication and often distortion of information between different geographical and industrial sectors of production; and (e) a lack of incentives due to the rigid principle of distributional equality, which could lead to economic inefficiency or low output.

Nuti (1988, pp. 11–13) indicates that, in the CPEs, there was both unwarrantedly high material intensity and low productivity of capital and labour, an excessively long gestation of investment projects due to too wide an investment front, and obsolete and unused capacity for various reasons. He also points to accumulating stocks of unwanted goods, waste in the consumption of necessary inputs due to excessive subsidies, the coexistence of overmanning and labour shortage, absurd biases in the quality and variety of output according to measurement units used in central targets, and so on. All these factors influenced the performance of the financial system, including the banking system, as the classical banking model moulded itself to the prevailing economic environment.

Macro-level banking problems

The state bank, while central in accounting terms in the distribution of credit, was effectively inoperative except through directives in the credit-granting decision process: it was all-important and yet unimportant. The economic system did not allow banks to play a more influential role in the management of assets, and funds could easily be rationed by plans and by the MoF.

The traditional banking system was managed mainly by credit-allocational plans directly from above, with the total volume and distribution of funds determined by the administration. The normal arrays of bank-control measures that work through market mechanisms – such as reserve requirements, discount facilities, the monitoring of default, risk assessment and changes in the terms of loans and deposits – were generally ignored. There were not enough indicators of either relative scarcity or relative rates of return for bankers to judge the direction of credits. Lack of information and slowness of reaction often resulted in losses.

An important problem was that there were not enough constraints on budget deficits and inflation, though the latter could be hidden or suppressed. The planners relied on printing money or adopting a policy of a high accumulation ratio. Concentrating the management of institutions and businesses in the hands of the national banks stifled competition and created bureaucratic inefficiency. Consequently, rigidity and inefficiency led to misallocation of credit.[9]

Being cashiers or tellers of the planning systems and the MoF, bankers always looked at credit indices and paid less attention to macroeconomic indicators. The heavy burden of commercial banking also meant that the national bank was unable to research macroeconomic policies.

Middle-level banking problems

Concentration of the banking system was far too intensive. Almost all credit lay in the hands of the national bank, which controlled or owned almost all the banking institutions, except those of the MoF. A large number of economic transactions were funnelled through the highly centralised agency. The statistical information system was relatively sterile and uninformative from the point of view of the economic information it imparted and the opportunities it afforded for analysis. Moreover the control function was largely limited to determining the amount of short-term credit available. It was highly circumscribed by regulations that gave little freedom of action to either the bank or its clients. In addition the bank's right to exert 'payment discipline' could become rather ineffective in practice.[10]

Micro-level banking problems

The sub-branches of the banks were managed by different administrative levels and could not exercise autonomy. The Chinese refer to 'big pots' – the problem of separating rights, interests and responsibilities between economic entities. For example employees' incomes did not differ even though their contributions were different. They also refer to 'iron bowls', the rigid management inside State-owned enterprises, where there is no risk of being sacked no matter how poorly employees perform. Thus there was insufficient incentive and discipline to promote efficient banking. All banks were administrative institutions rather than economic entities, lacking the motivation, vitality and freedom that was necessary to do their business. They had no mandate to change interest rates, and no matter how many deposits were collected they were forbidden from exceeding planned lending targets. There were few cross-bank operations, no market competition between banks and therefore no need for credit risk assessment. In addition there was little opportunity for bankers to make decisions regarding personnel.

Beyond these organisational problems, efficiency problems arose because money and investments were mainly allocated by the state budget. Bank credit accounted for a smaller proportion of credit than budget grants. The latter bore no interest charge, and therefore had little effect as a disciplinary or motivational instrument.

THE PARTIALLY REFORMED BANKING MODEL

The so-called 'partially reformed' banking systems are market oriented models, but they are not uniform. The banking systems of the former Yugoslavia and Poland incline towards Western banking models. The systems of Hungary and China are also market-oriented, but at the end of the 1980s they retained more characteristics of a planned system than the previous two economies. Yugoslavia and Hungary have been reforming their banking systems for a long period whereas the radical reform of banking in China has only been underway for about a decade. The radical Polish reform has been running since the latter part of the 1980s.

Banking system reforms in China

Financial reform in China has followed the national social and economic transition that has been unfolding since 1978, although the two are not closely related (see Chapters 3 and 4). Among the socialist economies, China is the second (after the former Yugoslavia) to have changed its mono-banking system into a system of diversified banks led by a central bank.

Changes before 1979

Since 1949, banking in the People's Republic of China (PRC) has gone through three distinct periods. The first, up to 1958, was one in which special arrangements for rural credit coexisted alongside monolithic centralisation of the economy's financial flows through the People's Bank of China (PBC). The second was the period of disruption, mainly during the Cultural Revolution, when the special arrangements for the rural sector in particular broke down into chaos. The third began with the reforms after 1978. Its main features were the reinstatement of special rural arrangements, above all through the reestablishment of the Agricultural Bank of China (ABC) in 1978; the introduction of a number of independent specialised credit agencies when the economy was opened up and decentralised; and the subdivision of the main central institution into a central bank and what amounted to a commercial banking network. Thus from 1949 to 1979 some institutions had their continuity of function disrupted by the Great Leap Forward (1958) and the Cultural Revolution (1966–76). They had become mainly rural credit institutions and thus had more specialised functions than previously though their names remained unchanged. Others were created after 1979.

Structural changes after 1978

The Third Plenary Session of the 11th Communist Party Central Committee in December 1978, which ended the Cultural Revolution, brought about fundamental changes in China's politics. Figure 1.3 shows the structure of the financial institutions prior to this key date. Figure 1.4, which depicts the framework of the *reformed* banking system after 1978, shows several significant changes. The administrative layers of the national economy were simplified by the removal of the State Economic Commission in 1987, but in the meantime the functional importance of the State Planning Commission and the institutional importance of the PBC had been strengthened.[11] To stimulate rural reforms, the Agricultural Bank of China was reestablished in December 1978. The Bank of China (BoC)

Figure 1.3 The framework of China's traditional banking system before 1979

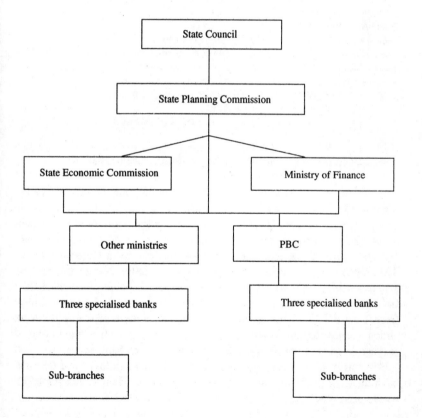

Figure 1.4   The framework of the reformed banking system after 1978

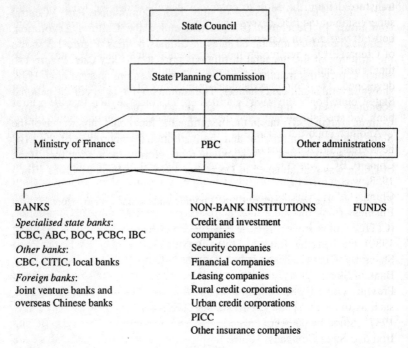

Note: Local banks were organised by local authorities, such as building trust and invesment corporations. 'Funds' are other-funds collection institutions.

was separated from the PBC in March 1979, coinciding with the establishment of the General State Foreign Exchange Bureau. The BoC became an independent bank specialising in foreign exchange business in September 1983. To collect funds abroad and conduct investment and credit business, the Investment Bank of China (IBC) was established in December 1981. The People's Construction Bank of China (PCBC) was established in January 1983, with its credit business under the control of the PBC. Industrial and commercial credit and deposit business has been transferred from the PBC to the Industrial and Commercial Bank of China (ICBC), which was established in January 1984. These five specialised banks play a major role and account for over 90 per cent of overall bank assets.

September 1983 was an important date in the modern history of China's banking. It was at this time that the State Council decided that the PBC would play the role of a central bank, with the PBC board as decision maker. The PBC has since become the leader of the Chinese banks, almost equal in stature to the MoF. Some of the banking institutions have been transferred from the MoF to come completely under the leadership and supervision of the PBC (except the PCBC, which receives supervision from both). It was also in September 1983 that the People's Insurance Company of China (PICC) became an independent non-bank financial entity. Since then, rural and urban credit cooperatives and many unit trusts have been developed. The temporary banking regulations of the PRC, issued by the State Council on 1 July 1986, clarified even further the roles that the central bank, the specialised banks and the other financial institutions should play.

Another important change is that many new financial institutions have been created in the space of only a few years. The Communication Bank of China (CBC), which had been set up in 1908 and merged with the PBC in 1958, was reestablished in July 1986, being the first shareholding bank in China. Other banking institutions were also established, such as the Business Bank of China International Trust and Investment Corporation (CITIC, China International Trust and Investment Corporation in spring 1980), the Xing Ye Bank of Fujien Province (November 1981), the Zhao Shang Bank in the Shekou industrial areas (August 1986), the Development Bank of Sheng Zhen (June 1987) and the Development Bank of Guangzhou Province (June 1988). A number of building societies were also established, such as those in Yentai City (October 1987) and Bongfu City (December 1987). Some banks were created by large companies, such as the Beijing Iron and Steel Company. Unlike the five specialised state banks, these are either shareholding or local joint companies, based in certain areas but without the restriction of regional allocation, and are developing very rapidly. The Hui Tong Urban Co-operative Bank was established in Sichuan Province in February 1985 (Tam, 1992), but it is not a private bank. A new commercial bank, Mingsheng Bank, was set up in 1995. It is a stockholding bank owned by private companies and households.

China's non-bank financial system is relatively weak; but it too is developing rapidly. Until recently there were two kinds of non-bank institution. Investment and trust companies still form one category, of which some belong to the banks while some are local. The second group consisted of financial corporates, which included the 55 000 and 4400 rural and urban credit corporates, respectively, mentioned above. However in 1995 the monetary authorities decided to merge these and reorganise them into urban and rural banks. There are other financial companies, such as leasing companies and insurance companies, including the PICC. By the end of 1989 there were 159 259 financial institutions in China employing 1.97 million people (Liu *et al.*, 1991). By the end of 1993 these figures had increased to 199 618 and 2.6 million respectively. The open-door policy has also brought in many overseas-Chinese, foreign and joint-venture banks. China's first international investment bank, China International Capital Corporation Ltd – in which Singapore Investment Corporation has a 7.5 per cent stake – opened officially for business, in August 1995.

Increased competition after the banking reforms has led to a loosening of credit criteria. Since the branches of the specialised banks are closely linked to their own regions, they are intended to offer 'political' loans, taking account of the needs of local governments and large SOEs, including loss-making firms. According to the 'Decision of the CPC Central Committee on Issues Concerning the Establishment of a Socialist Market Economic Structure' (14 November 1993), China intends to establish 'policy-lending' banks and to separate 'policy-lending' banking from commercial banking. The new banks will include the State Development Bank (SDB), the Import and Export Credit Bank (IECB), and the reorganised Agricultural Development Bank (ADB) of China, all handling strictly defined policy-related business. Meanwhile, to fulfil the need for a nationwide circulation of money and the requirements of centralised and unified regulations, the branches of the PBC are defined clearly as agencies of its head office and active efforts are to be made to create the conditions for setting up transregional branches. The State Planning Commission will be a macroeconomic advisor rather than a commanding body (see Figure 1.5).

By the end of June 1994, there were 19 Chinese banks, including four specialised state banks, 10 commercial banks, three policy banks and two building societies. There were also 391 trust and investment companies, 20 insurance companies, 54 financial companies belonging to company groups and 14 financial leasing companies. The asset contributors of the financial institutions to the total asset are: ICBC 34.4%; ABC 17.23%: PCBC 12.2%; B. C 3.2%; commercial bank 4.1%; non-bank 22.8%.

Functional reforms

The role of the central bank in macroeconomic control has been strengthened to allow the money supply to increase, within limits, to accommodate economic growth. Fiscal authorities have increasingly relied on issuing bills rather than money drawn from the central bank to finance the budget. The relationship between the central bank and the State Planning Commission has changed, giving the central bank certain rights to refuse to finance investments mandated by the SPC. A central bank law to clarify the central bank's powers and functions must soon be drafted in order to establish the central bank's authority and independence. Enterprises are becoming more efficient as they change their traditional attitude of relying

Figure 1.5   The framework of the banking system of China in the 1990s

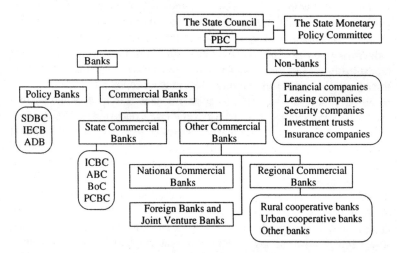

Notes: SDBC – the State Development Bank of China; IECB – the Import & Export Credit Bank of China; ADB – the Agricultural Development Bank of China.

National Commercial Banks cover the nationwide commercial banks, which are five. Other banks include eight or more local banks.

on grants to working mainly with interest-bearing credit from the specialised banks monitored by the central bank.

The past legacy of lending under the traditional system is reflected in the existing portfolios of the banks. In some bank branches over 60 per cent of loans are in arrears and 50 per cent of loans would be classified as non-performing by Western accounting standards. A large number of bank branches would have a negative net worth if their portfolios were marketed. Given these precarious portfolios, banks have been prevented from achieving their profit-earning goals (Sokil and King, 1989).

But how fast the specialised banks and other public financial intermediaries can be commercialised remains an unanswered question. The new term 'enterprisation of the specialised banks' suggests that banks should be reformed so as to be like Western commercial banks, which are responsible for their profits and losses just like other companies. However the notion has met with great difficulty in practice (Diao, 1990). Imperfect market mechanisms, excess demand, shortage of funds and lack of regulations have repeatedly forced the banks to ration their lending according to policies that were to some extent planned (see Chapter 2).

Interest rates have frequently been adjusted upwards, even though they are still set by administrative means. State and collective enterprises are preferentially treated and enjoy lower rates than ordinary firms. Certain priority sectors such as agriculture, energy, transportation and defence industries also enjoy preferential rates. On 1 September 1988 an interest rate subsidy scheme linked to the retail price index for savings deposits of three years or more was introduced to protect depositors from inflation. However it was not satisfactory given the annual rate of inflation (18.5 per cent). Thus another sharp increase in interest rates was announced on 1 February 1989, which induced an enthusiastic wave of deposits from the population in many areas (see Table 1.1).

Liu Hongru, vice-president of the PBC, said that the interest rate reform had to be sorted out step by step. If lending rates were to rise abruptly above inflation the cost increment would not be covered by enterprises themselves, but would eventually be passed on through increases in market prices.[12] The adjustment in August 1985 largely corrected the 'inversion' of interest rates, a long-standing problem that caused lending rates to be lower than deposit rates on savings (Li, 1987, pp. 170–2). Afterwards specialised banks and other financial intermediaries were given certain flexibility in adjusting their interest rates. Non-bank intermediaries such as investment trusts and urban and rural credit cooperatives were able to float their deposit and lending rates upward or downward by 20 per cent with respect to the rates of the specialised banks, who in turn were able to float their lending rates for working capital by 20 per cent with respect to the rates approved by the PBC.[13] The new policies in the 1990s will be discussed in Chapters 4 and 5. The interest rate adjustments since the reform are shown in Tables 1.1, 1.2, and 1.3.

The new banking reform policies

The reactivation of banks and other financial institutions was followed by the reopening of financial markets and relegalisation of negotiable financial instruments (Jao, 1990).

The interbank market was approved in principle by the PBC in October 1984 in order to end the previous vertical method of credit allocation. Interbank transactions in eleven cities totalled Rmb Yuan 352.9 million, at weighted average interest rates that varied from 10.44 per cent to 14.0 per cent per annum in the final week of March 1989 (Delfs, 1986).[14] Intereconomic-entity transactions amounted to 30, 230, 520 and 290 billion yuan in 1986, 1987, 1988 and 1989 respectively.[15] At the end of 1992 total interbank lending by the five specialised banks increased by 39 per cent from a year earlier to 507 billion yuan (Bank of Tokyo, 1994).

Table 1.1   Interest rate adjustments in China, 1979–91 (% per annum)

	4/79	4/80	4/82	4/85	8/85	9/88	2/89	8/90	4/91	5/93	7/93	1/95
Deposit rates:												
Sight deposits	2.16	2.88	2.88	2.88	2.88	2.88	2.88	2.16	1.80	2.16	3.15	3.15
Fixed-term deposits:												
6 months	3.60	4.32	4.32	5.40	6.12	6.48	9.00	6.48	5.40	7.20	9.00	9.00
1 year	3.96	5.40	5.76	6.84	7.20	8.64	11.34	8.64	7.56	9.18	10.98	10.98
Lending rates:												
WC 1 year	4.32	4.32	4.32	4.32	4.32	9.0	11.34	9.36	8.46	9.36	10.98	10.98
2 year	–	5.04	5.04	7.20	11.52	11.52	12.78	–	–			
FC 1 year	–	3.00	3.00	5.01	7.92	9.0	11.34	9.36	8.46	9.18	10.98	11.70
2 year	–	5.04	6.48	7.92	10.80	16.2	12.78	10.08	9.00	10.80	12.24	12.96

Notes: WC = *working capital*; FC = *fixed assets. The maturities are more diversified than in this table.*
Sources: People's Bank of China, Planning Division (1988) (Announcement of the People's Bank of China (1990); Industrial and Commercial Bank of China, annual reports (1989, 1991); the Chinese authorities (1995).

Table 1.2 China: interest rates on deposits, bonds and interbank operations, 1990–95 (in per cent)

	1990 (Apr.)	1990 (Aug.)	1991 (Apr.)	1991 (Oct.)	1992 (Dec.)	1993 (May)	1993 (July)	1994 (Dec.)	1995 (Jan.)
Individual deposits:									
Sight	2.88	2.16	1.80	1.80[1]	1.80	2.16	3.15	3.15	3.15
Three months	6.30	4.32	3.24	3.24	3.24	4.86	6.66	6.66	6.66
Six months	7.74	6.48	5.40	5.40	5.40	7.20	9.00	9.00	9.00
One year	10.08	8.64	7.56	7.56	7.56	9.18	10.98	10.98	10.98
Two years	10.98	9.36	7.92	7.92	7.92	9.90	11.70	11.70	11.70
Three years[2]	11.88	10.08	8.28	8.28	8.28	10.80	12.24	12.24	12.24
Five years[2]	13.68	11.52	9.00	9.00	9.00	12.06	13.86	13.86	13.86
Eight years[2]	16.20	13.68	10.08	10.08	10.08	14.58	17.10	17.10	17.10
Institutional deposits:									
Sight	2.88	2.16	1.80	1.80	1.80	2.16	3.15	3.15	3.15
Three months	6.30	4.32	3.24	3.24	3.24	4.86	6.66	6.66	6.66
Six months	7.74	6.48	5.40	5.40	5.40	7.20	9.00	9.00	9.00
One year	10.08	8.64	7.56	7.56	7.56	9.18	10.98	10.98	10.98
Two years	10.98	9.36	7.92	7.92	7.92	9.90	11.70	11.70	11.70
Three years	11.88	10.08	8.28	8.28	8.28	10.80	12.24	12.24	12.24
Five years	13.68	11.52	9.00	9.00	9.00	12.06	13.86	13.86	13.86
Eight years	16.20	13.68	10.08	10.08	10.08	14.58	17.10	17.10	17.10

Table 1.2 Continued

	1990 (Apr.)	1990 (Aug.)	1991 (Apr.)	1991 (Oct.)	1992 (Dec.)	1993 (May)	1993 (July)	1994 (Dec.)	1995 (Jan.)
Financial bonds	13.34[3]	13.34[3]	13.34[3]	8.50[3]	8.50[4]	8.50[5]	–	–	–
PBC rates:									
Loans to specialised banks									
Planned	9.00	7.92	7.20	7.20	7.20	9.00	10.62	10.62	10.89
Temporary	9.00	7.92	7.20	7.20	7.20	8.64–8.82	10.08–10.44	10.08–10.44	10.32–10.71
Deposits by specialised banks									
Required	7.92	6.84	6.12	6.12	6.12	7.56	9.18	9.18	9.18
Other	7.92	6.84	6.12	6.12	6.12	7.56	9.18	9.18	9.18
Government bonds:									
Six months	–	–	–	–	–	–	–	9.80	–
One year	–	–	–	–	–	–	–	12.00	–
Two years	–	–	–	–	–	–	–	13.00	–
Three years	–	14.00	–	10.00	9.50	–	13.96	14.00	–
Five years	–	–	–	–	10.50	–	15.86	–	–

Notes:
1. Effective 1, July 1991.
2. The inflation adjustment for deposits of three-year maturity and longer was 8.8 per cent in December 1994 and 9.84 per cent in January 1995.
3. One-year maturity: for two year maturity, 14.24 per cent; for three to five year maturity, one percentage point higher than that of individual deposits of the same maturity.
4. One-year maturity; for two year maturity, 9.2 per cent; for three year, 10 per cent.
5. One-year maturity; for two year maturity, 9.00 per cent; for three year, 9.50 per cent; for five year, 10.50 per cent.
Source: Data provided by the Chinese authorities.

Table 1.3   China: interest rates on loans, 1990–5 (in per cent)

	1990 (Apr.)	1990 (Aug.)	1991 (Apr.)	1991 (Oct.)	1992 (Dec.)	1993 (May)	1993 (July)	1994 (Dec.)	1995 (Jan.)
State industrial and commercial loans:									
Working capital	10.08	9.36	8.64	8.64	8.64	9.36	10.98	10.98	10.98
Fixed asset loans									
One year or less	10.08	9.36	8.46	8.46	8.46	9.18	10.98	10.98	11.70
One–three years	10.80	10.08	9.00	9.00	9.00	10.80	12.24	12.24	12.96
Three–five years	11.52	10.80	9.54	9.54	9.54	12.06	13.86	13.86	14.58
Five–ten years	11.88	11.16	9.72	9.72	9.72	12.24	14.04	14.04	14.76
Over ten years	11.88	11.16	9.72	9.72	9.72	12.24	14.04	14.04	14.76
Agricultural loans:									
Loans for collective crop production	9.00	8.28	7.74	7.74	7.74	8.46	10.08	10.08	10.08
Loans for collective crop investment									
One year or less	10.08	9.36	8.64	8.64	8.64	9.18	10.98	10.98	11.70
One–three years	10.80	9.36	8.64	8.64	8.64	10.80	12.24	12.24	12.96
Three–five years	11.52	10.08	9.54	9.54	9.54	12.06	13.86	13.86	14.58
Over five years	11.88	10.08	9.54	9.54	9.54	12.24	14.04	14.04	14.76
Loans financed by issue of Agricultural Bank of China bonds	12.096	10.80	9.72	9.72	9.72	11.25	13.18	13.18	13.18
Households:									
Agricultural production loans	10.08	9.36	8.64	8.64	8.64	9.36	10.98	10.98	10.98
Individual industrial and commercial loans	12.10	11.23	10.37	10.37	10.37	11.23	13.18	13.18	13.18
Loans for township enterprises working capital	10.08	9.36	8.64	8.64	8.64	9.36	10.98	10.98	10.98

Source: Data provided by the Chinese authorities.

However this lending is regionally fragmented and lacks a nationwide network and an adequate regulatory system. Therefore financial disorders can often be generated (see Chapter 4).

Establishment of the bond market commenced in 1981, when the government once again began to issue bonds in order to finance deficits and infrastructure projects. The specialised banks and enterprises were allowed to issue bonds on an individual approval basis in 1985. Initially the government bonds were unpopular because they were untradable, especially as their coupon rate was often lower than the inflation rate. In 1988 over-the-counter trade of government bonds to individuals was permitted, though the volume and type of bonds were limited and the price was set low to avoid excessive trading. The trading volume increased rapidly: total domestic bonds issued in 1988 and 1989 amounted to Rmb 9.2 billion and Rmb 5.6 billion respectively.[16] A secondary market for such treasury bonds existed in seven cities by the end of the 1980s (Shenyang, Shanghai, Harbin, Wuhan, Chongqing, Guangzhou and Shenzhen).[17] The discounting, acceptance and rediscounting of bills of exchange originated in Shanghai in 1980, and was formally approved by the PBC in December 1984. An experimental placement of government bonds through an underwriting syndicate brought success in April 1991, since when government bonds have usually been sold through such syndicates. Compulsory sales of government bonds were reintroduced in 1993, when stocks and financial and enterprise bonds offered higher yields. In 1994 the government took steps to finance the budget deficit by issuing bonds at home and abroad, suspending borrowing from the central bank. The PBC intends to initiate open market operations with government bonds. Short-term bonds were issued partly as a means of preparing for effective open market operations. However the volume of government bonds, which in 1994 was 150 billion yuan, is smaller than that of the interbank market. The effect of these operations in conducting monetary control will be very limited (Bank of Tokyo, 1994).

The establishment of a stock market followed the introduction of a stock company system. Corporate stock in China is a hybrid of bond and equity, or a kind of 'non-voting, redeemable, participating, preferred stock' in the terminology of developed market economies. It typically has denominations of Rmb 50 or Rmb 100 for individuals and Rmb 100 000 for institutional investors. Maturity is normally short, ranging from one to five years. The return typically consists of two parts: fixed interest pegged to the rates of the PBC, and a dividend linked to net profit. 'B shares', rather than domestically issued 'A shares', are issued to foreign investors. Bank debentures were issued by some banks in 1986, carrying coupon rates exceeding the one-year deposit rate by 1.8 per cent. Secondary markets in such stocks and bonds were reopened in 1986 in Shenyang, Shanghai and Guangzhou. On 12 December 1990 the Shanghai Stock Exchange was opened and the securities trading automatic quotation system (STAQS) was introduced, with a nationwide computer network, 25 members and 30 kinds of stock.[18] The monetary authority has recognised the urgent necessity of reforming the state-owned enterprises and of developing China's stock market, in spite of the fact that these are not short-term tasks.[19] Interest rates on bonds and interbank operations from 1990–5 are shown in Table 1.2.

Equally important, China has re-entered the world financial system. China rejoined the IMF and the World Bank in April/May 1980. In December 1984 it established formal business relations with the Bank for International Settlements. It became a member of the African Banking Group in 1985, and in 1986 it joined the Asian Development Bank. In 1979 China began to accept long-term loans, syndicated loans and export credits from foreign commercial banks, government agencies and international financial institutions. The BoC has rapidly extended its external network. It is now relatively easy for foreign banks to obtain permission to set up representative offices or branches in principal cities and the government has given approval for Western and Japanese banks gradually to establish branches inland.

The Communist Party Central Committee made the decision on 14 November 1993 to change not only the banking structure, but also banking policies. It declared that, as the central bank, the PBC should implement monetary policies 'independently' (but still under the leadership of the State Council). It should control the money supply and stabilise currency value, by changing from relying mainly on control over the scale of credit to using such means as reserve ratio on deposits, central bank lending rates and open-market operations. It should supervise and control various types of financial institutions, maintain the financial order and no longer handle business with non-financial institutions.

The Central Committee decided that banking business and securities business should be managed along separate lines. A monetary policy committee should be organised for the timely adjustment of monetary and credit policies. The commercial banks should engage in the management of assets, liabilities and risks. In the light of the changes in monetary supply and demand, the central bank should make timely readjustments of the benchmark interest rate and allow the deposit and loan interest rates of commercial banks to float freely within a specified range. The commercial banks should operate as independent and legal economic entities, with an integrated debt control system and a personnel system based on market mechanisms such as risk sharing, competition and incentives.[20]

The People's Bank of China issued its Administration of Financial Institutions Regulations on 9 August 1994. These regulations establish a more comprehensive regulatory framework for the financial sector and strengthen supervision and control over financial institutions. The People's

Bank of China Law (or the Central Bank Law) took effect on 18 March 1995, putting the central bank in a powerful position to regulate the national economy. This law addresses some important functions of the bank, especially in preventing budget deficits by overdrawing from the banks, and preventing local branches of the PBC from granting loans to local governments and other banks. The Commercial Bank Law of the PRC, adopted on 10 May 1995, aims at a proper banking system with a legal status. This Law is intended to increase banks' autonomy, strengthen supervision of bank staff and clients, and give depositors greater protection. The Negotiable Instrument Law was approved at the same time. On 30 June 1995 the Insurance Law was adopted by the National People's Congress. A series of other financial laws and implementation regulations for the laws are to follow.

The foreign exchange control system is also being reformed, leading to the establishment of a market-based, manageable, floating exchange rate system and an integrated and standardised foreign exchange market. To promote exports, local governments and enterprises have started to receive retention quotas for a portion of their foreign exchange earnings. Foreign exchange adjustment centres (FEACs) were set up in 1986 in major cities to enable foreign-funded enterprises to adjust their foreign exchange balances. A dual exchange rate system consisted of the official rate and the market rate at FEACs. In order to reenter the General Agreement on Tariffs and Trade, unifying the dual exchange rates is inevitable. On 1 January 1994 the yuan was set at 8.7 per US dollar, which represented a 33 per cent devaluation from the previous official rate of 5.8 per US dollar. A managed floating system was introduced. The PBC announces a daily middle rate based on the previous day's rate on the interbank foreign exchange market. The monetary authorities intend not only to unify the exchange rate but also to avoid market volatility. Chinese enterprises have to sell all their foreign exchange earnings to authorised banks and are forbidden to retain foreign currency. On the other hand foreign-funded enterprises are allowed to deposit their foreign exchange in foreign banks in China as well as in authorised banks. The aim of this differential treatment is to avoid a sharp drop in the value of the yuan caused by a strong demand for foreign exchange by foreign-funded enterprises. The yuan should gradually become a convertible currency.

Banking reforms in Hungary

Economic reform in Hungary began in 1957 with a revised economic policy. Socialist relations between production and ownership were manifested in the market mechanism, especially in the 1970s and the 1980s, although the Hungarian banking system retained features of the classical model until the end of 1986.

In the 1960s the banking system was very similar in structure and function to those of other CPEs in that it consisted of a small group of specialised banks, each controlling its own local branches. They were directly subordinate to the Hungarian National Bank, which combined the functions of commercial and central banking. The necessary intermediary action between household and enterprise money circuits took place through the state budget and not through the banking system. Investment projects were financed by the state budget, through the monobanks, without the regulatory role played by interest rates.

Before 1987 the channels through which all major financial transactions actually flowed in Hungary were found within the country's highly centralised banking system, which was attached to the National Planning Office and the MoF under the Council of Ministers. The banks, in line with the plan, exercised financial control of management, institutions and enterprises included in the single account system.

Banking reforms before 1987

Although there were no fundamental changes on the banking side, the economic reforms of the administration, of fiscal links between enterprises and central organs and of investment management in 1968 did have some influence on the banking system:

1. Commercial bank credit revived and some commercial banks served as lending institutions to enterprises and executors of government credit policies.
2. The government established a 'base rate'; that is, a general interest rate on short and medium-term commercial credit.[21] Credit policy was based on the policy directives formulated in detail by the Hungarian National Bank.[22]
3. Before granting loans, the banks had to scrutinise thoroughly the status and management skills of the applicants.[23]

Throughout the 1970s and the early 1980s there were debates on banking reforms and small, cosmetic changes were introduced. Among other things, banks were required to replace grants with loans, carry out creditworthiness analyses of clients and projects, and charge interest rates that were linked to surrogate market rates of interest (though there were no market clearing rates). In 1986 a new law on bankruptcy was enacted.

Even after the reform, however, Hungary still conformed to a 'classical prereform system' (Kornai, 1986). Certain types of money flow between different segments of the system were permitted while others were strictly prohibited. The state sector paid money wages to households but – with the exception of minimal, tightly restricted consumer credits granted by the monopoly savings bank – it could not give credit to customers. Households bought state-sector goods and services but could not make capital investments in the state sector. Even within the state sector money was 'earmarked'. Firms had at least three kinds of money: wage money, money covering current costs other than wages, and investment money. These categories of money could be used only for their assigned purposes. Some observers (for example Brus and Laski, 1989) have attributed the collapse of the new economic mechanism to a failure to create capital markets. The absence of a capital market had some implications for the effectiveness of the market system in goods.

Banking reforms in 1987

On 1 January 1987 a comprehensive banking reform strategy was launched in Hungary. The banking sector was substantially transformed and a two-tier banking system was established. The major objective of the banking reform was to introduce greater competition into the financial sector by allowing a broader range of financial institutions to compete in the mobilisation and allocation of financial savings. The key features of the banking reform programme were as follows:

1. The nature of the new system helped to bring monetary control to the fore. The central bank ceased to interfere in domestic commercial activities, while retaining its monopoly on foreign exchange dealings.
2. The central bank – the National Bank of Hungary (NBH) – established a regulatory system, consisting of policies on refinancing credit, central bank interest rates and compulsory reserve requirements.
3. The establishment of five commercial banks in 1987 represented an important development. They included the Hungarian Credit Bank (HCB), the National Commercial & Credit Bank (K&H or NC&CB) for agri-industrial enterprises and cooperatives, the Budapest Bank of Hungary (BB) for infrastructural activities and the energy sector, and two others (the OCB, which was known as the Hungarian Foreign Trade Bank, or HFTB before 1987, and the General Banking and Trust Company Ltd (GB&TC). These commercial banks were structured as stock corporations, with the MoF as the largest shareholder (Corbett, 1990b; Szekely, 1990).

4. From 1 July enterprises were permitted to open cheque accounts in more than one bank in order to promote competition in the banking system.
5. Several other financial institutions and a few foreign, joint-venture banks were reorganised.
6. The Ministry of Finance established a state banking supervision department in order to supervise the banking system through license registration, regulation adoption, data assessment and direct investigation: this was described in Act LXIX of 1990 on Financial Institutions and Financial Institutional Activities.

The structure of the newly reformed banking system is shown in Figure 1.6.

Banking reforms since 1988

The above reforms created the necessary conditions for a competitive commercial banking structure. However several problems arose, principally in the relationship between the new institutions and the new 'central bank', where political as well as market considerations continued to dominate. In addition, Szekely (1990) argued that the poor quality of the inher-

Figure 1.6   The structure of the banking system in Hungary in 1990

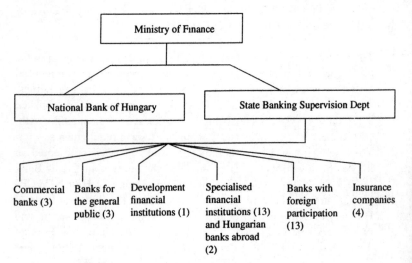

Note: After 1990 some further institutions were set up.
Source: The National Bank of Hungary.

ited loan portfolios, the high concentration of the system and the continued segmentation of the banking system posed serious problems.

The reform process that began in 1988 addressed some key issues. Commercial banks were allowed to issue certificate of deposits (CDs) to households in that year. The removal of restrictions on the capacity of banks to raise savings from households was a significant departure from the traditional separation of savings and enterprise financing in socialist economies. To counteract the problem of decreased household deposits and a decline in households' propensity to invest in domestic financial assets, interest rates on household deposits were increased. Separate agencies were set up to deal with concessional housing loans. The number of commercial banks (one new commercial bank and one new cooperative bank) and joint venture banks (two new ones) were increased by January 1990 while the National Savings Bank became a 'full commercial bank'. The deposit collection role of the post office was taken over by a new commercial bank. The big three banks increased their share capital, partly through share issues to households. The restriction on fee-based business and capital transactions by commercial banks was removed. In January 1989 the NBH's monopoly over foreign exchange business was broken. Commercial banks were allowed to collect foreign currency deposits from enterprises and individuals, and over the next twelve months restrictions relating to foreign exchange dealings were steadily relaxed.

The banking system's share capital had more than doubled by the end of 1989, its profitability significantly exceeding the average profitability of the economy. The banks also increased their risk reserves for prudential considerations. In 1989 the specialised financial institutes' equity increased by nearly 15 per cent.

Although the large banks continued to play a decisive role in the banking sector, the share of medium-sized banks increased with respect to total assets (+4.3 per cent), equity (+1.7 per cent) and profits (+3.0 per cent), and that of the large banks decreased by a similar rate. This resulted in keener competition among the banks and the development of a healthier banking structure. The National Savings Bank was the largest, with total assets of Ft 470 billion at the end of 1989. In its lending portfolio, long-term loans represented nearly 70 per cent (Ft 320 billion) of total liabilities.

The NBH required banks to maintain mandatory reserves with it. The mandatory reserve ratio was 16 per cent in 1991, from which the banks earned interest equal to 50 per cent of the base rate. Hungary was certainly trying to modernise its banking sector, but refinancing credit was probably still the most important instrument of monetary control by 1992. The NBH also influenced the level of interest rates by controlling the money supply and refinancing rates. From 1989 the NBH took an active part in open market operations. But it was unable to implement a market-based and unified interest system because: (1) preferential interest rates were expedient and beneficial to the transformation of the economy, particularly with respect to privatisation and the growth of enterprises and exports; (2) the budget received its credit at relatively preferential rates; and (3) some housing loans for households remained subsidised. The base rate in 1991 was 22 per cent. The charged rate to financial institutions for refinancing loans with a maturity of less than a year was 29 per cent and the rediscounting rate for drafts was 27–29 per cent.

The state's direct share in the share capital of the banks had gradually decreased to about 33 per cent by the end of 1990. Thirty-five per cent of the banks' capital was held by enterprises and cooperatives and 15 per cent was held by other financial institutions. There were sixteen banks with a foreign share in the capital, ranging from 20 per cent to 100 per cent (Balassa, 1992).

The new Act on Financial Institutions became effective in December 1991 and finally laid down capital adequacy requirements that conformed to Western standards. The law required banks to achieve and maintain an 8 per cent capital–asset ratio – corresponding to the Basle guidelines – by January 1993. A ratio of 7.25 per cent was set for the interim period. Individual exemptions were to be given until December 1994. Reserves in cash or liquid assets for risky loans taken out of untaxed earnings were fixed at 20 per cent for 'substandard' loans, 50 per cent for 'doubtful' loans and 100 per cent for 'bad' loans. Reserves could be taken out of profits. The state-run banking inspectorate suspended the operations of three banks in the first half of 1992.[24] Although the Act allowed universal banking activities, investment fund management was excluded from the permitted operations of banks. Moreover export credits could only be given after licensing. By January 1993 a mandatory deposit insurance system was to be established.

Creation of the financial market

Capital markets were stressed during the reforming period. From the first issue of bonds to households in 1983 the bond markets experienced an excessive demand as bond rates were higher than those on time deposits and exceeded the inflation rate. In addition the state carried full responsibility for bond risks and bond yields were exempt from tax. A secondary market for bonds was created in 1984 before any legal framework had been established. However in 1988 the economy deteriorated and consumer price inflation soared to 15.7 per cent, pushing up deposit rates and lending rates to 9 per cent and 13 per cent respectively – higher than bond rates. Furthermore the state ceased to guarantee bonds. All these factors contributed to the collapse of bond markets.

In 1987 twenty-two financial institutions, including the NBH, signed a cooperation agreement in order to promote securities trading in Hungary. Regular secondary market activities commenced from January 1988 and an information centre began to operate. A limited share market existed, comprising 40 different shares to the value of Ft 30 billion. Securities market law covered the establishment of a securities supervisory body, a stock exchange, rules for trading, information disclosure requirements and specific aspects in the area of investor protection (such as those related to insider trading). Commercial banks were authorised to extend credit and sell bonds to households from January 1988. The growth of the commercial bill market had been fostered in part by NBH regulation, which offered favourable terms for rediscounting.

In March 1988 the money market was opened to households with the introduction of treasury bills, whose interest rates had been substantially increased. In December 1989 the NBH started to auction three-month treasury bonds using Western auction techniques. Bond financing was allowed to develop according to the creditworthiness of the issuing company.

New laws on business corporations (1988/VI) and their conversion (1989/XIII) paved the way for a functioning capital market. Equity shares were being issued by the end of 1988. The Law of Association (1989) and the Law on Foreign Investment (1988) permitted individuals and foreign investors to participate. Shares of some Hungarian firms were introduced into foreign stock exchanges and some foreign corporations were founded to invest in shares of Hungarian companies.

A new company law introduced a uniform profit tax framework for all enterprises. A new tax code came into force to promote long-term financial savings through private financial intermediaries and established a tax credit for individuals' contributions to private pension plans. Facing the necessity of an increase in the interest rate on housing loans and household deposits, housing mortgage funds were established to deal with the existing stock of such loans. Subsidies to eligible recipients for new housing loans were administered through the budget rather than through the banking system. Thus a source of distortion in bank interest rates was removed and the total subsidy made more transparent.

Two acts passed in 1991, the Act on Accounting and the new Bankruptcy Law, were expected to bring about fundamental changes in the operation of the microeconomy from 1992. The acts state that all business entities will have to create reserves from pre-tax profits against potential losses (for instance on doubtful receivables), and filing for bankruptcy may become compulsory in cases of default on any liability for more than 90 days. Furthermore, creditors will be able to initiate liquidation proceedings if the debtor is in default for more than 60 days. Registered bankruptcy declarations were 2258 and 3658 in the first quarter and during the first eight months of 1992 respectively (Estrin *et al.*, 1992).

CONCLUSIONS

Although the mechanisms of CPE banking systems differ from those of market economies in some ways, the essential functions are the same, notably the financial control function. The character of the financial system, including the passiveness of money, was dictated by the economic system, which the former merely helped to control in different ways. In spite of the fact that such a control function might be 'formative' or limited under the traditional system, banks did follow and assisted planners and official investors to control, supervise and manage the production system. In certain periods the cooperation of the banks helped to bring about high economic growth, low inflation, full employment and equal income distribution. In the CPE model, corporate governance was characterised by the subjection of economic agents to different levels of administrative principals. Banks were the secondary masters of enterprises. The control function of the banking system was limited by the subordination of the banks and the SOEs to enterprises' primary masters – the planners and the MoF. The centralised institutional structure allowed the headquarters of the financial system and the central government to control banks. The corporate governance structure of the planned regime was supported by the joint and contingent control mechanisms of the political party system and the planning system.

It was the control-oriented nature of the planning system that placed the national banks in a less important position than the fiscal system. This avoided systemic conflict within the economy. The centralised economy needed a centralised banking system, and therefore central banking and commercial banking were conducted by the national banks simultaneously, regardless of their ability to do so. It was unnecessary for them to play to the full the role of central banks in the West. Another important difference between the two banking systems was that, for convenience of control, the functions of the socialist banks, including the branches of the state bank and the specialised banks, were limited to certain businesses or sectors under planning. There is no need for the commercial banks of some Western market economies to operate under such a restriction. The legal framework and central bank supervision allow them a freer rein.

The traditional banking system had many problems, arising both externally and from within the system. Reform was inevitable. The CPEs gradually saw the banking reform process being accelerated by economic reforms. The main trend has been to decentralise the highly centralised banking systems. Banking system reforms in countries adopting the partially reformed model introduced a certain degree of competition and efficiency. The establishment and reestablishment of two-tier banking systems in the former Yugoslavia (since the 1960s), China (since 1984) and Hungary (since 1987) were designed to introduce market mechanisms and resolve the problems of low efficiency, rigidity and the absence of adequate incentives and competition. On the one hand national banks have become central banks focusing on monetary policies. On the other, the commercial banks have been reorganised and compete with joint-venture banks. Interest rates show a general rising trend and a certain flexibility. Banks have been active in interbank lending and borrowing. Financial markets have been and are being created enthusiastically and international stock exchanges are being introduced. A legal framework for such a system has emerged, which has also helped to discipline the new financial system to enter into the world market.

A commercial banking system has emerged steadily in China since 1986. However this trend was reinforced only after a successful nationwide stabilisation programme. It is noticeable that the original banking system was relatively weak in fulfilling its regulatory and control functions. Once the economic system as a whole has changed (become marketised) the reform of the banking system should be structured in such a way as to strengthen it.

2 Problems of Selected RCPEs

The trail-blazing western companies which started to invest in Hungary at the end of the 1980s are beginning to ponder what they should have done differently .... Should they have committed less money? Less precipitately? In a different location? Or not invested at all? (N. Denton, 'Hungarian investors think again', *Financial Times*, 14 September 1992.)

INTRODUCTION

Banking reforms are only justified to the extent that they benefit the economy. This chapter examines the prevailing financial and economic situation in two countries, Hungary and China, after reforms had been implemented. It attempts to discover whether there is any link between banking reforms and economic outcomes. Does the banking system serve the economy well or not, and why? This chapter seeks the answer by looking directly at both the economic situation and the financial situation after the fundamental changes had taken effect in the two countries.

The two economies differ not only in size, but also in the nature and methods of the reform policies that were implemented. Hungarian economists often describe their reform approach as 'gradualism' because it avoided abrupt changes (Riecke and Antal, 1993, p. 108). In comparison with the rest of the Eastern European economies and the USSR, this is an accurate description. China, too, has adopted a gradualist model. However, whereas public ownership remains dominant in China with no moves being made to privatise the large number of SOEs, in Hungary even the state banks are likely to be privatised. We are studying two vastly different economies. But we are interested in whether the radically commercialised banking system in Hungary performs better than the still state-owned and specialised banking system in China in the areas of corporate finance and monetary control, and in what theoretical arguments can be brought about from the studies.

Before the reforms, China was basically an agricultural economy, in spite of the fact that a strong industrial base had been established in 1949.

Before 1979 the Chinese government had adopted some flexible policies of decentralisation and recentralisation to cope with certain immediate problems. But those policies had never touched the fundamental elements of the CPE model. The radical Chinese reform programme started with the agricultural reforms after the Cultural Revolution (1979). The problems of the industrial system were tackled only after the effects of the agri-reforms became evident. The policies of the urban reforms were designed with great care under the careful control of the central government. The banking system was reformed even more cautiously. Indeed, commercialisation of the banking system was not even put on the agenda until the 1990s. The political framework remained unchanged. From the outset, however, the strategists followed a clear principle that reform programmes must lead to economic improvement and bring increased prosperity to the majority.[1] There were some economic fluctuations during periods of political and social turmoil (1989). However the principle of initially experimenting on a small scale in certain regions, and then applying the experience gained to large-scale programmes is sound and has proved beneficial to the economy as a whole.

Like some Eastern European economies, such as Poland and Czechoslovakia, Hungary questioned the fundamentals of the CPE model both in theory, as shown in the work of the Shortage School initiated by Kornai (1980), and in practice, manifested by the radical reforms experienced in the 1950s and the 1960s (theoretical issues will be discussed in Chapter 5). However nationwide radical reforms came into effect only in the mid-1980s, later than in China. No distinction was made between agri-reforms and industrial reforms. Moreover privatisation programmes and commercialisation of the banking system (1987) followed hard on the heels of fundamental political and economic changes. Hungarian reformers stress the importance of learning from western models and of constructing a legal framework.

The economic results of these two countries are the best test of reform policies and banking reforms. The two have also proved to be fundamentally different. Though it is often regarded as a one of the better economies of the former Eastern European bloc, Hungary has been in economic crisis since the mid-1980s. Between July 1990 and July 1992 real GDP fell by 12 per cent. Consumer price index (CPI) inflation accelerated to 35 per cent and the level of unemployment stood at 8.5 per cent at the end of 1991. In contrast China's economic problems can be divided into temporary ones, such as inflation, and fundamental ones, such as structural problems. However the Chinese markets have been flourishing. During the period 1979–92, the average annual economic growth rate reflected in such figures as real national income (8.8 per cent) and real GDP (9.1 per cent) were the second fastest in the world after South Korea. The nation-wide annual CPI increase was only 6 per cent. Annual average wages increased by above 10 per cent. Foreign investments amounted to US$5 billion in 1991 and $33 billion (including $20 billion of direct foreign investment) in 1993. Ten thousand newly established foreign investment projects were approved and registered by the Chinese authorities in 1993.[2]

The economic problems involved are so complicated that it is necessary to focus on those relevant to financial reform, some types of which may be common among the RCPEs. This chapter is divided into three main sec-tions. The first and second discuss the problems of the Hungarian economy and the Chinese economy respectively. The third looks at the financial effects of decentralising the banking sector and appraises whether a com-mercialised banking system really improves corporate finance, especially long-term investment, and whether ownership and type of bank are more important than central bank regulation and supervision during transition.

THE ECONOMIC PROBLEMS OF HUNGARY

Were domestic input and foreign borrowing properly channelled into investment by the banks? Clearly, in the case of Hungary this was a problem. The discussion that follows concentrates on the problems encountered during the 1980s, a period that allows a reasonable compari-son with China. Since then the economic developments of these countries have retained the same trends.

Low investment rate and economic stagnation

Hungary differed from most of the CPEs in its emphasis on consumption and social welfare, even at the expense of necessary investment.

Low investment rate

Investment is a crucial variable on the supply side of the economy as it is the means by which changes in the real capital stock are brought about. The investment rate (investment as a percentage of GDP) stood as high as 30–40 per cent in the 1970s[3] but showed a declining trend thereafter, falling from 28.9 per cent in 1980 to only 21.1 per cent in 1988 and 19.5 per cent in 1989. Total final consumption remained roughly constant throughout this period (NBH, *Annual Report*, 1989, p. 30).

The accumulation of capital is a vital element in economic growth. The essential feature of capital is that its creation requires the sacrifice of labour and other resources that could be used for present consumption.[4] Although total investment declined only 1 per cent in 1989, investment by public and cooperative organisations, which formed part of the total, fell by 2.9 per cent while private investment grew by 7 per cent. Investment in housing and the building of holiday homes accounted for the overwhelming majority of this increase (NBH, 1990). Investment in Hungary, Poland and the CSFR fell sharply during the period 1988–91 (WIIW, 1993, p. 18). This illustrates that the low economic growth rates were due to the low investment level.

Backward economic structure in a stagnating economy

GDP indices show growth rates falling from 2.9 per cent in 1981 to –0.2 per cent in 1989 with three years of negative growth rates since 1980 (1985, 1988 and 1989).[5] The fall in the gross material product in 1990 was –5.5 per cent.[6] Industry growth rates dropped from 5.0 per cent in 1981 to –3.4 per cent in 1989, with only the period between 1987 and 1985 showing positive growth. The annual percentage change in gross industrial production was –0.3 in 1988, –2.5 per cent in 1989 and –4.5 in 1990 (ibid.) Construction and agriculture fluctuated between positive and negative growth in successive years (NBH, 1989, p. 106).

Another consequence of the low rate of investment was the backwardness of the economic structure. The contributions of industry and the total value of the industrial-material production sector to GDP production decreased by 0.1 per cent and 0.3 per cent respectively during the period from 1980 to 1988, while that of the non-material production sector increased only 1.3 per cent (though it accelerated faster than that of the industrial-material production sector after 1985) (NBH, 1989).

The market situation at home and abroad had changed greatly. However the pattern of the industrial structure in 1989 was roughly similar to that in 1975. With respect to the number of employees, there were increases of only 2.9 per cent, 1.2 per cent and 1.0 per cent respectively in food products, machinery and chemicals in 1988. In mining, electricity and construction, employee numbers remained more or less unchanged.[7] The volume of industrial production stagnated in 1988 and dropped by 3.4 per cent (2.2 per cent per work day) in 1989 compared with the 1986 level. Agricultural production went down by 2.3 per cent in 1989 (NBH, 1989, pp. 27–28).

During the period 1980–89 exports accounted for 36–42 per cent of GDP and imports for around 33–41 per cent (ibid.) In total, exports of

non-rouble settlements, raw materials, semi-finished products and parts
increased from 36.6 per cent in 1980 to 44.4 per cent in 1989, while the
proportion of machines, vehicles and other capital goods decreased from
12.3 per cent to 10.4 per cent over the same period.

Trade reorientation led the Hungarian industrial structure to shift
towards a higher share of less sophisticated, more energy-consuming production. According to some incomplete data from Mizsei (1993, p. 171),
the machine industry suffered from the worst decline (34.9 per cent) in
1991. Its share of total industrial production fell from 20.8 per cent in
1990 to 17.2 per cent in 1991. Within the industry, the decline was steep-
est in the more high-tech industries such as electronics, as well as the
strongly CMEA-dependent car industry. In these sub-branches, production was down more than 40 per cent from the previous year. The collapse was also strong in the metallurgical and construction materials
industries.

Inflation after radical decentralisation

Inflation rose to extraordinarily high levels only when more radical reform
steps were taken after 1986, when the banking system was substantially
transformed and a two-tier banking sector established. Before 1987
inflation fluctuated between 4.5 per cent and 8.2 per cent. National statistics show that the annual percentage change in consumer prices had grown
from 15.5 per cent in 1988 and 18.8 per cent in 1989 to 28.9 per cent in
1990. Generally speaking, Hungarian consumer price inflation was
inversely correlated with the growth rates of industrial production (see
Figure 2.1). Production prices seemed to be far more closely correlated
with the growth rates of consumer prices than that of wages, except for the
period 1982–5. Since 1985 both have taken roughly the same direction
(see Figure 2.1).

Foreign debts' crisis

When the first oil crisis occurred, domestic users in this oil-importing CPE
did not automatically pay the higher oil prices. There was no 'tax' effect
and no fall in domestic incomes, employment or output, and thus no
induced fall in imports. Hungary did not cut wages and did not increase oil
prices. Nor did living standards stall. Money was easy to borrow on the
world markets at the time as interest rates were low. Hungarian net debt
grew from US$1.4 billion to US$5.4 billion between 1974 and 1980 and to
US$7.3 billion by 1982 . By the spring of 1982 the accumulated total debt
of the previous ten years was equal to the total amount of GNP in that

Figure 2.1   Price, wage, production and employment, Hungary (annual % change)

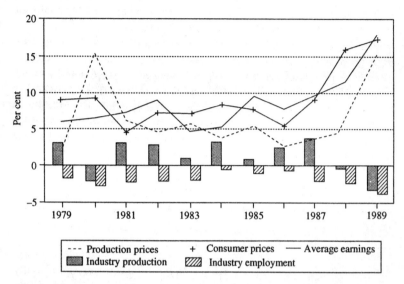

Source: International Financial Statistics Yearbook (1989,1990); IMF.

year.[8] By 1990 the country's debt had more than doubled: gross debt reached US$21.2 billion and net debt grew to US$15.9 billion in that year. Gross debt was US$22.3 billion at the end of 1991while foreign reserves stood at US$4 billion (Riecke and Antal, 1993, p. 113). According to the maturity breakdown of Hungary's long- and medium-term debt in convertible currencies, more than 80 per cent of the debts were financial loans. Trade-related credit made up a small proportion. Real per capita GNP was US$4000, compared with US$600 in China. However the amount of foreign debt per capita was US$2100.

Company insolvency and 'queuing-up'

In the 1980s a large number of companies were unable to meet their payment obligations.

The 'queuing-up' phenomenon

According to several surveys taken in 1989, about 30–40 large SOEs made up a 'hard insolvency core', which in turn eventually caused approximately 400 companies to fail to meet their payment obligations. This created a problem that in Hungary is called 'queuing up'. The balance that could not be paid due to insufficient funds was reckoned to be at least Ft127.6 billion (some estimates put it at about Ft200 billion) at the end of 1989, constituting 7.5 per cent of GDP. Of this amount, 57 per cent (Ft72.7 billion) represented the sum of the debts of 313 companies whose lack of funds had been both grave and persistent (Table 2.1). This situation worsened, with the number of persistently and seriously insolvent SOEs increasing by 60 per cent to 282 per cent during 1990, according to the NBH. By 1992 the amount of queuing up in the economy was estimated at Ft 125 billion plus another Ft 115 billion 'kept in drawers' (that is, not submitted for collection at banks); together these items roughly equalled the total of deposits from enterprises in the banking system (Estrin, *et al.*, 1992).

Table 2.1   Total amount of 'queuing-up' credits

	1/88	6/88	12/88	6/89	12/89
Unpayable loans between companies (billion forints)	17.5	19.4	45.5	57.4	72.7
Total number of companies in the queue*	80	119	208	239	313

Compared with some developed market economies, the capital gearing or financial leverage ratio of the Hungarian companies (that is, the proportion of total liabilities minus equity to total liabilities) was very low and their self-financing ratio was very high (Table 2.2). This indicates that the role played by financial institutions in the Hungarian economy was very limited. Consequently companies – particularly small and medium-sized ones – faced serious liquidity problems due to insufficient commercial credit.

Excessive commercial credits were easily accumulated, which made it impossible to quantify the financial position of companies. If companies are classified according to return on equity[9] – state-owned capital plus enterprise retention from net profits for internal finance – the most profitable companies had to grant the highest amount of commercial credit to the loss-making companies. Thus money was pumped from the profitable to the less profitable.[10] In July 1992, 573 enterprises were declared insolvent and were registered on a so-called rediscounting refusal list. The central bank refused to rediscount bills of exchange drawn by these enterprises.[11]

Table 2.2   The capital gearing ratio in some selected countries, 1986 (per cent)

Japan	85
France	70
FRG	59
UK	55
USA	39
Hungary	30

Source: OECD (1988).

High inventory accumulation

In a competitive market economy, companies must keep their excess stock below a certain level to avoid liquidity problems. The ratio of stock to GDP was much higher in Hungary (1.9–6.4 per cent) in 1989 than in Western industrialised countries (0.6–1.6 per cent) over the last decade. The value of all stock on 31 December 1989 was more than twice the total industrial output, or 61 per cent of total GDP (NBH, 1990, pp. 31–32).

Increasing loss-makers

Among the customers of the industrial department of the Budapest Bank, the number of loss-making companies increased from 8 to 101 and total losses increased from Ft909.5 million to Ft5135.6 million (US$82.2 million), an increase of 464.6 per cent in the period 1986–1988.[12] The national situation of loss-making companies in 1988 is shown in Table 2.3.

Among loss-making and tax-owing companies, about half were small companies. A significant number of large and medium-sized companies were loss-makers, especially in the industrial, construction and agricultural sectors. The amount of unpaid taxation was Ft12.2 billion (US$195 million), which was 53 per cent of the state budget deficit (Ft23 billion) in 1988.

Inefficient monetary policy and the inability fully to enforce bankruptcy law

In the transitional period, monetary policy was considerably less effective in controlling aggregate demand than it was in market economies. When policy was tightened, financial discipline over firms was generally weak and enterprises did not adjust their spending behaviour.

Table 2.3   Loss-making companies in Hungary (end of 1988)

Sector	Losses made		Taxation unpaid	
	(No. of companies)	(Ft. mn)	((No. of companies)	(Ft. mn)
Industry	196	5452	362	7198
Of which food	10	110	29	213
Construction	107	1355	226	1582
Agriculture	107	957	194	1074
Transport	8	37	22	1238
Trade	61	640	95	490
Others	68	286	135	626
Total	547	8727	1034	12199
Of which small enterprises	263	889	530	1141

Note: All the companies listed were state-owned.
Source: Research Institute, Hungarian Financial Ministry (1990).

Hungary might be regarded as a 'bank-oriented' economy since the channels of obtaining financing on the capital markets were only in the process of being created. If they were unable to finance themselves, firms had to apply to the commercial banks for credit. Between 1986 and 1988, money supply, represented by the ratios of M1/GDP and M2/GDP, significantly decreased.[13] However the restrictive credit policy could also result in indebted companies not repaying trade creditors or the banks.

The experience has been that undeclared bankruptcies generally remained unsettled. Bankruptcy regulation was applied satisfactorily on smaller units but liquidation proceedings against large state companies remained exceptional (Table 2.4). The majority of bankruptcy proceedings in fact became compulsory rescuing and restructuring by the authorities. Credit losses and the interest on delayed payments had to be written off when a company was liquidated, and this of course affected the financial position of the creditor and the bank. It was inevitable that bankruptcy would influence other sectors considerably.

Generally speaking, Hungary was in a serious economic crisis. This was intensified by worsening internal and external disturbances towards the end of the 1980s, of which the West became fully aware only after 1990. More radical reforms, instigated from 1987, had not eased the economic depression with respect to economic stagnation, inflation, company insolvency and foreign debt. Financial liberalisation in such circumstances had, at best, not improved the situation, and could indeed have worsened it.

Table 2.4   Liquidation Cases in Hungary (in per cent, up to the end of 1989)

Small cooperative	63
Housing and garage cooperatives	15
Others[1]	18
Large state enterprises[2]	2

Notes:
1. Includes different ventures, traditional cooperatives and smaller companies.
2. Large SOEs were liquidated in six cases only.
Source: Kuti and Mora (1989).

THE ECONOMIC PROBLEMS OF CHINA

Before 1979 the Chinese banking system faced the following economic problems, some of which were similar to those of Hungary.

Budget deficits and tax reform

In China, budget revenue as a proportion of GDP decreased from 33.6 per cent during the period of the First Five Year Plan to 32.9 per cent in 1979. It again fell sharply to 22.4 per cent in 1988 and 22.2 per cent in 1989. Meanwhile the ratio of budget expenditure to national income was higher than during most of the 1980s (Figure 2.3). The budgetary management system had been reformed by a method of responsibility classification according to level of administration, commonly known as 'having dinners through different pots' *(fen zao chi fan)*.[14] This method had provided some incentives to both the central government and the local administrations. However it had also brought about two problems: one was the creation of an economy split and blockaded by new 'dukes and princes under an emperor'; The other was that central government revenue had fallen to a level where the conducting of macroeconomic policies had become impossible. The proportion of revenue in the central budget to total revenue fell from 45.4 per cent in the period of the First Five Year Plan to about 15 per cent in the period from 1971 to 1980. It then recovered a little to 30.3 per cent in the period of the Sixth Five-Year Plan and 39.8 per cent in 1988 (Figure 2.2).

The proportion of central government expenditure to total expenditure declined in line with other expenditures in most years, in spite of the fact that a significant proportion of central revenue was reallocated to local expenditure each year.

Table 2.5 Three pricing systems since 1990 (percentage of the gross of social commodity retail sales)

Specification	Control agents	(A)				(B)				(C)			
		1990	1991	1992	1993	1990	1991	1992	1993	1990	1991	1992	1993
Retail sales commodities	Total	29.8	20.9	5.9	4.8	17.2	10.3	1.1	1.4	53.0	68.8	93.0	93.8
	Central	16.3	11.9	3.3	2.5	5.4	2.8	0.2	0.4	–	–	–	–
	Provincial	9.7	5.6	2.2	1.9	8.6	4.7	0.6	0.6	–	–	–	–
	Local	3.8	3.4	0.4	0.4	3.2	2.8	0.3	0.4	–	–	–	–
Agricultural products and byproducts	Total	25.0	22.2	12.5	10.4	23.4	20.0	5.7	2.1	51.6	57.8	81.8	87.5
	Central	23.8	20.2	12.3	9.3	9.9	9.4	3.3	1.1	–	–	–	–
	Provincial	0.9	1.2	0.1	1.0	11.7	7.6	1.4	0.6	–	–	–	–
	Local	0.3	0.8	0.1	0.1	1.8	3.0	0.8	0.4	–	–	–	–
Production materials	Total	44.6	36.0	18.7	13.8	19.0	18.3	7.5	5.1	36.4	45.7	73.8	81.1
	Central	33.4	26.7	14.5	10.4	12.5	11.2	5.6	3.4	–	–	–	–
	Provincial	8.5	6.9	3.1	2.4	5.0	5.6	1.7	1.3	–	–	–	–
	Local	2.7	2.4	1.1	1.0	1.5	1.5	0.2	0.4	–	–	–	–

Notes:
1. 'Central' means the central authorities; 'provincial' means the provincial authorities; 'local' means regional and city level authorities.
2. 'A' indicates the proportions of the values of the commodities under state pricing control in the total values specified, respectively. 'B' indicates those of commodities under state pricing guidance in the total values. 'C' indicates the proportions of the values of free market commodities in the total values.

Source: Guo (1995).

Figure 2.2   Changes in the state and central budgets

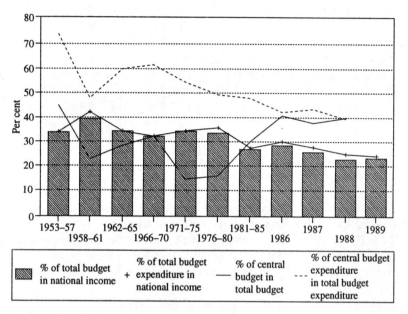

Source: *China Statistical Yearbook* (1990, 1991).

Enterprises repaid their bank loans before paying taxes. This repayment increased from 0.46 per cent of the national income in 1979 to 2.54 per cent in 1988, 108.5 billion yuan having been accumulated by SOEs. Part of this amount, if repayment was made before the payment of taxation, should be regarded as a significant loss to the budget compared with the tax revenue that would have been collected if the loans had been repaid after tax payments (Chai, 1990).

There were widespread inefficiencies in tax administration, tax evasion and even resistance or violence against tax collectors. The 'contract management system'[15] encouraged bargaining and gamesmanship at the expense of legal compliance and financial accountability. The same process also characterised revenue sharing between central government and local governments.

The decrease in the ratio of government revenue over national income by 18 per cent between 1978 and 1989 was almost entirely accounted for by the decrease in the flow of direct taxes from the enterprise sector into the national income (Hussain and Stern, 1991).

As far as extra budgetary funds[16] are concerned, the amount of extra state budgetary funds increased to 227 billion yuan in 1988, which was 91.2 per cent of state revenue for the year (Figure 2.3). Both in terms of revenue and expenditure, the extra budgetary funds of local governments were larger than those of central government departments from 1982–7. The expenditure of extra budgetary funds of the former was much larger than revenue compared with similar expenditure by central government departments from 1985 to 1987 (SSB, 1990, p. 242). After deflation, budget expenditure growth rates were negative in 1988 and 1989, and the proportion of total budgetary subsidy in budget revenue increased.

Price reforms and inflation

Reform of the pricing system is an important cause of inflation. Great changes have taken place since the economic reform in 1979 (see Table 2.5). The gross index of commodity retail prices is the main indicator of price fluctuation in China. In 1987 the planned growth rate of the index was 6 per cent but it actually reached 7.3 per cent. In 1988 the planned

Figure 2.3   China's budget and extra budget funds, 1979–89

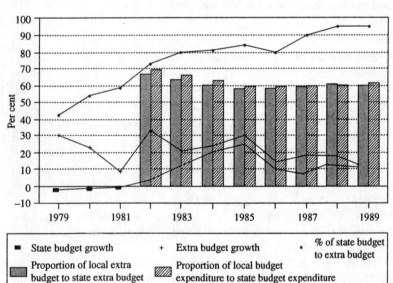

Source: China Statistical Yearbook (1990, 1991), pp. 242–3.

target was again 6 per cent, but it reached 18.5 per cent. In 1989 the target was 10.5 per cent, but after frequent adjustments the actual figure was 17.8 per cent (*China Statistical Yearbook*, 1990, p. 249). The figure planned for 1990 was 14–16 per cent, however the result in the first half of the year was only 3 per cent and that for the whole year was only 2.1 per cent (*People's Daily*, 17 January 1990, 17 February 1990). Although massive price increases by firms were stopped, the price structure and price system were still unreasonable and there remained a serious distortion of prices. Following the large-scale pricing liberalisation in 1992, in 1993 the state further liberalised the price of some important production materials, such as refined oil, part of state-allocated coal, most of state-allocated steel, part of iron ore and cement. The sales and purchasing prices of grain and oil were generally free from state control. The proportions of the value of the commodities under state pricing control in the gross value of social commodity retail sales, in that of purchased agri-products and byproducts, and in that of the income of production materials were only 4.8 per cent, 10.4 per cent and 13.8 per cent in 1993, respectively. The proportions of the value of the commodities under state pricing guidance[18] for the values mentioned above were only 1.4 per cent, 2.1 per cent and 5.1 per cent, while the proportions of the value of free market commodities were 93.8 per cent, 87.5 per cent and 81.1 per cent in 1993, respectively.

Price reform of the primary products such as grain, cotton, oil and coal was planned to take about twenty years from 1979, contributing to structural price increases of 3–5 percentage points annually. Among the consumer price growth rates in 1994 over 1993, the following prices were above 20 per cent: food (31.8 per cent), commodities for residents (21.3 per cent) and service items (25.7 per cent). Among foodstuff, grain increased by 50.7 per cent, poultry and poultry products by 41.6 per cent, vegetable oil by 64.1 per cent, seafood by 20.3 per cent, and fresh vegetables by 38.2 per cent. Compared with the growth rate of the price to producers of industrial products, which was 19.5 per cent, the retail price of agricultural production materials and the purchase price of agricultural products increased by 21.6 per cent and 39.9 per cent respectively. This clearly indicates that the radical reform of the pricing system in 1994 was one of the main causes of inflation in that period.

After a period of fluctuation, prices climbed to 27.7 per cent in October 1994 and annual inflation reached 21.7 per cent that year. The price increases of cotton, grain and other agri-products in 1994 caused a 43 per cent increase in the cash expenditure of the state banks when purchasing these products from January to October. Although this reform was widely welcomed by farmers,[19] the drastic raising of prices led to price-increase manipulation, especially as the backward circulation system for commodity sales became a mess and the price adjustment function of state commercial companies was weakened. This could indicate that the situation in China does not allow a radical and simple price reform policy. In his report to the recent annual session of the National People's Congress Premier Li Peng admitted to underestimating the repercussions of measures such as releasing the price control on many goods. He promised that no new price reforms would be adopted in 1995 (*Straits Times*, Singapore, 6 March, 1995).

According to the State Statistical Bureau of China the reform of the price system did not greatly benefit budget revenue in 1990, accounting for just 3 per cent of the nominal price increases. Over 75 per cent of the price increases was due to increases in industrial production costs. Fifteen per cent was caused by increases in agricultural production costs and the costs of trading, and only 7 per cent went to welfare funds of enterprises and their employees. The growth rate in revenue from taxation was 6.95 per cent, 4.59 per cent and 1.4 per cent in 1986, 1987 and 1988 respectively, which was much lower than the rate of growth of national income.

Dramatic changes had taken place in the composition of national income and the proportions contributed by state revenue, enterprise retention and household income (Table 2.6). Workers' wage income growth was faster than that of enterprise retention. On the other hand budget revenue fell sharply during the reform period.

Table 2.6   Distribution of the national income (per cent of national income)

	State revenue	Enterprise retention	Household income
1978	39.8	10.2	49.6
1988	18.6	11.3	70.2

Source: Chu Yan, mimeo, August 1990.[17]

Household income in 1989 increased by 280 per cent over the 1983 level, with an annual growth rate of 17 per cent, much faster than that of national income over the same period (10 per cent). (SSB, 1990, pp. 36, 131). 'Purchasing power outstanding' (SSB, 1990, p. 614, for example) covers 'cash in hand' and 'deposits', which can be regarded as the emission of money – from 1984–8 this accumulated to 113.5 billion yuan.

Enterprise costs and profits also push up inflation from the supply side. The responsibility system in state enterprises encouraged managers to increase the wages of workers faster than profits and taxes (Table 2.7).[20] The banking system failed to control the wage increases of enterprises.

Table 2.7   Taxation, productivity and wage comparison

	1985	*1986*	*1987*
A	1:0.73	1:1.015	1:1.12
B	2.5	7.2	9.9
C	20.0	13.1	23.1

Notes:
A = proportion of the taxes paid by the state enterprises to their total profits.
B = growth rates of the labour productivity of industry (per cent).
C = growth rates of the gross wage income (per cent).
Source: PBC, 1990, mimeo.

Structural imbalance of the economy

From 1984 the industrial processing sector developed at a very fast rate, putting great pressure on the agricultural sector, which was a main supplier of raw materials for industrial purposes. From 1985 to 1988 the average annual growth rate of industry was 17.8 per cent while that of agriculture was 3.9 per cent. In 1989 industry grew by 8.3 per cent while agriculture grew by 3.3 per cent (a ratio of 2.5:1). The output value of the processing industry was 46 per cent of industry as a whole (Wang, 1990).

Then there was the matter of investment. Agricultural investment came mainly from budgetary resources and bank credit. The proportion of agricultural investment to total investment in the national economy in 1980 and 1986 was 5.3 per cent and 3 per cent respectively. In 1985 national investment as a whole increased by 44.4 per cent while agricultural investment decreased by 0.5 per cent. At the same time, investment from local governments was even less than that from the central government.

As far as basic industry is concerned, the growth rate during the 1980s was not low, especially in the coal mining, electricity and steel production sectors. Electricity generation grew from 8.3 per cent in 1985 to 9.6 per cent in 1988, which alleviated some of the shortage in the electricity supply. However the amount of investment was still relatively low (Figure 2.4).

Figure 2.4   National income index of China (annual % changes, 1952 = 100)

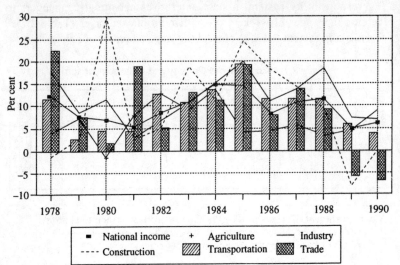

Source: China Statistical Yearbook (1990,1991).

Company insolvency and economic efficiency problems

Company insolvency had become a serious national problem by the end of the 1980s. To deal with this, the State Council set up a debt clearing office to lead a national programme. The office estimated a total debt of about 150 billion yuan in bilateral debts and about 300 billion yuan in multilateral debts – more than 31 per cent of total national income in 1989. By 10 October 1990 the debts that had been cleared, excluding those in capital construction projects, amounted to 110 billion yuan.[21] The office continued to deal with capital construction project debts.

The question was then raised of why the economy had this serious problem. Whether the clearing programme could solve the problem will be discussed in Chapter 4.

First, tight monetary policies brought protests from enterprises that there was a shortage of money. However in 1989 the money supply increased significantly compared with 1988, when the credit scale was already very large. The highest growth rates of the money supply, due to the whole banking system and the credit cooperatives, were 28.9 per cent and 28.7 per cent in 1984 and 1986 respectively. The highest growth during the twelve year period was in 1989 (Figure 2.5).

But why was there a working capital shortage in the enterprises? This could be explained by a number of factors: (1) inflation, which had offset

Figure 2.5   Uses of funds of banks and creditors, China (annual % changes)

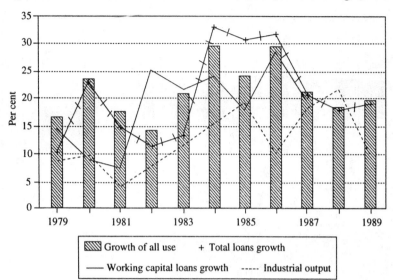

Source: China Statistical Yearbook (1990).

the increase in the money supply; (2) the high level of stock, which delayed the transformation from commodities to money and severely influenced the regular circulation of capital; (3) the expansion of commercial credit beyond the banking system (we will discuss this issue in Chapter 4); (4) the demand for bank credit, which exceeded the lending ability of the banking system (Figure 2.6); and (5) the various 'appropriations' paid by enterprises,[22] amounting to 20 billion yuan each year.

Second, the efficiency problem, characterised by relatively high inputs compared with outputs, had become increasingly alarming and provided one of the most important motives for reform. Taking industry as an example, the amount of profit and tax from each hundred yuan of capital input in to industrial enterprises that held 'independent accounting systems'[23] decreased from 25.6 yuan in 1980 to 20.53 yuan in 1988 and 18.24 yuan in 1989. The amount of fixed working capital (rationed by the state) used to produce each hundred yuan of output increased from 27.44–29.2 yuan in the period 1980–5 to 31.65–32.2 yuan in the period 1986–8. The growth rates of costs, in constant prices, of state enterprises with independent accounting systems increased year by year from between 0.38 per cent and 1.97 per cent in the period 1980–4 to 20 per cent in 1989 (SSB, 27 March 1990, mimeo).

Figure 2.6   Growth of working capital credit and GNP, China (average index)

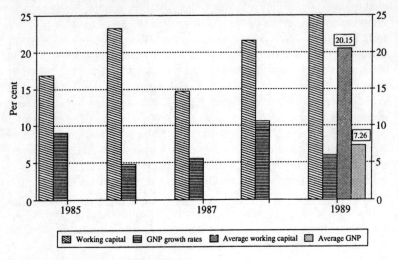

Source: People's Bank of China, 1990.

This situation worsened in the economic recession of 1989. One of the most important factors behind the decline in economic efficiency was that firms had been stimulated by profit and tax maximisation targets, which had been set in terms of output quantities by planners without examining the methods enterprises could employ to make profits.

* * *

The preceding sections have described the major problems in Hungary and China. Both economies experienced structural problems that were directly due to insufficient investment in specific sectors. The difference was that the level of total investment was low in Hungary but high in China. Hungarian banks lacked the capacity to invest due to the low level of national savings. Chinese banks, in contrast, had the more welcome problem of following correct investment policies. Clearly the situation in Hungary was of a different order of seriousness and is aptly summarised by the aphorism 'when there is no firewood, there is no point in discussing how to make a fire'.

A banking system has several different functions. Banks serve the economy as intermediaries, transforming savings and deposits into investments with varying maturities. Banks also guide their chosen borrowers to make efficient and profitable uses of their lending. Money can either be used to invest in medium and long-term projects or go into short-term consumption and/or riskless but profitable projects. Both the cases of Hungary and China show that it is relatively easy for a decentralising economy in a changing political environment to become myopic – to meet short-term needs such as the wage demands of the population and profit retention by firms. The desire to improve living standards could soon be jeopardised by a backward economic structure, especially a deficient infrastructure, leading to high unemployment and/or high inflation. The difference between China and Hungary was that the Chinese authorities discovered the problems quickly and were able to adjust by planning, thus keeping the economy growing rapidly. In Hungary heavy borrowing from abroad worsened the economy, which had been in the throes of its deepest recession since the 1930s.

In decentralising the economic systems, centralised public expenditure was bound to be reduced. A less obvious but more serious phenomenon was that public income might fall more sharply than public expenditure, the direct consequence of which (as happened in China) is an increase in the budget deficit. In addition, it was not obvious which part of expenditure should cut and which should be left intact. The real objective of decentralisation is to bring about efficiency, not necessarily to bring down state revenue. Otherwise there would be insufficient expenditure on necessary investments – such as those in infrastructure and structural adjustment – during the decentralisation process. Meanwhile the budget deficit would increase, causing inflation.

Whether it was right for the RCPEs to deregulate their banking systems during the transition phase remains in question. Decentralisation of the economies often resulted in financial disorder. The problems of Hungary and China also occurred in other RCPEs. The former Yugoslavia decentralised its banking system even earlier and more radically than the rest of Eastern Europe (see Dimitrijevic and Macesich, 1973). However the economic situation there deteriorated. The problem of inter-enterprise debt became very serious in many RCPEs in the 1990s, while banks became passive in dealing with these debts. They were unable to harden the credit constraint for various reasons, which will be analysed in Chapter 4.

BANKING DECENTRALISATION DURING TRANSITION

The banking system is important during transition for two main reasons. Firstly, the central bank is responsible for making monetary policy and banks are responsible for implementing that policy. Secondly, banks are an important intermediary in channelling financial resources into industry. Most of the reforming economies face structural adjustments that need investment. Long-term investment is desperately needed during transition while the financial market remains undeveloped and the production system relies heavily on bank financing. Banks may thus be central to the provision of long-term finance. Some related issues merit further discussion here.

The performance of different banking systems operating in different economic environments cannot be easily compared. However their contributions and problems are worth assessing individually. We intend to see whether a commercialised banking system really helps long-term finance, and whether ownership and type of bank are more important than monetary control during transition. It is difficult to evaluate the quality of banks' assets from published statements. However, with the help of the banking literature, we are able to discuss five issues, namely central bank control, commercial banking, the specialised banks, long-term financing and SOE financing.

Central banks during transition

When an economic system is transformed from a CPE to a market system, most of the responsibilities of financing the economy are inevitably shifted from the state budget to the banking system. Just as the banks in a market economy need a central bank (Goodhart, 1989a), an RCPE needs a central bank to conduct monetary policy and regulate the whole system. National banks shift from financing the production system directly to supporting the banking system (thereby serving the production system indirectly).

The key issues are whether the central banks can exercise control and how to implement that control. A financial effect of the reforms is the creation of a control vacuum for the central banks to fill. In CPEs the control power lay in the ability of the budget and the monetary authorities to allocate funds. 'A baby loves its mother for her milk' (Chinese idiom) – if the central bank has no 'milk' to offer, will the economy obey its regulations? A market economy obeys for two main reasons. Firstly, the central bank is the monetary authority and hence has administrative power. Secondly, the central bank has a set of effective instruments such as the base rate and its role as lender of last resort. But in the case of RCPEs if interest rate policy is not effective, and the administrative power of the government is ignored, the central bank may face problems of control. This is exactly what happened in the RCPEs. It is argued that the People's Bank of China

(PBC) does not have the necessary market-type instruments to control banks efficiently (see Shi and Cai, 1993; Fang and Li, 1993).

Refinancing credits from the National Bank of Hungary (NBH) were an important source of funds for the Hungarian Credit Bank. In the 1980s the proportion of refinancing loans in the liabilities of commercial banks generally exceeded 50 per cent (70 per cent in the case of certain large banks). In 1990 this ratio decreased to an average of 15 per cent (NBH refinancing was much lower than average in the case of short-term loans and higher in the case of loans with maturities exceeding one year). In 1991 the relative regulatory influence of the refinancing loans remained significant (Balassa, 1992). Central bank credit was important to the Chinese banking system – one third of bank loans (36 per cent in 1988) came from the PBC and 80 per cent of total PBC credit went to specialised banks (Figure 2.16; see also Dai, in Ma *et al.*, 1990, p. 802).

Refinancing credit to banks is necessary in the immature market economy not only as a support but also as a method of control or regulation by the central bank when the interest rate mechanisms are not effective. However this may give the central bank the appearance of a hybrid between a central bank and a commercial bank. When I investigated the NBH in Budapest in 1990 the central bankers told me frankly that refinancing credit remained the most effective instrument of NBH control over the banks. Why? Refinancing loans come from base money, which is composed of cash and reserves. When examined from the point of view of the economy as a whole, it is clear that credits create cash flow and the sources (deposits) of the banking system. Based on the linkage 'loans → deposits → cash', control of refinancing loans is an effective way of controlling the total loans of the banking sector.

Another issue is central bank independence during transition. Budget deficits are financed most easily by central banks, but central banks have a responsibility to restrict the budget deficit in order to control inflation. From 1987, when the banking system was radically liberalised in Hungary, inflation accompanied banking reform. There were seven years in the eleven-year period after banking decentralisation in China when Chinese government borrowing was larger than its deposits into the PBC. This means that the budget account in the banking system was overdrawn, indirectly indicating the budget deficit situation. In some years inflation either accompanied or followed such overdrafts. This indicates that a government facing great pressures during transition may need the help of a strong central bank on the one hand. Increasing the independence of central banks may help to restrict budget borrowing and overdrawing from the banking system on the other hand.

It may be better to increase independence more gradually. The Bank of England, the world's first central bank, founded in 1694, has not been allowed to become fully independent. Hong Kong, one of the most successful economies in the world, has never had an official central bank. From an historical perspective, central banks were created by a combination of political and economic factors in which the political were generally predominant. The responsibility for major decisions rests 'inevitably on the government of the day' (Cairncross, in Tonido, 1988). The independence of the Federal Reserve System in America is real but 'it is fragile' (Sylla, in ibid.). Although the Bundesbank is today the most independent central bank in Europe, its predecessor, the Reichsbank, was never really independent of the government of its time. The purpose of these examples is to illustrate that any institutional policy cannot be overstressed.

Commercial banks in transition

The basic task of a banking system is to finance the economy. A creditworthy banking system can solve the problem of the demand for investments by collecting deposits, organising funds, pooling savings and directing them to well-managed investment projects after proper assessment of their viability. Have the reforming banking systems performed this function well?

After the establishment of a two-tier banking system in Hungary in 1987, the amount of non-performing loans in the banking system grew from Ft2.8 billion to Ft43.3 billion in 1990, 89.6 per cent of the loans accumulating on the balance sheets of the large, state-owned banks. From the end of 1989 to the end of 1990 alone, uncollectable assets grew at a rate of 192 per cent, as did the proportion of total assets they represented. This grew from 1.78 per cent to 2.68 per cent.[24] In July 1992 the amount of bad debt was officially estimated at Ft60 billion, unofficial estimates put it at more than twice that amount. The system remained generally stable, simply because most Hungarian banks realised monopolistic profit margins as prudential regulations were weak.

The Hungarian problem was prolonged recession, the collapse of Eastern European markets and the Western recession exacerbating the situation. It is difficult to assess the banking system from the fluctuating values of assets and liabilities on the balance sheets of the Hungarian commercial banking group as a whole, but the balance sheet of the HCB shows a relatively clear deterioration. The fall in total liabilities in real terms has matched the decline in total deposits since 1987, the proportion of long-

and medium-term deposits falling by 50 per cent from 1987 to 1989. The HCB could not prevent the decrease in total assets in real terms, which must have constrained lending even if refinancing credit was able to be increased slightly from time to time. Short-term loans decreased sharply, without a sufficient increase in long- and medium-term loans (Figure 2.7). The other commercial banks had roughly the same experience. The commercialisation of the banking system in Hungary, therefore, did not really lead to an appreciable improvement in the collection of funds to finance the reconstruction of the economy.

Chinese banks differed significantly from those in Hungary. Benefiting from the fast growth in household savings and deposits from enterprises that had accompanied economic growth since 1978, the Chinese banks achieved an outstanding and continuous rate of growth in deposits. The commercial banks, such as the ICBC – the largest commercial bank – were also expanding rapidly (Figures 2.8 to 2.10). The banks' foreign currency assets increased extremely rapidly. The maturity structure of deposits and the liquidity ratios showed a significant increase in the banks' long-term sources. Therefore there was no need for the PBC to keep refinancing the banks to any great extent. The transformation of state-supported banks into independent commercial banks became not only desirable but also possible.

Figure 2.7   Some asset on the Hungarian Credit Bank balance sheet

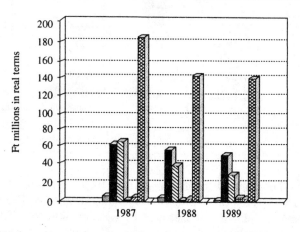

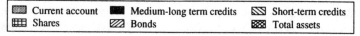

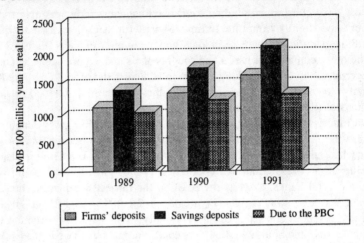

Figure 2.8   Firms' deposits, savings and People's Bank of China funds, Industrial and Commercial Bank of China

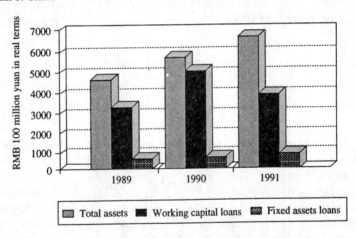

Figure 2.9   Working capital and fixed assets loans, Industrial and Commercial Bank of China

   Behind the financing task, the banking system performs a control function, ignorance of which can lead to serious problems. At the beginning of
1992 the estimated amount of bad debt in Hungary was around Ft50
billion, the vast majority of which was owed to the three big commercial
banks. Although a very large part of the non-performing loan stock of
these banks had been 'inherited' from the NBH, there was another reason

Figure 2.10 Total deposits, credits and net profits, Industrial and Commercial Bank of China

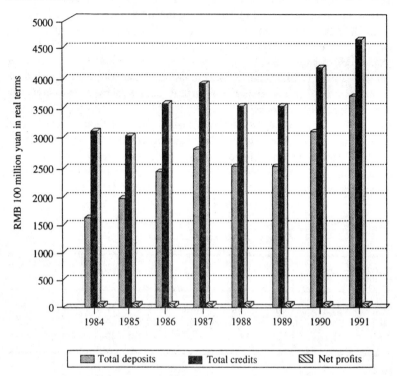

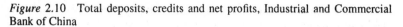

Source: Industrial and Commercial Bank of China Annual Rep[ort, 1989–91.

for the build-up: credit being extended without requiring any collateral. Such a practice obviously reduces even further the bankers' chances of recouping their loan losses (Estrin *et al.*, 1992).

Certain control problems in the development of Chinese banking are also revealed by the balance sheets of the state banking system. On the liability side, the growth rate of such items as enterprise deposits, the funds of banks and the profit and loss accounts were negative at the end of the 1980s. The growth rates of M0 were linked to inflation in some years, for example in 1984 and 1988. The financial statements also reveal that central government revenue weakened in the second half of the 1980s. On the asset side, the banks failed to control credit supply in certain years. Total bank loans showed a close and positive correlation with inflation in the period 1978–87 but the relationship broke down after the monetary authorities tightened the money supply in order to control inflation. Some off-balance-sheet factors since 1987, such as interenterprise debt problems and financial disorders, will be discussed in Chapter 4.

In 1988 the Chinese banks experienced a serious payments crisis. Lack of confidence in the Chinese economy led to panic buying and the hoarding of consumption goods by households. The PBC had to increase the money supply, which later caused inflation. Then followed a period of tight monetary policy, which was in turn followed by a recession that lasted about three years.

In 1988 the three ratios listed in Table 2.7 were at their lowest levels, indicating a crisis in confidence. They had already reached very low levels by 1987 but no action had been taken, which finally led to the payments crisis. Lin (1993) noted that the data in 1992 implied a similar trend. This was confirmed by the situation in 1993 (see Chapter 4).

Table 2.7   The ability to pay of the state banking system of China, 1985–92 in (per cent)

	1985	1986	1987	1988	1989	1990	1991	1992
RR	15.2	12.0	8.4	7.2	9.7	12.4	14.0	7.7
RC	27.0	24.1	19.9	19.3	22.3	25.2	27.0	19.5
LR	25.1	19.5	14.1	12.3	19.3	26.2	29.8	15.9

Notes:
RR = Banks' reserves/banks' deposits outstanding.
RC = Total banks' reserve capital/banks' deposits outstanding.
LR = Banks' liquid assets/banks' liquid liabilities.
Source: Lin (1993), Table 1, according to the PBC Annual Statistics Materials. The data for 1992 is estimated by Lin.

Specialised banks in transition

Zhou and Zhu (1987) argue that there are four differences between commercial banks in China and those in developed market economies. First, just as the overall political and economic management system in China is divided into geographic and sectoral management systems, so it is in banking. Local government at various levels and the relevant State Council departments are able to intervene in the credit business operations of commercial banks to a great extent. Second, central and local governments often instruct the commercial banks and their branches to make certain loans to conform with economic policies. The banks are obliged to do so. Third, because of the bargaining relationship between labour and management there is a critical shortage of bank supervision over the financial affairs of enterprises. People in enterprises are biased towards more bonus funds and less capital accumulation. The inflation of 1984–5 was at least partially caused by the relaxation of the banks' supervisory function. Fourth, the large specialised banks are not enterprises with an independent management and are not responsible for their own losses and profits. They therefore show no great concern about the efficiency of their credit operations.

A specialised bank differs from a commercial bank in that it prioritises government policy. Two questions may be asked. First, are the specialised banks still necessary? Second, how could a banking system dominated by specialised banks be transformed into a commercial banking system?

As far as the first question is concerned, there are specialised banks and venture capital investors in the West, and particularly in some very successful market economies such as Japan and Germany, where they are not only important but also profitable. The People's Construction Bank of China contributed to the economy by rapidly expanding investment under the policies of selective investment, vital energy, transportation, material production and high-technology projects being their investment priorities. The bank energetically pooled short-term funds into long- and medium-term investments, which formed the bulk of the portfolio. If the economy had lacked such banks to support it, development would not have been so successful.

If left to competitive market forces without the necessary support from the authorities at the start of transition, a specialised bank may either be weakened financially or change its nature by replacing macroeconomic interests with profit-maximisation as its priority. The total liabilities of the State Development Institute, including deposits, particularly long- and medium-term deposits, had been greatly reduced after decentralisation in Hungary. However, on average the proportion of profits to total loans was higher than that of a commercial bank in spite of the fact that the real value of long- and medium-term loans, and the proportions of total assets they represented, were drastically reduced in comparison with the increase in the proportion of short-term loans.

As the State Development Institute lost its original superiority in transforming short-term deposits into long-term loans, I reviewed the development of the State Development Bank, its predecessor, which had financed the production system relatively more efficiently by accumulating capital and reducing its dependency upon the state budget. The radical reforms in the second half of the 1980s brought a halt to this without achieving a satisfactory result. But the process seems to have succeeded in Chinese specialised banks.

However Chinese economists argue that, despite its fast expansion, the Chinese system is far from perfect. Firstly, the banks in China are specialised by sector rather than by specific banking business. They operate entirely within their own sector, which may cause unnecessary institutional expansion and inefficiency. Secondly, they have not been successful in coping with the repayment problem; at times they cannot collect the repayments due on their loans and credits from their debtors. For example loss-making companies in 1991 comprised 29.7 per cent of the total number of SOEs within the budgetary system. According to the Agricultural Bank of China at the end of 1990, 16.6 per cent of total loans outstanding were bad loans and delayed or suspended repayments. Meanwhile, 13.2 per cent of total PCBC loans outstanding were 'irregular loans' (Han, 1992).

Table 2.9 indicates that the growth rates of the free reserves (FR) of the specialised banks were all negative, and increasingly so. This suggests that the specialised banks lacked a capital-self-adjustment ability and had to rely on central bank credit. The economic expansion in 1988 and 1992 led to the lowest levels in the FR ratio. However the tight credit policy forced down the TC ratio to its lowest levels against the background of economic expansion in 1987, 1988 and 1992. Lin (1993) argues that the traditional control method of total credit ceilings should therefore be replaced. This sounds reasonable. There is an increasing necessity to find new and more effective

Table 2.9   Growth rates of free reserve and total credits of the state banking system of China (per cent)

	1986	1987	1988	1989	1990	1991	1992
FR	−25.0	−6.4	−27.1	−17.6	−11.5	−7.0	−29.9
BR	19.0	2.0	22.0	24.0	22.0	16.0	14.0
TC	29.4	20.3	17.0	17.9	22.8	19.8	17.9

Notes:
FR = Total bank reserves − reserves borrowed by banks (excluding interbank loans).
BR = Reserves borrowed by banks (including interbank loans) + the central bank loans to the banks.
TC = Total bank credits and loans.
Source: Lin (1993), Table 3.

methods of control. But the phase of transition is characterised by a certain ineffectiveness of the market mechanisms. If there is no effective replacement, control should be effected by the means available, including total credit ceilings. Regulations may help the specialised banks to keep the FR ratios at reasonable levels if the banks cannot adjust them effectively.

It would be wrong simply to conclude that large specialised banks are inefficient. In the last decade China's specialised banking system must have performed well in general, otherwise China would not have experienced such a relatively successful development. Taking the People's Construction Bank of China as an example, the bank helped the government to manage enormous investments that had been approved in the budget (Figure 2.11). It absorbed very impressively the increasing amounts of deposits not only from its traditional customers, the enterprise sector, but also from the household sector (Figure 2.12). Funds were mainly invested in fixed capital projects (Figure 2.13 and 2.14). This was also the case with another specialised bank – the China Investment Bank (CIB) (Figure 2.15). There were very few projects in the CIB that were not operated successfully.[25]

Recent literature shows that universal banking lowers financial costs. Calomiris (1993) compares the universal German banking system from 1870–1974 with its constrained US counterpart. He finds that large-scale universal banks that had long-term relationships with firms, provided low-cost

Figure 2.11   Selected liabilities, People's Construction Bank of China

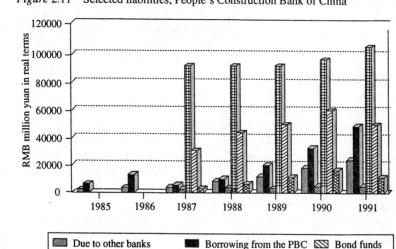

Figure 2.12   Total deposit and deposit structure, People's Construction Bank of China

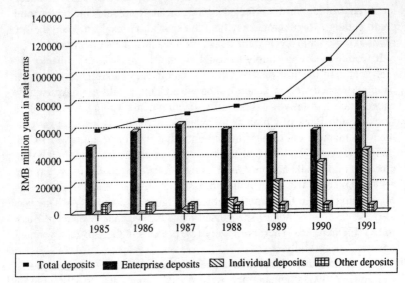

Source: People's Construction Bank of China, *Annual Report*, 1991.

finance to German industry. These low costs were reflected in lower investment banking spreads on securities and a higher propensity to issue equity relative to the US. A few large banks operated nationwide branch networks, lending directly to firms. Long-term relationships between universal banks and firms minimised the costs associated with monitoring and controlling the use of funds and distributing junior securities to investors willing to hold them. ('Junior securities' are a type of security with a claim on the assets and earnings of the issuer that is lower in priority, and contingent on payment to the holder of a 'senior security'). Even with good management, the Chinese banking system and its specialised banks cannot be transformed too radically, but instead may play a part in the industrial revolution during the process of transition, with the introduction of suitable reforms. Actually, in terms of its scale and degree of concentration the Chinese banking system is closer to the German banking system than it is to those of Britain and the US. Many economists agree that the German system is superior (see also Chapters 3 and 4). But banking in China has to remain separate from investment services until regulations are able to secure universal banking. This does not prevent banks from granting long-term credits.

As for the question of the transformation of the specialised banks into commercial banks, the newly-established policy banks need qualified staff.

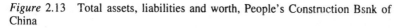

Figure 2.13   Total assets, liabilities and worth, People's Construction Bsnk of China

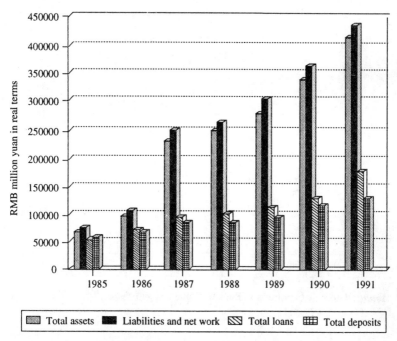

Source: People's Construction Bank of China, *Annual Report*, 1991.

This requires time for adequate recruitment and training. The state owned specialised banks also need time to gain commercial banking experience while accumulating their capital. Actually it would be relatively easy for a long-established specialised bank to conduct commercial banking business because it has staff with relevant banking experience. Moreover accumulated capital would help it to be financially independent. This has been the experience in the gradual transformation of some specialised banks in certain Asian NICs. An example is the State Development Bank of Singapore, which was a specialised bank completely owned by the government. With the development of its business in a fast-growing economy, the bank gradually diversified its portfolio, accumulated its capital and cast off its reliance on government financing.

Long-term investments during transition

Bank loans are an important financial source for industry. Banks are particularly central to the provision of not only short-term finance but also

Figure 2.14   Loan structure, People's Construction Bank of China, 1991 (RMB mn, nominal)

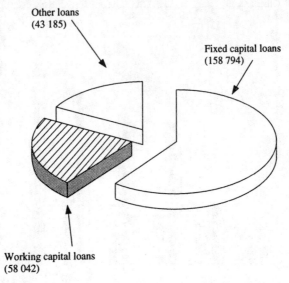

Other loans
(43 185)

Fixed capital loans
(158 794)

Working capital loans
(58 042)

Source: People's Construction Bank of China annual Report, 1991.

long-term investments. While there are economists in the CPEs who criticise the problem of excess long-term investment in their own system, some economists in the West stress the important role of long-term contracts in promoting long-term investment (see Chapter 3). The importance to industries of long-term investment over shorter-term funds has not been keenly stressed by some RCPEs since one of the reasons behind their reforms has been the need to cope with so-called excessive long-term investment. It is important to note, however, that once the planning regime is replaced, the situation may change significantly.

The idea that the time horizon of investors was too short in the UK goes back to at least the mid-1970s. Whether equity financing or debt financing is better able to cope with 'short-termism' has been debated ever since (see Edwards, 1987; Ball, 1991). When CPEs become RCPEs financial markets are not really helpful. It seems it is difficult to construct a system that bridges the gap between 'short-termism' and 'long-termism'. While securiy investment services are prohibited at this stage of the reform, banks should be encouraged to engage in long-term lending.

Figure 2.15   Distribution of Assets, China Investment Bank

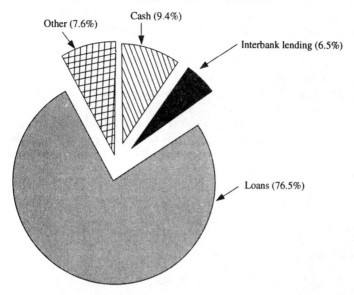

Source: China Investment Bank, *Annual Report,* 1989.

Not all banks in a market economy attach enough importance to long-term investments. Their ability to do so depends on the structure of the banking system and the policies of the authorities. Empirically, because of the increasing competitive risks prevalent in markets, commercial banks have a tendency to be myopic. Long-term investments may not be profitable in the short-term. Chinese banks such as the Industrial and Commercial Bank did not stress profits as much as the Hungarian banks. But they were, and still are, profitable. As the banking system is liberalised, competition and financial risks may force banks to deviate from their former tasks and macroeconomic policies. For an independent commercial bank nothing is more important than its expected return. If information from markets is distorted in any way, and therefore cannot guide banks to make correct allocations, financial disorder and even turmoil can be precipitated by speculators.[26]

In such a situation a profit-oriented commercial bank, or even a state-specialised financial institution can become myopic after decentralisation, as in the case of the Hungarian State Development Institute. In actuality, the long-term investment solidus total assets ratio did decrease and short-term investment projects came to dominate the portfolio, while the profit solidus total assets ratio and the profit solidus total income ratio grew to be relatively high (short-term biased) (see Appendices 2.1 and 2.2). The projects of '*duan, ping, kuai*' (short-term, common products and quick profit return) were often more attractive to Chinese producers and bankers than those of energy, transportation and raw materials. Industry, especially some infrastructure sectors, suffered from low investment levels, which brought about a backward industrial structure and a low economic growth rate in some RCPEs, for example Hungary.

When we argue the importance of long-term financing, a traditional problem of the banking system should not be ignored, namely the long-term bias of some state banks and their tendency to ignore market risks when allocating loans. This can lead to the repayment problem that has been experienced by the Chinese banks. Once market mechanisms had been introduced they failed to use certain supervisory instruments for market banking, such as banks' liquidity and risk ratios.

SOE finance and banking supervision

An interesting issue is whether bank credits should be available to SOEs that find themselves in difficulty, as one third of all SOEs in China turned out to be loss-makers. If banks are not selective their profits are threatened, and they may be dragged into payment crises. But this is only one side of the story. According to Dewatripont and Tirole (1993, see Chapter 3), managers are rewarded in good times by letting relatively passive shareholders retain control. Adverse conditions call for tough interference by debt holders. There are not many private shareholders in the RCPEs. The state could be regarded as the dominant shareholder of the SOEs. Firms need help from debt holders in order to avoid bankruptcy costs and sunk costs. The SOEs and the key projects planned by the authorities are given priority in the allocation of bank credit in China, but not necessarily in Hungary. The latter shows more interest in privatising the SOEs than in rescuing them.

Actually, by way of financial support the banks gained control over the SOEs. This control helped the banks to supervise and monitor firms and this contributed to turning loss-makers into profitable enterprises. My field studies demonstrated that the People's Construction Bank of China supervised its customers thoroughly. The PCBC had a permanent staff in Beijing Renmin Jijie Zung Chang (BRJGP, a medium-sized SOE customer). A representative of the bank sat at important factory meetings and was entitled to check any financial records. The PCBC has well-designed regulations for credit, following government macroeconomic policy. The

Regulations for Technical Improvement Credits made by the Dongsi Branch of the PCBC applied the principle of '*zhuan kuan zhuan yong*' in lending[27] and set up detailed regulations and principles on management, objectives, conditions and the process of credit approval and supervision. There was an increasing amount of 'special project funds' on the balance sheet of BRJGP, which had to obey this principle (Table 2.10). The problems of the economy, revealed in the previous section, demonstrate that this principle may not always be followed advantageously by the banking system as a whole.

The banks had to control and supervise debtors during periods both of prosperity and adversity. Loss-making was due not only to efficiency problems but also to problems of information and inflation typically found during transition. Companies which are attractive from a macroeconomic point of view may not be efficient from the microeconomic angle. Profit makers may report losses to reduce tax payments. Apart from the loss makers, the other two thirds of the Chinese SOEs were still making profits, especially most of the large and medium-sized companies. Supporting the profit makers and helping the loss makers may be a better strategy than simple privatisation. In this situation, helping means active control, supervision and even restructuring rather than the passive granting of credit.

CONCLUSIONS

Since economic conditions vary from country to country, any banking model applied by RCPEs cannot be simply analysed in the phase of transition. The radically commercialised Hungarian banking system suffered greatly from the recession and performed not much better than its predecessor. But the Chinese banking model, still dominated by state-owned specialised banks even after decentralisation, experienced an expansionary

Table 2.10   Funds balance sheet of BRJGP (million yuan at end of year)

	1980	1983	1988
Fixed capital	12.8	29.3	58.9
Working capital	13.5	26.0	54.3
Special project funds	2.3	14.1	53.1

Source: BRJGP (1990).

period in financing the economy. But there was also a close relationship between economic problems and the developments in banking, as reflected in the financial statements of the banks and the literature. The full extent of this relationship is not visible in the financial statements because of the limited information provided in them. Some off-balance-sheet factors obviously played a part. Financial disorders and interenterprise debt problems need to be analysed further (see Chapter 4), taking these elements into account.

The arguments generated from these studies are that ownership and type of bank are less important than central bank regulation and supervision, and that the reforms have reduced long-term investment provision to enterprises, at least in Hungary. It is important to deal with this problem. But commercialisation of the banking system may not be the only means of improving corporate finance.

Ideally, banking reforms should gradually increase central bank independence, improve the regulation of state banks and strengthen banking supervision of the production system. The separation of 'policy banking' from commercial banking through the establishment of state policy banks in China may solve some of the problems, but this needs careful design and steady implementation. Banks should, of course, avoid payment crises if possible. Firms are likely to face financial distress during transition, but there is no simple solution to this. The historical task of long-term investment remains the banks' foremost responsibility. The fulfilment of these tasks needs a capable central bank to regulate banks and control money. It also requires diversified banks, including some policy banks, to finance the economy, with proper supervision and monitoring.

APPENDICES

Appendix 2.1   Comparison of investment indications (per cent)

	1987	1988	1989	Mean
Hungarian Credit Bank				
Long investments/total assets[1]	38.9	42.4	35.0	38.8
Short investment/total assets[2]	34.8	26.2	22.2	27.7
National Commercial and Credit Bank				
Long investments/total assets	36.4	43.9	37.1	39.1
Short investments/total assets	42.9	39.0	28.9	36.9
Budapest Bank of Hungary				
Long investments/total assets	34.1	32.8	35.2	34.0
Short investments/total assets	36.9	26.6	25.6	29.7
Hungarian Foreign Trade Bank/				
Overseas Credit Bank of Hungary[3]	(HFTB)	(OCB)	(OCB)	
Long investments/total assets	5.4	9.3	17.1	–
Short investments/total assets	13.4	13.2	8.9	–
General Banking and Trust Company				
Long investments/total assets	30.7	31.3	24.2	28.7
Short investments/total assets	26.7	22.9	15.0	21.5
All Hungarian banks				
Long investments/total assets	30.2	31.3	24.6	28.7
Short investments/total assets	32.7	22.9	15.0	25.3
State Development Institute				
Long investments/total assets	28.6	20.8	5.6	18.3
Short investments/total assets	43.1	34.0	42.5	39.9

Notes:
1. Investments of five years or longer.
2. Investments of less than a year.
3. Two commercial banks that issued balance sheets only for 1987, and for 1988 and 1989, respectively.

Appendix 2.2   Comparison of profit indicators of the Hungarian banks(per cent)[1]

	1987	1988	1989	Mean
Hungarian Credit Bank				
Profit/equity capital	72.2	47.7	62.8	60.9
Profit/total asset	3.2	3.4	4	3.5
Profit/total income	27.6	24.4	23.5	25.2
National Commercial and Credit Bank				
Profit/equity capital	68.7	53.9	49.9	57.5
Profit/total asset	3.2	4.8	4.5	4.2
Profit/total income	29.5	28.8	24.5	27.6
Budapest Bank of Hungary				
Profit/equity capital	61.1	62.4	56.6	60.0
Profit/total asset	3.8	5	4.2	4.3
Profit/total income	34.6	33.5	23.6	30.6
Hungarian Foreign Trade Bank/				
Overseas Credit Bank of Hungary[2]	(HFTB)	(OCB)	(OCB)	
Profit/equity capital	72.0	49.1	88.9	–
Profit/total asset	2.5	3.7	3.7	–
Profit/total income	25.9	37.5	23.5	–
General Banking and Trust Company				
Profit/equity capital	18.8	–	–	–
Profit/total asset	3.3	–	–	–
Profit/total income	28.2	–	–	–
All Hungarian banks				
Profit/equity capital	67.1	51.8	72.2	63.7
Profit/total asset	3.1	4	3.9	3.7
Profit/total income	28.9	29.9	23.6	27.5
State Development Institute				
Profit/equity capital	24.1	24.7	35.8	28.2
Profit/total asset	4.8	5.9	4.4	5.0
Profit/total income	29.5	41.4	29.9	33.6
State Development Bank	*1984*	*1985*		
Profit/equity capital	196.0	117.6	–	–
Profit/total assets	0.8	0.9	–	–
Profit/total income	16.6	17.5	–	–

Notes

1. Data calculated in nominal values.
2. Commercial banks that issued balance sheets only for 1987, and for 1988 and 1989, respectively.

Source: PENZGUGYI ADATOK, pp. 327, 333, 345.

3 Financial Development and Banking Control

As we have acquired powers of control over physical nature, it is now essential for us to acquire powers of control over man himself and over his development. And as the first was acquired by the application of strict methods of observation and deduction, so must the second be. Science will not be checked (Radcliffe-Brown, 1979, p. 134).

INTRODUCTION

Economic development is usually accompanied by financial development. Financial development can be defined as an increase in financial intermediation and is reflected in an increased separation between savers and investors. This separation has consequences for the sectoral balances in the economy and for the stability of the economy. The former are affected because net savings and net investment are not necessarily equally distributed between the various sectors of the economy. This increases the scope for discrepancies between planned savings and investments. A system of financial flows, involving financial intermediation, becomes necessary. A means of regulating this system also becomes important in order jointly to satisfy the interests of lenders and borrowers. With economic development, the financial system of a country also grows.

Goldsmith (1969, 1983) finds that (1) in the early stages of economic development the financial superstructure grows faster than the economy; (2) the level of the indicators of financial development and their change with time can differ between countries. It depends, for example, on differences between the rates of economic growth and differences in the economic structure (such as concentration of production in larger corporations that are dependent on external finance, or in household firms relying on self-finance); and (3) financial development tends to start with the banking system and then gradually spreads to non-bank financial institutions. Goldsmith presents this as a rule. In the case of RCPEs, the development of the financial system is being undertaken as a condensed phase with rapid reform occurring as a result of consciously designed strategies rather than slowly evolving historical changes.

Since, as described in Chapters 1 and 2, RCPEs are restructuring their financial systems extensively, the question arises of whether their banking reforms have been well designed. This chapter examines theories of financial development and of banking as a basis for making such assessments, and it is particularly concerned with the light shed by the theories on banking control and the control of banks.

Here, *banking control* embraces two important functions of the banking system: internal self regulation and control and externally monitoring the non-bank production system. *Control of banks* refers to the policies conducted by governments and by the monetary authorities (the central banks). The issue covers macroeconomics in relation to monetary policies and microeconomics with regard to the nature of the relationship between the banking system and the production system.

The above issues are treated in a theoretical discussion. After a general review of financial development theories, some typical models from the theories are selected aids to understanding the special nature of the RCPEs during transition. This is followed by a review of some extremely interesting Western literature on the functions of the banking system as a theoretical basis for our hypothesis of monetary control through the banking system during transition. We then look at some Western and Chinese literature on credit rationing that is relevant to the argument about the ineffectiveness of the free interest rate and on the necessity and possibility of controlling financial development in RCPEs.

HOW TO TREAT THE MARKET: A REVIEW OF FINANCIAL DEVELOPMENT THEORIES

An issue repeatedly tackled by modern financial development theories is how to model the market, which turns on the question of how markets are cleared.

A key issue is how reliable the interest rate is in clearing financial markets. On this point, modern financial development theories can be divided into two basic schools. One believes in market efficiency through interest rates while the other cites various other ways of adjustment rather than relying mainly on interest rate clearing.

Tobin (1965) discussed the role of monetary factors in determining the degree of capital intensity. Households allocate their wealth between money and productive capital assets. The return on capital relative to money correlates positively with the ratio of capital to money, the capital/labour ratio, labour productivity and per capita incomes. Reduction of the relative yield on money (either by increasing deposit interest rates or by taxing money) causes capital/labour ratios to rise, accelerating the rate of economic growth.

By imposing loan rate ceilings, public sector deficits can be financed at lower cost (although the private sector is hindered when competing for available funds, according to Fry, 1973). Development planning models have been especially common in CPEs as well as in developing countries, using selective or directed credit policies to implement planned sectoral investment programmes with institutional loan rate ceilings.

Such a strategy of low, controlled interest rates and financial repression is challenged by McKinnon (1973) and Shaw (1973), who provide theoretical frameworks for analysing the role of financial development in the process of economic growth. McKinnon uses outside money in his model while Shaw uses inside money; in McKinnon's model real money balances are complements to, rather than substitutes for, tangible investment. Both models lead to the view that financial liberalisation is a growth-enhancing economic policy. Their views will be discussed in the next section.

Financial liberalisation gives a central role to increased interest rates. However Taylor (1979, 1981, 1983), Van Wijnbergen (1982, 1983a, 1983b, 1985) and other neostructuralists argue that raising interest rates increases inflation in the short run through a cost-push effect, and at the same time lowers the rate of economic growth by reducing the supply of credit, in real terms, available to finance investment. Under their assumptions, financial liberalisation eventually brings down the growth rate. Their assumptions include (in different combinations) exogenous wage determination, intermediate imports, cost-pushed pricing, determination of aggregate saving by income distribution, and the coexistence of formal banking and informal credit markets.

Another increasingly popular body of literature is on asymmetrical information. Marked discrepancies that may take a long time to adjust exist not only in the productivity of factors, but also in capital markets (Stiglitz, 1993, p. 346). Imperfect information can lead to excess demand and/or supply. Unemployment and credit rationing may occur (Stiglitz and Weiss, 1981, p. 409). There are inefficiency problems in the financial system (Tobin, 1984) and in financial markets (Wadhwani, 1988). Thorne (1989) uses twelve cases to show why a market solution to a financial crisis might not be feasible. One conclusion links successful development programmes to an important role for the government (Stiglitz, 1993, p. 347). Harris (1988) argues that the lesson to be drawn from the South Korean case of the 1965 reforms would be that growth resulted from an increased role for the state, rather than the simple liberalisation of market forces.

ARE FINANCIAL LIBERALISATION MODELS USEFUL TO
REFORMING CPES?

Some of the pre- and post-reform problems encountered in the CPEs are
similar to those experienced by less developed countries (LDCs). Since
1973 the most influential financial development theories have been
embodied in the financial liberalisation models put forward by McKinnon
and Shaw. Because this literature does not deal with short-run consequences, nor with their possible conflict with the professed long-run
targets, local economists in many market-based LDCs, who cannot afford
to ignore these problems, have often resisted the recommended policies
(Van Wijnbergen, 1983a, p. 434). However radical reformers in Eastern
Europe and some people in Asia have been attracted by this type of argument. Indeed the models applied in Eastern Europe may be theoretically
underpinned by the financial liberalisation literature, in spite of the fact
that McKinnon himself has revised his theory, especially in relation to the
problems of RCPEs (McKinnon, 1991).

There are strong arguments for financial liberalisation. Before going on
to assess them, some key differences between CPEs and LDCs are
identified in the next subsection. It would also be interesting to identify
where and why McKinnon has revised his views, and this will be done at
the end of this section.

Some economic differences between CPEs and LDCs

Financial development theories are based on issues pertaining to LDCs,
which differ fundamentally from CPEs. One such difference lies in their
economic systems. Most LDC markets are dominated by private ownership, with different degrees of state ownership of property. CPEs were
entirely centrally planned and the whole economy dominated by state
ownership. 'Virtually all economic activity in such systems was directed
(albeit imperfectly) by the state, and private enterprise was illegal except
in a narrow set of clearly delimited spheres' (Burkett and Lotspeich,
1992). The importance of this characteristic is that governments may play
a much more useful role in an RCPE than in an average LDC, if the
country remains politically stable during transition.

The financial structure of CPEs differs from that in poor countries,
described by Goldsmith (1969) as follows: (1) SOEs in CPEs relied more
on bank financing than do the 'individual economic units' in LDCs; (2) no
primary securities were issued in CPEs except (a few) government bonds,
and (3) there were no 'organised' markets for such primary securities as

bonds (even government bonds), mortgages, or common stock before the recent economic reforms. There is another difference between CPEs and LDCs that was not discussed by McKinnon (1973). In 'underdeveloped economies' the demand for real cash balances and the demand for physical capital are highly complementary in private asset portfolios, but this is not the case in CPEs due to their two channels of money and income control policy (see Chapter 1). There was almost no private investment and whether there was a determinate optimal real return on money (Ibid., p. 67) remains questionable.

Therefore the possible effects of financial development models need to be carefully assessed in the case of a CPE even if they are appropriate to LDCs. The context of financial relationships and the role for central banking institutions should be addressed anew, since financial control during marketisation involves a unique set of political–economic problems (Burkett and Lotspeich, 1992).

McKinnon (1973) built up his original model based on an understanding of market fragmentation in LDCs and by criticising the neoclassical and Keyensian hypothesis of homogeneous capital. Therefore unification of the capital market should come first and foremost. He suggests a kind of economic development generating high rates of saving and investment and 'accurately reflecting social and private time preference' (Ibid., p. 9) by means of free interest rates.

Three points are relevant to RCPEs. First, regarding the assumption that higher deposit rates will increase the savings rate, low rates of saving and investment were not a problem in CPEs prior to the reforms. Although household deposits were low, saving was manipulated to very high levels by the government by extracting profits directly from the SOEs and keeping household incomes low. The aggregate saving problem arose only after the tax system had been weakened in the decentralisation reforms. Second, informal finance was illegal and simply did not exist in the strictly established CPE model. There was basically no private sector access to investment funds. Therefore a fragmentation problem in terms of market organisation did not exist. However McKinnon defines fragmentation more rigorously as the existence of widely differing marginal returns on physical investments undertaken in different enterprises; it is not clear whether that problem did exist in CPEs, but in principle it would be incompatible with the planning system. The LDC-type fragmentation and curb markets have been developing in the RCPEs since the economic reforms in recent years. In these markets, prevailing prices need not reflect true economic scarcity. However it may be more easily solved by an RCPE that has just started to experience the problem than an LDC that has suffered from the problem for a long time. Third, unlike the firms in a market economy, producers in CPEs are largely state owned and are often monopolies. The increasing costs from interest rate rises may not force them into bankruptcy, and it may be easy for them to pass on the costs to their consumers by raising prices (see Chapter 1).

McKinnon's additional argument points to the importance of financial intermediation. Higher time deposit rates will lead to an influx of deposits into commercial banks. This 'raises the real size of the banking system and hence the net flow of real bank credit to finance investment', and helps long-run growth. The increased availability of funds for working capital purposes will also increase output and so reduce inflationary pressure for a given level of aggregate demand.

Neostructuralist economists argue with this, citing the existence of 'flourishing unorganised money markets' in LDCs (Van Wijnbergen, 1982, 1983a, 1985). If the public can lend directly to industry or agriculture in curb markets in an LDC, then time deposits are not closer substitutes for cash, gold and so on than they are for loans extended on the curb markets. There were no money markets and no capital markets in CPEs. Yet imbalance in terms of economic development did exist, and still exists, being the combined result of historical development, government policy and the economic system. The development-stage imbalance remains mainly within the public sector and between economic areas, rather than among the population or between firms and households. Imbalance may have the same effect as fragmentation upon price determination – prevailing prices need not reflect true economic scarcity.

What we have gained from such analyses is controversial. As the banking systems in most CPEs are more organised and more powerful (in terms of working-capital financing of firms) than those in LDCs, McKinnon's and Shaw's assumption of the importance of financial intermediation to these economies is reasonable (nevertheless they do not have curb markets). The problem lies in utilising the advantages of the existing banking systems while minimising their drawbacks, that is, how to bring in the banking system when implementing a stabilisation policy. The characteristics of RCPEs bring into question the traditional view on monetary policy. A high rate of interest may not necessarily be the key determinant of economic growth when market immaturity, firm monopoly and economic imbalances coexist between areas and sectors.

Is the liberalisation remedy feasible in RCPEs?

It is necessary to review the original McKinnon and Shaw literature because of its influence upon the RCPE reforms. 'Shallow finance' in

Shaw (1973, pp. 3–4) and 'financial repression' in McKinnon (1973, pp. 68–77) refer to the situation in LDCs where indiscriminate distortions of financial prices, including interest rates and foreign-exchange rates, reduce the real growth and the real size of the financial system relative to non-financial magnitudes. This stops or gravely retards the development process.

However financial restriction policies conducted in Portugal from 1962 to 1973 (Lundberg, 1964; Banco de Portugal, 1963), Turkey from 1963 to 1970 (Fry, 1971) and Korea since 1965 (Min, 1976) appear to have been successful in cases where a higher proportion of funds from the financial system was transferred to the public sector. A higher income elasticity and a lower cost elasticity cause income velocity of circulation to be low and falling, permitting a greater public sector deficit to be financed at a given rate of inflation and a given level of nominal interest rates.

CPEs were financially restricted but they were also successful in handling this policy during their periods of industrialisation. The banking systems and money in CPEs were favourable in controlling both the production sector and the private sector (see Chapter 1). Obligatory holding of government bonds and even household deposits could be imposed at zero or often negative interest cost, in order to tap this source of saving to the public sector. Private bond and equity markets were completely removed not only for the non-extraction of seigniorage, but also for well-known systemic reasons. The imposition of interest rate ceilings (or subsidised rates) and foreign exchange controls stifled competition to public sector fund-raising from the private sector and increased the flow of domestic resources to the public sector without higher tax, inflation or interest rates. Selective credit policies followed the national plans to encourage banks to invest according to priority targets.

McKinnon and Shaw also pointed out the problems that existed in CPEs. For example low or negative deposit rates induced by administrative manipulation discouraged bank deposits on the part of the population (although the low rates did not discourage obligatory enterprise deposits). Low loan-rate ceilings encouraged irresponsible misappropriation of loans on the part of financial institutions. Under the regime guided by planners' rationale, a certain proportion of potentially high-yielding investments might be rationed out, and great discrepancies in rates of return might certainly be unavoidable.

In LDCs low interest rates produced a bias in favour of current consumption and against future consumption, but in CPEs, where demand was under control, planners took more advantage of the low-rate cost to allocate long-term investments in favour of future consumption. Some favoured SOEs, which were able to borrow all the funds they wanted from banks at low rates, chose relatively capital-intensive projects. It is important to recognise that once the systems were radically decentralised, the same economic distortion under interest rate ceilings in LDCs could also exist in the reforming CPEs. A typical example is loan delinquency. Subsidised loan rates discourage prompt loan repayment. High delinquency and default rates reduce the flexibility and increase the fragility of financial systems, an issue taken up specifically in Chapter 4. Because of the low rate level, potential lenders may engage in relatively low-yielding direct investment instead of lending by way of depositing money in a bank. Firms are therefore restricted to mainly self-financing and interenterprise lending and may avoid bank supervision to generate payment disorders.

According to McKinnon (ibid., p. 124), savings rise as the attractiveness of money and near-monies increases. 'Stocks of monetary assets will be high relative to income if the real return on holding money is high'. Whether this is workable in LDCs is a question for others to investigate. However it is certainly questionable in the reforming CPEs. As indicated in Chapter 2, investment declined sharply from 1988–91. According to WIIW (1993, pp. 11–20), investment is the major component of S (savings), together with government deficit (D) and trade balance (E). The savings ratios ($s = S/\text{GDP}$) in Hungary, Poland and the CSFR were all decreasing under the high interest rates during 1988–91, as Table 3.1 shows.

Savings in CPEs, as elsewhere, were determined by a combination of diverse factors, such as GNP, real wage rate (and therefore inflation) and employment, as well as return on money. In addition, without the substantial development of security markets and the access of the population to the markets, the rise of the return on money would not be sustainable, since the latter would lose its signalling function. Private savings were not sensitive to the real return on holding money and its stability. Given the consumption inelasticity of income caused by the supply constraint on some consumption goods and/or the specific consumption type, savings should be relatively stable regardless of the return on money. The collapse of economic growth in most of the Eastern European economies since the liberalisation of their banking systems has been caused by low investment, and thus savings, according to Table 3.1. The rise in Chinese savings since the reform has been due largely to economic growth and growth in real wage rates, rather than to simple increases in deposit rates. Several Asian countries have experienced a fall in savings following the abolition of credit ceilings as households have responded to the relaxation of liquidity constraints by taking on more debt (Andersen, 1993).

Table 3.1   Savings ratios and components of savings for CSFR, Hungary and Poland, 1988–91

	s CP	P	S CP	I	GDP CP	D	I	E
			(previous years = 100)		*(S as % of GDP)*			
CSFR:								
1988	0.253	0.247	106.0	97.7	102.6	0.30	22.4	2.6
1989	0.256	0.246	102.5	103.6	101.4	0.80	22.9	1.9
1990	0.211	0.211	82.2	109.1	99.6	−0.90	25.1	−3.1
1991	0.229	0.247	91.3	67.9	84.1	1.10	20.3	1.6
Hungary:								
1988	0.208	0.209	100.9	97.3	9.9	0.70	18.0	2.2
1989	0.240	0.255	115.6	105.8	100.4	2.80	18.9	2.3
1990	0.212	0.217	85.3	93.1	96.7	0.03	18.2	2.9
1991	0.189	0.193	78.7	75.9	88.0	4.40	15.7	−1.2
Poland:								
1988	0.298	0.292	107.3	112.6	104.1	0.20	26.0	3.5
1989	0.346	0.389	116.4	114.4	100.2	3.50	29.7	1.3
1990	0.298	0.321	76.1	63.3	88.4	−0.20	21.3	8.7
1991	0.255	0.237	79.2	90.2	92.4	3.82	0.7	1.0

Notes:
P = current prices; CP = constant prices: CSFR – CP of 1986, Hungary – CP of 1985, Poland – CP of 1990; S = savings ratio; s = savings; D – government deficit; E = trade balance; I = investment.
Source: WIIW estimates.

Both McKinnon and Shaw argue that a system of directed credit and low interest rates discourages lending to riskier and longer maturity loans, hampers competition within the financial sector and contributes to credit rationing with no guarantee that credit will be granted to the more productive projects. However, in fact, liberalised or free market rates in RCPEs and some developed economies, including the UK, may not necessarily overcome the short-sightedness of investors. Even in the West, interest rates are not free of limit action and control. The main difference lies in the methods of interest rate management.

McKinnon's revised views

The main message of McKinnon's 1973 book was that finance and trade liberalisation with borrowing and lending at substantial real rates of interest was made possible by a stable price level. This was not easy to achieve, particularly due to the difficulty of government control over the rate of expansion in nominal cash balances (merely mentioned in the 1970s, but increasingly stressed in recent years). At the end of the 1980s, however, he admitted that his message was 'full of potential pitfalls' and that he was now more inclined to emphasise the pitfalls (McKinnon, 1989). Cho (1984, p. 7) indicates that 'without substantial development of security markets, full scale financial liberalisation would not be sustainable since there would be strong incentives for the government to intervene in the credit market'. This is certainly valid in the case of an RCPE. But McKinnon also notes other difficulties.

Liberalised or controlled?

McKinnon acknowledges some differences between an economy emerging from Stalinist central planning and a more typical LDC, such as differences in generating government revenue (1993, pp. 936–7). It was the problem of financial control in RCPEs, especially in Russia, that most concerned McKinnon. This problem was also vital to the Chinese reforms and will be further examined in the next chapter. The issue of *how* to tackle the problem is another matter. A key question is whether RCPEs should be advised to let their financial systems be fundamentally liberalised or controlled.

Is the banking scheme workable?

Control was difficult in the early stage of the reforms, when many SOEs operated with soft-budget constraints and the government ran deficits because of subsidies. In some circumstances the inherited excess supply of money ('monetary overhang') contributed directly to inflation. Having been branches of the state bank initially, commercial banks had to stop liberalised enterprises from wasting capital and divert them from possible moral hazards (McKinnon, 1991, p. 138). McKinnon has proposed that this control could be achieved by simply disconnecting firms and banks.

McKinnon's most recent argument is that there should be an explicit distinction between 'liberalised' and 'unliberalised' or 'traditional' firms. They should operate under quite different rules (which would change as the sequence went from stage to stage) in order to implement monetary control and avoid financial crises early in the reform process. In stage one there should be no bank lending whatsoever to firms of either kind, so that liberalised enterprises 'are confined to self-finance and to borrowing from the non-bank capital market'. In stage two, commercial banks should be allowed to conduct 'fully collateralised short-term lending' to these firms (ibid.)

However it is difficult to distinguish which enterprises have been liberalised and which are completely traditional. Most of the SOEs have been affected by the reforms. Many of them have been semi-liberalised. With a heavy burden of interenterprise debt, they are very unlikely to be able to finance themselves without external help. Having been the major financier of the working capital, the banking system is increasingly involved in fixed capital investment in the SOEs. Removing the foot from the accelerator could stop the engine. Even if this works, firms may face lengthy delays in achieving self-reliance during the first stage. The non-bank capital (or 'curb') market allowed by McKinnon could take years to mature. It is also difficult for firms in RCPEs to develop their highly overstated assets in order to make possible the liquidation of stock.[1]

McKinnon (1991, p. 7) suggests that 'the authorities should move cautiously, perhaps waiting for some years before establishing independent commercial banks that are only indirectly regulated or controlled by the central bank. Indeed the bad (uncollectable) loans of the existing state banks may require a major recapitalisation of both banks and enterprises before privatisation – or even decentralisation – can safely take place'. These remarks are correct, but what should be done immediately? It is argued that the problems posed by the overhang of enterprise bad debt and the correspondingly weak capital base of the banking system must be attacked directly and urgently (see Chapter 4). Limiting lending to that which can be justified under an appropriate version of the real bills doctrines was precisely the rule of crediting applied under the classical CPE system. Therefore Portes argues in his review (1993) that bad habits will doubtless persist.

Liberalist or structuralist?

The introduction of curb markets into McKinnon's analysis is an amendment of his previous disregard of their function in LDCs, moving his model closer to that of the structuralists, who will be discussed later. In McKinnon's view, curb market lending activity is benign with regard to the stability of currency and the financial system. It would be 'virtually automatic' for self-financed firms to reach bankruptcy if their internal cash flows became negative for any significant length of time (ibid., pp. 130–40). Besides the effects of the prevailing political climate on the relative power of creditors and debtors and the limited experience of the judiciary in enforcing private debt contracts (Mitchell, 1993), the fact that the newly established curb markets are operated by relatively inexperienced financial companies and under limited financial supervision by the appropriate authorities may generate inflationary tendencies and moral hazard problems (Burkett and Lotspeich, 1992, pp. 75–6). Should we not have paid more attention to the creation of formal capital markets than to the curbs? It may be more efficient and less risky to organise formal markets, considering that interenterprise debts have already created so much trouble.

In reviewing McKinnon, Taylor (1993) finds that under ongoing or macroeconomic instability, 'deposit-taking commercial banks have to be particularly tightly monitored and regulated ... some degree of "financial repression" coupled with credit-rationing may be warranted' (p. 41). As these policies had been roundly criticised by McKinnon (1991), Taylor (1993, pp. 279–280) states: 'McKinnon has changed his mind!' Perhaps, but it is commendable for economists to revise and improve their thinking in the light of experience. By analogy, it would be very unfortunate if a doctor insisted on prescribing a medicine that had been proved ineffective.

CPE reform involves deep and wide socio-economic conflicts that need comprehensive political–economic analysis. With respect to financial inter-mediation, the Keyensian 'traditional role of the government' has a particularly strong potential for combatting loss of financial control in McKinnon's revised views. The differences of RCPEs compared with LDCs may not only create difficulties, but also offer opportunities. It is probably easier to write a better article or to draw a more beautiful picture on a blank page than on a used one. Without curb markets, formal financial markets may still be properly organised and may indeed achieve greater efficiency. On the other hand it seems better to liberalise the RCPE financial systems gradually. This should have two effects: first, it introduces a certain degree of competition in order to improve efficiency; and second, it allows the monetary authority and the banking system to implement monetary policy by means of certain monetary instruments, such as meaningful interest rates. But financial control appears more important than simple liberalisation. The conventional market solution – a substantial increase of interest rates – is not the only policy or even the key to higher and more efficient investments, as demonstrated by McKinnon (1973, pp. 56–61) and Shaw (1973, p. 8). What really affects economic activity may be not so much interest rates on money markets (the rate of interest on government securities) as the availability of credit from banks and other financial institutions, and the terms on which credit is made available (Stiglitz, 1993, p. 350). With bank financing there must be effective ways of controling the banking system and allowing banks to control the non-bank production sector. Furthermore the authorities ought to contribute as much as possible to the establishment of a new set of mechanisms.

THE CONTROL OF BANKS AND BANKING CONTROL

This is a theoretical exposition of models of banking, monitoring and corporate control in relation to the main issues of this work. RCPEs are introducing market mechanisms into their economies and are transforming their banking systems from a typical state apparatus designed mainly to satisfy government plans to a system that faces the problems of a market economy. What roles should the reforming banking systems stress? How should these roles be brought fully into play, and how should the system be made to act as a stabilising factor in the economy? These are important issues and theoretical research on the relevant issues by Western analysts has supplied rich insights.

Banks in all modern economies are well known as intermediaries, performing four functions: (1) they provide portfolio management services; (2) they use their liabilities as a means of payment; (3) they transform liquid into illiquid assets; and (4) they monitor borrowers. Chapter 1 has shown that CPE banking systems have played similar roles, in spite of being limited in their activities.

However the reason for banks' existence is explained in a variety of ways. In the West, the question 'why do banks exist?' has a long intellectual history. The extensive literature may be classified into seven types. Besides some general arguments discussing the effects of the capital structure of a firm and some microeconomic properties of banking, the information literature has provided a rationale for the necessity of financial intermediaries and models of their operation in terms of imperfect information. While information theories explain the conditions under which banks provide loans to firms, the control literature has explained the role of banks as delegated monitors and their provision of long-term finance. A particular subset of the control literature is based on contract theories. The asset transformation literature argues that the reasons for this are associated with banks that can raise deposits from investors. The 'run' literature explains why this gives rise to a need for regulation. The ownership literature explains the effect of reallocation of the existing resources.

The deeper the understanding of the nature of banking the more fundamental the control function of the banking system is found to be. Western banking literature has confirmed that banking control and the control of banks are vital to market economies. If these two aspects in CPEs were formerly not as important as in market economies, they should logically become vital when the economies introduce market mechanisms. There follows a general discussion of some banking theories and an examination of the control literature on the essential role of banks.

Some banking theories

The Modigliani–Miller theorem demonstrates that, under certain circumstances, the capital structure of a firm is a matter of indifference. It therefore follows that firms should devote no attention to the problem of optimal capital structure. That conclusion derives from the invariance of the cost of capital. However, in reality phenomena such as imperfect information, agency costs (Jensen and Meckling, 1976) and a number of other market imperfections ensure that the cost of capital, and hence the choice of technique and rate of capital accumulation, is affected by the debt–equity ratio. Mayer (1988) suggests that there are systematic differences in performance between financial systems in which banks play a prominent role and financial systems in which banks are not so prominent. Hellwig (1991) takes up this thought and assesses the economic significance of the distinction between the different institutional environments for corporate finance. The allocation of capital among capital goods also makes a difference. Whether a firm is financed through debt or equity leads to differences in its incentive and risk-sharing effects (Stiglitz, 1985).

In a classic CPE, the capital structure of a firm was determined by outsiders – the planners. State-owned firms (SOEs) were under full obligation to reallocate their profits, although they did not know how they were to be redistributed until the plans had been made and approved. The capital structure of a CPE firm was a matter of plan. However even in this case the capital structure, once planned, could determine who would supervise the firm and to what extent the firm should be controlled by either the different authorities or the bankers. Since the economic reforms, budget allocation has been increasingly replaced by bank credit in the capital structure of firms. Profits may be retained and shares issued by firms. Now, just as in market economies, capital structure does matter to a firm. In China and other RCPEs, firms deal with bankers much more frequently than with planners and budget allocators. Different capital structures have different effects on strategic decision making and on the investment directions of a firm through incentive and risk-sharing mechanisms. Thus capital structure exerts an important control function on a firm, which will be discussed further below.

Banks are necessary to deal with information asymmetries. Entrepreneurs possess 'inside' information about their own projects, for which they seek financing. There may be substantial rewards to borrowers in exaggerating positive qualities (Leland and Pyle, 1977). This is more serious in RCPEs, where SOEs and local governments often 'fish' investments from planners.[2] Thus it is often the case that, as the Chinese have it, 'babies who cry loudly get more milk than quieter babies'. The verification of true characteristics by outside parties may be costly or impossible. One possibility is that willingness to lend serves as a signalling effect to the credit market. Should signalling equilibria not exist or not be sustainable and economically efficient, poor projects are supported and venture capital fails (ibid.), in spite of the fact that banks have an advantage of lower costs in making loans (Fama, 1985).

But banks obtain valuable information about corporate borrowers (Fama, 1985; Lewis, 1989), which enables them to supervise and control firms. Economic reform can make this difficult. In some RCPEs, for example Hungary, firms have been free to choose their banks. Although this encourages competition, it also increases risks because banks' information about their clients becomes less certain due to the multiplicity of their accounts. To obtain better information about them relative to competing banks (Sharpe, 1990; Pagano and Jappelli, 1991; Rajan, 1991), banks have to screen and monitor their clients more carefully than before. As banks in RCPEs are typically large and the credit markets centralised, continuing long-term project failures should be avoided at all costs because the banks are in a position to finance a sequence of investments by borrowers (Dewatripont and Maskin, 1990). Banks can avoid public disclosure of information that may act to the competitive disadvantage of firms (Campbell, 1979). Therefore banks should share the responsibility of using the inside information supplied by firms to minimise agents' costs, especially bankruptcy costs. But since different financiers have differing incentives to protect the privacy of such proprietary information and its value (Bhattacharya, 1992), it is necessary for the central bank to set certain regulations to prevent possible information distortion through competitive trading.

Banks are usually well placed to undertake liability transformation of short-term deposits into long-term illiquid assets (Edgeworth, 1988). The law of large numbers allows them to make long-term investments on the basis of deposits. Long-term investments are particularly vital to RCPEs in transition (see Chapter 2). Structural adjustment and infrastructure construction need more long-term funds. Information is thought to be central to the provision of long-term finance. Recent theory has explained why this is so (Grout, 1984; Bray, 1986; Crawford, 1988). Banks can utilise binding contracts and take advantage of sunk costs faced by entrepreneurs to exploit information about their clients. As efficiency requires investment in relationship-specific capital, the role of long-term contracts may promote long-term investment by restricting parties to a particular time pattern of compensation for any given investment plan (Crawford, 1988).

In CPEs, long-term credit came from banks' credit plans approved by the authorities. These plans contained full descriptions of the uses and sources of funds and the clear obligations of the lenders. However the obligations of borrowers were less clearly defined. The standard contract should define the obligations and responsibilities of both sides, including penalties imposed for various breaches. The arguments here justify the switch from the traditional short-term credit plans in the banks of RCPEs to a kind of standard long-term contract, which can enforce the responsibilities of both borrowers and lenders in order to promote long-term investments in these economies.

Banks transform illiquid assets to liquid liabilities and provide liquidity (Diamond and Dybvig, 1983). The risk-sharing deposit contract leaves banks vulnerable to panic runs (Vives, 1991). A run on a single bank can prompt the collapse of other banks in a contagious fashion (Diamond and Dybvig, 1983), resulting in systemic failure (Aghion, Bolton and Dewatripont, 1988). The risk of runs and contagious collapse justify regulation (Tobin, 1985; Kareken, 1986). Though isolated bank bankruptcy is possible, it seems impossible to have a 'contagious' run on banks unless they are privatised in CPEs. However national payment crises did happen in Eastern Europe, such as in Russia in 1991 and 1992, and in China in 1985, 1988 and 1993 (see Chapter 4). As there are strong leanings towards the privatisation of banks and increased bank competition in the Eastern European RCPEs, it is useful to understand the vulnerability of competitive banking to crises of confidence (Matutes and Vives, 1992). While economic risks do increase during the period of reform, liberalising the banking system and encouraging competition among banks during transition could be dangerous unless well-established warning systems and lenders of last resort are incorporated into a system of effective banking laws.

The importance of ownership lies in the control mechanisms

The most fundamental difference between Western market economies and socialist market economies lies in the different ownership systems. China insists on the domination of public ownership, in spite of the fact that diversified ownership, including private and collective ownership, has been allowed to develop. Asset transformation literature, which explains why banks can raise deposits from investors for long-term finance, ignores an important feature of many Western financial systems, namely that banks hold equity. According to the following analysis, the real importance of ownership to economic reforms and development lies in the control functions.

Takeovers may be a costly mechanism

It is necessary to distinguish between the two main functions that banking systems perform in relation to their corporate sectors: they provide finance for new investment and they allocate existing resources. Reallocation of existing resources is normally associated with takeovers in securities markets: resources are redeployed from low- to high-return activities through competition for control. Some have argued that takeovers may be a costly mechanism for achieving this end. Shleifer and Summers (1988) argued that acquisitions with negative social return may be privately profitable because acquisitions break implicit contracts and expropriate returns from other stakeholders. Extreme forms of control may be unnecessarily taken, such as 'takeovers' or negative social return acquisitions, which may be costly mechanisms. The threat of takeover discourages long-term contracts and investment in firm-specific assets (Franks and Mayer, 1990). Investment in firm-specific assets, research and development and training, for example, may be discouraged in either of the above cases. If banks hold equities, they essentially hold part of the ownership, which enables them to control firms. This control in turn enables banks to block uneconomic and hostile takeovers.

The insider system appears to be a more effective form of corporate control

A deeper analysis of the ownership issue has been conducted by Corbett and Mayer (1991). Banks may prevent the emergence of markets under corporate control by holding equity directly. This may encourage implementation of contracts that are conducive to long-term investment while avoiding the effects of breaking implicit contracts.

Criticising Eastern European reformers who have put too much effort into privatisation programmes, Corbett and Mayer (1991) argue that many fundamental questions regarding the structure of the financial system have not yet been addressed. These concern the relationship of the financial sector to the non-financial enterprise sector. Despite significant differences in the structure of financial systems across industrialised nations, there are close links between the banking sector and industry in some countries, notably in Germany and Japan. These relations concern not only the financing but, more significantly, also the control of industry. This control can be by banks holding corporate equity, both on their own account and on behalf of private investors. Bank representatives may sit on the boards of firms, frequently in the position of chairman. This differs from corporate control in the UK and the US, which is exerted indirectly through takeovers, in particular hostile takeovers. The latter are costly in terms of managerial time and effort, they fail to reflect the wider interests of stakeholders other than shareholders and they weaken investors' commitment to long-term corporate policies.

German and Japanese systems are forms of control by 'insiders'. While banks play an important function in these systems, they are by no means dominant. Enterprises own and control each other through systems of cross-shareholdings. These cross-holdings protect insiders from outside intervention and encourage them to engage in mutual and active monitoring. These insider systems therefore overcome the 'free rider' problem that afflicts corporate control in the UK and the US by concentrating control among a small group of interested parties (for example suppliers and purchasers) and banks.

The insider system appears to be a more effective system of corporate control: it provides both commitment to long-term policies and a mechanism for penalising poor management. Its obvious risks are that it does not provide an adequate inducement to corporate efficiency and that it concentrates power within a small group of insiders. In practice these risks are avoided by promoting competition between control groups. Competition in product markets is an essential feature of successful insider systems. However competition in ownership through the takeover process is not perceived in the insider system as a substitute for competition in product markets (Corbett and Mayer, 1991).

Banks are better financiers and controllers

Unlike Estrin *et al.* (1992), who regard privatisation as 'the key element of the transition', Corbett and Mayer (1991) regard the UK and US styles of capitalism as the exception rather than the rule. Most equity in the UK is owned by non-bank financial institutions, which have provided no solution to the UK's control problem. In most capitalist countries, stock markets are of very limited significance: there are few quoted companies and even these are not subject to external control by outside investors. Banks, not stock markets, are the main source of finance for industry and there is little direct participation by individuals in the enterprise sector. It is implausible to expect significant amounts of external financing to be injected into the giant, conglomerate organisations of the Eastern European economies by a large group of dispersed shareholders. It may also be wrong to expect ownership to be transferred overseas by foreign purchasers of domestic enterprises, and to 'find it most efficient to import foreign banks to create their banking system, just as they have to import foreign machinery for their productive investments', as recommended by Rostowski (1992). True economic development requires the creation of an indigenous control system, though retention of public sector control may not be a reform at all.

The alternative policy of promoting the development of control groups of enterprises and banks has some merit. The involvement of banks means that they are better placed to raise substantial amounts of finance from the public at large than are equity-issuing institutions.

Public policy needs to be directed towards the avoidance of the abuses that can result from the creation of control groups. Industrial policy needs to be directed towards the creation of competition and anti-trust policy is required to maintain it. Bank regulation is required to ensure that banking systems are not threatened by banks' close involvement with industry.

How to reform SOEs in RCPEs is a topical issue. Many debates concentrate on the ambiguous issue of 'economic efficiency'. A more important issue is corporate governance, which relates to the control mechanisms of the economic system. A better system lies in a better solution of the problems of corporate governance and no economy can avoid the principal–agency relationship. As the already established banking systems in RCPEs are better organised and staffed than newly created banks, it is wise to let them play a full role in the reform. A close relationship between banks and firms should be encouraged. With banks financing and supervising SOEs and other firms, takeover costs may be minimised and long-term contracts ensured. So long as competition is allowed, state ownership of some banks may help to control banks during transition. The development of the specialised Chinese state banks supports this view.

The essential role of banks is to control

Attention has recently focused on (1) the monitoring function of banks and (2) liquidity transformation. Controlling and monitoring borrowers are necessary, but involve the principal–agent problem. However there are economies of scale that make it costly for individual investors either to screen the quality of entrepreneurs, due to ex-ante information asymmetries, or to monitor the performance of firms, due to ex-post information asymmetries. Control theories have explained the provision of long-term lending.

Banks have a net cost advantage in monitoring

Diamond (1984) indicates that banks are elected as a more efficient monitoring representative. Delegated monitoring of firms is fairly important to

RCPE bankers, although it could be argued that in an RCPE they represent the public in supervising the production system.

Diamond calls the information production task delegated to the intermediary 'delegated costs'. He analyses the determinants of the delegated cost and develops a model in which a financial intermediary has a net cost advantage relative to direct lending and borrowing. Diversification with the intermediary is the key to the possible net advantage of intermediation. It alters the incentive problems sufficiently to make it feasible to hire an agent (the intermediary) to monitor an agent (the borrower). Diversification proves to be important even when everyone in the economy is risk neutral.

The basic model is of an ex-post information asymmetry between potential lenders and a risk neutral entrepreneur who needs to raise capital for a risky project. It is possible for lenders (who contract directly with the entrepreneur) to spend resources to monitor the data, which the entrepreneur observes. There are economies of scale that make it costly for individual investors to monitor. Therefore, in order to reduce the cost of monitoring some security holders may monitor on behalf of others.

A financial intermediary must choose an incentive contract that provides incentives to monitor the information, make proper use of it and make sufficient payments to depositors to attract deposits. Providing these incentives is costly. As the number of loans to entrepreneurs grows, the costs of delegation fall, so that for some finite number of loans financial intermediation becomes viable, considering all costs.

For a financial intermediary to provide delegated monitoring services in an economy where everyone is risk-averse, it must have lower delegation costs than an entrepreneur. Similarly, if the intermediary can bear risks at a lower risk premium it will generally face a less severe trade-off between risk sharing and incentives, and thus a monitoring task can efficiently be delegated.[3] This is the potential role of banks in RCPEs.

Banks are able to impose penalties upon their borrowers via contracts

According to the optimal contract literature (see Townsend, 1979; Gale and Hellwig, 1985), the monitor should offer a 'standard debt contract' whereby investors are paid a fixed return and a penalty is imposed in the event of bankruptcy. By diversifying its portfolio a bank is able to offer investors a contract that guarantees a fixed return and avoids bankruptcy costs. Gale and Hellwig (1985) indicate that, as a monitor, a bank is able, through the 'standard debt contract', to impose a penalty in the event of bankruptcy. Under certain conditions the optimal credit contract takes the form of a standard debt contract with a bankruptcy clause. Furthermore, banks can observe and analyse the state of firms during the on-going process of bankruptcy. A standard debt contract is a contract that requires a fixed repayment when the firm is solvent, calls for the firm to be declared bankrupt if this fixed payment cannot be met and allows the creditor to recoup as much of the debt as possible from the firm's assets. The combination of economies of scale in monitoring and diversification of investments is the fundamental justification for the existence of banks in this model (see also Diamond, 1993).

This is an extremely important issue in the case of an RCPE. After they have been liberalised from planned regimes, SOEs should be given full responsibility for profits and losses. However it is often the case that they share only profits. Once payment problems occur their banks become passive (see Chapters 2 and 4), when in fact they should impose penalties upon borrowers. It is necessary to make this obligation clear in project credit plans and/or contracts.

Reputation helps banks to monitor

Risks are involved in raising funds and in lending. Banks' reputation and borrowers' credit records are both helpful. Diamond (1988, 1989) notes that monitoring by an intermediary may initially be required to establish reputations in order to avoid moral hazard problems. Banks' reputations may make monitoring more effective by threatening more severe penalties in the event of default. Once established, however, firms can avoid the costs of being monitored and issue debt directly. New borrowers borrow from banks initially, but at a later stage can issue debt directly without using an intermediary. When monitored by a bank, borrowers' credit records serve to predict how they will act when left unmonitored. This indicates that banks are particularly important in the early stages of the development of enterprises (see also Boot and Greenbaum, 1993).

Banks in CPEs had monopolistic power and therefore had no problem with reputation. In RCPEs it is important to maintain the reputation of banks, despite state ownership. That reputation may be established through their contribution to stabilisation, through their improved services to the economy, such as payment services (Harris, 1993), and through carefully recording, screening and monitoring borrowers.

Debtors' cash expenditure needs to be controlled by their creditors

The reason why creditors lend to debtors who have previously exceeded an agreed limit has been answered by Hellwig (1977), who shows that during uncertainty the availability of credit may be restricted to below that which would be predicted. A dollar invested in a project with outstanding debt earns additional returns by improving the quality of previous loans. Debtors appreciate that there is an incentive for creditors to refinance in circumstances in which it was previously denied. This is more likely to be the case in RCPEs where debtors and creditors are closely related under the same ownership. But in CPEs credit, whether used by firms for consumption expenditure or interest payment, was subject to constraints that were similar to those described by Hellwig,[4] such as a credit limit, although they never went bankrupt. It was the planners' power that forced them to limit their borrowing.

Whether a debtor is able to borrow continuously would influence the *ex ante* expected present value of lending. A creditor could refuse to lend in order to avoid lending too much. The underlying difficulty for the creditor is due to moral hazard, which enters with the assumption that the debtor is free to determine his rate of consumption. The difficulty stems from the dynamic structure of creditor–debtor interaction, rather than from market imperfection or information asymmetries. In practice creditors attempt to, and indeed have to, control a debtor's cash expenditure.

Under pressure from workers and with the encouragement of some liberal ideas,[5] the managers of SOEs in RCPEs are likely to force banks to give them cash to cover consumption expenditure and wage bills. Banks are also likely to ignore their traditional function of controlling consumption in the economy. Therefore the supervisory relationship between creditors and debtors could be dismantled in an RCPE.

Upon bankruptcy in a market economy, the agent's debt is cancelled and he loses access to the credit market. This suggests to RCPEs that 'bankruptcy, although costly, has a beneficial side: without it contracts would be even more constrained and welfare would be even lower' (Gale and Hellwig, 1985, p. 648). The attractiveness of borrowing rises with the decrease of the bankruptcy penalty, or with increases in the credit limit and the chance of becoming wealthy. If bankruptcy is absent, the only constraint on borrowing is the credit limit, according to Hellwig (1977). If this limit is abandoned, which often happens in RCPEs, financial disorders are inevitable.

The agent engages in active borrowing if, and only if, the optimal contingent time to bankruptcy, T^*, is finite, because this can allow savings on interest payments to his creditors (ibid.) A great problem arises when T^* is infinite, as in CPEs and RCPEs. The problem is often solved by waiving interest payments and/or the principal. T^* is an important indicator of an agent's borrowing policy. Bankruptcy can be delayed by letting the debtor believe that he will obtain less credit than he will actually get. A strategic element involved in this result is that the debtor's course of action depends not only on the credit limit that is actually enforced, but also on his anticipation of what that credit limit will be at various stages. A creditor may try to make use of this and influence the debtor's behaviour. Thus successive credit limits may differ one from another. The debtor has to understand the principle by which the creditor determines the credit limit.

Borrowers can either receive the grant or not, depending on the revocability of the creditor's precommitment. If the original announcement can be revoked by mutual agreement, the creditor may grant the debtor's request for the optimal announcement A^{**}, provided that in the meantime he finds it in his interest to do so. In the case of an RCPE, the creditor may obey or follow some government regulations or policies to do so. 'If the creditor can control the debtor's consumption, the creditor's objective function does not change over time, so that the discrepancy between the optimal initial announcement and naive behaviour disappears ... the debtor would never go bankrupt' (ibid., p. 1894) The debtor's rate of consumption determines how soon the credit limit is reached and with what probability bankruptcy can be avoided. Therefore Hellwig's model provides a rationale for bank control over borrowers. The fascinating relevance of this analysis to RCPEs is that banks in transition have to be much more cautious due to the risks and uncertainty, and therefore they must control debtors carefully. Meanwhile creditor behaviour is also essentially indeterminate (ibid., p. 1899).

The funding of long-term investments requires a power balance

The problem of encouraging repayment lies behind Hart and Moore's (1989a) model of debt contracts. They consider a model in which an entrepreneur invests in a project in the first period that yields returns in the two subsequent periods. The entrepreneur finances the investment by raising a loan in the first period that is due to be repaid in the second period. In their model the threat that the lender has at his disposal is liquidating the asset in the second period, thus preventing the entrepreneur from earning the third period's returns. The repayment that the lender can anticipate is therefore bounded by the returns that the entrepreneur expects to earn in the third period. Grout (1984), Bray (1986) and Crawford (1979) have pointed to the role of long-term contracts in promoting long-term investment. According to their idea, long-term investments involve sunk costs that cannot be recouped by reversing investment decisions. Faced with sunk costs, entrepreneurs are exposed to exploitation by providers of finance. The desire of borrowers to invest in long-term assets is conditional on investors being willing to restrain themselves from intervening before the investments come to fruition.

Combining the two arguments suggests that the funding of long-term investments requires a delicate balance between the powers that lenders and borrowers can exert. Lenders restrain themselves by offering long-term contracts. Borrowers subject themselves to the threat of lender intervention. This can occur not only when they are in default but also when they are in violation of the range of covenant restrictions that are a common feature of debt contracts. The lender can threaten to liquidate the borrower's assets so as to prevent the entrepreneur from earning the whole of the expected returns within a certain period (Hart and Moore, 1989b). Willingness to lend is accordingly governed by threats that can be credibly imposed on borrowers.

Debt contracts provide a trade-off between the problems created by excessive and insufficient lender control. A debt contract allows the entrepreneur to remain in control of asset allocation so long as he/she is not in default of his/her repayment obligations or covenants. When default or any violation of the debt contract occurs, however, control may be transferred from the borrower to the lender according to the debt contract. Aghion and Bolton (1987) suggest that debt contracts provide a trade-off between the problems created by excessive and insufficient lender control.

In a typical CPE model, borrowers had no need to provide a credit record when bankers lent them money. The latter had little concern about repayment because whatever the borrowers produced would belong wholly to the state, and whoever defaulted would be subsidised by the government. Penalty was possible but it did not necessarily go through the economic system, rather it went through the political system (the party organisations). Meanwhile the borrowers had no bargaining position simply because the planners took complete responsibility for lending. But once that model is replaced by the market system, the power balance and discipline imposition have to function effectively. The payments crises that occurred in RCPEs after the reforms were caused by such power imbalances.

The distinguishing feature of banks is their ability to exert control

Stiglitz (1985) indicates that managers of firms are partially controlled, directly and indirectly, through both explicit and implicit contracts and by both lenders and shareholders. The lenders exert control through the formal terms of their contract and their refusal to renew a loan; shareholders exert control through the voting process and their refusal to provide additional capital. Managerial incentives are affected by both the explicit pay schedule – the rewards offered by supervisors and tempting offers from rival firms, contingent on performance – and the implicit punishments provided by other firms in their treatment of those who are dismissed or whose firms go bankrupt. Among the three control mechanisms – banks, concentrated equity ownership and managerial reputations – control is exercised more by banks and lenders than by other agents. The distinguishing feature of banks is their ability to exert control. Thus there is no reason for the banking systems of RCPEs not to be fully utilised for stabilisation purposes.

There is a trade-off between the ability of diversified credit markets to raise large amounts of finance from a wide range of investors and the advantage that a closely held firm has in controlling the activities of managers: a free-rider problem is associated with the involvement of investors in monitoring and controlling corporations. Banks and trade unions may be able to exert the necessary control in order to combine the risk-sharing properties of securities markets with the control properties of closely held organisations. Unfortunately many reformers ignored this essential principle when they initiated banking reform programmes.

It is clear, then, that banks are not simple providers of services. They are essential economic controllers.

Banks help borrowers in financial distress to restructure or renegotiate

In RCPEs it is common for firms to face financial distress. What can banks do in these circumstances? Asquith, Gertner and Sharfstein (1991) studied the restructuring decisions of firms with large amounts of public debt. The firms issued long-term, junior junk bonds and later experienced financial distress. The theory predicted that in this case banks would not make concessions. 'Outside of bankruptcy proceedings, banks almost never (there is one exception) forgive the principal on their loans and they rarely provide new financing... *[Banks] often waive covenants and defer principal and interest payments, but they also often force accelerated payments and increase their collateral*' (p. 1, emphasis added).

Gilson, John and Lang (1990) examined a sample of firms in financial distress and studied the characteristics of those that successfully renegotiated their debt outside the bankruptcy court. Firms with and without debt were examined. It was found that firms whose bank debt was a higher fraction of their total debt were more likely to renegotiate, with the banks making concessions. The bank would make concessions if the amount of bank debt was high enough, and if concessions were in the mutual interest of lenders. A firm was less likely to reach a negotiated settlement if there were more distinct issues of debt, a proxy for the costs of renegotiation.

Davis and Mayer (1992) studied the world of Euromarket syndicated publicly traded bonds and bank loans. They discoverd that bank loans were of shorter maturity than bonds, even for firms that used both forms of finance. Larger firms and firms that raised less capital had longer maturity bank loans and were more likely to issue publicly traded bonds. The smaller firms were marginal firms that could not raise sufficient funds if they chose a structure that limited the banks' right to liquidate when it was in the collective interest of the lenders.

These empirical findings are consistent with Diamond's (1992) theoretical paper, which describes the implication of his models for the restructuring actions taken by various lenders when borrowers cannot meet their contracted obligations. The findings also illustrate how the ability to refinance from competing future lenders improves the set of contracts available to the borrower. The structure of debt contracts and the actions that lenders take when the borrower is in financial distress depend on the type of lender providing the funds. If the borrower combines bank loans with public debt, the model predicts that the bank loan will be shorter term and senior to the public debt. If the borrower gets into financial distress, the bank will not make concessions. Instead, it will use its power to force a restructuring, such as asset sales or liquidation. If all the debt is bank debt, possibly owned by different banks, then the priority prediction (of bank claims, which influence the liquidation decision) is not clear. Banks, especially those that are part of a syndicate for a given loan participation, can renegotiate rather easily. Because bank loans often have strict covenants that allow even long-term lenders to exercise control, banks usually have the 'right to liquidate'. If all the debt is bank debt, then in certain cases, the banks will make concessions, extending maturity or forgiving interest or principal (ibid., pp. 23–4).

An implication of these arguments for RCPEs is that both renegotiation and restructuring are necessary to help SOEs in financial distress. Renegotiation is not always negative or passive. The interenterprise debt problems described in Chapters 2 and 4 are closely related to banks rescuing firms in distress. If banks had been eager to make the liquidation decision there would have been massive bankruptcies, which would certainly have been harmful to the economies in transition. Thus the People's Construction Bank of China arranged billions of yuan to refinance SOEs in distress in 1990. At the same time, however, another function of banks, namely the restructuring of firms, cannot be ignored.

Debt holders and equity holders must be able to exert contingent control

We are often told that debt holders in RCPEs are passive with respect to interference (see the cases of interenterprise debt in Chapters 2 and 4). What happens in market economies? Dewatripont and Tirole (1993) find that debt holders always have a socially excessive incentive to interfere while equity holders are typically passive. Yet it is vital that one of these two asset holders is empowered to discipline managers in certain circumstances. Naturally managers are rewarded in good times by allowing relatively passive shareholders to retain control. Bad times require tough interference by debt holders. The transfer of control from equity holders to debt holders can be triggered by the inability of the firm to reimburse short-term debt out of period-one profits. Both in turbulent and in quiet times, the firm's allowed level of debt is an increasing function of *ex ante* verifiability.[6] This is because more debt softens the outsider's control and thus rewards the manager with more freedom.

The behaviour of the banks themselves is affected by their own status. When some verifiable bank performance measure (capital-to-loans ratio, reserves, riskiness of loans and so on) falls below a certain threshold – that is, when the bank's solvency deteriorates – equity holders in the bank are tempted to 'gamble for resurrection', especially if the threat of depositor involvement is not credible. Therefore control of the bank would be better placed in the hands of its creditors than its shareholders. This would justify some control measures. For instance creditors could prevent the bank from 'gambling for resurrection' by limiting borrowing, requiring the choice of safer loans, reducing the discrepancy between the term structures of loans and deposits, or liquidating the bank. More generally, in the absence of adjustments in borrowing, loans or recapitalisation, the mere resolution of uncertainty gives rise to undesirable incentives for the bank's claim holders (as well as for its management). Claim holders of a shaky or troubled bank have more incentive to be passive than claim holders of a healthy one. Recapitalisation in turbulent times and increased borrowing in quiet times can be used to counter this tendency.

The features of the optimal control structure of banks in the Dewatripont–Tirole model are: (1) following a good performance, control rests with (passive) equity holders; (2) increased bank fragility should be followed by more interventionist, but still accommodating, equity holder behaviour; and (3) poor performance should trigger depositor control, with excessively interventionist behaviour.

The distinctiveness of banks lies in the nature of the debt holders, who are small, dispersed depositors, typically unable to exert residual rights of control. This justifies a 'bad time' principal delegating depositors to intervene in management.

To make this meaningful to RCPEs, it is easy to conclude that it is necessary to develop equity markets. Nuti (1990) indicates that this development is possible in the state sector. Otherwise there is no possibility of comparing equity holders and debt holders. Once shares have been issued and purchased by the public, contingent control may become possible. Then the most interesting issue to remain unanswered is when should banks control and when shareholders? However, in an RCPE the state is the main shareholder in firms and may have some incentives in common with the shareholders in a market economy. It is equally interesting to debate when banks should exercise control and when this should be done by the state, including local government. A serious problem in some RCPEs is that the state has too much controlling power. The authorities become 'free riders', often directing banks to extend too much credit in good times while failing to make policy adjustments in bad times. One of the consequences of this is shown by the economic overheating in China after the reforms. If banks had had more say, the problems today might have been less serious.

It is necessary for a public agency to regulate banks

An important feature of banks is that their debt is mostly held by a group of dispersed and uninformed small depositors. Most of these bank creditors do not have the incentive, the information nor the competence to monitor and exert their residual rights of control over the bank. This seriously limits the intensity of monitoring and outside involvement in management (Dewatripont and Tirole, 1993). To remedy this, a large private or public monitor representing the interests of the creditors must exert these rights of control on their behalf. Because of informational and free-riding problems, this exercise can be performed only by a representative. The more fragile the bank, the more incentive its claim holders have to take risks, whereas an optimal governance structure would call for more conservative policies. It would also penalise the bank's management by a high level of interference in turbulent times! Thus, keeping assets and liabilities unchanged, the mere accrual of information about existing loans gives the bank's financial structure the wrong incentives.

There exists the limitation of *laissez-faire* in the banking sector: one cannot rely on equity holders to discipline management. They are essentially biased in favour of managers and can thus be relied upon only in good times (and even then the level of deposits should not be under their control). Debt holders have to take an active role in disciplining management in turbulent times. As small depositors cannot be relied upon to perform this task, this problem suggests a role for a public agency that would: (1) regulate banks *ex ante*, forcing adjustments in the liability structure to counter the perverse incentive problem; and (2) intervene *ex post*, thereby acting on behalf of small depositors in turbulent times. Keeping risky assets unaltered, recapitalisation makes claim holders tougher while an increase in the level of deposits makes them more passive. Therefore recapitalisation should take place in turbulent times and deposit expansion should be allowed in quiet times. Certainly there is a need for a powerful central bank.

The Dewatripont–Tirole model has extremely important implications for RCPE reforms. In both CPEs and RCPEs the authorities are equity holders of sorts, as discussed earlier. Here one stress is on the issue of restructuring the corporate governance of the economies. As argued in Chapter 1, the CPE model did have a corporate governance structure. In the planning regime, SOEs were controlled by a system of 'planner– financier– banker' under the leadership of party organisations (see Chapter 1). This governance structure required administrative efficiency and party power. Contingent control by the administration and the party guaranteed the working of the system. Once this regime had broken down, corporate managers and bankers needed contingent control of shareholders (mainly the authorities) and debt holders (mainly bankers or depositors). The reason is very simple. It is the representatives of the state (the authorities) and the lenders (bankers or depositors) who are keen to manage their assets. This applies to both corporate governance and bank governance. There are two significant implications of the model. One is that both corporate bodies and banks need this kind of contingent control. The second is that this kind of system can serve as a new governance structure in RCPEs where contingent control by the administration and the political forces have been extensively removed.

The suggested corporate governance structure in Figure 3.1 differs from the structure displayed in Chapter 1. The RCPE model is based on market mechanisms. The national plans made by the State Planning Commission, or whichever body is responsible, are crucial for macroeconomic equilibrium. Given political stability, financiers and shareholders have contingent control over the production and banking systems. Control is based on market mechanisms, within the legal framework and with the help of administrative regulations. With regard to firms, bankers are the financiers. However, as far as the banks are concerned the depositors' representatives are the financial controllers.

Figure 3.1   Suggested corporate governance structure for RCPEs

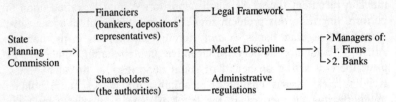

The transition of the corporate governance structure from the model demonstrated in Chapter 1 to the model shown here needs to be managed carefully. The success of the gradual Chinese approach is due to the fact that joint control by the political party and the planning system have not been suddenly abolished. Instead they are being used effectively until other mechanisms are ready to replace them. The radical reform approaches adopted in many Eastern European countries and the former Soviet Union have left a 'control vacuum' that is generating enormous problems. A 'control vacuum' means that for a certain period there is no effective control mechanism to hold the system together.

According to Dewatipont and Tirole (1993), firstly, the agency should not maximise *ex post* social welfare. Rather it should stand for the interests of depositors, if they were not being upheld, or the interests of taxpayers when depositors are secured. The agency's internalisation of bank or equity-holder welfare induces excessive passivity from the point of view of *ex ante* optimality. Such agencies should be encouraged to stand for taxpayers (assuming they ensure deposits) and not to attempt to maximise *ex post* social welfare. Here the independence of the agency might be a facilitating factor. Secondly, politicians are expected to be subject to pressure to internalise the welfare of the bank and its equity holders. Thirdly the welfare of the bank and its equity holders should be ignored. Fourthly, there is a limit to the regulatory efficiency embodied in the intrinsic tension between the two tasks allocated to the regulatory agency – monitoring and intervention. The conflict between monitoring and intervention suggests that it might be desirable to divide the tasks. The monitoring role could be given to a private or governmental rating agency; the intervention role might remain with a public agency. Finally, for an optimal governance structure the bank should be exposed to greater external interference in turbulent times: this can be accomplished, for instance, by forcing the bank to recapitalise or suspending the distribution of dividends and insisting that new loans be safe. An optimal governance structure also requires a shift of control to depositors in very adverse economic conditions, which again raises the issue of depositors having neither the information nor the incentive to exercise this control. Hungary established a State Banking Supervision Committee when its banking system was decentralised in 1987. This could also be an alternative in China.

Discussion

Having discussed some theoretical debates in banking that have mainly arisen in the West, it is time to summarise the main points in each case and turn to a more detailed discussion of the points that relate most closely to the hypothesis of my discussion.

Ownership literature has exposed the control mechanisms within the ownership system and found the 'insider' system to be more efficient than the conventional systems. But neither control literature nor information literature has touched on the essence of ownership; that is, the power of control over production properties, which eventually determines the control mechanisms. In a typical market economy the power to control production properties is in the hands of the rich minority – the share-holders – thus ignoring the wishes of the non-shareholding majority who should be involved in control. The contradiction between the increasing socialisation of production and the private ownership of production properties (which is one of the most fundamental reasons for asymmetric information) often forces economies to bear cyclical economic crises (see Marx, 1887). In a traditional CPE system the power of control over production properties lay in the hands of a minority of planners and political organisers. It was the restrictive planning control mechanisms supported by the political party (see Chapter 1) that prevented a market-style corporate governance structure from being established. Bureaucracy, corruption and the CPE planners' fundamental ignorance of the functions of the market led most of these economies to be less competitive and eventually to collapse one after another. Once an economic system is changed, the original control mechanisms may also be removed. A new corporate governance structure should then be designed. Public ownership is not in itself the essential problem in RCPEs. It is urgently necessary to establish a new control system that is superior to the two classical models, embracing not only government functions but a sound corporate governance structure in order to mobilise the majority into economic activity.

Control literature has established the economic control function as the fundamental reason for the existence of the banking system. The distinguishing feature of banks is their ability to exert control. Among the findings of the control literature, two are worth mentioning here. The first is that banks help borrowers in financial distress to restructure or renegotiate. This seems to suggest that banks should help the SOEs, some of which are loss makers. But there are two sides of this coin. On one side, banks should help SOEs in transition because they are in financial distress. Otherwise the problem could grow worse. However help can be given in different ways and renegotiation is not the only way forward. Bank control over firms enhances the power of banks in restructuring industry. This second point is often ignored by the government in its intervention and banks in their supervision in RCPEs.

Another issue relates to the most recent findings of Dewatripont and Tirole (1993): debt holders and equity holders need contingent control of firms, therefore justifying the regulation of banks by a public agency. The argument can be extended to the RCPE case. The authorities, including local governments, have a similar function to equity holders in market economies within this system. The restriction of banking control can leave the authorities 'free riding' during transition. This was never a problem in CPEs, where the planners had relatively, more say than bankers. It has, however, become a problem in those RCPEs where the authorities now have excessive influence and bankers not enough. A new corporate governance structure would allow bankers and shareholders to conduct corporate control on the basis of market mechanisms. Besides the need to develop equity markets, it is necessary for the authorities and banks to have contingent control over the production system. This also needs a powerful central bank to act as the leader and regulator of banks.

CREDIT RATIONING AND MONETARY CONTROL

Earlier in this chapter it was suggested that the interest rate has not been an effective method of control in CPEs and reforming CPEs, and that the quick solution of moving to a high interest rate has certain disadvantages. It was also suggested that controlled banking systems with a strong monitoring role are desirable. This raises a number of questions. As the banking system has been the major investor in RCPEs, are there any effective ways for the monetary authority to control the economy through the banking system? What transmission mechanisms would enable it to restrain investment and the economic overheating that usually occurs? Is there any way of directing investment into whatever structural adjustments and other important projects are undertaken? The Western literature of credit rationing and the Chinese literature of credit planning provide part of the answer. This section explains why credit planning is not only necessary but also superior to credit rationing. The contribution of this work is the view that credit planning should be used where beneficial rather than being abandoned.

Reasons for studying credit rationing

It is interesting to observe that excess demand for credit often occurs in market economies. Rationing is one way of dealing with this problem, and has been studied in the credit planning literature in the CPEs and by the credit rationing literature in the West.

The interest in credit rationing in the US originated with the debate over the 'availability doctrine' in the early 1950s.[7] The central idea underlying this doctrine was that monetary policy could be used to restrain aggregate demand. It was thought that this could be done without causing significant increases in interest rates, so avoiding any increase in the interest burden on the budget even if firms' demand for investment was highly insensitive to the cost of borrowing, as was widely believed to be the case. In particular, it was argued that a restrictive monetary policy would cause banks to reduce the availability of credit and to ration funds among borrowers rather than raise interest rates on loans. The federal Reserve would be able to abandon its policy of pegging the treasury bill rate and control private spending without generating a sharp increase in interest rates on government securities. Therefore credit rationing was regarded as a third 'channel of influence' over monetary policy in the 1960s, in addition to the conventional cost-of-credit effect on investment and the wealth effect on consumption.

In an RCPE, where monetary policy is exercised through a banking system that retains its former role of controlling the availability of credit (although now according to different criteria), one needs to examine how credit rationing would work under these new conditions.

The literature contains at least two approaches to credit rationing: rationing introduced by administratively imposed loan-rate ceilings (financial repression) differs from that arising from unconstrained profit maximising in the context of imperfect information – adverse selection (Arndt, 1982). In a market economy, government rationing in the form of concessional credit for target groups can, in principle, benefit low-income or relatively important but less profitable borrowers, while bank rationing, by its nature, favours those who are better off. The former can, in principle, alleviate some of the adverse effects of the latter. However, how far it will do so in practice depends on the integrity and efficiency of the bureaucracy and on the workings of the political process. Actually, government-directed rationing may, in principle, allocate credit in conformity with a social welfare function on a desired growth path while bank allocation, in the context of imperfect information, is more arbitrary.

Credit planning could be a typical example of combining the above two functions. As the most useful banking measure in CPEs, credit planning is practised in CPEs such as in China mainly for policy purposes, rather than for banks' expected return. Another difference is that central banks in RCPEs still ration a part of the credits directly,[8] while central banks in the West perform the regulation through the discounting windows. Credit planning is essentially rationing. In this respect there is no difference between socialist banking and market banking. Credit policies and credit regulations made and implemented in the Chinese banks serve as examples.[9]

Definitions of credit rationing

Credit rationing is more complicated to analyse than credit planning because it results from market mechanisms. It is broadly defined as a situation in which there exists an excess demand for loans because quoted loan rates are below the Walrasian market-clearing level. This certainly suits the RCPEs, where interest rates have at times become both meaningless and powerless.

However in a market economy the demand for credit cannot be determined without specifying the relevant price. Keeton (1979) defines two concepts of credit rationing. The first is said to occur whenever a customer receives a smaller loan than he would wish at the interest rate charged by the bank. An alternative definition is that rationing occurs whenever the total quantity of loans demanded by a class, with given characteristics at the complete set of loan terms, exceeds the total quantity supplied by banks.

Keeton demonstrates that these two types of credit rationing may also be observed in equilibrium situations and in the absence of government-imposed constraints on the setting of loan rates. In particular, equilibrium rationing may occur in the first sense if there is competition among lenders and a risk of default that increases with the size of the loan. It may occur in the second sense if there exists a moral hazard problem resulting from the lender's inability to monitor all relevant characteristics of the borrower's investment project.

Despite the low interest rate, these two types of credit rationing are well-known phenomena in China and the RCPEs. Sometimes none of the SOEs feel satisfied with the size of the loans they have received. Conversely it quite often happens that some SOEs receive higher amounts than they had applied for, while others in the same classification are refused credit by the banks. This disequilibrium may be caused by state-bank monopoly, the existence of government-imposed constraints on the setting of loan rates and the lack of default risk, or more essentially, bankruptcy. For the restrictive planning control mechanisms discussed in Chapter 1, credit rationing can be operated very well in an equilibrium situation.

If for some reason lenders were slow to adjust loan rates to changes in the cost or supply of loanable funds, rationing in one or both of these two senses might well occur as a temporary disequilibrium phenomenon. It is also well recognised that a ceiling on loan rates or a regulatory constraint on lenders' freedom to charge different rates to borrowers of different risk could lead to the rationing of credit.

Jaffee and Stiglitz (1990) define a number of different types of credit rationing, depending on how excess demand is defined, on whether the excess demand is temporary or continuing, and most importantly, on the factors that cause the loan rate to be depressed. They define 'interest rate (or price) rationing' and 'pure credit rationing' as being roughly the same as the above two types of credit rationing. 'Divergent views rationing' should be less important in RCPEs because of the relatively insignificant loan rates and incidence of default. 'Redlining' should also be unimportant because lenders in RCPEs often refuse to grant credit to borrowers when the lenders cannot obtain their required return at any interest rate. Moreover rate of return is not as vital as some state policies in RCPEs.

Credit markets with imperfect information

Credit rationing can be caused by imperfect information. Symmetric information is the situation in which borrowers and lenders have equal access to all available information. This symmetry could be approximately satisfied in classical CPEs, mainly because both sides were subjected to one comprehensive plan. The opposite case – which is called generally imperfect information – has many variants. Asymmetrical information, where the borrower knows the expected return and risk of his project, whereas the lender knows only the expected return and risk of the average project in the economy, is a particularly important case and is common in all types of economy (Meyers and Majluf, 1984). Information deteriorates as economies are forced to make fundamental changes that may be accompanied by instability and inflationary problems.

In loan markets, one imperfection arises from the fact that an increase in the loan rate raises the probability of default and increases the expected value of bankruptcy costs. It thus reduces the total expected return of the project, causing the lender's expected income to fall. Another type of imperfection arises when these resources consist of new capital for 'investment options' that would otherwise expire in Meyers' treatment (1977, and Meyers and Majluf, 1984). The third type occurs when increases in the loan rate cause the joint expected return to borrower and lender to fall and may even fail to increase the expected revenues of the lender. This phenomenon involves a moral hazard problem. All these imperfections exist in the loan markets of the reforming economies.

These imperfections have three implications. First, credit may be rationed. Second, although no firm may actually be denied a loan, firms that are relatively unaffected by the imperfections or have relatively large amounts of collateral to offer will tend to receive the greatest amount of credit. Third, when one of the imperfections is present it will generally be possible to increase the total social expected return on lending above that which prevails at market equilibrium by reducing the rate of interest, increasing the size of each loan and granting a larger number of loans. Each of the three imperfections involves a deadweight loss.

There are two basic reasons why the relationship between the interest rate charged and expected receipts may not be monotonic, and the adverse selection and incentive effects in turn cause lenders not to increase the interest rate charged, even when there is an excess demand for credit. The effect of adverse selection is that as the interest rate is increased the mix of applicants changes adversely; safe potential borrowers drop out of the market. The effect of adverse incentive effects is that as the interest rate is increased, applicants undertake riskier projects. Because monitoring is costly and never perfect, lenders must resort to indirect control mechanisms and the behaviour of a borrower is affected by the terms of the contract, including the interest rate. A key result of Stiglitz and Weiss (1987) is that the risk taking of borrowers rises as the interest rate they are charged rises.[10]

Whenever market mechanisms are introduced into RCPEs, the same effects, reflecting the advantages and disadvantages of markets, may also be introduced, and they tend to be stronger than in mature market systems due to lack of maturity. The disadvantages may be more obvious than the advantages at the beginning of the transitional period. This is another reason why the credit rationing techniques of the West have been stressed.

Banking control and credit rationing

Informational asymmetries are suggested by Leland and Pyle (1977) as a primary reason for the existence of intermediaries. The combination of economies of scale in monitoring and diversifying investments is the fundamental justification for the presence of banks in the Diamond model (Diamond, 1984).

In response to market risks and borrowers' attitudes, banks or lenders take the following actions to control risks in the West, some of which were also used by banks in CPEs and some of which should be noted by RCPEs.

First, since high levels of sunk costs are involved in gathering information to gauge the likelihood of default, lenders tend to specialise by making loans to particular industries. As a result there is a tendency towards natural monopoly – not in banking as a whole, but in the supply of credit to a particular person, firm or industry. There is an analogy here with the specialised banking model in China.

Second, since borrowers have an incentive to take actions that raise the probability of default, a lender can respond by placing restrictive clauses in a loan contract and by controlling the size of the loan and the related terms of the loan contract. This certainly favours the idea of strengthening banks' supervision in RCPEs during transition.

Third, several problems related to the public good are associated with any classification of creditors. A clause stating that the loan is in default (if any loan of the borrower is in default) will ensure that the lender can maintain control of the collateral and can represent his interests in the event of a reorganisation in the borrowing firm. These public-good problems become paramount when bankruptcy occurs and the majority of the creditors of any class have to agree to any settlement. There is a natural incentive to concentrate the sources of credit. This also indicates that the banking systems of the reforming economies should be alert to the risk of default and supervise rigorously the production system.

Fourth, ongoing customer relations provide the current lender with a distinct advantage over competitors in assessing the current riskiness of its customers. This implies that it may be necessary to withhold from enterprises the freedom to choose their banks in the reforming economies, especially when it is not possible to preserve absolutely the advantage of lenders as, for example, during a transitional period.

Fifth, since competitors may fear that winning a customer implies that the previous lender learned of adverse developments, Akerlof's (1984) 'lemons' principle is an important factor in loan markets. RCPEs may have to keep competition between banks at reasonable levels by means of legal restraints and maintain a relatively stable relationship between lenders and borrowers in the transitional period.

Finally, the threat of termination of credit plays an important part in encouraging firms to undertake less risky strategies during this period.

These 'moral hazard' problems can be better handled when there are exclusive relationships. This powerful instrument of threat, though it takes time to realise, should not be abandoned by the reforming banks.

Analysis of credit allocation by credit rationing literature

The credit rationing literature warns that analysis of credit allocation can go astray in trying to apply the standard supply and demand model. Despite their complexity and sophistication, financial markets are typically represented in macroeconomic models by just two variables: the money stock and the interest rate. In this respect the financial market is treated no differently from other complex markets, such as the labour market.

Credit rationing theory postulates that the interest rate alone does not adequately reflect the links between financial markets and the rest of the economy. Rather, credit markets deviate from the standard model because the interest rate indicates only what the individual promises to repay, not what he will actually repay (which means that interest rate is not the only dimension of a credit contract). The availability of credit and the quality of balance sheets are important determinants of the rate of investment; if credit rationing exists, quantity variables such as the amount of credit have to be examined in addition to price variables when appraising monetary and financial policy.

Credit has been considered to be an important transmission channel for the effects of monetary policy by various economists over most of this century. Among others, this 'credit' school of monetary policy includes Hawtrey (1919), Roosa (1951), Gurley and Shaw (1960) and Friedman (1981). Their shared view is that variations in the availability of credit can have a significant impact on real economic activity, both on the aggregate level and on its distribution among sectors and even individual projects. In addition, most would argue that monetary policy should be carried out, or at least measured and evaluated, with regard to its effect on the availability of credit.

The 'credit' school differs from the 'money' or monetarist school over whether monetary policy is based on the size of the money supply or on the availability of credit. This leads to different views regarding the implementation of monetary policy: how it should be measured, when and how it should be used, and what it might accomplish. Friedman (1981) has shown that a broad measure of credit stands at least on a par with money as an instrument that (a) the Federal Reserve can control and (b) forecasts future movements in nominal GNP, when the Federal Reserve has not used M1 as an operating target for monetary policy.

If credit rationing limits a firm's access to external finance, then the firm's liquidity and internally generated cash flow may determine how much of its investment demand is realised as actual capital investment. Furthermore credit rationing would have a larger impact on firms that have a higher ratio of investment demand to internally generated cash flow.

The relationship of capital investment to internal cash flow is the focus of research by Fazzari *et al.* (1988). Their analysis shows that the investment expenditures of certain firms display 'excess sensitivity' to variations in their cash flow. In response to lower interest rates or other factors that raise investment demand, the increase in the investment expenditures of these firms is closely tied to the amount of their internally generated cash flow. By implication, these firms do not have substantial and continuing access to external financing. Equity capital and trade credit are two alternatives to bank loans. This also occurs in China where inter enterprise debt became serious when monetary policy was tightened.

Stiglitz and Weiss (1981) believe that credit rationing will characterises imperfectly competitive lending markets as well as competitive lending markets. Therefore no RCPEs can escape rationing. How to formulate credit rationing models for the reforming economies in the midst of transition remains an interesting topic for research.

Relevant Chinese theories and credit planning in China

There are few works in China that analyse both the quantitative relationships of the variables of banking activities and the relevant economic variables. Credit planning and cash planning are stressed by Chinese economists, and together they are essentially similar to credit rationing.

In Li's book (1983) there is no separate chapter on credit planning, only a section discussing the comprehensive balancing of budget, credit, foreign exchange and production materials (Li, 1983, pp. 599–607). There credit planning and cash planning are subordinate to planning of the state budget. The factors influencing the level of bank loans are the levels of industrial and agricultural production, the management of enterprises and quarterly adjustment factors. Generally speaking, in the first half of a year there are more loan repayments and fewer bank credits, fewer rural deposits and more bank credits to the rural areas, and more loan repayments from commercial companies. In the second half of a year there are fewer loan repayments and more bank loans, more repayments and deposits from the rural areas and more bank credits to commercial companies. The factors influencing the cash supply by the banking system are the economic situation, the size of the commodity supply, budget expenditure and the management of wages and cash in hand. It seems that credit balancing is determined, first and foremost, not by the banking system, but by the state budget. Credit balancing in turn determines cash balancing (ibid, pp. 586–90). These rules certainly suit the framework of the prereform Chinese economy, which will be discussed later.

Peng (1985) edited a book that confirms that credit planning in banks is a process of comprehensive balancing that links the budget to the demand and supply of production materials. It was also demonstrated that cash balancing is subject to credit balancing. The situation of the economy and markets, as well as seasonal and regional differences, are the other factors influencing cash balancing. The book also indicates that, because of the equilibrium between the sources and the uses of the account transfer payments within the banking system, the disequilibrium between cash income and cash expenditure is always remedied by an additional money supply by the banking system (Peng, 1985, pp. 384–91). Cash quantity is determined by credit supply and the level of loan repayments (ibid, p. 286).

Sheng (1989) showed how the People's Bank of China (PBC) controlled money supply. There was a causal relationship between commodities and labour on the one hand and money on the other. They displayed a dynamic connection. There was also a relationship between the average stock of money and the flow of GDP – GDP being the aggregation of money stocks at different points (Sheng, 1989, pp. 285–8). Unfortunately Sheng does not support his analysis with any data.

Zhu (1985) wrote a book on sectorial banking business. He found an increasing proportion of bank loans in the expenditure of industrial working capital. There is an internal linkage between industrial working capital and industrial working capital credits, because (a) bank loans have their maturities, and working capital can also be refunded from sales income regularly; and (b) the demand for bank credits equals the demand for working capital minus company retentions. The amount of bank loans for working capital is determined by four factors: (1) a company's demand for additional working capital; (2) the potential of the working capital stock in the company; (3) the quarterly credit plan made according to the ratio of working capital over sales income and the working capital already obtained by the company; and (4) the capacity of the credits planned by the banks (Zhu, 1985, pp. 127, 161–6).

Some correlations were found empirically. Chinese economists such as Wang (1989, pp. 268–76) have studied the relationship between the sources of bank lending and the uses of bank loans. Their research found a positive correlation between the deposits of industrial enterprises and bank loans to industrial enterprises; a positive correlation between rural deposits and bank credits to commercial enterprises; a negative correlation between deposits of households in cities and in the countryside on the one hand, and cash in hand and bank credits to commercial enterprises on the other; and a positive correlation between bank deposits from the budget and bank credits, among other things.

Dai (1990, mimeo) used monthly data from 1981 to 1989 to run an OLS regression of industrial output on enterprise deposits. Although the mis-specification tests are missing, his conclusion is interesting. There is a high correlation between the two variables ($R^2 = 0.9348$). In the 107 months, on average an increase of one yuan in enterprise deposits is accompanied by a 0.5978 yuan increase in industrial output. The extent to which enterprise deposits restrain industrial output differs from period to period.

The theoretical analysis mentioned above supports the possibility of banking control in China. However the analysis has not been supported by enough statistical tests. Thus those theories offer us some hypotheses. We do, however, know that what Wang (1989) and the others have mentioned existed before the radical economic reforms of the 1980s.

Similar to Japan, bank credits in China are basically rationed or planned. How have they been rationed or planned in China? From 1953 to 1980 the credit management system was called '*tong shou tong zhi*'. This means that all deposits obtained by the banks should be handed over to the PBC headquarters, and that all loans should be planned compulsorily by the headquarters and implemented by the branches of the banks. Since 1950 the PBC has formulated the 'comprehensive credit plans of the state banks', which are regarded as important components of the national plan. These credit plans are composed of credit plan balance sheets and the accompanying instructions of the PBC (the central bank), the specialised banks and the commercial banks. These plans are drafted independently by tried and tested methods according to party and state policies, the national plan and the economic situation. When ready, the plans are transferred to the banks and their branches for implementation under the supervision of the PBC.

Under the CPE system, once the compulsory credit plans were in place the PBC shared the responsibility of financing the credits. But after the credit-system reforms in 1985 the plans managed by the PBC were separated from the credits managed by the state-owned banks. This meant that the banks had to find sources of credit by themselves. However money emission ($\Delta M0$) and loans for fixed assets investments – two important components of the credit plans – were managed rigorously as they were written into the compulsory plans. The extent of other credits could be decided by the banks according to the deposits they could secure.

The credit plans of the PBC system were compulsory – once the quantity of credits had been planned by the PBC, the banks had to implement them. The credit plans of the banks were managed according to the different management principles of the banks. The basic principles were that credits had to be planned uniformly, different levels of branches shared different responsibilities, and the quantity of credits had to be based on the quantity of deposits. Different banks, moreover, had some additional principles of their own. The annual credit spread plans of the Industrial and Commercial Bank of China arranged by the PBC were compulsory. The plans for the spreads between deposits and loans had to be fulfilled. The Agricultural Bank of China's borrowing plans, its plans for the reserves in the PBC and its fixed asset investments in the countryside were compulsory, while the separate items of the balance sheets were indicative plans, not compulsory ones. The annual borrowing plans and the loan plans of the capital construction projects of the Bank of China and the spreads between deposits and loans of the People's Construction Bank of China were compulsory. The balance sheets of the Business Bank of China International Trust and Investment Corporation and the Communication Bank of China were combined into the comprehensive credit plans of the state banks.

The PBC has drawn up the credit plans of the non-banks since 1989. Management of the credit cooperatives in urban areas follows the principle of lending according to deposits; that is, the more deposits obtained, the more loans can be advanced. However 10–20 per cent of deposits collected must be deposited at the PBC. A similar principle is imposed on the credit cooperatives in rural areas by the Agricultural Bank of China on behalf of the PBC. Since 1988 the PBC has asked them to follow two principles of management: that the proportion of deposits outstanding represented by loans outstanding should be kept below 75 per cent; and that the proportion of total loans to enterprises in townships and the countryside represented by additional equipment credit to them should be kept below 30 per cent. The PBC has also strengthened its administration of credit and trust companies. For example the total amount of fixed assets investments, loans and leasing values should be no more than 60 per cent of the total amount of the additional deposits, bonds and the real capital of an individual credit and trust company. In 1987 their reserves in the PBC were raised from 10 per cent to 12 per cent.

In 1989 the PBC ordered both banks and non-banks to transfer 5–7 per cent of their customers' deposits to the central bank. The PBC also uses refinancing credits and the interest rate to monitor the banks in order to control total credit.

Summary

Imperfect information in credit markets, which differ from goods markets, has led economists to research credit rationing as an important channel between banks and firms, in addition to the functions of market self-adjusting mechanisms and government regulating mechanisms. One implication of credit rationing is that the interest rate is not a reliable indicator of the impact of financial variables on aggregate demand. It is quite likely that quantity variables, such as the amount of credit, have to be watched carefully. Another, probably more important, implication is that financial intermediaries are crucial in coping with asymmetric information. The necessary screening and monitoring of the production system are the fundamental justifications for the existence of banks. Meanwhile central banks are also necessary for the regulation and control of banks.

Non-price allocation of credit does not necessarily have adverse implications for economic efficiency if market competition and regulations exist. An imperfect market may have to tolerate and utilise, at least temporarily, more rationing than a perfect market due to the possibility of more distorted information in the former than in the latter. Therefore the banking systems in the market-oriented RCPEs should fully utilise credit rationing as an important tool. It is not wise for them to abandon credit planning which is essentially the same as the credit rationing widely used in the West. If credit is planned properly, government rationing and bank rationing can be combined to achieve a compromise between macro- and microeconomic interests.

Credit has been considered an important transmission channel for the effects of monetary policy. Variation in the availability of credit can have large effects on real economic activity, both on the aggregate level and on its distribution among sectors and even individual projects. Money stock may not be a key factor in determining price level and output, instead the availability of credit and the quality of balance sheets may be important determinants of the rate of investment. This idea of credit rationing can be the most suitable transmission mechanism. It can act as a half-way house in decentralising the financial system. For instance the central bank can operate it using a mixture of market and administrative methods and can eventually abandon the latter.

CONCLUSIONS

In this chapter we have reviewed Western financial development theories and the modern banking literature. Financial development theories have been used to study some serious problems relating to the financial repression that exists widely in LDCs. Whether the remedies suggested by these theories are feasible for RCPEs remains questionable. The conventional market solution suggested by the financial liberalisation literature should be carefully assessed. A substantial increase in interest rates may not be the only policy and may not even be the key to a higher and more efficient investment blueprint, although it is true that interest rates should play an important role in the marketisation process. There exist significant differences between LDCs and CPEs and between CPEs and RCPEs that, among other things, have been ignored by Western literature.

The modern banking literature, especially the recent findings of banking theories, has given strong theoretical support to the central argument that it is necessary to control banks and to allow banks to control the production system during transition. Although the literature explains the nature of banking in various ways, this necessity was discovered very early on and the deeper the research into it the clearer the distinguishing features of banks have become. The information literature has explained the foundation of financial intermediation. Control theories have also stressed the provision of long-term finance, which is vital to the economic restructuring of CPEs. Banks can renegotiate loans easily, which is helpful to borrowers in financial distress. In arguing the reasons why asset transformation gives rise to a need for regulation, the 'run literature' has provided a solid basis for the control of banks. The ownership literature argues for a correct understanding of the effects of takeovers and capital reallocation.

It is vital for RCPEs to choose correct directions before radical steps are taken, since misunderstandings can create erroneous models. As CPEs already have powerful banking systems, it should not be too difficult to reform them. As stock markets are of very limited significance and not the main source of finance for industry even in many Western countries, more emphasis should be laid on bank financing instead of equity financing. Naturally banking control and the control of banks become extremely important, since marketisation generates risks and the possibility of bank runs.

As the recent literature explains, shareholders act as principals in 'good times' while debt holders act as principals in 'bad times'. Both financial markets and banks are necessary for a healthy modern economy. This gives RCPEs important guidance: the establishment of the former and the reconstruction of the latter are important factors in reforms. The process may be lengthy and require caution. There is an important issue of corporate governance, which had not been a problem in CPEs due to the restrictive planning mechanisms (see Chapter 1), but which has become a serious problem because of the control vacuum following the removal of central planning control.

A vital task of RCPEs during such a historic period of transition is to establish a new control system with sound mechanisms to incentivise all the involved agents, forge a compromise between macroeconomic and microeconomic interests, ensure commitment to long-term policies and provide a mechanism for penalising poor management.

It is worth experimenting with a contingent control system for enterprises and banks. The Chinese gradual reform approach is more convincing than the radical approaches attempted by many countries in Eastern Europe and the former Soviet Union because it can at least narrow the control vacuum left by the original system.

Meanwhile the authorities should promote competition between control groups in order to induce adequate efficiency and avoid overconcentration. It should be borne in mind that the authorities could become 'free riders' if they are not restricted by more intervention from banks in bad times. Meanwhile competition between banks should be limited. A powerful central bank and a well-established regulatory system will become ever more important in regulating and securing banks and in protecting the new corporate governance structure.

State ownership does not prevent shareholding and cross-shareholding systems from developing, according to the experience of China in recent years (see Nuti, 1990). If competition in ownership through the takeover process is not perceived in the insider system as a substitute for competition in production, the reforms should bring state ownership and cross-shareholdings into a more effective system of corporate control. Thus insiders would be protected from outside intervention, encouraging them to engage in mutual active monitoring and therefore overcoming 'free rider' problems.

As far as banking is concerned, some suggestions arising from theoretical results are worth repeating here. Given the risks involved, the cash expenditure of clients should be controlled carefully by banks. A public agency that regulates banks both *ex ante* and *ex post* on behalf of depositors is necessary. Politicians are expected to be subject to pressure. For regulatory efficiency, the monitoring role could be given to a private or government rating agency, while the intervention role might remain with a public agency. The banks should be exposed to more external interference in turbulent times. A new corporate governance structure was suggested in this chapter in order to realise these ideas in RCPEs.

The arguments for strengthening government economic functions and banking functions raise the issue of credit rationing. Money stock may not be a key quantity in determining price level and output. Instead availability of credit and amounts on balance sheets may be important determinants of the rate of investment. The combination of imperfect information and the immaturity of market mechanisms justifies the necessity and usefulness of credit rationing in the RCPEs. Banks can control the production system through controlling quantity variables with the help of credit rationing, which can be the most suitable transmission mechanism. Credit rationing can act as a half-way house in decentralising the financial system operated by the central bank by using a mixture of market and administrative methods, though the latter can eventually be abandoned. This interesting idea suggests a strong role for the reforming banking system in guiding transition. Therefore credit planning, once a very important policy in the traditional CPE model, will still be very useful during transition as it is essentially the same as credit rationing. If credits are planned properly, government rationing and bank rationing can be combined so as to allow a compromise between macroeconomic interests and microeconomic ones.

4 Financial Disorder and Banking Control

Tell the Queen, I am busy (Robert Maxwell).

INTRODUCTION

Chapter 3 argued that the control of banks and bank control can be rigorously justified by theoretical models. However it is necessary and instructive to show what may happen in the transitional period if proper controls of this kind do not exist. This chapter discusses the microeconomic functions of the central bank and its subordinate banks. Despite the benefits of banking reforms, financial disorder occurred in almost all the reforming economies immediately after decentralisation of the banking system. Why should this have occurred? The answer is directly related to the control functions of the monetary authority and the banking system. While in recent years there have been several studies of East European experiences of reform and subsequent financial disorder, this chapter discusses the Chinese experience, which hitherto has not been comprehensively studied.

Fiscal policy and monetary policy are two basic instruments of the state for macroeconomic adjustment and control. Coordination between the two embodies the relationship between the Ministry of Finance and the central bank. In mature market economies, monetary policy focuses on the role of a nominal anchor, essentially a medium-run objective. It also exerts a temporary influence upon the level and composition of aggregate demand; and on the stability of the financial system through banking supervision and financial regulation. Comparatively speaking, fiscal policy tends to adjust the economic structure and needs a relatively long time to work through. However, once fiscal measures are implemented their effects are felt relatively quickly, as in China. Monetary policy, on the other hand, tends to adjust certain aggregates, such as money supply and the total amount of credit, which are in themselves relatively flexible. Here, however, the effects of these mechanisms have a time lag.

The microeconomic function of a central bank is to provide support in the form of regulatory and supervisory services in order to maintain the health of the banking system. The support function via lender of last resort

131

assistance has never been an issue in China since no banks are facing insolvency. In effect there has been an implicit 100 per cent deposit insurance.

This chapter utilises the concept of 'financial disorder' to analyse China's experience. Financial disorder means that the behaviour and activities of the economic entities, especially the financial institutions (banks for example), are contrary to the regulations set by the authorities. Problems may arise from incorrect macroeconomic strategies and/or policies. The consequence can be financial crisis, bringing about monetary and macroeconomic disequilibrium. Generally speaking there have been four instances of national financial disorder since the economic reform in 1979.

Financial disorders, especially those in the payment system, frequently occurred when the banking system was being decentralised. The banks were deeply concerned about loan repayment because deposits had become more volatile, especially as an increasing proportion of liabilities were household deposits rather than funds allocated from the budget. The former were more unstable than the latter since the expenditure of the household sector fluctuated with expectations about inflation. The derivative deposits generated from the bank accounts of the enterprise sector were increasing. This caused difficulty in controlling the money supply. The lack or inadequate enforcement of regulation gave much scope for criminal activity.

In this chapter Jiangsu Province of China is used as an example to show the changing pattern of finance after the reforms. With this as a background, it will be shown that four national financial disorders have already been experienced by China, from which some lessons can be drawn. Interenterprise debt problems are then discussed and the causes of the problems analysed. Hengshuei region is used – with additional national data – to describe the third national financial disorder and to show empirically that banking control is urgently needed. This is followed by a study of the fourth financial disorder and the efforts to combat it. The subsequent discussion centres on why the control functions of the banking system were successful in the CPE model and why this control function is essential to decentralisation. We then turn to a comparison of the Japanese and German experiences of banking control. Finally, the central hypothesis concerning the necessity of banking control is assessed in the conclusion.

THE CHANGING PATTERN OF FINANCE: JIANGSU PROVINCE

Jiangsu Province is one of the most developed areas in south-east China. In 1989 it had a population of 65.36 million and a national income of 96.9 billion yuan – the highest per capita level in China at the time.

After ten years of reform, the banking system has replaced the Financial Bureaux of the governments at different administrative levels to become the main financier of the production system, and the banks manage and supervise capital flows among enterprises.

As shown in Figure 4.1, from 1978 to 1988 budgetary revenue as a proportion of national income declined more sharply than government expenditure. The difference between revenue and expenditure decreased, implying that transfers from local government to central government, as well as local government relations, also declined sharply. Furthermore the credit scale expanded rapidly. By 1990, 70–90 per cent of total working capital and 30 per cent of total fixed asset investments of enterprises in the province came from bank credit. From 1981 to 1988 the annual average growth rates of industrial credit and fixed asset investment credit were 23.9 per cent and 46 per cent respectively. That of credit to enterprises in towns and the countryside was 43.6 per cent. This suggests that banks lay at the heart of the problems that immediately followed the reforms.

The main reason for the problems was that planners were no longer able to control the budget and the banks. There are two ways of forcing banks to

Figure 4.1   Revenue and expenditure as a proportion of national income, Jiangsu Province, 1978–88

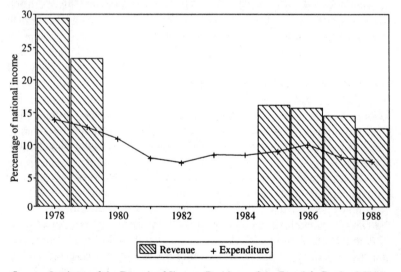

Source: Institute of the Branch of Jiangsu Province of the People's Bank of China, 20 April 1990.

increase credit availability. One is by local governments asking them to sustain the high GNP growth rate. The local budget frequently 'borrowed' and overdrew from the banks as much as it could. Another is by SOEs demanding that they meet the needs of the overheating economy. The second method was more likely to succeed in Jiangsu Province. The industrial output elasticity of the money supply ($\delta M/M$ over $\delta Y/Y$) during the period 1980–4 (the Sixth Five Year Plan) was 0.77, but rose to 4.05 in the period 1985–8.

The rapid increase in bank credit, especially the increase in fixed asset investment credit, directly contributed to investment expansion, which in turn induced consumption expansion (usually about 40 per cent of the fixed asset investment is generated by the investment). In Jiangsu Province the average annual capital accumulation rate, which is the ratio of accumulation funds over the uses of the national income,[1] was 33.1 per cent in the period 1980–4. It increased to 42.5 per cent from 1986 to 1988. The wage fund in 1988 grew by 525 per cent over its 1978 level, which was much faster than the GNP growth rate.

When supply and demand were unable to be balanced, certain functions of the budget system then being taken over by the banking system became risky. In Jiangsu Province significant amounts advanced by some major banks became either bad loans or fell into arrears in 1990. Much credit had in fact been transformed into grants, simply because many enterprises had become loss makers and the banks had to continue to support them. The accumulation of these non-performing loans was larger than the total amount of credit of the banking system in this province. The bankers were shocked by such a net debt (insolvent) situation.

FOUR NATIONAL FINANCIAL DISORDERS IN CHINA

Financial disorder as a national phenomenon has been admitted by the Chinese authorities and discussed in the Chinese literature only since 1989. However four national financial disorders have occurred in China since 1970.

The first, which occurred during the period 1979–80, was characterised by expansionary fiscal and monetary policies that stimulated money to grow much faster than GDP. Budget deficits totalled 29.81 billion yuan for the two years. National income grew by 7.0 per cent and 6.4 per cent in 1979 and 1980, and in the same year, net material product grew by 8.5 per cent and 8.4 per cent respectively. Currency in circulation grew by 26.3 per cent and 29.3 per cent, M1 by 24.4 per cent and 23 per cent and M2 by 26.2 per cent and 27 per cent.[2] The banking system relaxed its control on credit, causing money supply to be higher than economic growth. Given the roughly constant velocity, the excess total demand for money forced the international trade deficit to reach $2.01 billion in 1979 and $1.28 billion in 1980. Import control was also relaxed (Dai, in Ma *et al.*, 1990, p. 806). This was the first period when banking reforms threatened the authorities' ability to maintain price stability. Indexes of cash in circulation and savings deposits increased by 85.3 per cent over the period 1978–80 whereas retail sales at constant prices increased by only 25 per cent. A retreat from the various reforms was adopted towards the end of 1980 (Chai, 1981, p. 45).

The second financial disorder was characterised by credit-induced open inflation. Credit activities were out of control in 1984, the year that the People's Bank of China became the central bank. Total loans in that year increased by 100 billion yuan, equal to the total amount of the loans prior to 1979, with several billion yuan being over-issued into circulation. The central bank failed to control the money supply and made some policy errors, leaving the specialised banks to either misallocate funds or compete with each other, which caused extraordinary credit expansion. By abandoning administrative control too early, the central bank also experienced difficulties in controlling the specialised banks' branches in the cities and their sub-branches in the counties. In 1984 M0 was 26.2 billion yuan, an increase of 49.5 per cent over the previous year and equal to the total M0 of the previous 34 years (Chen, 1992). Economic overheating exacerbated the budget deficit, which accumulated to 27.54 billion yuan in 1984–8. During these five years M0 increased by 32.1 per cent, M1 by 20.5 per cent and M2 by 25.9 per cent on an average annual basis, while the corresponding rate of national income increase was only 11.2 per cent. Excess demand forced the international trade deficit to increase from $1.27 billion in 1984 to $14.9 billion in 1985 and $11.97 billion in 1988 (Dai, in Ma *et al.*, 1990). The inflation rate was 8.8 per cent in 1985 (Chen, in ibid.), forcing the government to restore order (Yang, 1988).

The third financial disorder, which took place in the period 1987–9, was characterised by substantial deregulation and interenterprise debt problems. Measures to alleviate the previous three financial disorders had never tackled the problems at their roots and therefore difficulties had accumulated. The fourth and the most recent financial disorder, which commenced in the first half of 1993, has been accompanied by serious economic crimes. The continuing national battle against this disorder must solve fundamental problems if economic reform is to succeed. The last two episodes will be analysed in detail in this chapter.

INTERENTERPRISE DEBT IN CHINA

Interenterprise debt has become a widespread phenomenon in Eastern Europe and some literature has recently appeared that deals with this issue. In China the problem is also serious, but with some particular Chinese characteristics.

Defining interenterprise debt

Interenterprise debt relates directly to trade credit lending between enterprises, which indicates that credit markets have formed in China since the reforms.

Standard (goods) markets differ from credit markets in two important respects. First, standard markets, which are the focus of classical competitive theory, involve a number of agents buying and selling an homogeneous commodity. Second, in standard markets delivery of a commodity by a seller and payment by a buyer occur simultaneously. In contrast, credit (in money or goods) received today by an individual or firm is exchanged for a promise of repayment (in money or goods) in the future. But promises are frequently broken and there may be no objective way of determining the likelihood of the promise being kept.[3] The need for credit is evidence of change: those who control existing resources, or have claims on current wealth, are not necessarily those best placed to use these resources. Thus they transfer control of their resources to others, in return for a promise. Trade credit serves as a substitute for bank loans.

The Chinese formerly regarded interenterprise debt which was not permitted by state regulations, as 'triangular debt'. Recently the definition 'linear indebtedness' has been advanced (Shu, 1992). It would be wrong to regard interenterprise debt as 'triangular' because it is not necessarily in a triangular linkage (A owes B, B owes C, C owes A). Debts that are in a triangular arrangement between enterprises are often not permanent arrears or defaults. It would be wrong to define all interenterprise debt as default simply because interenterprise debt is a common phenomenon in market economic relations.[4] Such debts only become problematic when enterprises persistently fail to meet their obligations. What A owes B and B owes A should net out.[5] Even in mature Western economies there is a considerable occurrence of such credit, by no means all of which is voluntarily extended. Although enterprises are not necessarily unable or unwilling to repay by any formal legal definition, the debts represent a failure to fulfil contractual obligations. This chapter defines interenterprise debt as that with no guarantee of repayment.

Before the mid-1980s such debt was not a national problem in China. But the difficulties have become serious and widespread since then, inter-enterprise debt often occupying huge amounts of capital flow and inevitably affecting production and sales. This has led to reduced tax payments, and hence budget revenue, and has hidden the problems that existed within indebted companies and non-performing banks, both of which were plagued with low-quality management while the former suffered additionally from extraordinarily high excess stock. Solving the problem is an urgent task if there is to be a healthy development of market mechanisms.

The facts

Serious interenterprise problems began in China around 1986, following a credit expansion in 1984 and tight monetary policy in the second half of 1985.

The data in Figure 4.2 has been collected from different sources, but unfortunately their records were incomplete. Banks should be able to ascertain the extent of the interenterprise debt problem simply because all enterprises hold bank accounts, but Figure 4.2 does not represent enterprise debt to banks. Data issued by the banking system excludes enterprises not yet investigated by the banks. For example, interenterprise debt in March 1990 was 270 billion yuan. Therefore it is likely that the data in the figure is bilateral debt, rather than triangular and multilateral debt. The former accounts only for arrears between two enterprises and ignores debt to a third party. Bilateral interenterprise debt was estimated by the State Planning Commission (mimeo, October 1990) as 150 billion yuan while multilateral debt amounted to about 300 billion yuan. Yan (1992) also confirms that the amount of debt was 300 billion yuan by the end of 1990. According to the incomplete statistics, at the end of 1986 interenterprise debt, in the form of money and goods and evaluated at current prices, had stood at 16 billion yuan, so in just five years it had increased more than tenfold.

The National Clearing Conference on Triangular Debt, held by the State Council in September 1991, reported that, among the important fixed capital investment projects planned by the state,[6] more than ten thousand projects involved interenterprise debt, which amounted to 38 billion yuan. Twenty-three billion yuan of bank money and 11 billion yuan collected from enterprises was injected into these enterprises through the banks in order to clear the debts. In spite of this effort a large number of new debts were created in 1991 (Yan, 1992). The State Council held a similar meeting in March 1992, stating that the clearing of interenterprise debt

Figure 4.2   Interenterprise debt in China (current prices in billion yuan)

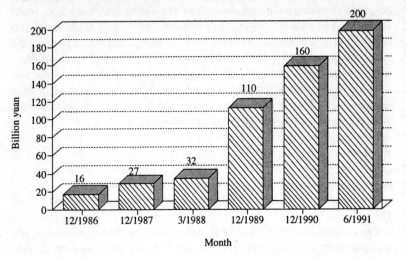

Sources: Shu Xin, vol. II, no. 377 (1991), p. 25; Li and Lin (1990).

had been 'very successful' and that reindebtedness had been 'basically stopped'. However the factors generating new debt still existed and were deeply rooted. The process of clearing them continued and the aim of preventing new indebtedness was emphasised. On 23 December 1992 the prime minister claimed that triangular debt had been cleared. Each one-yuan injection of clearing credit had sorted out 4 yuan of interenterprise debt. Enterprises and local governments were told they would have to share complete responsibility for any new interenterprise and fixed capital investment debt.[7] However recent news about the fourth national financial disorder (discussed later) seems to contradict the claim that reindebtedness has indeed been prevented.

Causes of the debt problems

Interenterprise debt was never a problem in typical CPEs, and this was not simply due to the non-existence of credit markets. There were financial regulations and banking control to avoid over-crediting and interagency lending. Moreover budget constraint was very strict.[8]

Credit markets in reforming economies may not function well – or at least they may not function as a standard market in allocating credit. Among other things, the existence of imperfect information can be cited as the reason for this. Credit rationing may arise whereby certain borrowers are denied credit, even though they are willing to pay the market interest rate (or more), while other apparently similar borrowers do obtain credit. Unlike firms in a market economy which can find an alternative to equity capital, firms in an RCPE have access to just one alternative source of working capital – each other, which creates the risk that they will escape bank supervision.

Trade credit is also a major element in the credit system: outstanding trade credit is almost as large as bank loans to businesses and corporate bonds in the US.[9] Whether national problems can be caused by trade credit does not depend on the maturity or otherwise of the market economy. Rather it is determined by the functional ability of market mechanisms. If market discipline fails to function properly, interenterprise debt can also occur widely in the West, especially during a recession.[10]

Various factors may have caused the debt problems in reforming China. For example, because of their inefficiency it was difficult for enterprises to generate the money to finance investment in new technology. Bank credit was affected by the reduction of enterprise deposits, especially when many enterprises became loss makers. The question is, which are the most important factors?

Are the 'expansionary economic plans' fundamental?

Interenterprise debt often occurred immediately after a period of tight monetary policy following a spell of credit expansion. Therefore planners were often blamed for projects that exceeded the investment capacity of the economy.

Such projects resulted in a 51.2 billion yuan shortage of funds to match the investment plans for the SOEs in 1990, a significant part of which became interenterprise debts as SOEs had to make up the shortfall by delaying payments to their partners (see Shu, 1992). Yet the shortage was generated not just by the tight economic policy in 1990. There was a 10 billion yuan gap between the credit scale planned in 1988 and the amount available from banks. In 1989 the gap doubled. A 20–30 billion yuan shortage was caused by the national investment plan in 1989 (Tang, 1990). According to an investigation of 4117 large state projects under the reconstruction of 1991, there was a 196.8 billion yuan shortage in the funds required to meet the planned investment target of 1068.1 billion yuan. The 18.4 per cent shortfall was transformed into 40 billion yuan of interenterprise debt (Yan, 1992).

However the above shortages represent only a small proportion of total debt. The previous section analysed the reasons for the shortfall and showed that state revenue was effectively crowded out. The national planners can hardly be blamed since they seldom set over-expansionary targets in the 1980s.[11] Indeed an excess demand for credit is common and applications for credit are frequently not satisfied even in developed market economies. The problem was that economic control had been relaxed after the reforms. It thus became easier for individual applicants to satisfy project appraisal and approving criteria, especially since different local administrations were authorised to approve projects up to varying amounts. Under pressure from applicants supported by local authorities, the banks grew more likely to approve projects. More than 50 000 new projects were arranged in 1990, and a further 2000 were arranged in 1991. Some applicants artificially reduced their design requirements and investment scales in order to gain approval to start their projects earlier than their rivals. After their applications had been approved, they readjusted their figures and asked for more funds. Eighty per cent of investment projects had not accurately estimated the costs of inflation and interest payments (Yan, 1992). Therefore it was not the expansionary plans that created the funding gaps, rather there is evidence to show that the economy lacked proper control.

Failure to control credit and keep bank loans performing

Tight monetary policy after a period of expansionary economic policy led to monetary growth. In 1984 total state bank credit increased by 28.4 per cent over the 1983 figure, which was much faster than the speed of growth in production and trade. According to the planning experience, the proportion of the annual outstanding value of bank commercial credit to the annual outstanding value of the commodity inventory of the trading companies[12] should be kept roughly constant, otherwise inflation may occur due to the disequilibrium of effective demand created by the credit over the quantity of commodities ready to be supplied. For example, from 1979 to 1982 the ratio was 1:0.97, but from 1983 to 1987 it fell to 1:0.72. Commercial credit increased by 171.8 billion yuan in 1987 compared with 1986, but the commodity inventories of trading companies increased by only 98.5 billion yuan. This meant that each one-yuan increase in bank commercial credit could only be backed up by 0.57 yuan of commodity inventories (Huang, 1989). These figures indicate that credit was out of control; that is, it had become easier for agents to obtain bank credit.

Once investment plans and credit plans had been formulated, work on the various projects commenced immediately. Interenterprise debt in such a situation was primarily a response to tight credit and monetary policy, which created financial difficulties for these projects and their relevant agencies. Completion of the projects had to be postponed and payments for purchasing contracts had to be cancelled. A series of backward and forward linkages were broken.

Figure 4.3 illustrates some features of the Chinese economy form 1987–90. Bank lending to SOEs increased substantially, although there was credit restriction in the period from the third quarter of 1988 to the second quarter of 1989, with relatively low growth rates following the fast credit expansions during the period from 1987 (third quarter) to 1988 (second quarter). This was followed by credit injections in the next period to save the economy from recession. M2 followed the same dynamic pattern. Interest rates[13] grew in the period from the restrictive level of 1989 until the beginning of 1990, and then started to fall. The credit restriction had not necessarily affected M0, although growth rates of M0 fell to below 0 per cent in the first three quarters of 1989, lagging about two quarters behind the starting point of the restrictive period. This picture clearly shows the failure of monetary policy – when policy was slack, the

Figure 4.3   Domestic credit, money supply, interest rate and inflation, China (% growth over previous quarter)

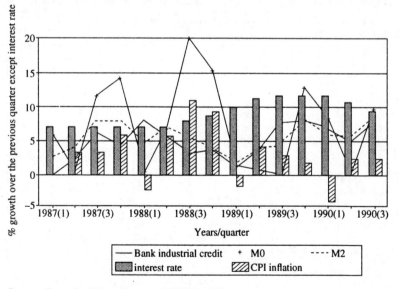

Source: State Statistical Bureau of China, 1990.

issuing of credit was liable to be out of control, but policy had to be relaxed after a short period of tight operation, which often induced inter-enterprise debt problems or recessions.

If goods could not be sold they were stored in either warehouses or shops. Recession is often characterised by extraordinarily high inventory levels. The plot of bank credit to industry against the inventories of light industrial companies and commercial companies, both in nominal values, shows positive correlations over the period (Figures 4.4 and 4.5). From the end of 1989 the inventories held by light industrial companies increased faster than their supply of industrial credits. This indicated recession and also implied that supply was not balanced by demand due to problems of quality and other conditions in the contracts. The market recession during the second half of 1989 and 1990 led to an accumulation of stocks and hence the conversion of working capital into semi-finished or finished goods. The regular linkages between production, trade and consumption were thus damaged. The nascent private sector and firms in small towns and in the countryside were damaged more seriously than the SOEs. All these factors prepared the ground for the creation of inter-enterprise debt.

Figure 4.4   China's bank loans to industrial and commercial enterprises (*ICL*) and the inventories of commercial enterprises (*SC*) in real terms

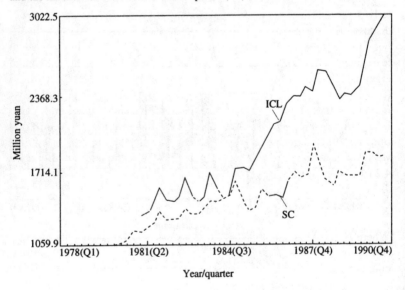

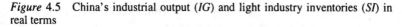

Figure 4.5   China's industrial output (*IG*) and light industry inventories (*SI*) in real terms

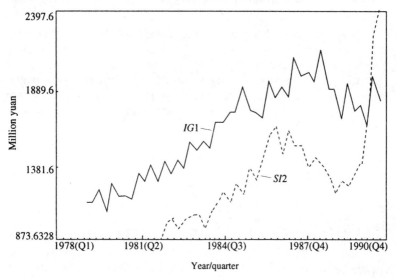

Note: *SI2 = SI* – 10

Two simple regressions may favour this analysis. The data used is quarterly data from the State Statistical Bureau of China. In Chapter 6 we will discuss the data in detail. With the help of the Johansen maximum likelihood procedure (see Johansen, 1988 and Johansen and Juselius, 1990), at least one cointegrated vector is approved by the LR test at the maximum eigenvalue of 0.60 with 31 observations for 1983 (first quarter)–1990 (third quarter) in the regression. The cointegrated vector with 4 VAR maximum lags for the adjustment is estimated using Equation 4.1 (the long-term equation). The cointegrating OLS regression with 34 observations for 1982 (second quarter)–1990 (third quarter) in log first differences with two dummies for the seasonal adjustment is estimated using Equation 4.2 (the short-term equation).

$$\log IL = 2.5 \log SI + 0.13 \log SC \tag{4.1}$$

Where *IL* represents bank loans to the industry, *SI* represents the inventories of the industrial sector and *SC* represents the inventories of commercial companies. They are all *I*(1) variables according to augmented

Dickey–Fuller (1) tests. Therefore we obtain the following cointegrating regression with two dummy variables (D_{t-j}):

$$\Delta \log IL_t = 0.06 + 0.20\Delta \log SI_t + 0.22\Delta \log SC_t - 0.03D_t\,2 + 0.08D_{t-3}$$

$$(4.2)$$

SE	0.01	0.09	0.11	–0.02	0.02
T ratio	(4.43)	(2.12)	(1.97)	(–1.81)	(–3.53)

$R^2 = 0.57$; $F(4, 29) = 11.94$;   SE = 0.04;   DW = 2.08.

Diagnostic tests:

Serial correlation: chi-sq(4) = 0.45
Functional form: chi-sq(1) = 1.77
Normality: chi-sq(2) = 1.41
Heteroscedasticity: chi-sq(1) = 1.94

Equation 4.2 passes CUSUM and CUSUMSQ structural stability tests, and the autocorrelation function and the unit root tests of the residual term show that the residual term is white noise.

The results of Equations 4.1 and 4.2 confirm that the inventories of the industrial sector and the commercial sector positively and significantly correlated with bank loans to industry. The correlation became even closer from 1985, influenced by the recessions in the restrictive periods. Increases in bank loans within certain limits could be transformed into stock, leading an increase in interenterprise debt. The coefficient of commercial companies' inventories in the short run is larger than that of industrial companies in comparison with the long-run equation. The situation is reversed in the long-run Johansen equation. This may imply that commercial companies' inventories are more sensitive to credit policy than that of industrial companies in a dynamic model, because the former are closer to the markets and they purchase the finished goods from the latter.

The above mentioned shortage of capital was, at times, even more serious before the reforms and in the mid-1980s. Why, then, had there not been any obvious interenterprise debt problem? Also, since shortage of funds often exists in a mature market economy, why have they not suffered problems similar to those of the reforming economies? Clearly there must be other factors generating interenterprise debt as such. There was a definite problem with enterprise payment mechanisms, and many other factors also contributed.

In Central and Eastern Europe there is a significant relationship between bank credit and interfirm credit. Interenterprise debt is essentially a symptom of inadequate incentives for banks to keep their loans performing. The greater the creditor passivity of banks, the more probable is creditor passivity in interenterprise debt. In China, creditors also show a lack of aggression in seeking satisfaction for their claims. When debtors default, creditors passively accommodate them by such actions as extending the payment period for loans and capitalising or evergreening unpaid interest, rather than pursuing their claims through bankruptcy or other means. The reluctance of creditors to pursue their claims had a drastic impact on the use of bankruptcy. It was in large part responsible for the ineffectiveness of the law, in spite of the fact that the law could be adapted to the prevailing financial conditions, such as in the case of China in 1986 and Hungary after 1987. This creditor inaction also appears in developing economies. For example the World Bank (1989) reports that in the decade preceding 1989, twenty-five governments came to the aid of distressed financial institutions.

Why are creditors passive?

That enterprise debtors meet promised payments of principal and interest to creditors – be these banks or other enterprises – is a mechanism by which budget constraints bite and the price mechanism works in the re-allocation of resources. Similarly, on the macro side 'failure to enforce credit obligations may render the effects of an orthodox macroeconomic policy ineffective at best, perverse at worst' (Begg and Portes, 1993). The price mechanism is not only unable to provide adequate incentives for new entries but may also be completely unable to enforce exit. Failures in credit and banking markets lead to resource misallocation, a weakening of corporate control, delay in restructuring and increased transition costs.

Although the reforms encourage them to be self-reliant and responsible for their profits and losses, many SOEs in China do not share the responsibility for losses because of society's failure to impose bankruptcy law. Managers believe that their direct boss, the state, and their indirect bosses, the banks, will ultimately help to save them (see Chapter 2). Decentralisation helps to soften the budget constraint of the SOEs. Facing the replacement of budget grants of working capital by bank credits, many SOEs ignored the need to accumulate capital from their retention. In recent years several billion yuan of working capital has been used by SOEs for other purposes (Tang, 1990). Once there was an investment boom they borrowed heavily from the banks and reduced the proportion of retention to total capital. Many of them suffered great losses due to either the quality and the structure of their products or an increase in prices and other costs. Therefore they became very weak in confronting any risks. This was the internal factor causing interenterprise debt under the tight monetary policy.

Having investigated all these complicated factors, it is not difficult to identify the central problem of the control vacuum left by planners after the reforms. Were it not for this, interenterprise debt would never have been a problem. The replacement is the new control system mentioned in Chapter 3.

Solutions to the interenterprise debt problem

The above causes and effects of interenterprise debt have also been identified by Chinese economists, but their solutions are different. The radical solution lies in the enforcement of bankruptcy laws because failure to exercise creditors' rights through these laws is the main reason for the crisis (Sung, 1991). This 'bankruptcy school' calls for the help of civil law and the establishment of a new 'debt economics' to constrain and manage the debts (Li and Lin, 1990). Another solution emphasises improvement in the internal mechanisms of enterprises, especially the SOEs, because the causes of the problem are rather complicated and enterprises share the important responsibility of promoting efficiency and avoiding losses (see Shu, 1992; Wang, *et al.*, 1991; and Yan, 1992). This 'mechanism school' notes, in addition, that adjustment of the economic structure is also important. Still others believe that the problem is caused by different factors and therefore the solution should lie in the joint efforts of at least three agents: firms, banks and the authorities (see Chow, 1990; Tang, 1990). The official attitude seems more pragmatic. Because the problem is long-term in its nature, comprehensive implementation of the bankruptcy laws needs, at the very least, a sound social security system, such as an insurance system. This is currently under preparation in China.

It is worth looking at two recent pieces of Western literature: one stresses bankruptcy laws and the other emphasises 'direct tackling' of the problems.

According to Mitchell (1993) a necessary element of financial reform, and consequently of economic reform, is implementation of bankruptcy laws. Bankruptcy is a keystone of reform, helping to strengthen firms' budget constraints. One general goal of bankruptcy strategy in any economic system is to specify clearly the rights of a firm's claimants in the case of default on debt. Bankruptcy laws are an important component of property rights and should have clear and enforceable definitions. Another goal of bankruptcy laws is that of efficient resource allocation. Bankruptcy laws have potentially significant incentive effects with the help of financial markets. The implementation of bankruptcy depends not only on the terms of bankruptcy status but also upon financial institutions and political constraints. Successful implementation requires adapting provisions of bankruptcy laws to prevailing financial conditions and modifying financial institutions to render them more compatible with the application of bankruptcy laws. Mitchell's reasons for creditor passivity are examined in her paper.

Given the planned credit target, interenterprise debt can deprive the household sector and new private business of bank credit. They impose an implicit (heavy) tax on savings and investment, at least in Eastern Europe. In China they have turned banks into loss makers. Continuous rescheduling of SOE debt to banks preempts other opportunities for bank lending. The problem has not only affected management incentives within SOEs, but has also impeded many forms of bank legislation designed to make credit enforcement effective (Mitchell, 1993). Failure to initiate bankruptcy proceedings has often been due to the fact that the expected value of the debtor's assets was less than the cost of enforcing bankruptcy, or that there was an option value in waiting. Taking action against creditors might signal the extent of the bank's existing non-performing loans. The asset side of banks' balance sheets have become increasingly devalued.

According to Begg and Portes (1993), it is essential to make the banking sector work more efficiently in order to impose budget constraints. Treating microeconomic failures as given, since we know that almost no SOEs have been forced into liquidation, it is more attractive to tackle the problem directly. Debt write-offs for enterprises are likely to deal with a symptom and not a cause, unless or until (1) bank lending is replaced by open fiscal subsidies and (2) privatisation occurs; otherwise further debts are likely to emerge rapidly. Cancelling SOE debts to banks leaves them insolvent. Recapitalising the banks can be achieved only by a government injection on the asset side or by default on household deposits on the liability side. The former is preferable, but must be accompanied by much closer banking supervision. Recapitalisation with indexed bonds would be the clearest commitment to a sound banking system and would raise the credibility of monetary policy. A future government faced with fiscal difficulties would then be forced to seek its savings elsewhere. The procedure of recapitalisation is introduced in the Begg–Portes paper.

Once banks are recapitalised and solvent, the monetary authorities are able to delegate most everyday credit concerns to commercial banks.

Policy makers are then able to confine their attention to aggregates, thereby simplifying the informational demands on central bankers and finance ministers. The programme also helps the development of domestic financial markets, which allow at least the short-run divorce of monetary and fiscal policy and also mitigate the bluntness of the transmission mechanism of monetary policy according to G. Calvo and J. Frenkel (1991a). Delegation and marketisation would help the implementation of monetary policy.

The Mitchell approach can be grouped with the bankruptcy school mentioned above, which is a long-term programme. The Begg–Portes approach requires urgent action to tackle the banking problem but ignores the insolvency of the production system, which is fundamental. What China has done is to inject credit, through the banking system, from the monetary authorities to the SOEs. Once the enterprises are able to pay their debts, their banks, as intermediaries, can also participate in solving their problems, as demonstrated in Chapter 2. The most recent news from China indicates that the above approaches may also be combined. On the one hand China is improving its market foundation by all available means and preparing the social insurance system for the impact of the bankruptcy laws. On the other hand the commercial banks are emerging and separating themselves from the specialised policy banks. The establishment of policy banks is planned in order to share the responsibility for policy investments that are not purely profitable projects. The commercial banks will then have to take responsibility for their own solvency and for imposing market discipline on the SOEs and other debtors. Until this is effective, new debts can be created over and over again. This highlights the need for a new control system, the organisation of which may benefit from the following experience.

THE THIRD NATIONAL FINANCIAL DISORDER: HENGSHUEI

Besides interenterprise debt problems, there are other forms of financial disorder. We now turn to a specific example.

Hengshuei is a district, which is administratively higher than a county but lower than a province. It forms part of Hebei Province, where Beijing is situated. Financial disorders in such an area may reflect similar problems elsewhere in the economy. In spite of the many achievements of the financial reforms, financial disorder seriously affected economic development in Hengshuei in the following ways.

Competition and regulation

Many banking institutions were set up without adequate regulation. To cope with the inefficiency problems, competition between banks was encouraged in 1985. The Agricultural Bank encroached on city business while the Industrial and Commercial Bank stretched its operational units into the countryside; the Bank of China (the foreign exchange banker) tried to expand its domestic businesses and the Post Offices also opened banking windows. In addition the Construction Bank started to deal with lending beyond its usual sphere of capital investment. As competition was encouraged, regulations were not closely followed. Financial institutions proliferated rapidly (Table 4.1),[14] suggesting that entry was easy while exit was difficult or impossible. Some local governments, administrative agencies, enterprises and public units also carried out credit transactions, trust and insurance business, and even opened unlicensed credit and trust companies.

Competition and costs

Banks and non-bank financial intermediaries competed with each other to attract deposits whilst ignoring the costs. In order to attract deposits from the accounts of other banks, some intermediaries sent customers gifts. Almost unbelievably, having sent 45 965 gifts valued at about 95 654 yuan, one bank gained only 579.25 yuan more deposits, according to an investigation in the district in 1987. Another way for financial institutions to compete was to increase interest rates to levels that were several times greater than the regular rates. In 1987 the lending rates to firms in some areas were 30–40 per cent while the annual inflation of the country was 21.7 per cent (SSB, 1989).[15] This indicates that competition between financial intermediaries should be carefully organised during transition.

Table 4.1   The number of financial institutions in Hengshuei

	31/12/1985	*30/09/1989*	*growth (%)*
Deposit institutions	29	308	962
Total financial institutions	405	729	80

Source: Hengshuei Branch of The People's Bank of China, mimeo, 30 March 1990.

Misallocation of money

Money and customers' tax payments were blocked and misappropriated by some financial institutions. Bills were unreasonably returned and credit or commercial letters were postponed without justification. Large remittances were stopped by some banks and then transferred elsewhere for two to fifteen days. Credit arrears were substantial. According to the statistics, by the end of March 1988, 425.84 million yuan – about 22 per cent of the outstanding credits of the local banking system – became interenterprise debt among 1328 enterprises in Hengshuei. Certain banks in three counties of the district stopped 56 tax payments being transferred to the budgetary system, equivalent to 250 000 yuan over the period of an investigation.

Lack of supervision

As a result of desperate measures to attract customers, cash management in some regions was out of control. Some financial managers reduced or even ignored the conditions for approving cash payments. In some financial cooperatives there were no regulations for cash-flow supervision. One particular bank offered its customers forty cash payments amounting to 93.6 thousand yuan with no plan or approval. Transactions in large sums should have been conducted by cheque, however a plant bought 5000 tons of raw materials for about 30 000 yuan paid entirely in cash. Some financial institutions allowed firms to grant bonuses without limitation.

Escaping regulations

According to the state regulations, an enterprise could hold only one clearing account in the banking system. In reality enterprises could choose their banks and banks could choose enterprises as their customers. The number of accounts held by each enterprise increased.[16] A company in Hengshuei opened a deposit account with the Bank of China, a clearing account with the Industrial and Commercial Bank and obtained loans from the People's Construction Bank and the Insurance Company of China.[17] It became very easy in such an unregulated environment for companies to escape bank supervision.

Interbank lending and interenterprise debt

According to the regulations, interbank lending should have solved the banks' problem of short-term illiquidity (about one to thirty days).

However, encouraged by profit-seeking in an overheated economy, many financial intermediaries used interbank borrowing to satisfy excess demand and even to invest in long-term fixed capital projects.[18] As long-term borrowing matured, debts were paid by further short-term borrowing, therefore increasing short-term interest rates.[19] Illegal commissions paid and received in transactions further increased costs. Some company subsidiaries also joined in, thus intensifying the risk of default. The main sources of interbank loans were temporary credit payments by the central bank and the seasonally idle capital of the specialised banks. Long-term interenterprise debt forced the central bank to inject additional money.

Immature money market

As tight monetary policies struggled to cool the overheated economy, enterprises faced a shortage of money. They turned to other sources to fund both their working capital and their fixed capital investments. This movement, however, became an uncontrollable tide. Ideally enterprises should raise funds from society under the supervision of banks that have been authorised by the state to assess and approve their applications to do so. In fact, in Hengshuei 539 enterprises raised 42.75 million yuan of funds by the end of November 1989. Among these enterprises 240 obtained permits only after they had raised 28.93 million yuan. Two hundred and ninety-nine enterprises (55 per cent of the total number) collected 13.82 million yuan (32 per cent of the total amount) without obtaining permits. Those funds could certainly have not been supervised by banks.

Unregulated lending

Although non-bank institutions were not allowed to conduct banking business, according to Provision 4 of The Temporary Regulations of the Banking Management, interfirm lending, interhousehold lending and lending directly from people to firms was freely developed at interest rates higher than those of banks. The Hengshuei Budgetary Bureau also joined in to set up a credit and trust company with the People's Construction Bank in order to do financial business.[20]

Summary

Due to the lack of legal guidelines and necessary financial discipline, as well as the unwillingness of economic entities to obey financial regulations, Hengshuei District experienced serious financial disorders during the period 1987–9, which reflected a similar situation nationally. The disorder contributed to economic overheating, which has led to inflation and economic fluctuation since 1988. This indicates that banking competition and freedom in the early stage of transition may not only be inefficient but rather risky and even chaotic. This is because there is no valid legal framework, no serious banking supervision and no effective financial discipline within a sound market infrastructure.

THE BATTLE AGAINST THE FOURTH NATIONAL FINANCIAL DISORDER

Since 1992 the Chinese monetary authorities have been conducting a set of financial redisciplinary policies. Is this the correct approach? If so, why has China chosen these policies? Is it a temporary tactic or a strategic decision?

At the beginning of this chapter four national financial disorders that occurred in China after economic reform were briefly introduced. The first happened immediately after the first banking reform, and each was closely linked to the banking system, although they had distinctive characteristics. The struggle against the disorders also took different forms, and the problems of the first three were never solved. Problems accumulated in the economy, placing the government at a crossroads with respect to the reforms. It could either abort the reform programme and restore central planning, or solve the problems at their root. However, reform was irrevocable, so the only choice it had was to solve the problems. The macroeconomic decision makers finally realised that the banking system had a control function during transition and a national struggle against the financial disorder was launched, mobilising the efforts of the planning, budget, banking and legal systems, with the support of the economic entities and the people.

Background

The struggle against the third national financial disorder in China ended with recession in 1990. People were warned that they would have to live frugally for an appreciable period. An enormous injection of bank credit led to the economy recovering from the recession by 1992. The growth rate of real national income was 15 per cent and 20 per cent in 1991 and 1992, respectively. The annual inflation rate was 2.9 per cent and 5.4 per cent respectively. However, from the second half of 1992 the economy started to overheat. By 1993 the problems were becoming obvious.

On 15 March 1993 Li Peng, the prime minister, delivered the Government Report on the First Plenary Session of the Eighth National People's Congress, in which he made no mention of financial disorder and developing inflation. Rather he emphasised the economic task for the next five years, which was to quadruple GNP by the year 2000. In order to realise this 'great plan', which had been suggested by Deng Xiaoping, the targeted average annual economic growth rate of 6 per cent, originated in the Eighth Five Year Plan, was adjusted to 8–9 per cent. It may have been reasonable to expect the whole economy to develop at such a speed if equilibrium could have been kept under macro control, but as local governments and the SOEs intended to grow even faster than this (in Chinese this is called '*cen cen jia ma*'), economic overheating seemed unavoidable.

According to the State Statistical Bureau (19 July 1993), from January to June the growth rates of industry, fixed capital investment and GDP continued to grow by 25.1 per cent, 61 per cent and 13.9 per cent respectively over the first half of 1993. Real per capita urban household income increased by 13.5 per cent and real per capita rural household cash income increased by 7 per cent. However, the scale of fixed capital investment projects under construction was too large. In the first half of the year 22 161 new projects were started, an increase of 3059 over the previous year. The investment planned was 125.7 billion yuan, more than double the amount for the same period in the previous year. The budget deficit was increasing while deposits in banks were insufficient to support the development. The bottleneck was narrowed by the supply difficulties of steel, electricity and transportation. CPI inflation of the household sector was estimated at about 12.5 per cent, while inflation in the big cities was even higher.

At such a critical time banking control and the control of banks became crucial. However some newspapers came out once more in support of further liberalisation of the banking system, taking the conventional line that banks should be decentralised to become 'real companies'. In January 1993 the deposits in the Industrial and Commercial Bank decreased by 60 per cent compared with the previous January. In March there was a negative rate of growth. The top banks in Jiangsu, Shandong and Shanxi saw a reduction in their deposit takings at about the same time.

On 3 August 1993 Zhu Rongji, president of the central bank, indicated that the yuan exchange rates had declined sharply since the second half of 1992. That trend was accelerated in 1993. In mid-June 1993 the US dollar exchange rate fell to 11 yuan from 7.4 yuan at the beginning of the year.

The main causes were economic overheating and the financial disorder, including financial trading mobilised by market speculation.

The fourth national financial disorder

The *People's Daily* (25 July 1993) described three kinds of financial disorder:

1. Fund collection disorders: funds were collected by the authorities, the collective organisations, individuals, provinces, cities and counties. Collected funds in the first quarter of 1993 amounted to 50 billion yuan, effectively removing deposits from banks. Some of the money was used to trade in housing markets or to smuggle goods.
2. Inter-lending disorders: some banks lent money to non-bank institutions for profit-making purposes because bank lending rates could be charged in contravention of the regulations. This also increased the supply of money.
3. Banking disorders: some banks set up economic entities for profit-making investment, calling this 'a combination of banking and trading with varied business'. The State Council published a series of documents to stop these, but the power to do so by administrative methods was limited as it required further steps to reform the banking system.

Besides using some old methods, people started to utilise the imperfections of the new transitional legal system, using the name of reform to take chances on institutional changes in the administration. Legislative institutions, law implementation institutions and some monopolist companies were more likely than others to create these problems. According to the Xin Hua News Agency (13 July 1993), many public utilities undertook business transactions without regulation. Even banks were changed into building societies overnight, and some became security traders. The financial markets in many places became chaotic (Wu, 1990). Money intended for key construction projects was lent elsewhere for profit or commission.

Fund collectors from different companies offered interest rates ranging from 20 per cent to 50 per cent, attracting money from the household sector and the banks. To get deposits back, some banks paid bonuses and commissions as well as high rates. Trading became frenetic. People traded in anything profitable, including steel, cars, petrol, property, housing, land, dollars and even tickets to popular concerts. Some foreign investors were also involved in the financial disorder.

On 25 July 1993 Zhu Rongji complained that money had not been properly used in the key projects that were necessary to structural adjustment. In the first half of 1993 deposits declined because large amounts of money were siphoned off for security trading in the open-door coastal areas. Zhou Zhengqin, vice-president of the PBC, also indicated on 21 October 1993 that the shortage of money was not caused by the tight monetary policy. Enterprise deposits had already decreased by 28.7 billion yuan in June – before the tight policy had been implemented. They continued to decrease until September. It was in fact the expansion of fixed capital investment that caused the shortage. This expansion, accompanied by financial disorder, interrupted the normal capital flow and crowded out simple production, leading to sharp decrease in deposits. Money supply growth in the first half of 1993 reached a record-breaking level. The banks' ability to pay was weakened. Prices soared. The money planned for key investment projects was dispersed for other uses.

An important feature of this financial disorder was the increasing incidence of economic criminal cases. According to the *People's Daily* (28 September 1993) the criminals were ambitious and the losses caused were huge. Their crimes were committed over a lengthy period, highlighting the inadequacies of the management system. Most of the offenders were aged between 20 and 30, suggesting that young staff were inadequately supervised. Criminal collaboration between the staff of financial institutions and non-bank businessmen was more likely to succeed during transition, when the supervisory system and regulations had not been perfected. Once the offenders found themselves in danger they were able to take advantage of the open-door system to flee the country, leaving the authorities no hope of recovering the large amounts of stolen money.

According to the Criminal Investigation Bureau of the Ministry of Public Security (12 July 1993), more than ten cases involving foreign investment had been investigated, the fraud amounting to hundreds of millions or billions of dollars. For example Mei Zhifang, an American Chinese, embezzled US$10 billion simply by using an informal letter of credit.

The struggle against the fourth financial disorder

Economic 'overheating' means excess aggregate demand. One solution to this problem might be to increase interest rates. The lessons from the previous three financial disorders seemed to discount this market-type solution. The problem was attacked with the use of four sets of policies:

administrative control, legal regulation, economic levers (such as interest rate regulation) and banking-system reforms.

Administrative and planning control

The Chinese administrative system has traditionally been efficient. The battle against the fourth financial disorder was launched by the central government around April 1993. Administrative control included the announcement of State Council and Communist Party Committee regulations, planning control, the mobilisation of control by local governments, and foreign exchange regulation by the authorities. It is worth mentioning that these regulations known as the 'Sixteen Regulations', were drafted by the State Planning Committee, thus demonstrating its importance at such critical moments.

Under the leadership of the State Council, a nationwide investigation of tax payments and financial accounts was conducted. Ten investigative teams were sent to help in twenty provinces, autonomous regions and cities. By the end of September 3.476 billion yuan of irregular payments were discovered that should have been paid to the state revenue. Fines were imposed on 5874 production units and 282 individuals, and 11 people were jailed.

The China Security Issue Assessment Committee was established on 23 June 1993 under the China Security Supervision Association in order to improve the transparency of the assessment process of security issues and the quality of security issuing companies. It is a relatively independent institution composed of experts from the security administrations and relevant institutions. The committee shares the responsibility for assessing the reports of companies intending to issue securities.

Banking control

Market mechanisms, including interest rates, are useful and usable by banks, though they cannot be relied on in isolation. On 5 May 1993 the People's Bank of China raised deposit rates by an average rate of 2.18 per cent in order to cope with the decline in household deposits. In the past these had amounted to only 18.6 per cent of total deposits, but latterly had grown to about 50 per cent. This rise in interest was minor compared with inflation, since in recent years interest rates had been cut to cope with recession.

On 11 July 1993 the People's Bank decided to raise deposit rates again by an average of 1.72 points and lending rates by 1.38 points. It also adopted a policy of value guarantees on time deposits that guaranteed interest payments to depositors would be no less than inflation, based on the CPI of the whole economy. The increase of the time deposit rates was 10.98 per cent for one-year deposits, 11.7 per cent for two years, 12.24 per cent for three years and 13.86 per cent for five years. Preferential lending rates for some thirteen basic construction sectors were also arranged, including the key projects of energy and transportation.

Another important step was that Zhu Rongji was nominated to replace Li Gueixian (originally an engineer) as president of the People's Bank in accordance with the resolution of the second session of the Standing Committee of the National People's Congress of the PRC (2 July 1993).

The monetary authorities used other methods besides economic levers. The Ministry of Finance held a national finance conference from 5–7 July, when Zhu Rongji asked the leaders of financial companies to obey three regulations: (1) the immediate cessation and clearance of all irregular inter-lending, such loans to be retrieved by the banks within a specified date; (2) no financial institutions would be allowed to raise deposit and loan interest rates, nor launch a 'deposit taking battle' or to take any commission from debtors; (3) the immediate cessation of credit to economic entities established by the financial institutions themselves – banks should separate themselves from the varied economic entities they had established. Zhu Rongji made it clear that this period of macroeconomic adjustment and control did not represent a national financial retrenchment.

On 13 July 1993 the presidents of the branches of the Industrial and Commercial Bank, the Agricultural Bank, the People's Construction Bank, the Bank of China and the Communication Bank met within their individual organisations to discuss financial discipline. The task was to concentrate enough funds in the banks to finance key investment projects. Above all, funds supporting projects related to energy, transportation and raw materials had to be specifically arranged by banks (in Chinese '*dai mao xia da*'). This called for improvement of the stock management system, the credit structure and financial services. Payments should not be delayed further. The credit scale had to be controlled and services improved. A responsibility system to discipline branch leaders was suggested.

On 21 October 1993 Zhou Zhengqin, vice president of the PBC, revealed that with the increase in household deposits, cash issuance had decreased by 19.2 billion yuan in the third quarter compared with the same period in the previous year. The reserve ratio of the specialised banks increased to 7.2 per cent. Meanwhile total loans to the specialised banks advanced by the People's Bank amounted to 100.8 billion yuan, 100.3 billion of which was used by them to increase loans to enterprises. Thirty billion yuan more than had been envisaged in the plan was lent to help the state with key construction projects, mostly infrastructure projects. Total loans by the banks in the first half of 1993 increased by 99.3 billion yuan, 26.3 billion yuan less than in the equivalent period in 1992. The People's Bank designated 100 billion yuan as base money or high-powered money in August and September 1993 compared with only 14.6 billion yuan in the same period in 1992. This indicated that the PBC was not simply conducting tight monetary policy.

Budget control

On 11 August 1993 the Ministry of Finance decided to raise the yields of three- and five-year government bonds from 12.52 per cent and 14.06 per cent to 13.96 per cent and 15.86 per cent respectively, an average increase of 1.72 per cent and 2.0 per cent. The MoF also adopted a value guarantee policy on bonds issued since 7 November 1993. The total amount of bonds was estimated at 300 billion yuan in 1993.

The national finance conference ordered the budget institutions of the authorities to obey three directives: (1) to restrict tax waiving and tax reduction; (2) to control budget expenditure tightly and to stop the practise of delaying payments to the banks; and (3) to refrain from commercial banking without the approval of the People's Bank (23 July 1993).

Legal method of control

The United Conference, held by the Preparatory Ministry of the Communist Party Central Committee, discussed the punishment of corruption, bribery and other economic crimes in order to develop a socialist market economy (26 July 1993).

The People's Courts of Justice stressed the need to tackle major cases and meted out severe punishment to wrongdoers. Some of the most serious offenders were sentenced to death. Regardless of the difficulties and obstacles, and no matter how influential the offenders' supporters, the Supreme Court required cases to be investigated thoroughly and criminals to be punished. A conference was held by the Supreme People's Court of Justice, attended by the heads of the high courts of justice, to discuss measures against serious economic crimes and corruption. According to the conference (27 July 1993) the prosecution of 155 100 criminal cases had been concluded legally, leading to the punishment of 187 700 offenders in the first half of 1993. The other 9550 economic cases had been completed, resulting in the punishment of 9120 offenders in the same period. Local authorities were asked to investigate any cases of tax evasion, default and fraud (for export tax returns).

Several important laws were approved by the central government:

– 9 August 1993: the Regulation of Enterprise Debt Management, which makes clear the process and qualifications of the enterprise debt issuance.
– 2 September 1993: the Anti-Trust Law of the PRC, which defines unfair competition and makes clear the supervision, investigation and legal implications of unfair competition.
– 6 September 1993: the Law of Economic Contracts of the PRC, which strengthens the management of economic contracts and makes clear the implications of any violations of the contracts.
– 19 September 1993: the Current Regulation of State Public Servicemen of the PRC, which makes clear the responsibilities, rights, awards, disciplines and penalties for all staff employed by public service agents.

Achievements

The macroeconomic policies were quickly rewarded by the restoration of economic order, July 1993 being the turning point. At the Third Session of the Standing Committee of the Eighth National People's Congress (31 August 1993) Zhu Rongji reported the following successes. First, irregular interbank lending activities had stopped and by 15 August 1993 72.7 billion yuan had been recovered, representing one third of total inter-bank loans. Second, illegal fund collecting activities had been controlled and the decline in deposits reversed. Deposits rose 39.6 billion yuan in June and July compared with the same months in the previous year. Since July money supply had been slowed down. Third, the yuan exchange rate had become acceptable to foreign investors (8.8 yuan per US dollar). Fourth, money was being concentrated in key state projects. The funds to purchase the summer agricultural output were also guaranteed. The money demand for working capital for large and medium-sized SOEs and export-ing industries was being satisfied. Fifth, open-zone establishments and the trading of housing and land markets, once too active, had been stabilised, and the prices of houses and land, once artificially inflated, had declined.

According to the State Statistical Bureau of China (19 October 1993), in the first three quarters of 1993 GDP and industrial output had grown by 13.3 per cent and 24.1 per cent respectively, relatively slower than before, but still too rapid. The sales output ratio was 94.5 per cent. Over the same period the fixed capital investment of state entities had increased by 66.4 per cent (which was still relatively high). Compared with the same period in the previous year, the growth rate of investment of the state entities had decreased by 9 per cent; the number of new projects had declined by 3300 due to a reduction in the proportion of self-collected funds in total investment sources from 86 per cent in June to 76 per cent in September; investment in transport, the postal system and communication had increased by 4 per cent; and the price of gold, imported consumption goods and production materials were all decreasing. Total sales value decreased from 49.5 per cent in the first half of the year to 27.3 per cent in the third quarter. Retail sale price and household consumption price increased by 12 per cent and 14 per cent respectively. In thirty-five large and medium-sized cities the latter was 18.9 per cent, in spite of the fact that the household income in cities and towns and cash income in rural areas in real terms increased by 17 per cent and 5 per cent respectively. Household deposits increased month by month.

Lessons

The financial disorders that have taken place in China can teach us some important lessons.

First, such disorders are not an extraordinary phenomenon. Economic overheating stimulated by overambitious targets for government investment projects and SOEs often causes disequilibrium and creates bottlenecks. Once supply is unable to meet demand, the conditions are set for disorder. This indicates that correct planning is still very important at the macroeconomic level and that correct macro planning helps to restore equilibrium in development.

Second, during transition disorders take place when a control vacuum is created by the removal of central control. Planning may be replaced by market sovereignty, while the market mechanism is not ready to discipline the behaviour of firms. If planning and administrative tools are removed completely, leaving nothing to control the situation, financial crises are apt to erupt repeatedly. Macroeconomic equilibrium requires a certain amount of financial control to be maintained.

Third, the most appropriate controllers are bankers. Banking control should go hand in hand with budget control. Once the major financial responsibility has been shifted to bankers, credit control must be handled very carefully by the banking system. The banks themselves also need to be supervised, regulated and controlled. Enormous efforts were made by the government and the monetary authorities to regulate banks and other financial intermediaries in 1993. Had they not done so the struggle would not have been successful.

The plan has been to transform the Chinese banking system into a state-owned commercial banking system accompanied by some 'policy banks' and financial markets under the supervision of a 'real central bank', according to Chen Yuan (28 September 1993). China has the environment and ability to realise this plan. The question is how long the reform should take. To avoid other national financial disorders, financial control and discipline cannot be regarded as temporary tactics, rather they should be important strategies throughout the transitional period. Experience so far argues for a new control system that combines the efforts of the administration, the banking system, the budget system and the legal system. The joint efforts of these bodies may allow a well-designed corporate governance structure to work through the phase of transition.

A new problem: the management of foreign investments

Foreign investment can be classified into borrowings from abroad (including foreign government loans, loans from international financial institutions, export-supporting credits, and foreign bond and share issues) and direct foreign investment (that is, cash, materials and technology invested by foreign investors when establishing companies, economic organisation and individual ventures, joint ventures and cooperative development projects in China).

Foreign investment in China has soared. According to the State Planning Commission, borrowings from abroad accumulated to 83.5 billion yuan and total direct foreign investments amounted to 76 billion yuan during the period 1979 to June 1994. By the end of 1994 the two had reached 83.4 billion yuan and 110 billion yuan respectively. Prior to 1992 foreign investment was mainly borrowings from abroad. After 1992 direct foreign investment assumed major importance (Table 4.2).

If the financial sector had been mature the monetary authorties could have effectively 'sterilised' the inflow of foreign capital by selling bonds or by introducing some 'swap' arrangements, as in Western economies. But it was not. In addition such short-term money market instruments as swaps might not have been able to solve the long-term surplus of large amounts of foreign capital. Investment growth can push up the prices of associated materials products, which can in turn push up the prices of consumer goods.

In 1994 the number of registered foreign companies reached 206 000, having increased by 40 000 according to the State Statistical Bureau. A large amount of foreign investment went into housing projects and fixed asset investments. The new foreign currency balance system after the

Table 4.2   Structural changes in foreign investment in China

	Total foreign investment (100 mil. yuan)	Borrowing from abroad (100 mil. yuan)	Proportion of total (%)	Foreign direct investment and other investment (100 mil. yuan)	Proportion of total (%)
1979–82	124.57	106.90	85.82	17.67	14.18
1983–89	453.28	286.31	63.16	166.97	36.84
1990	102.89	65.34	63.50	37.55	36.50
1991	115.54	68.88	59.62	46.66	40.38
1992	192.02	79.11	41.20	112.91	58.80
1993	367.73	107.50	29.23	260.23	70.77
1994	458.00	120.00	26.70	338.00	73.30
Total	1806.03	834.04	46.18	979.99	60.91

Notes:
1. Total foreign investment is roughly divided into the amount of foreign currency borrowed from abroad and foreign direct investment.
2. Borrowing from abroad includes foreign government loans, loans of international financial institutions, export-supporting credit, and bonds and shares issued abroad.
3. Foreign direct investment includes the cash, materials and technology invested by foreigners to establish companies, economic organisations, individual ventures, joint ventures and cooperative development projects.
Sources: Cao (1995); State Statistical Bureau (1995).

foreign exchange system reform allows the convertibility of the renminbi. Enterprises can change into yuan not only their foreign currency earnings, but also their borrowings from abroad, partly because renminbi interest rates are higher than those of foreign currencies (see Table 4.2). This caused a sharp increase in renminbi deposits.

The proportion of gross net foreign assets in M1 was 7 per cent in 1993, rapidly increasing to 20.8 per cent in September 1994, while the proportion of net bank credit (total bank loans minus quasi-money and other liabilities) in M1 dropped from 91.5 per cent to 68.2 per cent in the same period. The sharp increase in time deposits and demand deposits (which together form quasi-money) by 41 per cent and 10.2 per cent in nominal and real terms, forced the banks to maintain extraordinarily high bank reserves in September 1994 – about 10 per cent compared with the 5–7 per cent required by the Central Bank (Hua, 1995). Although the fixed asset investment loans of the state banks were under the control of credit plans, the self-collected funds of enterprises and foreign investment were beyond the credit regulations, and greatly expanded the scale of fixed asset investment.

According to Cao's calculations (1994), which were based on a 1:1 ratio of foreign investment to injection of the renminbi,[21] foreign investment accounted for about 2.4 per cent of inflation through fixed asset investment and about 3–5 per cent through consumption in 1993. Based on his method, the same effects could be 2.99 per cent through investment and 6.2 per cent through consumption in 1994 considering that foreign investment in 1994 increased by 24.5 per cent over 1993. These influences upon inflation are significant and therefore cannot be ignored.

Some Chinese companies borrowed short-term money from joint-ventures to engage in financial market speculations with foreign investors. A large amount of foreign capital from foreign exchange markets found its way into the state's foreign exchange reserves, which recorded a more than US$20 billion increase and formed a large part of the central bank's base money. There was a US$5.3 billion foreign trade surplus in 1994. To prevent the renminbi exchange rate from increasing, the PBC had to buy foreign currency and sell renminbi. This was the main cause of the sharp increases in net foreign assets and base money, according to *Money Outlook* (PBC, 1995). This certainly affected inflation.

Some serious steps have been taken by the Chinese monetary authorities to control money. Besides the approval of the People's Bank of China Law in March 1995, the central bank has regularly published a set of statistical data for supervising the money supply. In one of China's biggest bank scandals, the central bank sacked or disciplined 11 senior state bank officials and rescinded a business licence after they violated a credit squeeze (*Business Times*, Singapore, 22 March 1995).

China is to promulgate the first national unified legislation on loan management, to be implemented by the PBC, in order to strengthen its control over the loan market. This will be binding on all financial organisations and commercial banks and will involve loan scale, loan period, and the interests and liabilities of both lenders and borrowers. The law will be formulated according to the experiences of foreign commercial banks and the actual situation in China and will conform to international practice.[22]

Controlling inflation is not just the concern of the monetary authority. The State Planning Commission has recently put forward four measures concerning overseas loans. (1) Besides loans from the state financial organisations and bilateral loans between governments, cash loans, convertible stocks, bonds in the compensation trade and capital raised from overseas funds are also bound by reimbursement terms of contract and run the risk of debt, and therefore must be included in the foreign capital expenditure plan of the state administration. (2) There is to be strict control over the overall scale of international commercial loans. (3) Sino–foreign funded, cooperative and overseas-funded projects will be subject to state industrial policies and regulations. Single projects will not be allowed to be dissected into several parts in order to evade the necessity for state approval. (4) Once an international commercial loan is assured, the applicant must entrust a financial organisation approved by the state to borrow the money overseas. No government department may act as guarantor or issue guarantee certificates.[23]

Current monetary development

According to Zhou (1995), M0, M1 and M2 at the end of 1994 increased by 24.3 per cent, 26.8 per cent and 34.4 per cent over those at the end of 1993 respectively. By the end of 1994, total outstanding nominal deposits amounted to 2932.8 billion yuan, having increased by 794 billion yuan or 37.1 per cent from the end of the previous year. Of this enterprise deposits represented 1146.7 billion yuan, an increase of 273.5 billion yuan or 31.3 per cent. The total deposits of urban and rural residents amounted to 2151.9 billion yuan, having increased by 631.5 billion yuan or 41.5 per cent. Money in circulation (M0) was 728.9 billion yuan, having increased by 142.4 billion yuan of newly issued cash.

Compared with the growth rate of GDP, which was 11.8 per cent, the annual growth rate of money was above 30 per cent in 1994. It seems that there was an excess demand for money in the economy as a whole, which forced the banking system to increase the money supply, in spite of the fact that money shortages did exist in some SOEs, industrial sectors and regions of the economy. By the end of October 1994, total enterprise deposits had increased by 315 billion yuan or 2.6 times those at the beginning of 1994, among which, enterprise time deposits had increased by 53.6 billion yuan.

The problem might not have been due to enlargement of the planned scale of bank loan. All kinds of bank loans, except those for purchasing agri-products and by-products, were within the planned targets, according to Dai (1995). Table 4.3 shows that the total amount of bank loans in 1994 was only 9.8 per cent higher than the figure planned for that year, bearing in mind that this is in nominal terms.[24] Even non-bank financial institution loans were kept largely within the targeted amounts. The total amount of nominal outstanding loans was 2342.8 billion yuan, an increase of 516.1 billion yuan or 19.5 per cent (the growth rate in real terms was only 14 per cent), of which short-term loans were 1109.4 billion yuan, an increase of

Table 4.3   Targets planned and fulfilled in 1994 (in nominal terms)

Target items	Planned	Real	Changes (%)
GDP (per cent)	9.0	11.8	+2.8
of which			
Primary industry	3.0	3.5	+0.5
Secondary industry	10.7	17.4	+6.7
Tertiary industry	11	8.7	−2.3
Total fixed assets investment (billion yuan)	1300	1592	+22.5
of which			
SOEs and state institutions	875	1135.4	+29.8
Collective and private investors	425	457.2	+7.6
Net government deficits (billion yuan)	66.9	63.8	−4.6
Gross government deficits (billion yuan)	129.2		
Total bank loans (billion yuan)	470	516	+9.8
Total imports ($US billion)	100	115.7	+15.7
Total exports ($US billion)	100	121.0	+21
Inflation (per cent)	10	21.7	+11.7

Source: The State Statistical Bureau (1995).

19.3 per cent, and medium- and long-term loans were 717.3 billion yuan, an increase of 20 per cent. Even the increase of money in circulation was well within what had been planned.

The nominal growth rate of M0 (month on month over the previous year) declined from its peak in the middle of 1993, when a tight monetary policy and a financial regulating strategy were adopted by Zhu Rongji, the Central Bank governor. The real growth rate of M0 started to decline even earlier (in April 1993). Both rates presented a declining trend for the year until June 1994, and that year they failed to return to their peak levels, in spite of the fact that they experienced growth after the middle of 1994. The equivalent rates for M1 also started to decline in February 1993, but with more fluctuations. The equivalent rates for M2 have moved smoothly upwards since the beginning of 1994. This can be attributed to the significant increase in household deposits. The rates for M1 and M2 in real terms over the same period were much lower than in nominal terms. Money data curves do not show a simultaneous correlation between inflation and money supply.

These money growth patterns show that the monetary policies of the central bank have been successful, generally speaking. Since the beginning of 1994 the PBC has prohibited its local sub-banks from granting direct loans to local authorities or their local branches in order to deal with the overexpansion of their money supply that had been facilitated by local governments. This has proved to be a wise move in controlling money supply.

It cannot be ignored that loans for projects were not properly assessed by some banks' branches, resulting in a significant number of loans going to the wrong projects or not being repaid on time. There was no clear distinction between banking business and that of trusts and securities. Some banking funds were diverted to stock markets and mortgage markets while the capital market in China was still far from developed. But these are microeconomic issues and are irrelevant to macro monetary policy. Bank loans were just 32.4 per cent of total fixed assets investment in 1994, and the former was not the main cause of the increase of the latter.

Thanks to the government's 'thorough implementation' of price control measures (*International Herald Tribune*, Singapore, 17 April 1995), China's inflation rate continued to fall from its peak of 27.7 per cent in 1994 to 18.7 per cent and 12.3 per cent in March and August 1995 respectively. The year-on-year retail price index does not include services and utilities. The consumer price index has followed the same pattern in spite of the fact that price rises in some regions have been excessive and that the inflation rate has continued to rise in others. The February 1995 figure dropped below 20 per cent for the first time since June 1994. Reducing inflation was the government's major goal of 1995, and the premier set the target for price increases at 15 per cent in 1995. If the Chinese government continues with its tight monetary and fiscal controls, this target is likely to be realised.

The central government's measures to curb inflation are working, as evidenced by the declining subsidiary interest rate for bank deposits, whose interest rates are pegged to inflation.[25] The People's Bank has announced that the subsidiary rate for inflation-proof deposits maturing in April 1995 was 11.47 per cent, 0.4 percentage points down from the 11.87 per cent subsidiary rate in March 1995, an encouraging sign of decreasing inflation (*People's Daily (Business Weekly)*, 19–25 March 1995).

CENTRALISATION AND THE CONTROL FUNCTION OF THE BANKING SYSTEM

Comparing the original CPE banking system with the reformed version, it may be asked how problems were prevented with the help of the centralised banking system in the unreformed model, why certain problems occurred after the reforms and why the banking system should be kept under control during transition.

How were problems prevented in the centralised banking system?

Unlike economies without a financial sector, CPEs were a form of modern state with not only a financial sector, but also a system of financial intermediaries. The latter transformed direct claims into indirect financial claims, which were not held by financial firms as in market economies, but by the state banks. Like market banking systems, deposit-taking institutions played a central role in the payment system and were regulated by the authorities. But the household sector, with its limited savings, had no more opportunity to borrow from financial institutions than under a financial sector with no financial intermediaries. It is worth investigating the reasons for this.

An important justification for the existence of financial intermediaries is the relative advantage they confer in transforming risky, long-term, illiquid direct claims on borrowers into the safer, shorter-term, liquid claims that savers prefer. The CPE banking system achieved this by removing financial markets and competition. The conventional problems of imperfect marketability did not exist and there was no risk of bankruptcy. Therefore holders of indirect claims (depositors) did not have to evaluate the solvency of a deposit-taking institution to affirm that the market value of its assets exceeded the promised value of its deposit liabilities. There was no need for households to be cautious and no need for bankers to be 'precautionary' in competing for yields. Also, no real reserves were required by the central bank, thus no high-powered money was generated.

This system was necessarily centralised. Prices and the demand for goods and labour were planned. Banks had to conform with the plans and were not allowed to extend more or less credit than set out in the plans. The quantity of money was automatically adjusted. As part of the central administration, banks became monopolistic and were under the strict control of the authorities. The structure of the management system warranted the subordination of the banking system to the financial system, at the expense of banks having financial control over the production system. But they were the authorities' second eye and ensured that enterprises and public utilities did not use more funds than the plans allowed. Wage bills were tightly controlled by bankers, who had to keep a watch on the books of the whole economy.

Difficulties of the decentralised model during transition

What does decentralisation mean? Some commonly used definitions of the terms centralisation and decentralisation contradict each other.[26]

Decentralisation of a CPE banking system in the transitional period has at least four meanings, which may not be easy to verify in practice.

First, the separation of central banking functions and commercial banking business changes the relationship between the banking system and the government (MoF). It creates a new three-way relationship between the MoF, the central bank and bank and non-bank institutions that is similar to the relationships in a typical market economic banking model. The question here is how close they can be. Banks and non-bank financial institutions may ignore or avoid the supervision of the authorities simply because of the lack of proper regulations (and the obligation to obey the regulations that do exist). Another problem is how far the central bank can be separated from the MoF: as the budget deficits in Hungary and China were so high, the central banks had to finance them.

Second, after the above fundamental development, a significant step may be to give the banks more autonomy: credit freedom is the most obvious means. The commercial banks and the specialised banks can determine the amount and direction of their credit activities (loans) to alternative borrowers (clients). However problems may occur when there is insufficient unbiased market information, such as efficient prices and interest rates, to direct credit correctly and allocate resources in the interests of both agents and society. The impossibility of bank runs contributed to credit being over-extended in China in 1985 and 1988.

Third, the most important contribution of the reforms to increased efficiency should be enhanced competition among banks. Market orientation should steadily create an environment in which decisions are made according to the requirements of lenders and the number of borrowers. The range of available financial instruments should be widened and the number and types of financial institution increased. However competition may function inefficiently in an immature reforming economy if a legal framework and pricing system are not in place. Encouragement of competition under these conditions resulted in financial disorder in China and Eastern Europe.

Fourth, the relationship between banks and borrowers should also be changed. Three elements are involved: (1) decentralisation should not root out necessary institutional concentration; (2) the reforms should lead to a greater share of assets being allocated by the banking system rather than the budgetary system; and (3) banks should play a more important role than before in the financing of non-financial corporations. The question is, how can banks realise these objectives if there are large amounts of bad debt and company arrears but no effective economic enforcement, such as bankruptcy laws?

Why have problems occurred since decentralisation?

Decentralisation brings in market mechanisms and competition, and therefore risks and imperfect marketability. Meanwhile a fundamental change brought about by economic reforms is the reduction of the administrative power of the state over the economy, formerly embodied in compulsory plans and regulations. In RCPEs the scope of compulsory plans has been reduced to a minimum (Hungary has removed all compulsory plans), providing more and more autonomy to enterprises. Enterprises can now determine a certain proportion of wage rates, including bonuses, staffing levels, and the price of many products and their capital investment (through either retention or borrowing), which together were the essential elements of classical national plans.

Shortages and excess demand still exist. Indeed they cannot quickly and easily be made to disappear. Decentralisation has removed direct control over supply and demand. Meanwhile free markets have become legal, with state markets being freed, in terms of price, to a certain extent. Unrealised purchasing power pushes up prices, which in turn generates higher wage demands than before. Higher interest rates may not be effective in bringing them down during transition (see Chapter 5). Companies are often thirsty for investment, even with a hard budget constraint.

The two-tier banking system and the universal banking of the commercial banks now integrate the two types of money that were used by two sectors through two monetary circuits. Banks now have the autonomy to decide where and how much they would like to invest. They seem always ready to extend loans, not only in the pursuit of profit-maximisation but due to their inability to enforce enterprise bankruptcy. Credit is biased towards short-term investment projects, ignoring the sectoral problems created.

Monetary control is never easy, but today it has become even more difficult in RCPEs. The structure of financial institutions has changed, commercial banks have become independent and compulsory plans have been abandoned. There are no useful instruments (such as economic penalties or bankruptcy) to link them with the monetary authorities and the state financial and planning organisers. There are insufficient banking laws and market mechanisms with which to discipline them. The planners are impeded by a 'Great Wall' of autonomy: they are unable to help the economy even if they do manage to ascertain what is going wrong. The central bank has given up its conventional administrative instruments, but the new 'economic levers' of a typical market environment, such as the discount rate and reserve requirement, have yet to become effective tools of control. Huge interenterprise debts have accumulated and await for creditors to eliminate them.

The direct relationship between wages and the money supply has not been completely broken, in spite of the fact that there is no plan to equalise the aggregate value of consumption-goods supply with household wage demand. The flow of income has increased sharply, leading the monetary authorities to supply additional money to the household sector. While micro monetary control has been abandoned, there is still no direct control over aggregate monetary variables, such as credit and total currency emission.

Then there are the major disorders. Over-extension of bank credit has overheated economies. The situation has been worsened by large and increasing budget deficits caused by unrealistic production goals, an excess demand for investment (urged by local administrations) and the impossibility of suppressing trade credit. As a result economies have suffered from long-term monetary disequilibrium with high inflation, a situation little better than in the pre-reform period. Confronted by high, open and official inflation, people who have been used to non-inflationary conditions still have to queue to exercise their purchasing power, but in an even longer queue than before.[27]

All this has happened in most RCPEs in certain periods. The experience has taught reformers a valuable lesson: when the production system is decentralised, the banking system should not simply follow but should be placed under careful control until industry becomes subject to market discipline.

SUCCESSFUL BANKING SYSTEMS ARE CONTROLLED AND HELP TO CONTROL: SOME SUCCESSFUL BANKING MODELS

The fortunes of nations rise and fall through history. 'Powers' travel on 'the stream of time', which they can 'neither create nor direct', but upon which they can 'steer with more or less skill and experience' (Pflanze, 1990).

The world's banking systems are so diversified that it is difficult to identify the absolute advantages of some over others. This forces us to look first at successful global economies and then relate their survival and development to features of their banking systems. However it is puzzling that the banking systems of the most successful economies appear to be not particularly modernised. Successful economies such as Japan, Germany and South Korea have been analysed by many economists, and the Japanese and German cases in particular have been highlighted by recent theoretical debates (see Mayer, 1988; Hellwig, 1991). Some of their conclusions are summarised here, with a further brief comparative assessment of the banking models of the UK and Taiwan.

Japan, Germany and South Korea have given banks a more important position in financing than security markets, as well as greater supervisory powers. The German universal banking system differed significantly from the US and UK commercial banking systems in the early period of German industrialisation (Calomiris, 1993). A few large banks had close relations with large and small firms and gave them financial support (Prais, 1979; Harm, 1992a, 1992b). The banking systems in Japan and South Korea appear rather simple or traditional in comparison, and a significant number of specialised banks were, and still are, state-owned (see Bank of Japan, 1982; Prindl, 1981a, 1981b; Suzuki, 1987; Tsutui, 1990).

It is necessary for central banks to regulate the banks carefully and for banks strictly to supervise the firms they have as customers. Greater monetary discipline in the Pacific Basin countries has been one of the factors contributing to their substantially higher rate of economic growth. The Asian success stories have been brought about by government policies and it was appropriate for Asian developing countries to ignore the euphoria of Western economists over financial liberalisation and continue on their own gradual paths towards financial development (Fry, 1988). In Japanese terms, monetary policy is essentially a control-based policy (Suzuki, 1987). There are no sophisticated methods. Credit is often rationed. Moreover it seems that a legal framework with relatively stable laws designed to fine-tune the system is very helpful for regulation and supervision.

Different schools may interpret the same example in different ways to support different models. For example South Korea's 1965 financial reform, which was marked by a significant rise in bank rates, was regarded by Shaw (1973) and McKinnon (1973) as providing notable support for their liberalisation recommendation. Harris (1988) saw this as only partial reform. Although interest rates were raised, financial markets were subject to considerable state control and intervention. The financial reforms were only part of a package of measures that *increased* the role of the state in the economy; if they were responsible for an increased rate of growth, it suggests that appropriate forms of strong state intervention in finance may have a positive impact. In South Korea the state has had a major influence on each of these components, as well as regulating interest rates and the financing that connects them. Moreover its role in all sectors increased substantially in the 1960s, including the creation of special state banks in

1961 and the great emphasis on its five-year plans for the economy. The lesson to be drawn is that South Korea's growth resulted from an increased state role, rather than the opposite.

Byung-Nak Song (1990, p. 146) once warned that 'the style of policy-making and implementation used in Korea in the 1960s and 1970s is effective only if it is carried out by capable and committed policymakers and only in relatively early stages of development when the market system still functions poorly. As the economy develops and becomes increasingly complicated, greater reliance on market forces becomes imperative and discretionary enforcement of policy decisions carries significant negative side effects'. Because of highly concentrated bank ownership and insufficient independence in bank lending decisions, even after privatisation of the banks, credit allocation is not sufficiently related to financial risk-return criteria in Korea and therefore the creditor banking sector seems incapable of exercising greater financial discipline over highly indebted firms. The financial sector is in sore need of reform. Nevertheless the South Korean style and experience can be of value to most RCPEs.

Corbett and Mayer (1990) have carried out a comparative study of the banking systems of the UK, Germany and Japan for the period 1970–85. Table 4.4 adds the South Korean and Taiwanese models to their study.[28]

According to Table 4.4, while the banking systems are competitive in all three developed economies, those in the two NICs are not. For the most

Table 4.4   Lending and borrowing in five countries

	UK	Germany	Japan	S. Korea	Taiwan
Is the banking system competitive?	Yes	Yes	Yes	No	No
Are banks general or specialist lenders?	G	G	G	S	S
Is there separation of investment and commercial banking?	No	No	Yes	Yes	Yes
Is there separation of savings and lending institutions?	No	No	No	No	No
Are there limitations on the forms of finance that banks can raise?	No	No	Yes	Yes	Yes

Source: Corbett and Hayer (1990).

part the developed economies offer general rather than specialist services, while the two NICs offer the latter. Although postal savings systems exist in almost all the economies, there is no separation of savings and lending institutions in any of the five countries. In this they differ from the description of banking in CPEs. In Japan, South Korea and Taiwan the banking systems have been more regulated than in Germany and the UK. Investment and commercial banking have been separated, imposing restrictions on the sources of finance available to banks and separating long and short-term lending.

Corbett and Mayer indicate that the main distinction between the banking systems of Germany and Japan on the one hand and the market system of the UK on the other is not the structure of their lending and borrowing but their ownership and control. As shown in Table 4.5, in Germany and Japan banks hold corporate equity and have representatives on the boards of firms. Unlike the UK, corporates and in some cases the state, also hold bank equity and there are more state-owned banks. The control reflected by ownership is even stronger in South Korea and Taiwan, where the authorities directly own many banks, large and small. Banks in South Korea can hold corporate equity either through participating in underwriting private placement or through purchase in the secondary market. Their representatives sit on the boards of firms, albeit usually as non-executive directors or non-standing auditors. Bank representatives also sit on boards of firms in Taiwan. The authorities held more than 50 per cent of the banks' shares before 1987 and some banks are still held by the authorities. In China the state banks sent representatives to sit

Table 4.5   Ownership and control in five countries

	UK	Germany	Japan	S. Korea	Taiwan
Do banks hold corporate equity?	No	Yes	Yes	Yes	Yes
Are banks represented on the boards of firms?	No	Yes	Yes	Yes	Yes
Do corporations hold bank equity?	No	Yes	Yes	Yes	Yes
Does the authority hold commercial bank equity?	No	No	No	No	No
Are there authority-owned banks?	No	Yes	Yes	Yes	Yes

Source: Corbett and Mayer (1990).

not only on the boards of their clients, but also to remain at the companies in order to supervise them.

Corporates in South Korea can hold up to 8 per cent of each bank's shares (their voting rights would be limited to 8 per cent even if they held more than 8 per cent). The government (MoF) of South Korea owns banks and holds commercial bank equity. Commercial banks are currently supervised by the Bank of Korea, although the bank holds no commercial bank shares. Therefore it may be said that the MoF is the higher-level supervisor. The MoF divested all its holdings in commercial banks a few years ago. Banks that specialise in government-directed financing are still held by the government, for example the Koon Development Bank, Korea Exim Bank, the Industrial Bank of Korea, Citizens National Bank and so on.

It can be concluded that the most successful (but not necessarily the most powerful) world economies, such as Germany, Japan and South Korea, have established banking systems that have suited the conditions of their economies at the different stages of their national development. These systems have been controlled by the authorities and have also helped the authorities to control and improve the economic situation, especially during their transitional periods. This is certainly helpful to us in understanding the advantages of having a controlled banking system in RCPEs during the transitional period. But there are limitations to the banking system. Appropriate government policies during the period of political stabilisation are also very important. This is indicated by the Japanese economy in its period of rapid growth in the last three decades.

CONCLUSIONS

This chapter has mainly looked at the question of why banking control is necessary during transition. Chapter 3 showed that control of and by banks is necessary from a theoretical point of view. This chapter has demonstrated what may happen in the transitional period if there are no suitable controls.

Radical decentralisation of the financial system has sharply reduced budget revenue in the RCPEs and shifted the major investment responsibility from the budget to banks. Credit activities can not be guaranteed merely by a commitment between borrowers and lenders. As market mechanisms have not been in place to discipline either borrowers or lenders, control of and by banks has become crucial. Banks were, and still are, able to plan, adjust, ration, supervise and regulate financial activities according to macroeconomic policies. Even after the development of non-bank financial intermediaries and financial markets, banks are still the most important financial institution and therefore the most useful financial control weapon of the monetary authorities. Chapter 3 showed that, in theory, banks themselves need to be carefully controlled. This requires correct government policy and regulation by the monetary authorities.

Four financial disorders have been experienced in China and these were closely linked to macroeconomic policy (particularly investment policy) and the reform steps taken by the banking system. Important problems arose from the failure to control credit and keep bank loans performing. Creditors were passive due to immature market mechanisms and the fragile legal framework. Many Eastern European economies have had a similar experience.

Will careful control of banks and bank control be necessary and helpful? Western bank control literature has confirmed the proposition, in spite of the arguments of the *laissez-faire* school. Economists find that a fundamental rationale for the existence of banks cannot be found in either portfolio management or the provision of a payment system. Instead it is the monitoring function of banks that is essential.

Observation of the banking systems in the most successful economies, such as Germany, Japan and some Asian NICs, also supports the bank control literature. Their banks are under the control of the authorities and the banking systems help to supervise and control the production system. The central banks support, regulate and supervise their banks rigorously and ensure that banks act to stabilise the economy.

Unfortunately this key issue has been either ignored or insufficiently stressed in some RCPEs. Because of the control vacuum left by both the budgetary system and the banking system, at a time when neither invisible hands nor legislation were ready to help, irregular trading and economic crimes proliferated. In such a situation, the more radical the decentralisation, the worse the economic disorder. Not only has bank credit been granted excessively, but trade credit has been encouraged outside the banking system, generating a severe payment crisis. Non-bank financial assets being traded in financial and other markets can be very damaging if it is not properly regulated and managed.

Excessively ambitious expansionary policies not only narrow the 'bottlenecks' but also provide scope for financial disorders and even serious crimes. Inflation and the shortage of funds have forced producers to accept high costs and risk losses. Corruption and monopoly aggravate disasters partly because of inadequate staff training and discipline. In this situation foreign investors should not simply seek short-term profits. They should work with the authorities and people in the reforming economy in question in order to establish a healthy and reliable economic environment.

The central argument of this work concerning the necessity of bank control during transition can therefore be supported by both theory and practice, based on the lessons and successes of banking in the East and the West. Liberalisation of the banking system should not be attempted as long as the industrial system is not subject to proper financial discipline. Given that the production system of an RCPE is decentralised, the banking system should be correspondingly controlled in terms of banking regulation, credit control and investment assessment. Without the control of banks and banking control, and a well-designed corporate governance structure, the economic and social costs of the reforms, such as inflation and/or financial disorder, will be increased. In open RCPEs, reformers and investors (including foreign investors) should cooperate closely in narrowing the control vacuum and building up a good corporate governance structure.

The recent struggle against the fourth financial disorder in China shows that the banking system is not the only regulatory tool, and neither is the interest rate. The successes of the Japanese economy and the Asian NICs are due also to relative political stabilisation and government policies. Complete success still depends on the integration of different control systems, including the planning, banking, budget and legal systems complemented by the support of economic entities and political stability.

5 Monetary Equilibrium and Disequilibrium

> The central controls necessary to ensure full employment will, of course, involve a large extension of the traditional functions of government (John Maynard Keynes, 1936, p. 379).

INTRODUCTION

This chapter serves as a link between the previous analysis and Chapter 6, which will discuss the possibility of controling – through econometric modelling – money in China. In Chapter 1 we reviewed the development of the banking systems of the RCPEs in the transitional period. Chapter 2 demonstrated that new problems were created while the old ones were being solved. Western financial theories justify the proposition of the crucial necessity of controlling banks and banking control (see Chapter 3). If the controls fail or are not implemented properly, the situation assessed in Chapter 4 could cause the reforms to falter or proceed in directions that are counterproductive. Overall these arguments give rise not only to policy implications, but also to some academic significance. The reforms are supported in order to introduce market mechanisms into the CPEs. While price and interest rate mechanisms should not be completely rejected in the RCPEs, the solutions to the disadvantages and the costs of decentralising the system must be examined.

This chapter discusses the issues of monetary equilibrium and disequilibrium from a macroeconomic point of view. A historical approach has been adopted in an attempt to understand the existing CPE and RCPE institutions, especially the banking systems. Institutions are shaped by history and customs, and are not merely the result of the deliberate designs of an individual or group of individuals. Institutional problems are often solved gradually. There is room for normative analysis to improve upon history by gradual reform.

The findings of the earlier chapters will be reiterated through a theoretical simplification. This chapter is divided into two main sections, the first of which deals with mechanistic issues of monetary equilibrium from a macroeconomic point of view. As the mechanisms of a stylised market economy may not work well in the RCPEs, not only because of the insen-

sitivity of the interest rate to investments, there may also be some alternative strategies for the RCPEs to choose. Considering these discussions, the
second main section clarifies how our central hypothesis applies to certain
RCPEs. It will take the form of a discussion of Peebles' two books on
financial developments in China and the socialist economies. The arguments will be supported by the illustrative cases of China, the former
USSR, Czechoslovakia (before 1993), latterday Russia and the Czech
Republic.

MONETARY EQUILIBRIUM IN THE RCPEs

In CPEs it was mainly planning mechanisms that helped establish economic equilibrium (see Chapter 1). In market economies it is mainly
market mechanisms that discipline the behaviour of economic agents.
The equilibria in both models depend on the functions of the internal
(control) mechanisms. Even in market economies, market mechanisms
are not always effective. Government intervention remains an important
instrument. The crucial problem of the RCPEs is that they did not establish effective control mechanisms when abandoning the sovereignty of
planning (see Chapters 3 and 4). There are disorder costs during transition and, as Chapter 4 showed, these costs can be higher than
administrative costs.

Macroeconomics

The liberal financial school once argued that interest rate flexibility and
financial liberalisation serve as keys to economic equilibrium and growth
(McKinnon, 1973; Shaw, 1973; see also Chapter 3). The shortage school
(Kornai, 1980) argues that 'soft-budget constraints' caused chronic excess
demand in the CPEs. The disequilibrium school (Portes, 1989) finds no
chronic excess demand in the household sector of CPEs before the economic reforms. It is the control mechanisms within the economic models
that really matter. Different economic systems can hold equilibrium
growth by different control mechanisms. Disequilibrium becomes a
serious problem in RCPEs due to the control vacuum (see Chapter 3). The
argument here has implications for both macro- and microeconomic
levels. Some theoretical support for this is found in the Western financial
and banking control literature reviewed in Chapter 3.
    In this subsection we analyse the mechanisms that function in three dif-
ferent models: namely the market economy, the CPE and the RCPEs.

These will help us to understand the importance of monetary control to monetary equilibrium during transition.

Monetary equilibrium

'Monetary equilibrium' means a balance between the demand for money and the supply of money. Economic growth influences the equilibrium directly. Growth that is too rapid is often accompanied by excess money demand and may bring about inflation, as in the Chinese case. Conversely growth that is too slow is marked by a low investment rate, as was the case in Hungary, and may signal recession. The rate at which growth should occur depends not only on resource constraints and political pressures but also on the methods of financial management. Monetary equilibrium is not easy to achieve. On the one hand it becomes difficult to balance demand and supply in a decentralised situation without effective controlling mechanisms, while on the other hand there is uncertainty and asymmetric information. Markets are segmented and it is difficult to integrate the money, goods and labour markets. Inflationary pressure should help to solve the standard problem of a high-investment, low-consumption 'socialist' growth model analysed by some observers (Ofer, 1991). How much the system can tolerate inflation or the minimum levels of the real wage (w) is country-specific, therefore the equilibrium point (E) at any particular time, being influenced by social and political as well as economic factors, is also model-specific.

Though money growth (m) in the long run is translated fully into inflation, according to monetarist analysis, sustained monetary expansion typically expands output in the short run. The interest rate in real terms (r) and output (Y) return to the full-employment level (Y^*). Expectations play the role of distinguishing between the short run and the long run in determining the dynamics of inflation (π). Only under rational expectations and with full wage and price flexibility does monetary expansion translate instantly into a more rapid rate of inflation without impact on output (Dornbusch and Fischer, 1987). However this may not be realistic.

A stylised market economy

The market economy presents a great step forward from the subsistence economy in which each family produced almost everything it consumed. The capitalist system, based on private ownership, coordinates economic entities through an interlocking network of markets and prices. Price serves as a balance wheel within each market. The textbook IS-LM model incorporates asset markets as well as goods markets, and it lays particular stress on the channels through which monetary and fiscal policy affect the economy. There are interest rate mechanisms in developed financial markets that allow monetary policies to play greater roles than in the CPEs. Dornbusch and Fischer (ibid., pp. 624–57) stylise the market economy for simplicity, which may help us to understand how the mechanisms in an ideal market economy work. It is time to examine whether these mechanisms work in the RCPEs.

In a textbook model, at the long-run full-employment equilibrium output level, Y^*, inflation, π, equals money growth, m, where the real interest rate is allocated. When $\pi > m$, real balances are falling and hence Y is declining together with demand. When $\pi < m$, Y is rising. Meanwhile, at Y levels above Y^*, π rises, and at Y levels below Y^*, π declines. If real aggregate demand depends on the real interest rate, r, a higher r lowers aggregate demand and hence reduces Y^*, as shown by the IS schedule.

Chapter 3 discussed how to treat the market. Sik and Sling (1976) once argued that the limitation of the market was that it never behaved as a perfect market. In the later phases of capitalism, monopoly has introduced substantial inequalities and defects. This is one of the reasons why there are no unregulated market economies.

A stylised CPE

The market crisis contributed to the creation of the CPE system. According to Marx and Engels, a socialist economy based on public ownership should be characterised by direct *ex ante* regulation for the equilibrium of supply and demand in physical units, and by centralisation of savings and investment decisions. Bureaucracy and central planning tackle market failure directly, though they may do so by introducing other forms of inefficiency.

In a stylised CPE model the state is the major investor in the economy, and banks are working capital suppliers and cash monitors. The two contribute to the money supply in spite of the fact that banks are less important than the state budget (see Chapter 1). Firms realise economic growth. From a macroeconomic point of view the planner is the only active agent to determine the locations of the control points. Through two channels of money (to enterprises and to households) and direct price control (see Chapter 1), planners are normally able to allocate resources to reach the equilibrium (E) where economic growth would not generate inflation.[1] Political stabilisation and planners' experience should bring about relatively high rates of growth and infrequent fluctuations.

This is the so-called 'planner's sovereignty mechanism' (Fan *et al.*, 1990), under which only the planner is in a position to determine resource allocation and economic variables. As planners handle economic equilibrium without the interruption of π and the use of r, economic growth relies purely on the accuracy of plans and predictions.

Chapter 1 discussed in general terms the disadvantages of this system, which was theoretically challenged by von Mises (see Brus, 1972, pp. 65–71) and Hayek (1935, pp. 92, 104), but was supported by the 'Lerner–Lange solution' and by Dobb (1928) and Baran (1957). In reality, certain factors such as the resource constraint, planners' misunderstanding of economic dynamics, incentive and information problems, and political pressure can divert growth away from the equilibrium path. The Lange–Lerner *model* was rejected by post-1989 reformers and is under review.

The relative insensitivity of investment to interest rates in RCPEs

In a model of an RCPE the 'Planner's sovereignty mechanism' is replaced by the 'multi-sovereignty mechanism' (Fan *et al.*, 1990), under which certain other agents are also able to play direct roles in the determination of economic variables, such as primary income distribution, investment, output level, enterprise expenditure and so on. The problem is that the mechanisms demonstrated in the stylised system are not effective in the RCPE case. A key question is whether investment is sensitive to interest rates, which depends on the slope of the IS curve.

In terms of empirical research, the Chinese Academy of Social Sciences carried out a production and financial survey of 300 large and medium-sized industrial SOEs over the 1984–8 period. Managers had an investment-insensitive response to the question 'how much would you reduce your demand for loans if the interest rate were to increase by 5 to 10 percentage points?' (see Table 5.1). In 1989 between 65.7 per cent and 85 per cent of managers did not want to cut loans in response to a 5–10 per cent increase in interest rates.

Table 5.1 must be interpreted with care. Firstly, there was no trend in the response as this was the only questionnaire to have been done by the end of the 1980s. Secondly, interest rates as a monetary instrument had just been used after a long period of central planning. It took time for the sensitivity process of interest rates to develop. If interest rates did not reflect the correct prices of financial assets, why should the managers follow them closely? Thirdly, the evidence of the recession in 1990 and the slow-down in investment in 1993 in China show that tight monetary policy and significant increases in interest rates made a certain amount of sense to managers of enterprises.

Table 5.1   Interest elasticity of demand for loans

Extent of expenditure reduction	Frequency	Per cent	Cumulative percentage
Response to a 5 per cent increase in the interest rate			
No cut	240	84.8	84.8
Cut 10–20%	20	7.1	91.9
Cut 20–30%	15	5.3	97.2
Cut 30–50%	2	0.7	97.9
Cut 50% or more	6	2.1	100.0
Response to a 10 per cent increase in the interest rate			
No cut	184	65.7	65.7
Cut 10–20%	42	15.0	80.7
Cut 20–30%	19	6.8	87.5
Cut 30–50%	14	5.0	92.5
Cut 50% or more	21	7.5	100.0

Source: Fan and Woo (1993), Table 5.

Theoretically the sensitivity of investment to interest rates is determined by the hard budget constraint of the investor. If budget revenue is not given, or the investor (an SOE) can increase revenue by applying for investment projects, the demand for loans or investment cannot be restricted by an increase in the interest rate. If additional investment can bring in more employment opportunities and income, if local governments and enterprises can benefit from the addition, if the interest and principal payments can be transferred to the next generation of managers, and if the losses can be sub-sidised, or if there is no financial discipline, then the demand for investment will not be reduced by increasing interest rates alone.

The sensitivity of investment to interest rates is reasonably low in RCPEs. The role of interest rates in bringing equilibrium to the supply and demand of financial resources is asymmetric, as an interest rate increase can induce more personal savings but hardly reduce the demand for investment. The degree of sensitivity is country-specific. The higher the level of the interest rate needed to bring down the growth rate of money (m), or the larger the possible costs of investment, the more difficult for the monetary policy to bring about equilibrium.

A textbook market framework does not work well in RCPEs

Once reforms are underway, RCPEs experience enormous difficulties in developing stable national economies. This situation has arisen in Hungary and Poland since the 1960s, in the other Eastern European economies and the former Soviet Union since the end of the 1980s, and in China during the period of the four financial disorders (see Chapter 4).

An examination of two RCPE cases will illustrate whether a textbook market framework works or not. China provides an illustration of an *overheating* RCPE, where macroeconomists worry more about overheating than recession (see Chapters 1 and 2). Chapter 3 suggests that the functions of market mechanisms are far from perfect in RCPEs. This assumption can destroy the basic mechanisms demonstrated above in a stylised market economy.

For about six years during the period 1979–90 the NI growth rates in China were above 10 per cent. Inflation was not very high before 1985 (Figure 5.1). Since 1984 the NI deflator growth rates have fluctuated between 5 per cent and 14 per cent regardless of the levels of nominal lending rates. The slope of the IS curve turns out to be very steep, which could be a result of the growth in the lending rate in 1988–9. The increases in lending rates by 38 per cent in 1982 and 29 per cent in 1989 did not prevent domestic credit from rising (Figure 5.2). When π and *m* locate on a high level where *Y* is above *Y** (for example above the 8 per cent that was planned), real balances should fall. But demand stubbornly continued

Figure 5.1   China's NI, inflation, credit and interest (NI and credit in real terms; NI deflator, 1985 =100)

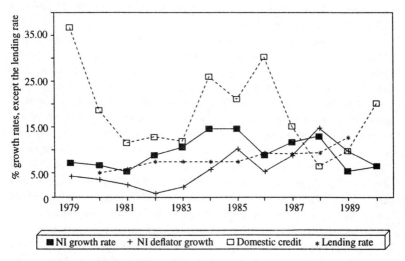

Source: IMF, *International Financial Statistical Yearbook*, 1990–4.

Figure 5.2   China's NI, inflation, credit and interest (NI and credit in real terms; NI deflator, 1985 =100)

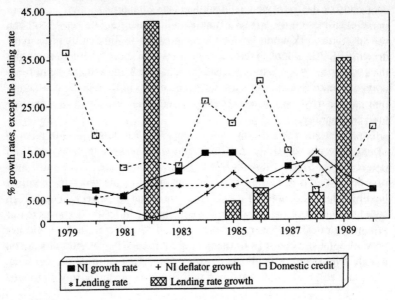

Source: IMF, *International Financial Statistical Yearbook*, 1990–4.

to increase because of the attractiveness of profits and the absence of effective bankruptcy procedures.

Banks could 'passively' satisfy (Mitchell, 1993) the credit demand of SOEs due to these same factors. The credit curve of China in the period 1983–6 demonstrates this (Figure 5.1). Real domestic credit grew very rapidly from 1984. The sharp decrease in credit in 1987 and 1988 was not caused by lending rates, rather by credit rationing and tight monetary policies. Then credit rose again, together with the interest rate. Planners and budget makers have been unable to change this situation since the liberalisation reforms. The central bank also lacks the instruments to control the situation and there are no effective penalties. Therefore the banks cannot decide when firms should not be credited according to the mechanisms explained by Hellwig (1977). The banks expand deposits in both quiet and turbulent times without implementation of the strategy recommended by Dewatripont and Tirole (1993), which has been explained in Chapter 3.

Total real deposits fluctuated violently from 1985, showing a negative relationship with inflation but no clear correlation with the deposit rate

(Figure 5.3). This is not what McKinnon and Shaw's models predict. However increases in the deposit rate by 25 per cent in 1985 and 20 per cent in 1988 did raise domestic deposits significantly, though such large increases in the interest rate cannot often be utilised (Figure 5.3). The sensitivity of deposits to inflation was real and generated a 'deposit withdrawing shock' that caused the bank payment crises in 1985, 1988 and the 1990s (see Chapter 4). Inflation continued to grow (see the NI deflator curve in 1987–8 in Figure 5.4), threatening political stability by reducing real income. The consequence could be either recession, caused by very high interest rates combined with quantitative control (for example the administrative cut-off of investment projects in 1990), or the continuation of economic overheating (as happened in 1985), leaving the equilibrium point of economic growth beyond reach. Without traditional administrative intervention the system could be at risk. In June 1989 the Chinese government did intervene and economic growth fell sharply, causing an unusual recession. But the cycle could be repeated in the absence of effective control instruments.

A *recessional* RCPE case can be found among the RCPEs of Eastern Europe and the former Soviet Union, where recession was sometimes

Figure 5.3   China's NI, inflation, deposist and interest (NI and deposits in real terms; NI deflator, 1985 =100)

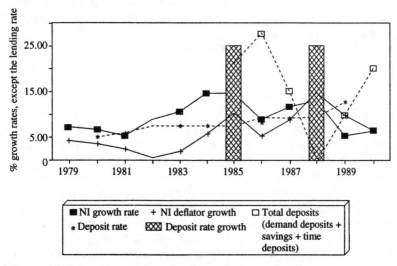

Source: IMF, *International Financial Statistical Yearbook*, 1990–4.

Figure 5.4   China's NI, inflation, deposits and interest (NI and deposits are in real terms; NI deflator, 1958 =100)

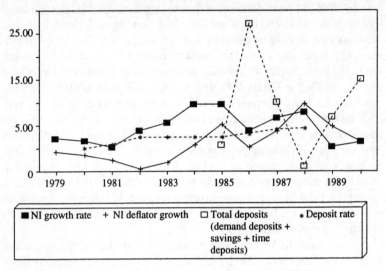

Source: IMF, *International Financial Statistical Yearbook*, 1990–4.

accompanied by inflation. In the Hungarian case, investment was not necessarily the cause of inflation. Consumption demand, currency exchange rates and the debt situation were important (see Chapters 1 and 2). The growth of real GDP had stagnated and fluctuated between 0 per cent and 4 per cent, eventually falling to –4 per cent in 1990. But when inflation is lower than equilibrium money growth ($\pi < m^0$), investment does help Y to grow. Theoretically, when $\pi > m^0$, investment slows down at a point of high interest rate, r. Figure 5.5 shows some positive correlation between GDP deflator growth rate and the annual interest rates after 1979. Both of them correlated negatively with GDP. These facts seem to support the well-known Fisher hypothesis of interest rate effects. The problem was that inflation continued to rise while the economy slipped deeper into recession. A similar 'deposit shock' also happened in Hungary. Regardless of the steady growth of the deposit rate, total real deposits fluctuated violently, especially after the decentralisation of the banking system in 1987 (Figure 5.6). This again contradicts the hypothesis of the McKinnon–Shaw models. It also reflects uncertainty and inflation expectations during transition. From 1987–90 the lending rate increased but total real domestic credit decreased sharply (Figure 5.7). The economic growth curve fluctuated below the equilibrium Y^* under the high π and r (Figure 5.8).

Figure 5.5   Hungary: GDP, inflation, interest and deposits (GDP and deposits in real terms; GDp deflator, 1985 =100)

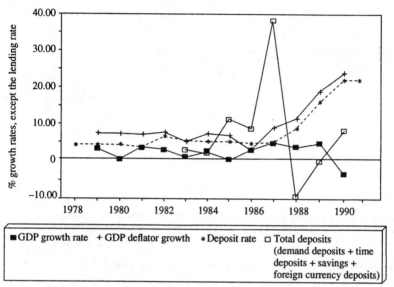

Source: IMF, *International Financial Statistical Yearbook*, 1990–4.

Figure 5.6   Hungary: GDP, inflation, interest and deposits (GDP and deposits in real terms; GDp deflator, 1985 =100)

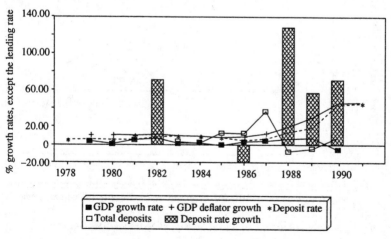

Source: IMF, *International Financial Statistical Yearbook*, 1990–4.

Figure 5.7   Hungarian GDP, inflation interest and credit (GDP and credit in real terms; GDP deflator, 1985 =100)

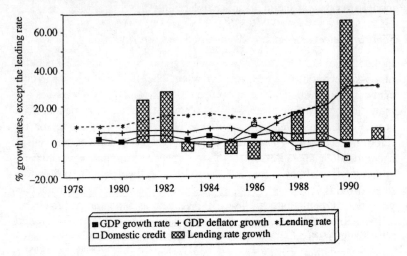

Source: IMF, *International Financial Statistical Yearbook*, 1990–4.

Figure 5.8   Hungarian GDP, inflation interest and credit (GDP and credit in real terms; GDP deflator, 1985 =100)

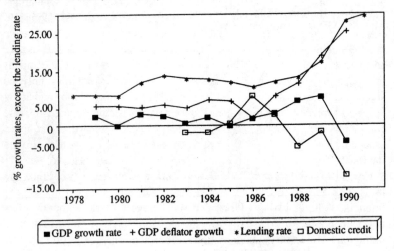

Source: IMF, *International Financial Statistical Yearbook*, 1990–4.

The conclusion is that neither an overheating RCPE nor a recessional RCPE can solve their problems in the pure market context of the stylised model after they abandon planning sovereignty.

Some arguments on banking competition and centralisation

In the light of the above analyses, some arguments on commercial banking in market economies are worth reviewing. They relate to two basic concepts: competition and centralisation. Wadhwani (1988) stresses the inefficiency of financial markets that 'do not mirror fundamentals'. He argues that bank financing may be a better major alternative for the reforming economies. Though competition is a very important mechanism, a *competitive* financial system does not merit complacency and self-congratulation either in the industry itself or in the academic professions of economics and finance. Nor are its shortcomings entirely attributable to government regulations and likely to disappear as deregulation proceeds.

In a competitive decentralised system where individual banks are chasing what seems to them to be 'profitable', they will end up with fragile loans – with 'speculation' prevailing over 'enterprise' (Keynes, 1936, p. 158). If competition is unleashed in the banking system, inflationary forces elsewhere in the economy may be readily confirmed by banks. Higher rates often bring about stagnation rather than the end of inflation. In an analysis of twelve cases, Thorne (1989) shows why a market solution to a financial crisis might not be feasible. Mayer (1988) points out that competition in financial markets can discourage commitment and the creation of incentives to risk taking and sharing. The most competitive financial markets in the world appear to be the most deficient at funding their industries. If economic models fail to take adequate account of intertemporal effects, the immediate benefits of competition can be overemphasised. The benefits of competition may only be attained at the expense of longer-term economic prosperity. Gurley and Shaw (1960, Chapter 6) find that when the monetary system comprises private commercial banks seeking profits, a system of control over their activities, especially when banks are subject to rigorous competition from uncontrolled intermediaries, may in time create problems for the monetary authority.

Cargill (1988) argues that although financial liberalisation since the mid-1970s is said to have increased the role of competitive forces in the financial systems of both Japan and the US, enhanced competition has never been a major objective of financial reform there. Competition, as a market structure, plays an ambiguous role in the financial reform process because a competitive financial system is likely to conflict with several major goals of financial regulation. Regulatory reforms have occurred in response to forces that demanded a more flexible financial system, and as a result regulatory authorities have played a reactive role to these forces.

Some recent literature has shown that too much competition between banks on the microeconomic level may have negative effects on the macro level (Vives, 1991). Financial intermediation may not increase social welfare and the banking industry may be characterised by a zero-rent monopoly structure (Yanelle, 1991), or equilibrium may fail to be established (Smith, 1984). When competition among financial intermediaries is modelled it tends to yield generally counter-intuitive results, particularly in banking. A bank resembles a network, and many different outcomes of the competitive process are possible, depending on the expectations of depositors. These become central to the explanation of the fragility of banking (Matutes and Vives, 1992). Even if rate regulation has costs and tends to generate over-investment in services and the possibility of regulatory capture (Vives, 1991), it does have some benefits if deposit insurance is deemed necessary. This is probably the reason why competition reforms that were started with a desire to combine the merits of the two systems – the CPE and the market – have often ended up combining the defects of the two. A certain amount of competition is necessary to improve efficiency, but this should be managed carefully.

Another issue is linked to centralisation. Institutionally, there is great variety across different banking systems, partly as a result of accidents of historical evolution. Lenin (1917) recognised the historical development of the monopoly of the banking systems in Germany and Russia, and its close relationship with the production system at the imperialist stage of capitalism, and he laid the theoretical foundation for Gosbank monopoly. His analysis was based on Hilferding's findings (1910; see also Chapter 1). Prais (1979, pp. 33–50) confirmed the trend of *centralisation* of the Western financial systems in his analysis of the banking systems of three countries – Germany, Britain and the US. Lewis *et al.* (1987) confirmed this trend as a general orientation in the West, even in the case of the US. The comparative studies in Chapter 4 also discuss this. To make control easy and reduce costs, is it necessary for the reforming banking system to retain a certain degree of centralisation in transition, while gradually changing the overcentralised monopoly of a CPE model? As the production system is being decentralised, it seems unnecessary to decentralise the banking system in such a simple fashion.

The choices of RCPEs

When the issue of decentralising the banking system is assessed, it is easy to look at its benefits rather than its costs. Moreover, when the costs are assessed it is easy to think just of administrative costs, ignoring disorder costs. By disorder costs we mean costs brought about by economic disorders, especially financial disorders. A possible reason for ignoring this is that these costs are often impossible to measure quantitatively. However the costs could be unimaginably high, and it is these costs that often jeopardise economic reform programmes (see Chapter 4). Here it is argued that disorder costs are likely to be higher than administrative costs. An understanding of this argument relates to the strategic choices of the RCPEs.

Definition of the three 'bests'

We assume three situations: a 'first-best' situation – under which the aggregate resource is the only constraint and there are no administrative costs at all – is hardly realistic. A 'second-best' situation may occur in the form of an environment in which the authorities can enter into a binding policy commitment before certain economic variables are set. For example, the government can choose the price level before those who set wages choose wage levels, with employment being determined last. There is administration but no discretion, therefore the disorder costs may be higher than that in the first-best scenario, but lower than a 'third best', under which discretion is also possible. Discretion has to be allowed over some or all of the policy instruments, therefore increasing administrative costs. Equilibrium policy in a discretionary regime will typically yield a worse outcome than equilibrium policy in a commitment regime, according to Persson and Tabellini (1991). But if the normal situation is jeopardised, the former may not yield a better outcome than the latter. The question is how to modify the incentives and constraints defining the policy optimisation problem in order to obtain a more desirable institutional framework and government policies in equilibrium.

Disorder costs could be higher than administrative costs

An RCPE is a CPE that is introducing market mechanisms during the process of transition. There are at least three separate elements of this definition. First, the RCPE was formerly a centrally planned system with a large state-owned production sector and a strong banking system. Second, planners have been largely removed by the reforms. Investment allocation is being shifted from the budget to the banking system. SOEs have been vigorous in their investment and wage decisions. Third, transition implies that there are no mature market mechanisms. Budget constraints can be softened, while the functions of interest rates and prices in signalling information are limited. A legal framework is being prepared. But there are not enough experienced and qualified staff in management and marketing.

Administrative costs in regulation, supervision and intervention are created by the principal (the authorities). Suppose that the smaller the effort expended in regulation, supervision and intervention, the lower the administrative costs (B_i where i is the ith 'best'), and vice versa. The total administrative costs for the first-best choice are the lowest. The administrative costs for the second and third best are increasing since they involve a commitment to discretion. The administrative cost function is

$$B_1 < B_2 < B_3 \tag{5.1}$$

However administrative costs are not the only costs. There are various kinds of disorder costs (D_i, with $i = 1$–3), which are created by economic disorders arising from inadequate administration. Disorder costs can be sudden and damaging, such as bank runs or economic turmoil. They can also be slow, such as massive, dispersed, irregular activities. Disorder costs can be generated, for example, by financial chaos, and can be higher than administrative costs. Ignoring these costs often leads to the reduction of financial regulation and economic administration, bringing about financial disorder or even national catastrophe (see Chapter 4).

We assume, for simplification, that regulation and administration are rational, therefore additional regulations and supervision, including the additional administrative agencies that join in, can improve information, management and efficiency.[2] In the same three alternative cases, the disorder costs are decreasing as

$$D_1 > D_2 > D_3 \tag{5.2}$$

We argue simply that the third-best choice may be the most efficient one in terms of overall costs, C_t, that is,

$$\partial C_t / \partial C_m < 0 \tag{5.3}$$

where C_m is the management costs
Cost functions will be discussed in detail in the appendix to this chapter.

The third best can be the best

The first best is a choice in which independent firms compete for profits without any intervention from other agents. This is the production-system-centred case, with the maximisation of profits. Generally speaking there is no control. Encouraged by the demand for high employment and wage rates, firms tend to increase production. Without sufficient supervision or intervention from state planners, the banking system supplies as much money as firms require. The consequence can either be economic over-heating or recession. Financial disorder increases D, with $D > B$, and can generate turmoil (see Chapter 4). The experiences of the RCPEs in Eastern Europe and the former Soviet Union show that the economic situation can be worse than in the pre-reform period.

A constraint in the second-best case is that the government conducts only policy commitments or exerts only partial control – letting planners, the budget or bankers control SOE investment, without sufficient help from and coordination with other agents in the economy. However inflation can still mobilise political pressure against economic growth because policy commitments or the control power of the individual system is limited (see Chapter 4). China experienced this situation at the time of the first three financial disorders and therefore seems unable to cope with transitional problems. Disorders remain and disorder costs exceed admin-istrative costs $(D > B)$. It is still difficult for the economy to maintain the process of equilibrium development.

In the third-best case, when the interest rate cannot clear the markets, a visible hand in the form of government intervention and policy regulation is necessary. When policy commitments are not enough, discretion becomes the rule. Not only does the banking system control the production system in its investment, but the planners and the budget also jointly help the banking system. Economic growth can also be secured by an improved legal framework in conditions of political stability. The agents and the principal (the planners) are united in a common goal of mobilising the whole team. The availability of credit is a decisive constraint of a firm, according to Hellwig (1977). If the banking system controls firms, it decides when firms should be rewarded with credit and when they should go bankrupt. Recapitalisation in turbulent times and increased borrowing in quiet times can be used to counter the perverse incentives of banks, according to Dewatripont and Tirole (1993). A public agency is selected to represent depositors and regulate banks. This interference brings about a better situation since we suppose that additional administrative efforts may improve information and management. Rationing or credit planning is still useful. All this contributes to a stable environment for firms to compete in order to maximise their profits. This situation is preferable. Prices are under control and political disturbance is reduced to the minimum because of the joint efforts of the agents and the principals. This has been the

Chinese experience since the most recent battle against financial disorder (see Chapter 4). Disorder costs are minimised, though administrative costs are relatively increased. It has been encouraging that government functions in making macroeconomic policies and implementing regulations have helped some economies to develop successfully (Stiglitz, 1993).

Summary

The above discussion has been simplified to facilitate a clear picture. RCPEs cannot be generalised: the factors causing inflation in an overheating RCPE differ from those in a recessional RCPE. An RCPE can have economic crises and even turmoils that reflect inefficiency even compared with a CPE. World developments have shown that, in general, there are disadvantages as well as advantages to decentralisation and have pointed to the increased importance of the signalling mechanism. When an economic system has been highly centralised and bureaucratic, the advantages of introducing market forces, cash constraints and more flexible prices are likely to be considerable. In order to introduce market forces, the banking system has to change from being an accounting system to an agency that imposes planning horizons and cash-flow performance requirements over those horizons.

However it must be recognised that market forces decrease collective action while increasing competition. As the imposer of market forces, the banking system may also be short-sighted, conventional in an inappropriate way and speculative. It is by no means obvious that flexible interest rate structures are always advantageous. It should of course be noted that when individual financial agencies become freer to take credit-granting decisions in the light of market interest rates (rather than simply following directions), there is the possibility of some 'disintermediation'. In other words, flexible interest rates do not necessarily ensure proper control over aggregate effective credit.

The technique lies in the operation of the banking system and its coordination with the other agents and principals (the budget and firms, as well as planners) when market mechanisms are initially introduced. Therefore the lowest intervention costs of the first-best scenario render it unreachable. The third best, with discretion and multi-sovereignty under proper control, can be a favourable alternative due to its low disorder costs, in spite of the relatively higher administrative costs $(B < D)$. The key issue among these choices is the control mechanisms functioning inside the economy.

It is bankers that are stressed here because the banking system becomes the major investor and supervisor when the production system is in an imperfect market environment. As the banking system is changed in order to play a more important role in industrial cash-flows and disciplining economic agents' behaviour, it becomes ever more important to regulate the banking system itself. In doing so, it becomes particularly important to identify its operation correctly (which is why a broader measure of the money supply is required). Awareness of what is happening to interest rates and credit distribution is also necessary as it is needed to improve the efficiency and ensure the responsibility of banks while the system is tightly controlled.

Equilibrium in both the stylised CPE model and the market model depends on the functions of their respective internal mechanisms. The crucial problem among RCPEs is that they did not establish effective control mechanisms before abandoning planning sovereignty (see Chapter 3). This has both macro- and microeconomic implications. On the macro level, the banking system has a special control function of implementing stabilisation policies. On the micro level, RCPE banks can help to establish a new corporate governance structure. In sum, monetary equilibrium is ever important. The control of banks and banking control are essential for macroeconomic stabilisation, regardless of what form the system takes. Full utilisation of price and interest rate mechanisms is not to be rejected, however. With both the invisible hand (r) and the visible hand (government functions), RCPEs may work better than before.

LIBERALISATION OR CONTROL? PEEBLES AND THE 'SHORTAGE SCHOOL'

There has been extensive literature on macroeconomic issues in CPEs and RCPEs, some of which deals specifically with China. Peebles' two recent books on money, one on China (1991a) and the other on Eastern Europe and former Soviet Union (1991b), have provided some interesting descriptions under the hypothesis of 'chronic excess demand'. However, if we read Peebles' books carefully it is not difficult to find that his views are fundamentally wrong. Since the control functions of planners in CPE regimes did contribute to macroeconomic equilibrium, it is the control vacuum left by the withdrawal of planners after the reforms that has brought about financial crisis and inflation in the RCPEs, and therefore I argue that bankers should largely replace planners as controllers during transition. Some proponents of the Shortage School and its followers, such as Peebles, challenge this view. Peebles' views will frequently be referred to here, not because of their intellectual significance, but in order to develop my theoretical arguments. My criticism of Peebles leads to some further comments on the interesting and important debates among these schools.

The following discussion relates some of the analyses of banks to macroeconomic issues. This requires a brief review of the debates concerning the economics of CPEs as well as a discussion of relevant issues and theories. Evidence will show no support for the chronic-excess-demand hypothesis. We then go on to distinguish the RCPE model from the CPE model in more detail and show the real nature of the financial crises in RCPEs. Because Peebles' books deal not only with China but also with other 'socialist economies', evidence from both will be presented in order to ascertain why a serious monetary overhang has occurred since the radical reforms.

Disequilibrium or shortage?

Behaviour and policy in the stylised CPE have been explained in various ways. Since the mid-1970s the Disequilibrium School, advanced by Portes and his colleagues (1978 to 1989), and the Shortage School, represented by Kornai (1980 to 1986), have attracted substantial interest. They have been surveyed by Davis and Charemza (1989) and reviewed by Brabant (1990). In *A Study of the Soviet Economy* by the IMF, the World Bank, the OECD and the EBRD (IMF, 1991, pp. 380–1), the two schools are distinguished by their method of defining the concept of aggregate excess demand in the presence of many goods and price controls.

According to the Disequilibrium School, the step from a one-good economy to an economy with many goods is not a difficult one. If, at the current price vector, aggregate demand for goods and services (the sum of demand in all markets) is greater than aggregate supply (the sum of supply in all markets), then the economy is in excess demand and, with sticky prices, it is subject to repressed inflation (that is, the absolute price level is too low to clear the market). If, instead, aggregate demand and aggregate supply are in equilibrium, the contemporaneous existence of excess supply and excess demand in different markets requires an adjustment in relative prices, but does not imply the need to adjust the price level. Certainly, in the presence of both shortages and surpluses, the measurement of excess demand may present some problems; however these problems can be tackled econometrically.

The Shortage School argues that the concept of aggregate disequilibrium, which is legitimate in market economies, becomes ill-defined in economies characterised by 'chronic' shortages. Two specific points are raised. First, agents who are unable to buy the goods they desire almost always end up buying substitutes; rarely do their savings rise involuntarily. Second, the volume of voluntary savings may be directly affected by the existence of chronic shortages at the micro level; the precautionary reserve of purchasing power (stored mainly in monetary assets) increases, artificially inflating the savings rate.

Charemza (1989) classifies disequilibrium and shortage models of CPEs into three categories: testable excess demand (the Portes school), disequilibrium indicators,[3] and Kornai's economics of shortage. He argues that some disputes are not caused by the theoretical features of the models but rather by utilisation of different estimation methods that are not directly comparable. Therefore he suggests that computational techniques and the statistical hypothesis testing theory be improved.

The contradictions between the methods may not cover the deep reasons behind the debate. Charemza's argument cannot explain the fundamentals behind the debates and why the direct policy suggestions of different schools are different: the Shortage School notably calls for fundamental changes of the non-workable CPE into a market economy, while the Disequilibrium School, according to Peebles, suggests certain adjustments under planning (although the leading writers of the Disequilibrium School did not make such suggestions). They would argue, however, that the 'classical' CPE did exercise effective monetary control, despite excess real demand in the producer goods sector, and that the inflationary pressures in the household sector in several CPEs in the 1980s came from relaxation of that control.

The issues

The differences behind the debate are very fundamental: how to treat markets, how to treat planning, and how to reform the planned economy if reform becomes inevitable.

Peebles writes: 'The chronic-excess-demand hypothesis, and particularly Birman's prediction of financial crisis in the Soviet Union that was based on it, *have been shown to be correct. Events have shown that the chronic-excess-demand hypothesis was a better description of the situation in the planned economies than anything else available.* Therefore the approach of this book [*A History of Socialist Money*] will be to explain events in these countries in the framework of this hypothesis' (Peebles, 1991b, p. 5, emphasis added).

Here three questions are raised. Has the theoretical debate between these schools ever been clearly concluded? If not, have events proved the hypothesis of chronic-excess demand? If not, can the events in these countries be explained by such a framework?

Besides those quoted by Peebles (1991a, pp. 70–72) against the traditional excess-demand hypothesis and the important papers that Peebles missed (Portes *et al.*, 1987; Burkett, 1988), other subsequent papers supporting the Disequilibrium School are worth mentioning here, such as Ofer (1991), Cottarelli and Blejer (1992) and the above-mentioned work coauthored by the IMF (1991). Even Chang's model (1992) does not reject the argument that there is no chronic excess demand. Peebles also considers that it is very difficult to decide between these two schools because 'all the available evidence is compatible with either view' (Peebles, 1991a, p. 71). Excess demand may be measured by different data in different ways with different formulas, and may of course achieve different results.

The socialist economy is superior to other economic systems with respect to structure of output, income distribution and efficiency, according to Mandel (1968) and Dobb (1970). The actual performance of CPEs, however, has been quite different among the countries in different historical periods. Pervasive disequilibria in markets and shortage of labour and commodities have occurred due to a combination of factors, including objective conditions, specific institutional arrangements and policy choices (Davis and Charemza, 1989, p. 5).

The radical transformation of the CPEs at the end of the 1980s and the beginning of the 1990s sounds favourable to the Shortage School. This point is clear in Brabant's survey (1990). But as Portes (1989) warned, the changes (in Poland) could not have distorted the model for the whole period since the 1950s, and the problems of transformation suggest we may question the initial analysis. If the Shortage School is correct, the radical approaches in Eastern Europe and Russia should have brought about good economic results in general; however the potential for inflation, recession or financial disorder – or all three – has disturbed the reforms from time to time (see Chapters 1 and 4 above). Perhaps the fundamental changes were not organised properly or the analyses of the Shortage School (and others suggesting similar policies) were incorrect.

The theories

First of all, it should be clear whether or not the main problems of the CPE (not the RCPE) model pointed out by the Shortage School have already been proven true. This ought to be discussed theoretically and shown by some empirical evidence.

In the Shortage School's writings there is often an ambiguity concerning aggregation. Given their arguments about forced substitution and the coexistence of shortage and slacks at the micro level, writers such as Kornai sometimes deny the possibility of measuring aggregate demand and supply[4] (but it can be inferred that the concept of 'resource-constrained economy' is an aggregate one). '[T]he most fundamental and important issue is the aggregation problem', which leads Shortage authors to suggest not only that the measurement problem is, in principle, insoluble, but also that neither monetary theory nor macroeconomic policy are of any interest in considering disequilibria in CPEs (Portes, 1989, p. 31).

The Shortage School rejects the ability of planners to maintain macroeconomic equilibrium. Thus socialist planned economies are invariably characterised by excess demand for goods as well as for labour, and this view is a cornerstone of Kornai's interpretation of the functioning of those economies (Kornai, 1980).

The CPE system can be defined in variety of ways, but the essential character of the CPE was that the planning authorities had enough power to control the balance between supply and demand on both microeconomic and macroeconomic levels. The central decision makers could control enterprises through production plans and direct profit control. They could control household consumption through wage plans while also controlling inflation through fixed price policies. Finally, they could control the supply of money through credit plans. They had the power to direct both the budget system and the banking system to fulfil the national plans (see Chapter 1). That is why equilibrium at the macroeconomic level was generally maintained in the classical CPEs, in spite of the fact that excess demand or excess supply might temporarily occur on both macro and micro levels. A simple question might be asked: if planners could 'control the growth of household monetary incomes so that these incomes accord with the growth in the supply of retail goods' (Peebles, 1991b, p. 42), and if they were able to prevent the overflow from the non-cash circuit to the cash circuit in the form of excessive payments of wages (this is what a 'CPE' means, partly or essentially), why should there have been permanent excess demand? Thus the CPE was an economic regime within which the central planning system could control and maintain macroeconomic equilibrium. If there was *chronic* excess demand, however, the fundamental character of central planning disappeared.

In fact some Disequilibrium writers do not doubt that there was excess real demand within the state production sector in CPEs, in part imposed consciously by the planners to elicit more output. Nor do they question that this could generate excess demand in the markets linking the state production sector to the household sector: the markets for consumer goods and services as well as labour. 'But for these markets the planners have always stressed the importance of macroeconomic equilibrium because the effects of excess demand here are so clearly dysfunctional. The "balance of money incomes and expenditures of the population" (BMIEP) is a key element in the planning process, and the planners dispose of powerful policy instruments to achieve its targets' (Portes, 1979; see also Rudcenko, 1978; Portes and Winter, 1980).

Kornai (1982) argues against the discrete switching model of a non-clearing market used by Portes and his associates at an aggregative level because shortage and slack may coexist, with 'discouraged consumers' (Kornai, 1980). Burkett (1988), however, distinguishes between actual and potential shortage, and defines the latter as the shortage that would exist if consumers were not discouraged. His use of a hyperbolic relation rather than the 'min condition' simplifies estimation, especially when disturbances are serially correlated, and yield estimates of gross shortage and slack, as well as net excess demand. Applying these techniques to the consumer markets of five East European countries, Burkett cannot reject the discrete switching hypothesis, and he does not find chronic excess demand.

Theories on China

The absence of macroeconomics from Shortage School analysis is its obvious weakness in its dispute with the Disequilibrium School. Peebles seems to understand this. Based on the 'purchasing power approach' invented by Perkins (1966) and Jao (1967–8),[5] Peebles constructs an index of purchasing power imbalance (PPI) as excess demand, which is measured by the increase in money incomes of the population minus the increase in real net material product (all in percentages). Its exact definition is in terms of growth rates (Peebles, 1991a, p. 179), where PPI = pdSPP – pdRNI.[6] SPP is a Chinese term meaning 'the social purchasing power', and RNI is the real national income, the growth of which is a proxy for the growth of consumer goods supplies. PPI is used to explain both increases in currency in circulation and increases in administered prices. If it exceeds zero, planners can choose either money accumulation or list-price increases to combine monetary overhang with some price increases (ibid., Chapter 6).

Peebles uses simple bivariate econometrics to support his proposition with a few very basic tests (t-ratios, R^2, s, and Durbin–Watson). The maximum number of observations is 34, and some regressions have only nine observations (ibid., p. 176). This is because he 'firmly believe[s] that any explanation of the relationship between money and prices and any other variables should be shown to be supported by quantitative analysis over a long period' (ibid., p. 4), in spite of the fact that there are no quarterly and monthly data for such a long period in China. He 'also believe[s] that the theories proposed should stand up to examination using the simplest of techniques with unadjusted annual data' (ibid., p. 4). It is not always necessary to mine data, especially in a small sample case. But in his regressions on pdLP (or $\Delta \log P$, where P is the price term) with 30 annual observations for 1953–85, R^2 is low (0.43) while the standard error of the regression is very high (1.8). In the regression on pdP, R^2 is again low, and s is extremely high.

Although there are different approaches to econometrics, and not all are sophisticated, Peebles' econometric exercises are superficial, and the empirical findings are difficult to interpret. These results do not prove that there is a 'close correlation'. There are no unit root tests and causality tests, yet he clearly concludes that there was no causative relationship between growth in the monetary stock and open inflation. He believes that they were both the consequences of PPI; money supply changes and budget deficits are not independent primary causes of open price increases; PPIs are the primary exogenous change to which the monetary sector, and particularly monetary planners, have to react; monetary change itself is one of the consequences of these imbalances (ibid., pp. 219–20). His theoretical analysis and some simple scatter diagrams indicate that the PPI approach provides some insights regarding money in China, but he admits: 'List prices were hardly ever increased during the period 1963–78, not because planners froze prices irrespective of the state of excess demand, here PPI, but because the PPI indicator was generally well controlled' (ibid., p. 180). In his own framework, that means excess demand was well under control, though the extent of retail list price increases in years of positive PPI was not sufficient to restrain the growth of the ratio of currency to retail sales (ibid., p. 183). Thus there should not have been chronic excess demand.

Peebles (ibid., p. 125) finds support in the fact that the predictors of crisis often share similar views to those held by economists in the countries under study. Quite a few writers who upheld the chronic-excess-demand hypothesis are citizens or former citizens of the countries they are discussing. However indigenous observers do not always have a better understanding than outsiders. A famous Chinese poet in the Sung Dynasty wrote: 'You never know the true face of Lu Mountain, because you are inside the Mountain' (Su Dongpo, 1037–1101).

Just as Western writers may be divided into different schools, such as the Disequilibrium School and the Shortage School, there are a variety of views amongst the writers in the countries under study. Peebles (ibid., p. 121) indicates that 'Chinese economists ... admit the applicability and existence of the soft budget constraint to the enterprise sector and that there was excess demand for consumer goods throughout the 1980s'. Here he makes a similar mistake as Goldman (1984, p. 113) in generalising the views of economists of a huge country 'without naming them'.

Some have discussed the issue with a preconception that China is an economy in shortage. Yin and Zhang (1987) is one example. By estimating the parameters of a simple OLS equation, they conclude that excess demand in China had been increasing since 1980 (see Table 5.2(D)). But there is evidence that there have been years when aggregate demand has been less than aggregate supply in China, even in the 1980s. Guo (1990) takes a different approach without any preconceptions. He distinguishes 'aggregate balance' from 'equilibrium', while the former indicates a balance between GDP and gross domestic expenditure, the latter is a perfect balance in a particular situation. According to his view, in the previous forty years the aggregate balance had *never* broken down. Even in the period of 'the Great Leap Forward', GDP always equalled gross domestic expenditure. The problems of the previous analysis were often caused by ignoring the statistical differences between stock variables and flow variables. Those who espouse the excess-demand hypothesis use prices from the previous year to calculate excess demand while aggregate demand is calculated using current prices. Guo investigates in detail the correct method of calculating household consumption, GDP, aggregate investment and savings. In a study covering the period 1979–88 he finds that macroeconomic aggregates had always been in balance in China, in spite of the fact that there had never been perfect equilibrium (see Table 5.2(A)).

It appears from these Chinese approaches that the excess-demand hypothesis can hardly stand if the excess demand preconception is removed. Liu (1991) conducted a comprehensive estimation of aggregate demand in China for the period 1952–89 to test the chronic-excess-demand hypothesis. He believes that any concept must be adapted to Chinese reality. For example, effective aggregate demand should be replaced by 'disposable aggregate demand', which excludes the part of demand that consumers can satisfy through self-reliance. The 'narrow market' should be replaced by the 'broad market', which covers not only the free market but also the market under the intervention of the authorities. It is necessary to avoid duplication or even multiplication of calculations in measuring aggregate demand.

Liu finds it important to estimate not only the demand for consumption, including household consumption and the consumption of the public sector (including the demand for goods, labour and services), but also the investment demand of the SOEs (including fixed-assets investment and inventory investment) and net export demand (including goods, labour and services). He also uses a 'national income coefficient adjustment and factor deduction approach', which can be illustrated by the following aggregate supply equation:

$$AS = NI\,(1.13 + B_3/300 + B)-Z$$

where AS is the aggregate supply counted by current prices; NI is nominal national income; B_3 is the proportion of the number of employees in the tertiary sector[7] over the total number of employees in society; B is the coefficient of the net factor income from abroad;[8] and Z is the self-financed consumption of peasants.

Although this approach may incorporate some inaccuracies over such a long period, Liu has done some adjustments according to the differences between economic sectors and between the prereform period and the post-reform period. While the methodologies are very different, his results are remarkably close to those of Portes and Santorum (1987). Another advantage relative to Peebles is that his approach has taken account of much broader factors affecting equilibrium in the estimated period.

The Chinese literature indicates that the chronic-excess-demand hypothesis has never been universally accepted in China. The approaches adopted by Liu and Guo challenge not only the Shortage School, but also the hypothesis of the 'generalised excess real demand' in the state production sector accepted by Portes (1989, p. 29). The Chinese economists have no problem with data availability. Their approaches are more comprehensive than those of the Disequilibrium School, which indicates that planners in China balanced demand and supply in respect of both consumption and production and were able to restore equilibrium if there were disruptions. If the CPE was a planning regime where producers had no initial incentive to generate chronic excess demand, there was no theoretical reason to allow chronic excess demand to stand before economic reform, and the chronic-excess-demand hypothesis may be fundamentally undermined.

Evidence from China

In China, as in many CPEs before the fundamental reforms of the 1980s, the income level of the household sector was kept low until the end of the

1970s and was often lower than economic growth. Income distribution was very equal which made the low wage income politically tolerable. Planners generally knew how much people could spend and therefore what quantity of goods should be supplied to shops. It was the planners who planned the level of income in order to save resources for industrialisation. Price increases forced people to save out of their fixed money income, with a fall in real income according to the writings of Wicksell, von Hayek and von Mises. In CPEs, savings had to come directly out of planned income without an indirect price mechanism. Therefore it is incorrect for Peebles to have judged that the 'forced saving' in the socialist system was purely a monetary phenomenon and did not imply any reallocation of resources between consumption and investment (Peebles, 1991a, p. 68).[9] There were problems of disequilibrium, as well as of shortage, when demand was too high, but this was only temporary because the planners were able to make adjustments (see the model of such adjustment behaviour in Portes *et al.*, 1987). The chronic-excess-demand hypothesis of the Shortage School 'has never been formulated very vigorously' (see also Peebles, 1991b, p. 3).

Chinese scholars and economic research institutes use different approaches to estimate aggregate demand and supply, and the results are different. Table 5.2 summarises some influential work that has not been discussed by Peebles. Row A shows that the figures always balanced (there was no excess demand or supply). Row B shows that five years out of the period 1979–86 were negative (excess supply). Rows C and D indicate that in some reforming years in the period, aggregate demand was greater than aggregate supply, indicating that the chronic-excess-demand hypothesis has not been accepted without question by Chinese economists.

According to the results presented in Liu (1991, Table 2–2), excess supply occurred in at least thirteen of the thirty-eight years of socialist economic development in China, and there were only twenty-three years when demand was in excess. Excess demand was continuous for fifteen years from 1976, the year of Mao's death. Another relatively long period of excess demand was experienced from 1959–64 during the Great Leap Forward and the period of natural disasters. In most other years there was excess supply. It is not true that the whole period since 1978 has been dominated by excess demand, because there were obvious market surpluses in the late 1980s.

There is also a large amount of literature in China discussing how to cope with excess supply; however Liu concludes that it is unreasonable to claim that China's macroeconomic development has been in a situation of chronic excess demand or shortage over the whole period. Thus 'Kornai's

Table 5.2   Different results in estimating Chinese aggregate demand and supply
(0.1 billion yuan)

	1979	1980	1981	1982	1983	1984	1985	1986
A	0	0	0	0	0	0	0	0
B	20	−43	−122	−66	−111	−190	187	55
C	n.a.	n.a.	757	776.2	694.8	989.5	885	n.a.
D	n.a.	485.1	691.3	996.7	1110.5	1867.1	2653.3	4684.8

Notes: Negative figures indicate excess supply.
Source: A: Guo (1990); B: China Economic System Reform Institute (1988) in
Lin (1991); C: Zhang (1988); D: Yin and Chang (1987).

doctrine' is not convincing (ibid., p. 32). But why China should have had
two such long periods of excess demand (if Liu's research is correct), and
why excess demand occurred in these two periods in particular, remain
questions of interest.

Evidence from other countries

The above argument does not mean that there was no disequilibrium or
excess demand at all, but no theory can be proposed without evidence to
support it. The evidence from Portes and Winter (1978, 1980) justifies
rejecting the hypothesis of sustained repressed inflation in the market for
consumption goods and services since the mid-1950s in Czechoslovakia,
the German Democratic Republic (GDR), Hungary and Poland. Even in
the GDR, the country where excess demand appears to have been the
dominant regime, it is fairly small and four years show excess supply.
Alton *et al.* (1981) show their alternative consumer price index (CPI)
growing faster than the official implicit CPI by 2.4 per cent per annum for
Bulgaria, 1.6 per cent for Czechoslovakia, 1.3 per cent for the GDR, 1.1
per cent for Hungary and 1.6 per cent for Poland. Therefore there was not
a significant amount of hidden inflation. Pickersgill (1976, 1983; Ofer and
Pickersgill, 1980) rejects the proposition that Soviet households save inor-
dinately large amounts of their income as a result of the lack of consumer
goods and services available for purchase. Asselain's (1981) theoretical
and empirical analysis concludes that, in the case of several CPEs, the full
set of characteristics typical of situations of forced saving are never found
together. The savings ratios were not high in Czechoslovakia by international comparison and did not seem to depend on supply-side events,

according to Klaus and Rudlovcek (1982). Even Peebles himself (1981, p. 75) finds an overall trend of decline in the currency-to-deposit ratio as elsewhere in Eastern Europe, and that 'Soviet liquidity is not excessive' in comparison with other CPEs.[10]

Portes *et al.* (1984a, 1984b, 1987) have found that various East European economies exhibited both periods of excess demand for consumption and periods of excess supply. Burkett's (1988) alternative approach, based on Kornai's arguments, finds that shortage – even when corrected for a discouraged consumer effect – was seldom as great as slack in the consumption goods markets of these four countries as well as that of former Yugoslavia. His estimates indicate that shortage ranged from 0.3 per cent to 7.6 per cent of consumer demand while slack ranged from 0.5 per cent to 60.9 per cent of supply. Potential consumer demand, purged of the discouraged consumer effect, commonly exceeded actual demand but seldom surpassed supply. Portes *et al.* (1988) tested Kornai's assertion that 'chronic shortage' characterises such CPEs by analysis of disequilibrium models and rejects both the all-excess-demand and all-excess-supply hypotheses advanced for the Polish case during the years 1955–80.

New evidence from the former Soviet Union and Czechoslovakia reveals some fundamental similarities between China and the Eastern bloc.

The Soviet Union   During the 1980s, a sizeable body of literature appeared on the extent of the disequilibrium in the Soviet Union. To prove the existence of chronic shortage in the Soviet Union, Birman (1980a, 1980b; Birman and Clarke, 1985), Pindak (1983) and Winiecki (1985) relied mainly on a supposed indicator of stock disequilibrium, namely the ratio between household financial holdings (in monetary form) and consumption or disposable income, which, as an increasing 'undesired accumulation' of monetary balances, has exhibited rapid growth during the last thirty years. Many authors criticise this approach, indicating that in countries with limited capital markets, money-to-income ratios have a different meaning than they do in economies with well-developed financial markets.

Ofer (1991) gives a comprehensive analysis of the case. According to Table 1 of his paper, the relative size of the budget started to increase well before the reforms were implemented (since 1971–5). Fiscal deficits before the reform were relatively small (2–3 per cent). The prereform period was characterised by a substantial ordinary budget surplus, or a more-or-less balanced adjusted ordinary budget. Therefore most of the budget deficit was created during the reform years and was not carried over from the old regime (ibid., pp. 311–12). Before the reforms the household sector had been in a state of excess demand, expressed mostly in the form of repressed inflation, since most prices were kept at given levels for extended periods. Whatever the extent of the inherited and accumulated disequilibrium in 1985, 'it was not very large' but 'it has grown significantly since then' (ibid., p. 321).

In the classical Soviet system, according to Ofer, typical life-cycle motivations for saving are much weaker than in market economies, which are concentrated in cash and saving deposits, and 'private saving is a relatively recent phenomenon'. While the stock of monetary assets to personal disposable income has been growing, 'it is very low' (ibid., p. 324).

Official price indexes in the Soviet Union were remarkably stable over a thirty-year period. Between 1960 and 1980 the official retail price index remained almost unchanged, and even in the 1980s official recorded inflation barely exceeded 1 per cent per year. The savings rate in the USSR does not appear particularly high compared with Western countries.

The remarkable stability of the Soviet savings rate up to the late 1980s has been used to suggest that if excess demand ever existed, it remained relatively stable (according to a joint study of the Soviet economy by the IMF, 1991). Econometric estimates of the consumption function find that the behaviour of consumption between 1965 and 1985 can be adequately described by the evolution of total (human and non-human) wealth; and that household wealth is predominantly 'human'. The estimated consumption functions are very stable until 1985 and present strong instability in the subsequent period. Given the limited share taken by the real component of savings in the last 20–25 years, almost all of the involuntary accumulation of savings is likely to have been in the form of financial, and specifically monetary, assets. During the second half of the 1980s (not before) continued price controls, coupled with an increasingly inadequate supply of goods relative to nominal household and enterprise incomes, stimulated the accumulation of a substantial amount of unspent purchasing power held in the form of monetary assets.

Cottarelli and Blejer (1992) argue that the money-to-income ratio should be interpreted as a wealth-to-income ratio if money is the main store of wealth. The extent to which an increase in this ratio signals disequilibrium will therefore have to be assessed against the factors influencing the desired wealth-to-income ratio. An analysis of repressed inflation in the Soviet Union should start from an evaluation of forced saving and undesired wealth accumulation. It is revealed by panel data that the savings rate in the Soviet Union in 1965–85 remained approximately stable at a level close to 6 per cent for about two decades. Only in the second half of the 1980s did this rate start to rise rapidly.

Evaluation of excess money holdings requires a comparison between desired and actual wealth, or in terms of flows, between desired and actual saving. Cottarelli and Blejer (1992) estimate a consumption function on annual data between the mid-1960s and the mid-1980s. Their dynamic error-correction model involves long-run stability between consumption and total (human and non-human) wealth of Soviet households. That desired consumption and actual consumption were equal means there was no overhang. The estimated consumption function presents a high degree of parameter stability during the sample period. Cottarelli and Blejer also show that around the middle of the 1980s the stable relationship between consumption and wealth broke down as actual consumption consistently fell short of projected consumption. They attribute this development primarily to macroeconomic rationing in the consumer goods market. By cumulating the difference between desired and actual consumption, they also estimate that about 170–190 billion roubles of undesired wealth was being held in the Soviet Union at the end of 1990.

Czechoslovakia   According to Drabek *et al.* (1992), open inflation has been relatively insignificant over the last ten to twenty years. Rather suppressed, hidden inflation has been more typical for all sectors of the economy. In addition, overall macroeconomic disequilibrium has been much less pronounced than in other Eastern European countries and the former Soviet Union. Inflationary pressures were translated partly into open inflation until full price liberalisation in January 1991.

It is interesting to examine their explanation of the low inflation level. Firstly, in the interwar period Czechoslovakia had a tradition of tight monetary discipline (Kaser and Radice, 1985), and this tradition was continued in the centrally planned period. The tight financial policy has been demonstrated, for example, throughout the post-war period, including the 1980s, by strict wage policy reflected in relatively tight control of wages and other incomes. This can be verified by Czechoslovakia's relative success in keeping the growth of wages below the rate of growth of labour productivity. In 1985 the ratio of growth of wages to growth of productivity was only 0.51. The corresponding figures for 1986 and 1987 were 0.44 and 0.76, respectively. The loosening of central control in 1988 and 1989 resulted in convergence of both growth rates – the respective figures were 1.00 for 1988, and 0.99 for 1989. Even in these years, however, the growth of wages did not exceed the growth rate of labour productivity, thanks to a mix of direct and indirect control over the growth of incomes (ibid.)

These two cases show that if prices and wages are both under control, given no external shocks there is no reason for forced saving and monetary overhang to be chronic. In a stylised CPE the planners are able to control inflation directly through wage and price control. If the model is fundamentally changed, there must be something else to control the situation.

CPEs or RCPEs?

Some Western economists, together with some of their CPE counterparts, often bracket CPEs with RCPEs, in spite of the fact that great changes have taken place in the latter. There is a clear distinction between CPEs and RCPEs.

Pooling data makes Dengism equal to Maoism

Peebles never makes a clear distinction between RCPEs and CPEs. Yet he wants not only to review the past, but also to predict the future, so that his two books may offer guidance to RCPEs. He 'firmly believe[s] that any explanation of the relationship between money and prices and other variables should be shown to be supported by quantitative analysis over a long period' (Peebles, 1991a, p. 4). However the fundamental changes in Eastern Europe and China have been under way for only fifteen years. China started comprehensive reforms in 1979. Some similar reforming steps in Eastern Europe and the Soviet Union came even later. By 'fundamental changes' we mean the systematic transformation of a CPE into a non-CPE, with an economy based significantly on market mechanisms. The changes were so fast in China in the 1980s and 1990s and in Eastern Europe at the end of the 1980s and the beginning of the 1990s that the economic nature of these RCPEs is radically different from that of CPEs, though some of the economies may still be considered somewhat distant from the market model in certain respects.

Therefore it is impossible to discuss important current issues in the RCPEs or predict their future by conducting quantitative analysis over a long period. An RCPE may have removed its original budget constraint and released economic control, causing serious disequilibrium and excess demand or shortage when market disciplines were not properly applied in transition. This is likely to be the reason why Portes and Winter (1980) only extended their data base from 1955 to 1975, and why Portes *et al.* (1987) restricted their study of the Polish case to the period up to 1980. Unlike Birman (1980a) and Birman and Clarke (1985), they did not address the question of future events. Since then, however, more and more reforming policies have been implemented, changing the situation and the CPE model dramatically.

But this caution is mistakenly thought of as weakness (Peebles, 1991a, p. 127). Peebles based his theory heavily on the assumption of stable behaviour on the part of planners (ibid., p. 176). He pooled data on money, output, prices and money holdings in China for the period 1952–85. Even though his Figure 2.1 presents radical upturns in many important time series (such as currency in circulation, savings deposits held by households, cash holdings and their proportions over the annual value of retail sales respectively, since the end of the 1970s) (ibid., p. 12), he still agrees with J. C. H. Chai that the reforms had modified the economy but had 'not changed the basic characteristics of the Chinese economic system'. He cites Kueh's argument (1989, 1990) that much of the Maoist development strategy remained in Dengism, and then bravely states: 'For analytical purposes it is acceptable to assume that the economic and monetary systems were fundamentally the same during the entire period 1953–85' (Peebles, 1991a, p. 44). By further extending the period under study, his book on China becomes an 'examination of money in the People's Republic of China over the period 1949–88' (ibid., p. 1). In this respect he has made a crucial error in pooling data.[11] It is worth mentioning that many economists and econometricians have adopted the same procedure.

Ignoring the far-reaching effects of many important reforming steps, including the establishment of the two-tier banking system in China just before 1985, Peebles follows the above assumption to 'apply the same approach for the entire period' (ibid., p. 6), extending this framework to the Chinese case to cover the even longer period to the end of the 1980s. He informs readers (ibid., p. 126, emphasis added) that '*even in the 1980s*, Chinese officials distrusted money'. The Chinese monetary authorities held a continued preference for withdrawing currency from circulation by selling more commodities, rather than changing prices or interest rates (see Fry, 1993). From this, Peebles finds that 'the dominant paradigm of Western monetary economics, the Quantity Theory of Money, is inapplicable to China' (Peebles, 1991a, p. 6). The intention is to avoid an excessively simple application of Western economic concepts and models to RCPEs, but the underlying logic behind this conclusion is questionable.

The institutional surface hides the fundamental transformation in RCPEs

The Chineses economy as a whole is undergoing a gradual reform process, although the reforms in the agricultural sector are very radical. The problem with Peebles' discussion of the institutional setting is a lack of dynamic assessment. He begins Chapter 4 (1991a) with an analysis of institutions and policies. The developments he assesses took place in the period 1952–85, mainly before the fundamental reforms. Peebles would rather set China within the institutional framework of the centrally planned model, although the changes following reform have been substantial.

For example, a significant amount of monetary flow has been shifted from the budget to the credit system; direct profit collection from the SOEs has been replaced by taxation; and the deposits of the household sector have become more important than enterprise deposits on the liabilities side of the balance sheet. Market mechanisms have become the foundation of the economy. The 'two spheres of monetary circulation' noticed by many economists are now being integrated in urban areas. It would be misleading to overstress the institutional framework, ignoring significant functional changes beneath the surface. In Eastern Europe, reformers have paid too much attention to changing the external institutional structure, such as choosing the appropriate form of banking system or reforming ownership patterns, and too little attention to the reconstruction of internal functions and mechanisms (Corbett and Mayer, 1991). This is another major difference between China and some RCPEs.

As Peebles notes (1991a, pp. 211–12), since the adoption of the new approach to Chinese development at the end of 1978, fundamental reforms have taken place in the following areas: the agricultural system, including its terms of trade; the wage system; the price system; international trade; the foreign exchange system; government bond markets; the urban economic system, especially the reform of SOEs; and financial reforms, including the budget system and the banking system. All these contributed to a situation in which 'urban and rural markets flourished' in China (ibid., p. 211). Open inflation has replaced suppressed inflation. Interest rate policy has been used increasingly (see above Chapter 4). The new RCPE model is based not on central planning, but on an increasingly developed market system. All the assumptions held in the CPE model, such as central planning controls over prices and wages, and the separation of household money, have been removed completely.

One of the basic economic reforms in the RCPEs from the very beginning has been to give enterprises and farmers more autonomy, which means fewer quantitative directive plans. China has reduced those plans year by year. Already in the mid-1980s, about 50 per cent of goods, including producer goods and consumer goods, were free of state control. Agricultural products were purchased by the state wholly according to contracts, without any quantitative plan enforcing purchases. The number of industrial products planned by the state was reduced from 120 to 60, with the proportion of their value in gross industrial output reduced from

40 per cent to 17 per cent by 1987. The number of consumption goods with central plans was reduced from 188 to just 25. At the end of the 1980s about 90 per cent of goods were already subject to market prices. By 1993 the number of so-called mandatorily planned products of industries had been reduced to 36, the proportion of their value in gross industrial SOE output being just 6.5 per cent. The number of industrial products controlled by plans has been reduced to 25 per cent.[12] Many important daily necessities, such as food, oil, soy sauce, vinegar and milk and so on, have been completely freed from price control.[13] How then can China still be considered a planned economy?

Peebles' PPI approach could be an interesting means of analysing the monetary mechanisms under the hypothesis of excess demand. However one should be careful in applying this to an RCPE. In an RCPE context, the assumption of fixed prices has been removed. Peebles is wrong in stating that 'list price increases became a general feature of policy in the 1980s', when so many commodities are not on the listing. Similarly, it is not justifiable simply to set CPE institutional features as given for the current Chinese economy, and then to concentrate on purchasing power developments as the prime determinant of currency growth and retail price changes (ibid., pp. 218–19).

Peebles continues to use the same doubtful methods of simple econometric regressions to demonstrate a further test of the PPI theory for China in the 1980s, using only 11 observations. Four of the five regressions have DW statistics of less than 0.9. Although more sophisticated econometric techniques are not necessarily advised here, the correlation results obtained from pooling data series covering either 1953–85 or 1953–88 are very doubtful because at least two fundamental structural changes took place during these two periods – the Cultural Revolution and the reforms. His regressions take no account of structural changes.[14] I am sure that adding dummy variables does make a difference. Therefore Peebles' conclusion that the relationships he identified (1991a, Ch. 6) hold for the period until 1988 has not been proven convincingly.

Criticisms of the quantity theory lead to the necessity of monetary control being ignored

Peebles' discussion of money supply changes is based on the studies of some Chinese economists. These pertain to the mid-1980s, however, when the mechanism of money supply determination was also being changed. For example, his Equation 5 (ibid., p. 107) no longer holds when the wage incomes of enterprises in the countryside and towns and self-employed people in the informal sector are increased radically. Therefore traditional control methods, such as commodity *hueilong*[15] and the nature of the money supply mechanism argued by Peebles in Chapter 4 (ibid.), have to be altered. If the new method is insufficiently effective, means of planning control such as currency *hueilong* may still be unavoidable. As commodity sales contribute to about 70 per cent of total currency *hueilong*,[16] it is wise for planners and the monetary authorities to regard this mechanism as an important factor when determining the money supply, especially currency in circulation.

A basic theme of Peebles' book is that 'the Quantity Theory is an inappropriate mental framework for thinking about the relationship between money and prices in China.' In support, he points out that increased nominal expenditure can reduce the narrow money supply; and that money wages and other variables determining nominal income are not just passively determined in a competitive market, thus adjusting to prior exogenous money changes (ibid. p. 218).[17] But this situation in China can be and is being changed by reforms that have brought about increasingly flexible prices. The variables determining nominal income, especially wages and bonuses, can be brought under market control by adopting a hard budget constraint. Therefore the stability of demand for real balances is the main requirement for the feasibility of the quantity theory.

According to Xie Ping (Ma *et al.*, 1990, pp. 607–8), the traditional formula used by the People's Bank of China before 1979 to predict the demand for M0 was the planned total amount of social commodity retail sales divided by velocity (V), which was obviously based on the quantity theory. Since the economic reforms there have been five methods of prediction, among which the basic econometric formula is exactly the same as that of the quantity theory, that is, $M = PT/V$, though there are different ways of calculating V.

As the RCPEs are laying the foundations of markets, and market mechanisms are already functioning, though imperfectly, there is no reason why some suitable Western methodologies and Western economics should not be applied to the RCPEs, although such application requires careful modification and explanation. Peebles himself has done some work based on Western economic theories, including the quantity theory (Peebles, 1991a, pp. 76–82; 1991b, pp. 80–9).[18]

Another important weakness of Peebles' approach is that he ignores the contribution of enterprise deposits to money in contemporary China. These have been the biggest component of broad money, though they are being challenged by the increase in household deposits. Byrd (1983) remarkably stressed the contribution of the decentralised banking system to inflation in China at the very beginning of the economic reform. Because the banking system has replaced the state budget in financing the economy, the increase in deposits has a multiplier effect in increasing money supply, a mechanism well described by Western monetary theory. But this cannot be underestimated. Excess demand in post-reform China has often been generated by investment booms fired by either overambitious plans or the expansionary thirst of enterprises (a kind of 'animal spirits'?) It was only after the 1970s that household deposits became increasingly important to broad money. Focusing on the very narrow measure of 'money' (M0) also ignores the determinants of money from the supply side. Marketisation of the Chinese economy and decentralisation of the production system have made money active. Broader measures for money supply, including enterprise deposits, should be used (see the experiment in Chapter 6 below).

What is the financial crisis?

A 'sound' reason why Peebles supports the chronic-excess-demand hypothesis was the existence of so-called financial crises in East Germany and the Soviet Union (Peebles, 1991b, pp. 5, 72–3). The 'financial crisis itself' was the 'only evidence' enabling him 'to judge' between the Shortage School and the Disequilibrium School (Peebles, 1991a, p. 126). He did not analyse the reasons behind the financial crises and what these crises actually revealed, but simply stated 'it is hard to accept that this was due just to temporary excess demands and irrational relative prices' (Peebles, 1991b, pp. 72–3). He claims vindication of the predictions of crisis made by Birman (1980a) and Birman and Clark (1985), and complains that some leading economists in socialist economies have ignored Birman's important findings regarding the possibility of financial crisis after the reform.

Birman (1983, 1988) cites evidence of the declining effectiveness of monetary incentives and falling productivity in the Soviet Union. He predicted collapse, defined as falling output, and the fall of the communist regime. Of course anti-communist parties predicted collapse all the time (Birman, 1980b, pp. 590–1). His work 'had no theoretical foundation', but assumed 'a very simple indicator' supposing (untested) sustained excess demand (Peebles, 1991a, p. 124). Some economists strongly reject Birman's cumulative disequilibrium hypothesis (Pickersgill, 1976, 1980; Rosefielde, 1988, pp. 227–8, 231; Nove, 1988; Farrell, 1989; Ofer, 1991; Cottarelli and Blejer, 1992), concluding that 'neither neoclassical theory nor the preponderance of the evidence at present validate his surmise' (Rosefielde, 1988, pp. 234–5).

By financial crisis, Peebles means 'the situation when the government adopts policies to abandon the traditional Soviet monetary system or when it adopts policies the traditional system was designed to make unnecessary' (Peebles, 1991b, p. 1). This definition is arbitrary and does not make sense. Modifying systems or changing policies is one of the main functions of any authority. The economy is developing dynamically. It would be dangerous for a government to maintain the same policy package and stick to one kind of institution without any (fundamental) adjustment. If it does, crisis will surely follow.

According to the Shortage School, the CPE system is essentially wrong. Without 'fundamental changes' of the non-workable CPE into a market economy, the problems cannot be solved. Therefore financial crisis should not only be an inevitable consequence, but also a logical solution to the problems of the model. Here both the Shortage School and Peebles oversimplify the situation.

Far more complicated causes, both economic and political ones as well as the well-known problem of rigidity, led the CPE systems to change fundamentally. However we cannot say that the changes themselves are financial crises simply because they are not 'part of the traditional system'. Otherwise, how could we explain so many reforms in the past, such as those in the 1980s, and how could we explain the relatively successful reforms, including banking reforms, in socialist China? It is not impossible for a socialist economy to solve by reforms those problems that once concerned Birman (1980b), such as the opportunities for household investment, insurance against casualties and monetary incentives to secure agricultural sales to the state.

The policies of deep financial reform were adopted far later than the general economic reform policies in almost all the RCPEs. For example the two-tier banking system was established in China five years after the start of the economic reform. Similar changes occurred even later in Hungary (1987), Poland (1988) and Czechoslovakia (1991), and the financial crises described by Peebles all coincided with or immediately succeeded periods when these economies were adopting radical reform programmes. Peebles indicates that the financial crisis definition 'clearly' applied to East Germany when it abandoned its own currency in July 1990. In October 1990 Gorbachev adopted the last stage of his two-year, four-stage reform programme, calling for full convertibility of the rouble. Poland in 1990 and Czechoslovakia in 1991 made their currencies convertible just as Hungary was doing likewise. Actually the 'financial crises', in terms of inflationary pressure, in the Soviet Union started in 1987–8 after Gorbachev (1) restricted vodka, thereby cutting tax revenues;

(2) started the process of excessive investment; and (3) decentralised some investment and wage setting. In Poland, high inflation began in 1988. All these 'crises' imply that there must be some causal factors behind the events.

Why does serious monetary overhang occur?

The IMF's (1991) econometric work on forced saving and repressed inflation in the former Soviet Union confirms that the relationship between observed consumption and the regressors in the equations progressively broke down in the second half of the 1980s. Enormous monetary overhang started to accumulate. The absence of chronic excess demand under the CPE framework suggests that many Eastern bloc economies had shifted to a situation where excess demand and serious shortage coexisted. Why?

The Soviet Union

Reform turned the extremely centralised Soviet Union into an extremely decentralised region. After the liberalisation of the banking system, over 1000 banks were created by enterprises and local governments, and they were independent of the central bank. The banks in the newly independent states had the right to create rouble-denominated Russian bank money. Money supply became out of control, and excess demand became a serious problem immediately following the weakening of financial discipline and banking control.

The following financial disorders were experienced. First, prices did not discipline enterprises when their transactions and accounts were monetised. When combined with the demand for inputs by newly created private and cooperative enterprises, and with the existing sellers' market in producer goods, this situation turned a sector with a manageable physical disequilibrium into a narrow market with a significant excess monetary demand (Ofer, 1991). Second, the partial liberalisation of the banking system added to monetary expansion without an adequate expansion of production (Bunich, 1988; Bochkov, 1989; Levchuk, 1989; McKinnon, 1989a, 1989b). Low and even negative real interest rates added nothing to borrower discipline. Banks were forced to grant unreasonable amounts of credit to the wrong clients (Ofer, 1991). Third, there was a clear general tendency among SOEs to allow far higher wage increases than were justified by the additional contribution to production. The total nominal wage fund increased by 7.1 per cent in 1988 and

8.4 per cent in 1989 (Zoteyev, 1989, p. 23) with little effect on production. Finally, in the highly monopolistic structure of the Soviet production sector with irrational prices, firms chased profits by shifting production away from low-profit products towards high-profit ones at the expense of macroeconomic interests. With no significant hardening of the budget constraint by the authorities, and no serious challenge from markets and competition, agents found it easier to simulate success and avoid failure rather than perform according to the real intentions of their principals. The goals, signals and rules of the game became less clear and at times erratic (Ofer, 1991).

The former Soviet Union has also experienced an interenterprise debt explosion in recent years (Table 5.3). Between 1 January and 30 April 1992 interenterprise debt in Russia grew from a few dozen billion roubles to 1800 billion roubles, the equivalent of GNP for the first four months of the year, according to a Russian government report to the IMF. Roughly the same relationship between interenterprise debt and GDP was observed in Latvia in June 1992, suggesting that in both countries about half of all transactions were not being paid for. By the end of June interenterprise debt in Russia had reached 3000 billion roubles. In the first six months of 1992, in nominal terms it increased almost 100 times, and the real increase was about eight and a half times, while the ratio of interenterprise debt to bank credit increased from almost zero to over two (Rostowski, 1993).

Table 5.3   Credit and interenterprise arrears in Russia, 1992
(billions of rubles)

End of month	Nominal bank credit	Real bank credit	Nominal arrears	Real arrears	Arrears/ bank credit
12/1991	450	450	39	39	0.078
1/1992	510	148	141	41	0.277
2/1992	700	147	390	82	0.558
3/1992	920	149	800	129	0.870
4/1992	1050	139	1800	239	1.710
5/1992	1050	125	2050	243	1.952
6/1992	1400	140	3000	299	2.143
7/1992	2300	207	1190	107	0.517

Source: Russian Centre for Economic Reform.

CSFR

The evolution of events in Czechoslovakia in 1990–1 differed completely from the development in the second half of the 1980s. The new government started the transition to a market economy in early 1990. The policy of price liberalisation, the deep devaluation and the severe exogenous shocks after the break-up of COMECON and the collapse of the Soviet Union fuelled price increases by 10 per cent in 1990 and 57.9 per cent in 1991. The 1.8 per cent decrease in GDP in 1990 was followed by a record 15.1 per cent fall in 1991 and a further 8.5 per cent decrease in 1992. GDP in real terms in 1992 was only 75 per cent of its 1989 level.

Besides some macroeconomic problems similar to the above Russian case, constraints in the banking sphere were important. In 1990, almost all banks were severely undercapitalised and at the same time burdened with inherited non-performing loans and/or credits extended at artificially low interest rates. According to Hrncir (1993), after the start of the transition in 1991, one quarter to one third of outstanding loans were estimated to be either bad, non-performing or carrying a high risk. The non-performing and risky loans were not confined to domestic clients.

Substantial increases in interenterprise loans were registered in 1981–2 and again in 1987, when the monetary authorities tried to tighten credit policies. An unprecedentedly sharp increase developed, however, from the second half of 1990. The trend accelerated even further in the course of 1991 and at the beginning of 1992. At the end of 1991 the identified sum of interenterprise indebtedness amounted to CSK170 billion, the equivalent of 25 per cent of total bank credits extended to enterprises; 4723 firms from a total of 11 043 (43 per cent) were in arrears in their payments to other firms. The volume continued to increase in the course of 1992, peaking at around CSK250 billion (ibid.) In Czechoslovakia, interenterprise debt constituted about 18 per cent of GDP at the end of 1991, double that of the beginning of the year (Table 5.4). There was no doubt that mass interenterprise arrears, coupled with bad loans in bank portfolios and credit contract failures, were a destabilising factor that hindered the transition.

The above examples suggest that it was financial disorders, or a lack of financial control, that caused the increasing amount of monetary overhang.

China

Liu (1991) finds two periods of excess demand in China both of which occurred during periods of financial disorder (except a subperiod of natural disaster in 1960–2 with the supply constraint dominant). The Great Leap Forward period (around 1958) was characterised by overambitious

Table 5.4   Credit and interenterprise arrears in CSFR, 1989–91
(billions of crowns)

End of month	Nominal bank credit	Real bank credit	Nominal arrears	Real arrears	Arrears/ banks credit
12/1989	578	578	7	7	0.012
03/1990	569	569	11	11	0.019
06/1990	579	579	14	14	0.024
09/1990	588	588	28	28	0.048
12/1990	583	490	54	45	0.093
03/1991	618	358	77	53	0.125
06/1991	664	367	123	68	0.185
09/1991	694	391	147	83	0.212
12/1991	732	407	155	86	0.212

Sources: Begg and Portes (1993).

plans and investment thirst. As Peebles noted, changes in the monetary system in China in the 1980s were moderate. China merely 'modified' its banking system, with the state-owned specialised banks remaining as its banking base. The existence of such a state-owned banking system and the policies as a whole could not be termed a 'financial crisis' in accordance with Peebles' definition. The reason for the financial imbalances was the release of financial control without compensatory support by other means; in other words a control vacuum was left by the removal of central planning and radical changes to the corporate governance structure. It was after decentralisation of the systems (including the monetary system after the radical changes in the 1980s) that problems such as lack of regulation, indiscipline and soft budget constraints occurred, exacerbated by imperfectly functioning market mechanisms.

Financial crisis and financial control

Chapter 4 compared the original CPE banking system with the reformed version, and it answered why problems were prevented with the help of the centralised banking system in the unreformed model, why certain problems occurred after the reforms and why banking systems should be kept under control during transition.

Financial crises should be generally absent from the CPE model because planners were able to balance and control, and bankers were able to monitor firms' budget constraints (see Chapter 1). Even during the Chinese 'three-years of natural disasters' (1960–2) and the Cultural Revolution (1966–76) there had been no such crises. Bank runs were also absent. Burkett and Lotspeich (1992) criticise McKinnon's (1991) financial prescriptions for the RCPEs by indicating that RCPE reforms present a new array of financial policy problems and that financial control during marketisation involves a unique set of political–economic problems.

It is widely held in the literature that the financial crises resulted from a complex set of factors, notably fiscal deficits and collapse of the money-to-GNP ratio (not in the case of China), along with loss of control. The previous chapters have discussed at length the patterns of growth and income distribution, interest rate policy and so on. Sachs and Woo (1994) and McKinnon (1993a), from different perspectives, both observe that, unlike in Eastern Europe and the former Soviet Union, China's fiscal deficits and bank credit expansion have not resulted in explosive inflation largely because households have greatly increased their real money balances. There is no space for us to discuss further the factors accounting for the increase in savings, interest rate policy or income growth. However inflation became the main problem after the turmoil in 1989. Inflation stood at 14.7 per cent in 1993, soaring to 24.1 per cent in 1994.

McKinnon (1993b) analyses financial control under classical socialism, which prevented the macroeconomy from inflation, and points out that it was during transition that financial control broke down. 'The ability of the reform government to collect taxes and control the supply of money and credit is unwittingly undermined by the liberalisation itself' (ibid., p. 223). Losing central control over firms leads from microeconomic disorders into macroeconomic chaos.

According to the Shortage School (Kornai, 1980; Winiecki, 1985; and so on), the 'soft budget constraint' is a structural feature of CPEs. If this is correct, why did it not have these inflationary consequences before 1986 in the Soviet Union, before the end of the 1980s in Hungary, or at all in Czechoslovakia until 1990? No evidence can be found to support the chronic-excess-demand hypothesis. There was no significant excess demand in Hungary nor rapid inflation until the end of the 1980s. The 'soft budget constraint' appeared there *after* relaxation of bank controls! The question is whether it operated in respect of wage payments leading to inflation before the financial 'reforms'.

Financial crisis can be caused by lack of financial discipline, regulation and control. It is a special economic situation in transitional RCPEs. This in turn can actually cause excess demand and serious shortages, since the original hard budget constraint has been removed at the institutional level. Peebles notes such control problems in his two books. Unfortunately he does not recognise these as the real causes of the financial crisis. Instead, chronic excess demand is blamed as the cause. In fact excess demand is only a surface phenomenon, beneath which financial disorders exist.

For the micro-level institutions of RCPEs, the softening of the budget constraint has made it easy to generate serious economic problems such as investment hunger and wage/bonus over-expansion. This requires variety of regulations to strengthen financial discipline. The experience of the reforming economies taught the reformers a valuable lesson: when the production system is decentralised, the banking system should not simply follow, but should be placed under careful control so long as the production system is not subject to market discipline. Actually the experience of some successful banking models shows that successful banking systems are those that are controlled and help to control (see above Chapter 4). Financial control and regulation may help to solve disorder and inflation problems and restore stabilisation in RCPEs.

Summary

The Shortage School, whose arguments Peebles advocates in his books, misunderstands the CPE model. The Disequilibrium School understands the management power of planners, at least in consumption, and emphasises the support of data evidence for hypothesis testing. The Disequilibrium School may have relied too much on econometrics, which by itself is not sufficiently illuminating. Chinese economists have not unanimously accepted the chronic-excess-demand hypothesis. By removing the preconception of chronic excess demand, they have tested the hypothesis in different ways and have not necessarily relied so heavily on econometrics. Some of the results challenge the hypothesis of 'generalised excess real demand' in the state productive sector, which is accepted by Disequilibrium writers (Portes, 1989). The hypothesis could have been undermined fundamentally if China had not experienced chronic excess demand in the production sector. Further and more comprehensive investigation into the model is strongly recommended.

Both Peebles and the Shortage School tend to define 'financial crisis' inaccurately, thereby overlooking financial control mechanisms during transition. Certain radical policy changes cannot simply be regarded as the crisis of the previous system. The real crisis is represented by financial disorders caused by the lack of certain control mechanisms and financial disciplines within the new system during transition. A review of some important debates between the Disequilibrium School and the Shortage School has made the crucial argument clear: financial crisis is essentially a kind of financial disorder caused by lack of financial discipline and control. Therefore, besides improving the newly established market systems, financial control and regulation may help to solve the problem and restore stabilisation.

The Chinese authorities have been more cautious than the inexperienced Eastern European governments when selecting policies. This does not necessarily mean that Western or modern theories have been useless to the reformers. To the contrary, the market foundation being established there may form an economic basis that is fundamentally identical to that of market economies, so Eastern reformers can use modern Western economic theories. But planning should not be simply abandoned. Nowadays all economies have controllers, just as all economies have bankers. If planning and market mechanisms are combined properly in suitable forms, Byrd's concern about the problem of controlling inflation in a situation of increasing savings deposits can be gradually removed (Byrd, 1983, p. 74).

In short, it can be argued that (1) the chronic-excess-demand hypothesis has by no means been shown to be correct; (2) the work of chronic excess demand will have difficulty in translating micro behaviour (soft budget constraints, investment hunger and so on) into macro phenomena (permanent shortages, chronic excess demand and so on) so long as it does not explain the determination of money demand at the aggregate level (the roles of planners and households); (3) important differences between CPEs and RCPEs in terms of the nature and functioning of economic institutions should not be overlooked; and (4) financial crises in CPEs/RCPEs are outcomes of a set of complex factors (notably the decontrolling of the financial and banking systems) that are not reducible to chronic excess demand. These arguments are supported by evidence from China and the former Eastern bloc countries.

As far as econometrics is concerned, models and regressions should be separate for CPEs and RCPEs; that is, it is wise to separate the data base for reforming periods from that for unreformed periods. As the reforming period is so short, econometrics may run the risk of limited power of explanation due to some structural changes and the lack of observations. Some econometric regressions in Peebles' books are based on very limited observations and few tests. Although empirical econometrics should not necessarily be sophisticated, his econometrics is insufficient and the empirical findings are therefore difficult to interpret. Simple graphs may be more useful than regressions. Quarterly or monthly data, therefore, are recommended in the case of China.

CONCLUSIONS

This chapter has discussed macroeconomic issues in terms of a theoretical simplification, and argued with the theories put forward by the Shortage School. The main argument is that the disorder costs of decentralising the banking system during transition should be recognised, and that these can be higher than administrative costs. Ignoring this could jeopardise reform programmes. Both Peebles and the Shortage School inaccurately define 'financial crisis', thus overlooking financial control mechanisms during transition. A review of some important debates between the Disequilibrium School and the Shortage School has made the crucial argument clear: financial crisis is essentially a kind of financial disorder caused by lack of financial discipline and control. Therefore strengthened administrative measures, besides market mechanisms, financial control and regulation, may help to solve the problem and restore stability.

Foreign investors are strongly recommended to adopt long-term strategies in their dealings with emerging RCPEs. Great effort should be made to cooperate with local authorities and entrepreneurs to bring about a well-designed corporate governance structure and a healthy national environment for economic development.

APPENDIX 5.1: THE COST FUNCTION

Against the theoretical background developed in this chapter, a cost function can be illuminated by the following analytical framework. The total costs of an economy, C_t, are assumed to be a combination of administrative costs, C_m, and disorder costs, C_d. The former could be the administrative expenditure of the state budget. The latter could be variety of variables, such as the extra-ordinary costs of producers due to a financial disorder, which could also be caused indirectly by inflation. Therefore,

$$C_t = C_m + C_d \tag{5.1}$$

The degree of the disorder, K, rests on the situation of the market environment, λ, and the management costs, C_m:

$$K = K (\lambda, C_m). \tag{5.2}$$

Our arguments in this chapter show that λ, the efficiency situation of the market environment, is relatively poor in transitional RCPEs in comparison with mature market economies. This assumption has been justified by our studies. Obviously from this assumption, $\partial K/\partial \lambda < 0$, $\partial K/\partial C_m < 0$, and $\partial^2 K/(\partial \lambda \partial C_m) > 0$.

Meanwhile the disorder costs are closely related to the degree of disorder of the economy. That is,

$$C_d = C_d(K) \tag{5.3}$$

$$C'_d(K) > 0$$

The following equation is developed,

$$\partial C_t/\partial C_m = 1 + C'_d(K) * (\partial K/C_m) \tag{5.4}$$

Equation 5.4 indicates that the change in the total costs of the economy relative to the increase in management costs is determined by two factors: $C'_d(K)$ and $(\delta K/\partial C_m)$, where K's increase will lead C_d to increase, while the increase of ∂C_m leads ∂K to decrease. Obviously,

$$C'_d(K) * (\partial K/\partial C_m) < 0 \tag{5.5}$$

Therefore, with the *inefficient* market assumption, the negative value of Equation 5.5 would be high enough to reduce the result of Equation 5.4, especially in a chaotic situation. This means that an increase in administrative costs would decelerate the total costs of the economy. That is:

$$\partial C_t/\partial C_m = 1 + C'_d(K) * (\partial K/\partial C_m) < 0 \tag{5.6}$$

Equation 5.4 with the *perfect* market assumption may produce the opposite result.

6 Modelling Money Demand and Supply in China: Dealing with a Small Sample Size

That which has been proved by tests cannot be undermined. However, that which has been proved by theoretical studies cannot be established as a theory if it has not been proved by tests (Professor Ding Zhaozhong, winner of the Nobel Prize for Physics, translated from his original Chinese speech in Nanjing, 5 July 1992).

INTRODUCTION

Monetary policy is important to a market economy. It therefore becomes important to RCPEs when central planning is increasingly replaced by market mechanisms. Chapter 1 implied that monetary control can be both possible and successful in a CPE when implemented directly by planners from both the demand side (wage control) and the supply side (credit planning). Chapters 2 and 4 showed, however, that once decentralisation reforms have taken place, control is questionable. Chapters 3 and 5 argued from a theoretical point of view that market mechanisms, typically interest rate mechanisms, may not be so reliable during transition and therefore monetary control has to be implemented from both the demand side and the supply side by all possible means.

The effectiveness of monetary control depends on the existence and stability of an appropriate demand function for money (and other factors). Therefore this chapter presents and evaluates econometric evidence on money holding functions in China.

It is widely noted that a disparity exists between the practice of applied econometrics and the econometric methodology that is taught. Therefore it is useful to construct a framework that takes account of practical, theoretical and econometric considerations using the criteria of relevance, consistency and adequacy (Pesaran and Smith, 1985). Since Goldfeld (1976) brought widespread attention to the poor predictive performance of the standard demand for money function in the West, a large volume of literature has introduced new variables and/or transformations of the old ones (Cuthbertson, 1991), and both standard and empirical models have been questioned (see Appendix 6.1).

In the literature on modelling the demand for money there has been a considerable dispute about the relative importance of fit (R^2, significant coefficients, passing misspecification tests) and the theoretical interpretation of the various models (for example see the dispute between Hendry and Ericsson (1991) and Friedman and Schwartz, in Hendry and Ericsson, 1991). In fact Cooley and LeRoy (1981) argue that, by choosing appropriate additional variables, one can get almost any coefficient one wants. There is also evidence that equations that are obtained by 'data mining' have good fits and significant coefficients, but forecast poorly. To avoid these problems a different strategy can be adopted. A number of theoretically derived models are estimated in all the measures of money: a multivariate rather than a univariate regression model can be used. This not only allows us to evaluate the sensitivity of the results to the measure of money used, but also to make comparative judgements of the plausibility of coefficients between measures.

Modelling the demand for money in China is still at a primitive stage. Chow (1987) estimates a simple money demand function derived from quantity theory. Using annual data (1952–83) Chow concludes that the quantity theory 'provides a reasonable first approximation' in explaining the demand for money in China (ibid., p. 325). Portes and Santorum (1987) use a more general specification with currency and a measure that includes savings deposits, to test the homogeneity of the demand for money with respect to price level and real income. They argue that currency is the preferable measure. Feltenstein and Farhadian (1987) find that demand for real balances, defined as the broader measure, is a function of real income and expected inflation.

The previous studies suffer from two common shortcomings. One is merging the prereform period with the reform period, which ignores the fundamental changes that have taken place within the Chinese economic system, so the conclusions drawn are often misleading. A typical example is the claim that the Chinese economic system in the 1980s was fundamentally the same as in the prereform period (Peebles, 1991a). The institutional changes and structural shifts of the data forced Ma (1993) and Yi (1993) to conduct structural adjustments. Hafer and Kutan (1994) use Chinese data to suggest that M2 provides a long-run guide to monetary policy that is consistent with recent results using US data, in spite of the fact that their economic and financial systems are vastly different. The other short coming is the lack of systematic assessment in most previous studies of the demand for money in China. By using a single equation, or by a simple comparison between two equations, the studies try to judge whether narrow money or broad money is the preferable measure. The first shortcoming relates to the second. The sensitivity of the models to small sample size, with limited observations, forces the modellers to rely heavily on data mining. Advanced methods may obtain some excellent test results that, however, may be still unconvincing (see also Appendix 5.2).

In this chapter a systematic approach is adopted in order to examine

1. The influences on the alternative measures of money in China.
2. The use of levels and first differences.
3. The influences of money supply shocks.
4. The benefits of using disaggregated transaction measures.

We shall use identical theoretically derived models for different measures, and use the data base covering the reform period only. Because of the shortness of the period, possible data deficiencies and structural changes over the period, the results can only be indicative. However the application of a range of theoretical models will illustrate the likely factors influencing monetary control and how China has controlled money in order to achieve cautious but rapid economic growth and a relatively stable price movement. Having discovered the essential economic dynamics, the relationship between demand for money and supply of money in conducting stabilisation policies can be understood, and this helps us to discuss the possibility of monetary control by the banking system.

This approach does not include data-instigated 'specification searches' of the Hendry form. It focuses on examining how well the theoretical models perform in explaining all the measures of money, rather than experimenting with ad hoc specifications to obtain good fit and significant coefficients.

THE THEORY

Before turning to the model it must be made clear how monetary policy has been conducted in China and what main factors affect monetary control. Similar questions, but with respect to the West, are discussed by Cooley and LeRoy (1981) and summarised in Appendix 6.1.[1]

How has monetary policy been conducted in China?

Though the final objectives of monetary policies in an RCPE are similar to those in a market economy, for example price stabilisation and/or economic growth, monetary policy in the former may have a different content or emphasis. This is because the economic situation is different and policy is determined by the effectiveness of the instruments chosen rather than by any theoretical soundness. Though price stabilisation may be more important to a central bank in the West than in a CPE, planned economic growth with fixed prices was more important to the latter. Price stabilisation has become increasingly important to the RCPEs, simply because inflation was their most serious problem immediately after the introduction of market mechanisms. Current debate in China centres on whether the People's Bank should still have economic growth on its agenda. The central bank has been aware that its major target is to cope with inflation rather than targeting inflation and economic growth simultaneously. Monetary policy in China during the 1980s was operated according to the following simplified process:

Instruments	Operating Targets	Policy Targets	Final Objectives
Credit plan			
CB credits	SB reserves	Total credits	Economic growth
IR policy	Money base	Money supply	
Reserves		Cash emission	Price stabilisation

Notes: CB = central bank; IR = interest rate; SB; specialised banks.
Source: Dai in Ma *et al.*, 1990, p. 798.

This model shows that monetary policy implementation in China has relied mainly on supply-side instruments such as credit plans, central bank credit and the deposit reserves of the banking system. The interest rate started to increase only after reform (see Figure 6.4) and has become effective, step by step, only since the second half of the 1980s. Open-market operations and the discount window have not yet become as important as in a market economy, such as the UK. The operational targets are the deposits of the specialised banks in the central bank and the money base. Closer to the final objectives, three policy targets are measurable: total credit, total money supply and cash emission. Cash control has been regarded by the People's Bank as most effective and it remains an important measure for control. However, as non-cash payments are increasing, total bank credit has been another monetary target for the People's Bank since 1984. In fact total credits and reserves of banks are regarded as more effective than other instruments for central bank control of money in China (Dai, in Ma *et al.*, 1990). The People's Bank's *primary credits,* equivalent to *refinancing credits,*[2] are regarded as a 'water gate' since these credits come from base money and are easier for the central bank to manage than other instruments (Zhung, in ibid., p. 809). These central bank credits amounted to about one third of total credit (36 per cent) in 1988.

Besides these factors, the intervention of local governments plays an important role in government monetary policy (see Dai, in ibid., p. 804). Local governments try to increase their revenue, which reduces central government revenue (see Chapter 2). Only since the adoption of a regulation in 1994 has the situation changed. Since 1994 the local branches of the People's Bank have no longer had the authority to grant loans to either the local authorities or the local branches of any banks.

With the deepening of China's economic reform, '[t]he Central Bank will increasingly utilize loans, deposit requirements, interest rates, exchange rates, open-market operations and other measures to effect a gradual shift from direct to indirect control' (Chen, The Higher, 9 July 93). But this will take time. The supply of money, in terms of bank credit, was extremely important in China with respect to monetary control in our research period. This important feature of Chinese monetary policy in the current transition has been ignored by some previous econometric models. The transition highlights the increasing importance of monetary control.

The main factors influencing monetary control in China

The principal factors that have influenced monetary control in China are revealed by the Chinese literature (Ma *et al.*, 1990).[3]

First, fiscal policy and monetary policy became almost equally important after the reform. In the past the Chinese description of the system was '*Da jiwei, xiao caizheng, jiage chuna*' (a big Planning Commission, a small budget system, plus some cashiers – the banks). Now only about 5 per cent of industrial products are under the planner's control. More than half of all investments are channelled by banks, yet the budget system remains important. The banks have separate policy targets, though their final objectives are about the same. The importance of fiscal and monetary policies does not necessarily mean that, when tight monetary policy is conducted, the financial policy of the state budget must necessarily be as tight. But the possible mismatching of policies between the two may create problems. It is especially dangerous to relax both policies while there is excess demand. This was the case in the periods 1979–80 and 1984–8. In the former period the budget deficit grew to 29.81 billion yuan, M0 increased by 29.3 per cent, and M2 by 27 per cent. In the period 1984–8, the budget deficit reached 27.54 billion yuan, M0, M1 and M2 increased by an annual average of 32.1 per cent, 20.5 per cent and 25.9 per cent respectively, but economic growth had never been so rapid. Inflation could be a consequence of this disequilibrium (and in turn affected the demand for money).

Second, incomes policy. Inflation can be pushed up by either the direct price-linked factors (for example price monopolisation) or wage cost increases. Wage costs can push up product costs, which leads to inflation if wage growth is faster than productivity growth. In a CPE wages are controlled tightly through labour and wage plans, which are a part of the financial and national income plans. After the reform, firms were given the autonomy to decide their wage levels and various kinds of bonuses. However labour market mechanisms in RCPEs are not mature and firms do not easily constrain themselves in terms of their sensitivity to interest rates (see Chapters 2, 4 and 5). Banks can control credit directly, but it is difficult for them directly to control the uses of credit, as in the case of firms' income distribution, in spite of the fact that money income is a major component of banks' working capital credit. Rapid income growth (wages and various kinds of bonuses) may lead to extraordinarily fast expansion of consumption demand. Since September 1988 banks have been ordered by the monetary authority to control the consumption funds of their customers directly, according to the level of the previous actual allocation of the funds in August that year. This has proved fairly effective.

Third, industrial (sectoral) policies, including policies for infrastructure construction, industrial resources allocation, and sectoral and intersectoral organisation, have always been important in China. China and Japan have laid emphasis on government policy for the optimisation of resource allocation and the rationale of industrial sectoral organisation. These semi-macro and semi-microeconomic policies restructure economies effectively while also stimulating investment demand, which can affect monetary policy through pressures on the supply of credit. According to Dai (in Ma *et al.*, 1990, p. 804), M1 in China correlated closely with industrial output with a lag of two to three months. The banks were asked to rank their customers (the firms) according to the priorities of the industrial development policy.[4]

The three main factors revealed by the Chinese literature influencing the demand for money in China are investments (which may be investments in fixed assets), government expenditure and household income or consumption (see Appendix 6.2). Other factors, including foreign exchange reserves and expenditures, should be included if the topic is broadened. Such a modelling theory should have this reality as its foundation and should stress the monetary movements during transition, bearing in mind that it is modelling neither a market economy nor a planned one.

Demand for money functions and their stability are a major focus of interest in applied macroeconomics and Western economic theories have gone far in modelling them. Economists in the RCPEs have also tried to model them with respect to CPE or RCPE cases. Some economists believe that demand and supply schedules (or functions) are themselves well-defined 'only in equilibrium', though they admit that 'most economic phenomena seem to be in permanent disequilibrium' (Hendry, 1982) partly because of non-instant clearing, limited information and a myriad of innovations. In the presence of rational expectations, the modelling of the demand for money function seems sufficient to find the equilibrium points. However, even given that effective demand and supply will be equal on average, it is by no means certain that they always be equal. In the short run, prices do not adjust adequately to clear markets. While the adjustment is going on, discrepancies between demand and supply persist and short-side rules are in effect. In relation to Chinese reform, no one-sided research can discover equilibrium, and one-sided management cannot achieve equilibrium (see also Chapter 4). This is theoretically similar to the buffer stock approach and may lead to disequilibrium methods. But it is not necessary to become involved with the debatable 'min condition' (see Appendix 6.1).

Assumption of optimising behaviour by individuals, subject to certain constraints, is a principle of Western economics. Whereas in the West it may be reasonable to assume that individuals are on money demand curves, in China supply shocks may mean that they are holding more or less than they desire. We wish to investigate this transaction demand for money function by including measures that capture money supply shocks from government borrowing and overdrawing from the banking system. In addition, it is not obvious on theoretical grounds what the appropriate measure of transactions should be. Therefore it is necessary to experiment with total income (industrial output) and disaggregate it into consumption and investment. As is standard in the Western literature, transactions (income) and the interest rate will be regarded as exogenous. The results may be in line with some theories, but may also be difficult to interpret due to either the specialty of the case, the uncertainty of transition or simply the small sample size.

THE MODEL

The Chinese demand for money literature (see Appendix 6.2) has provided a Chinese model that is surprisingly similar to the Western traditional demand for money function. Western theoretical arguments on the modelling of demand for money functions are presented in Appendix 6.1. Classical and Cambridge economists have concentrated on the determination of the transaction demand for money. Keynes accepted the transactions and precautionary motives of the Cambridge approach, but introduced the speculative motive with uncertainty about the future yield on bonds. In Friedman's restatement of quantity theory, demand for money is placed in the context of the choice between money and a wide range of other financial and real assets. When there are shifts in demand, money supply adjustment can bring about a relatively stable velocity (Kaldor, 1985, pp. 17–36). Many early empirical studies used annual data and therefore the issue of adjustment lags tended to play a minor role. The basic equation of the static demand for money function is summarised by Laidler (1977) as follows:

$$M = \alpha_0 + \alpha_1 X + \alpha_2 r + \alpha_3 P + \varepsilon \qquad (6.1)$$

where M is nominal money balances; P is the price level; X is a scale variable, usually taken to be current income, financial wealth or permanent income; and r is the opportunity cost of holding money (either a rate on short-term assets or a rate of interest on long-term bonds). The own-rate on money is included in later studies. The variables are in logarithms (except for r occasionally). Western studies for the period prior to the 1970s suggest a well-determined, fairly stable demand for money function. Broadly speaking, stability applies under different definitions of money for different interest rates and over different periods. The traditional Western approach interprets the equation as a demand for money function. It can be extended to allow money supply influences to enter, interpreting the equation as a disequilibrium adjustment process.

Our models start with a simple demand for money function:

$$MD_t = \alpha_i + \beta_i Y_t + \delta_i R_t + \eta_i P_t + \varepsilon_t \qquad (6.2)$$

where MD_i is the ith category of money stock in China, which will be defined in the next section; R is the nominal interest rate.

Y is a function of investment, I, consumption, C, and government expenditure, G, in Western economics. But this cannot easily be applied to China, where national income is a combination of consumption and 'accumulation' plus the difference between imports and exports. They are the 'utilised values' (*shiyong e* in Chinese) rather than the I and C planned by the State Planning Commission, which should be the 'undertaking values' (*fasheng e*). The latter is the short-term data and has not yet been fully realised, while the former is the long-term (annual) data and has been fulfilled. Often, one third to 40 per cent of I is transformed to consumption, such as bonuses and wages. I and accumulation, however, cover the investment part of government expenditure. The differences between the West and China are the importance of the public (or state) sector in production and the extent to which the government invests in the SOEs. The SOEs are the main producers and government investments remain important in China.[5] But there are further government expenditures, such as those on public utilities and various subsidies.

Equation 6.2 can be rewritten approximately as

$$MD_t = \alpha_i + \beta_i I_t + \phi_i C_t + \psi_i G_t + \delta_i R_t + \eta_i P_t + \varepsilon_t \tag{6.3}$$

The approximation arises because the identity is linear, but the model is logarithmic in real values except R and P. P is introduced for an investigation of the costs of holding money. Because of the inadequacies in the data for the GDP components, it is necessary to use proxies in disaggregated analysis. Note that this disaggregation is what the Chinese DFM literature maintains (see Appendix 6.2).

No data on G is available. Government borrowing and overdrawing from the banking system (GB)[6] can indirectly tell us something about the budget situation. GB is a stock variable. Theoretically, government expenditure (G) minus tax revenue (T) should equal government bonds additionally issued (ΔB) plus money printed by the central bank or the additional money supply (ΔMS), within which ΔGB – additional government borrowing and overdrawing from the banking system – is a significant component. Actually the Chinese government counts ΔB as a 'soft deficit' since it is often regarded as a part of 'budget income', while the difference between expenditure and revenue is regarded as a 'hard deficit' since it must be financed from elsewhere. Another part of ΔMS relates to economic growth and the monetisation process of the economy.

$$G - T = \Delta B + \Delta MS \tag{6.4}$$

The money supply (MS) is

$$MS_t = MS_{t-1} + \Delta MS_t \tag{6.5}$$

From Equation 6.4:

$$\Delta MS_t = (G_t - T_t) - \Delta B_t \tag{6.6}$$

The growth of money supply should include bank credit and loans to collective and private businesses, as well as peasants. But no data are available. It is better to use a poor proxy than ignore the effects completely. Therefore $\Delta GB_t = \Delta MS_t$.

With the minimum condition (Portes and Winter, 1980; also see Appendix 6.1) for the money balance $M = \min(MS, MD)$, the disequilibrium equation of money balance changes (ΔM) is a weighted average of desired demand growth and supply growth

$$\Delta M = \lambda\Delta MD + (1 - \lambda)\,\Delta MS = \lambda\Delta MD + (1 - \lambda)\,\Delta GB \qquad (6.7)$$

This means that the money stock of an economy changes when both demand for money and the supply of money change in a disequilibrium fashion. Note that Equation 6.7 could be confronted with problems in a switching-regime situation, for instance. Suppose $MS_{t-1} < MD_{t-1}$ and $MS_t > MD_t$, then, according to the short-side principle, $M = \min(MS, MD)$,

$$\Delta M_t = M_t - M_{t-1} = MD_t - MS_{t-1}$$

In such a case, the value of λ could not lead Equation 6.7 to the above equation. In addition, this value equals either zero or one in an equation $M = \lambda MD + (1 - \lambda)\,MS$, according to the short-side principle.

But a model of our form (Equation 6.7) can be derived if we aggregate over many micro markets, some of which are on the demand side and some on the supply side, referring to the various pieces of work by Portes and Winter.

From Equation 6.3, and by assuming $\tau = (1 - \lambda)$, we can get

$$\Delta M_t = \beta_i\Delta I_t + \phi\Delta C_t + \psi_i\Delta G_t + \delta_i\Delta R_t + \eta_i\pi_t + \tau_i\Delta GB_t \qquad (6.8)$$

π is defined as the growth rate of prices. We have to assume roughly that government expenditure, G, moves proportionally to C and I in $Y = C + I + G$ (see Equation 6.3), as a first approximation given the inadequate data:

$$\Delta G = a\Delta C + b\Delta I + u \qquad (6.9)$$

where u is an error term. Equation 6.7 can therefore be written as

$$\Delta M_t = (\beta_i + b)\,\Delta I_t + (\phi + a)\,\Delta C_t + \delta_i\Delta R_t + \eta_i\pi_t + \tau_i\Delta GB_t \qquad (6.10)$$

Equation 6.10 is not a traditional money demand function, but a disequilibrium adjustment relation in which measured money responds to both demand and supply determinants in a simple equation. Unlike standard equations for Western countries it does not assume instantaneous market clearing.

The equation we estimated is a reduced form that includes a set of all potentially relevant variables to allow the data to decide which are important. If they are not relevant they will appear with insignificant coefficients. Keeping the full set of variables is necessary to maintain adding up and comparability across measures in the results.

The assumption is that *GB* is exogenous. Investment comes from both output (profit retention) and loans. But if it is assumed that banks are able to control the investments of the state owned sector, *NFI*, and therefore *IG*, through the control of total bank loans, these regressors are all exogenous. Although Chinese state-owned enterprises have the freedom to distribute bonuses, wage levels in the public sector – which are much higher than those in the West – are still under government control. Therefore the per capita rural consumption level (RC) and its counterpart in urban areas (UC) are generally exogenous. These assumptions do not ignore their flexibilities after the reform. But if these variables are all exogenous variables, we then get a theoretical model:

$$\Delta M = f(\Delta I, \Delta C, \Delta R, \Delta GB, \pi) \tag{6.11}$$

Considering the ambiguity of the results of the augmented Dickey–Fuller tests for stationarity in Appendix 6.3, and also that these have low power, particularly on short runs of possibly poorly measured data, the analysis will be conducted under two assumptions: levels regressions (appropriate for stationary regressions or cointegrating regressions) and first difference (appropriate for non-stationary or non-cointegrating regressions), with different categories of money measurements in China. Equation 6.12 is an OLS regression in log levels.

$$\log MD_t = \alpha_i + \beta_i \log I_t + \phi \log C_t + \delta_i R_t + \eta_i P_t + \tau_i \log GB_t \tag{6.12}$$

Whether Equation 6.12 is a cointegrating regression depends on the augmented Dickey–Fuller tests of the residuals of the regression. Since some variables are stocks, and because of the possible problem in stationarity, we can take the differential of the variables:

$$\Delta \log MD_t = \beta_i \Delta \log I_t + \phi \Delta \log C_t + \delta_i \Delta R_t + \eta_i \pi_t + \tau_i \Delta \log GB_t \tag{6.13}$$

The exercise can be started by using the classical demand for money function in log terms and then letting the terms be in first differences:

$$\Delta \log MD_t = \alpha_i + \beta_i \Delta \log Y_t + \delta_i \Delta R_t + \eta_i \pi_t \qquad (6.14)$$

π is an $I(0)$ variable already and there is no need to difference it further. It is inflation that seems most important (in first differences).

Different economic theories explain the contributions of the variables to the demand for money models in different ways, and there are different econometric results of applications of the models (see Appendix 6.1). Our disequilibrium money function is determined by the equations in reduced forms, which mix demand and supply influences. The variables I, C, R and π are the determinants of money demand, and GB – the amount of government expenditure to be financed through newly printed money – is the determination of money supply. We intend to see whether Y or C, I, GB, inflation, π, and nominal interest rate, R, are the significant variables for monetary control in China during the period of transition. They may be expected to have the following properties. First, in general Y, or I, C and GB should be positively related to M in the long run. Second, the effect of π could be negative on household deposit money, at least in the short run, since high inflation often causes panic purchasing or the hoarding of goods[7] if the interest rate cannot clear the money markets instantaneously. Replacing repressed inflation, open inflation could be positive with respect to broad money in the long run (in unit proportion?) according to some textbooks (Cuthbertson and Taylor, 1992, p. 151).

Third, the sign of the coefficient of R is rather more complex than output, GB and inflation. According to the Keynesian School it should be negative since there is a link between bank rates and the yields of other financial assets. The interest rate, however, is not a free market rate in China. It is under the control of the monetary authorities and the banks are allowed to exercise only a certain degree of flexibility. Its effects cannot be simply compared with those in market economies. Nor is it the original planned interest rate (see Chapter 1). In the 1980s China had not developed financial markets. The high level of deposit rates should have increased household deposit money, since the households were creditors. But they should have negatively correlated with enterprise deposits since the latter were debtors. Tight monetary policy induced interenterprise debt problems (see Chapter 4), which also had negative effects upon enterprise deposits. From a macroeconomic point of view, interest rates should negatively correlate with broad money, at least in the short run, since tight monetary policy reduces money supply and cuts off investments. The increase in interest rates may also reduce cash since M0 could be depressed by both an increase in deposits and cutting sources. In the long term, however, it is difficult to say. The interest rate started to increase from a meaninglessly low level after the reforms. It might not have correlated with inflation so closely. Therefore the sign of the coefficients of interest rates will vary depending on the definition of money and the time schedule.

ESTIMATION

Data definitions

All the following variables are in real terms deflated by the official quarterly CPI except R which remains in nominal terms.

Target variables

All the following are $I(1)$ variables (see Appendix 6.3).

- UD = real urban household deposits outstanding, including demand and time deposits.
- RD = real rural household deposits outstanding, including demand and time deposits.
- ED = real enterprise deposits outstanding, including demand and time deposits.
- M0 = real value of currency in circulation of the whole economy.
- M1 = M0 + ED.
- M2 = M1 + UD + RD.

There are different ways of measuring money in the West (see Emmanuel, 1989) and in China (Xie, in Ma *et al.*, 1990, pp. 607–8). M0 is a traditional measure of money in a CPE model. M0 in China often does not separate household cash and enterprise cash, and cash is very limited in CPE enterprises. It is still necessary to examine M0's behaviour because of its importance to the economy, including its sensitivity to the consumption goods markets and prices.

According to Dai (in ibid., p. 806), M1 = cash + enterprise demand deposits + public units deposit accounts + rural collective units deposit accounts. M2 = M1 + enterprise time deposits + household savings deposits + other deposits. M1 is more liquid than M2, even though these definitions may ignore the fact that household deposits are increasingly important after the reforms. According to the most recent official definitions of money (Dai, 1995), money in China has four classifications:

1. M0 = currency in circulation or cash.
2. M1 = M0 + enterprise deposits + deposits of public service institutions and the army + deposits of rural organisations + deposits with individuals' credit cards.
3. M2 = M1 + deposits of rural and urban citizens + time deposits of enterprises + foreign currency deposits + deposits of leasing and trust companies.
4. M3 = M2 + financial bonds + commercial bills + certificates of deposits, and so on.

M1 is the so-called liquid 'narrow money'; M2 is 'broad money'. 'Quasi-money' is the residual between M1 and M2, which is less liquid; and M3 consists of recent financial innovations that have not yet been measured. With a less developed financial market, M0 is above 30 per cent of M1, and the classification of M2 remains rudimentary (see *China's Banking*, no. 403, 01/1995, pp. 4–5). It seems that M1 is more closely related to inflation than M2 in the Chinese case, according to Dai (1995).

Here, the definitions of money differ because of the unavailability of quarterly data: M1 here is not necessarily more liquid than M2 because enterprise deposits in M1 are the total deposits of enterprises, and household deposits in M2 include savings and demand deposits of households. We are assessing the influence of regressors upon narrow money (cash) and broad money in different economic sectors (either enterprises or households, or both), not those on money of the standard definitions.

Control variables

– Y = total real output, which is replaced by an available flow variable, *IG*.
–   *IG* = the real value of industrial output. It is an $I(0)$ according to the augmented Dickey–Fuller test(1).
– I = total real investments, which is represented by an available flow variable *NFI*.
–   *NFI* = the real value of investments in SOE fixed assets. This is compatible with *IG* since most of SOEs are industrial enterprises. It is an $I(0)$ variable according to either Dickey–Fuller(1) or augmented Dickey–Fuller(1).

- C = total real consumption, which is disaggregated by two available flow measures (both are $I(1)$s).
- RC = real per capita rural household consumption levels.
- UC = real per capita urban household consumption levels.
- GB = real outstanding value of borrowing and overdrawing from the banking system by the state budget.[8] This is an available stock variable of $I(0)$.
- R = nominal interest rate, which is the nominal household one-year annual deposit rate. It is an $I(1)$.
- π = inflation, which is an $I(0)$, being the growth rate of the CPI index, which is an $I(1)$.

It would be wrong to use the real interest rate, r, here (see an example in Appendix 6.2). The nominal rate, R, should be the opportunity costs of holding money.[9] Together with inflation, it indicates how real money is affected by both, and how real output relates to the regression. If the nominal demand for money can be $MD = aY^{\beta}(1 + R)^{\rho}P^{\delta}$ and $\delta = 1$, the real demand for money can be written as $M/P = aY^{\beta}(1 + R)^{\rho}$, where R is the nominal return on the alternative asset. The real rate of return on the alternative assets is $(1 + R)/(1 + \pi)$. The real rate of return on money is $1/(1 + \pi)$.

The nominal rate is used also because financial markets in the RCPEs are not mature. There are very few alternative financial assets for people to choose. The opportunity costs of holding money may force depositors to withdraw money for (durable) goods storage, such as the panic purchases in China in 1988. Therefore the authorities have to raise the nominal rates when inflation rises. While the CPI index shows an upward trend, the interest rate is generally upward in the Chinese case.

Discussion of the data

All the data comes from the State Statistical Bureau of China. Official data often have some drawbacks. In such a rapidly changing period it is difficult to let the selected variables, such as those of per capita consumption, reflect all the information that the variables in Equation 6.3 should reflect. However the Chinese statistics may be more reliable than their Eastern European counterparts. The relatively stable political situation supports the consistency of the data on the one hand and the well-organised statistical system in China also improves the quality of the data.

Figures 6.1 to 6.4 illustrate the dynamics of the data and reveal the interrelationship between the selected variables, either in levels or in ratios

Money in Figures 6.1 to 6.3 is in line with our definitions above. The graphs tell of the instabilities of the M0 ratios, but it is not clear which components of money were relatively unstable. Figure 6.4 shows that inflation fluctuated greatly, while the interest rate required five major steps to become effective in controlling inflation. Around 1989 there was a period of social upheaval.

To reach the dynamic relationship, we take the first differences of the log terms of the variables. There are certain positive correlations between the growth rate of industrial output and different components of money, but the frequency of the fluctuations of output looks higher than money. The interest rate does not appear meaningful until 1988. There is an obvious negative relationship between inflation and rural and urban deposits. The relationship between enterprise deposits and M0 is less clear, but was positive before 1985. All this certainly affected the relationship between inflation and broad money. There are obvious positive correlations between government borrowing and overdrawing from the banking system (*GB*) and different components of money. A similar positive correlation exists between the former and both rural and urban per capita consumption levels. But the correlation between the fixed-asset investments of the state sector (*NFI*) and money is sometimes positive and

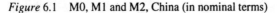

Figure 6.1   M0, M1 and M2, China (in nominal terms)

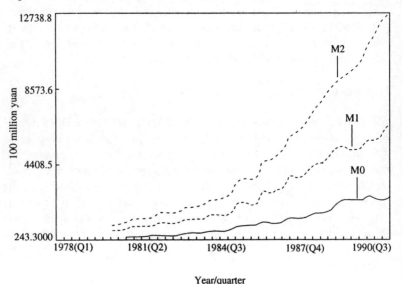

Year/quarter

Figure 6.2   Ratio of M0/M1 and M0/M2, China (in nominal terms)

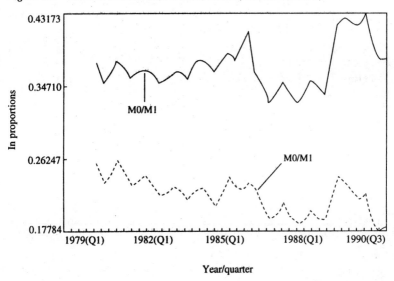

Figure 6.3   Peasants' (*PD*), urban household (*UD*) and Enterprise deposits (*ED*), China (in nominal levels)

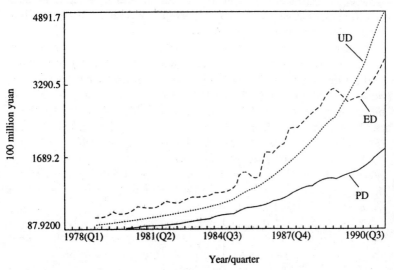

Figure 6.4   Inflation (*P*), nominal interest rate (*IR*) and real rate (*RIR*), China

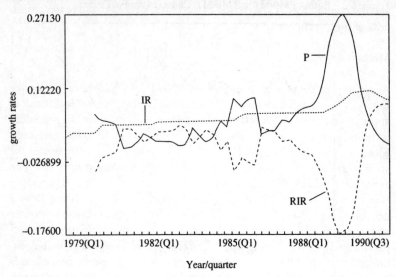

sometimes negative. There are clear seasonal patterns in the variables and the possibility of time lags. The urban consumption level does not necessarily correlate with the rural consumption level, and that former is more dynamic than the latter. Yet the growth rates of both are positively related to different components of money (These dynamic relationships are illuminated in Yang, 1994b).

The sample size of the period from the first quarter of 1979 to the third quarter of 1990 is very small. Therefore unit root tests here may have low power. Causality tests (Granger, 1969) on such a small sample are also too weak to try. Appendix 6.3[10] shows that some variables, such as *GB*, *NFI* and even *IG* in log levels pass the unit root (*DF* and *ADF*) tests with trend,[11] and therefore they can be regarded as *I*(0) variables. The *MD* variables, such as *RD*, *UD*, *ED*, M0, M1 and M2, and some others, such as *R*, *RC* and *UC*, are stationary only after first differencing, which means that they are *I*(1) variables. Three dummies are added initially to the regressions to pick up seasonality effects. The variables and the ratios are in real terms before logarithms are taken.

The tests for unit roots and cointegration have very low power (that is, there is a low probability of rejection of the null hypothesis of non-stationary *I*(1) residuals even when it is false). Therefore, since we are uncertain, we shall do both OLS regressions. The levels are appropriate if they are cointegrated or stationary; the first difference is appropriate if they are $I(1)$ and not cointegrated. Comparison of the two allows us to judge the robustness of the conclusions.

Methodology

According to some studies (Qin *et al.*, 1992), the uncertainty over the exact degree of non-stationarity of individual variables makes it difficult to apply Johansen's (1988) system estimation procedure, since the procedure is quite sensitive to changes in the numbers of variables and lags. Moreover the small sample size is likely to give biased estimates of the static regression (long-run) coefficients by the Engle–Granger two-step estimation method (1987). One way of overcoming this is to apply Hendry's general to simple reduction approach (1991), starting from a general linear dynamic equation with lags for each explanatory variable and seasonal dummies. This equation is then gradually reduced and re-parameterised until a parsimonious *ECM* is found, nested within an economically interpretable long-run relation. Finally, Johansen's procedure is used mainly as a weak endogeneity test of the single-equation results obtained, since Hendry's procedure depends crucially upon weak endogeneity. According to Gonzolo (1994), the Johansen tests have better properties in small samples compared with several other methods of cointegration.

This has been a relatively good approach. However, although increasingly popular it may be questioned when the sample size is very small. According to Schwert (1987), the maximum lag length was set equal to the integer portion of $12*(T/100)^{0.25}$ where T is the number of observations. By this criterion, about nine lags are necessary in our sample. However the well-known rule for the maximum number of variables, k, that can be included in an OLS regression – $Y = X*\beta + u$, where X is a $T*k$ matrix – should be less than $T/3$. The period allowing us to model the Chinese case is very short (from 1979 onwards) and the data available is limited (to the end of 1990). Annual data for such a short period is inadequate for a time series regression. As argued in Chapter 5, it would be better to separate the prereform period and the reform period (see also Appendix 6.2) and to use the available quarterly data. Accordingly, the sample here allows 12–15 regressors only. The inclusion of seasonal dummies does not allow a sufficient degree of freedom to include lagged values of the regressions. But there is insufficient reason to use fewer lags for the seasonal data base due to the small sample size.[12] Many previous equations built up by econometricians[13] have passed the tests, only to break down afterwards. The data may be fitted closely into the sample by exploiting chance correlations in small samples. But such correlations are unlikely to persist, so 'data-mined' equations will have a poor forecasting performance. Once the data and/or sample periods are changed, the model could break down. Thus there is a trade-off between data mining, which runs the danger of producing incorrect results, and having some unavoidable misspecifications.

Another issue is that demand for and the supply of money in China should be assessed from different points of view rather than using one definition of money (see Chapter 5). The conventional way is to model M0 since about 70 per cent of China's consumption demand was realised using cash, and cash was 21 per cent of M2 in 1989 compared with 7–8 per cent in some Western countries (Dai, in Ma *et al.*, 1990, p. 801). Additionally, cash is not easy to control. Economists in China in the early 1980s tended to use the ratio of cash to enterprise deposits for the prediction of money, as this ratio was relatively stable at the time. As the economy has monetised rapidly, they have found it increasingly difficult to use this ratio for prediction. For example, in 1981 cash amounted to 30 billion yuan while enterprise deposits were in short supply. In 1988 M1 increased by 24.3 per cent over 1987, while M0 increased by 46.7 per cent. It cannot be simply concluded that monetary policy was – or was not – tight because of a change in any single component of broad money. Therefore it may be inappropriate for some economists (for example Peebles, 1990a; see also Appendix 6.2) to adopt the approach of modelling only the 'narrow' demand for money.

Therefore the approach adopted here is to analyse a system that explains each of the components of Chinese money in order to assess differences in the behaviour of different components of money demand. Because of the shortage of data, we are confined to running simple models with a limited number of regressors.

The OLS technique can be used to run a set of simple equations without lags due to the sample-size constraint. Seasonal adjustments are conducted by adding a few dummy variables. The tests should not be trusted completely, but those that are necessary should be assessed carefully. The objective is not to demonstrate modern econometric techniques, but to investigate the factors that are likely to affect the supply of and demand for money in China and examine how these factors may affect different components of money. With the same regressors explaining the different components of money, this approach enables a comparison of the effects of the regressors upon different moneys between regressions. This is superior to a single equation and may be more honest and stronger than the data mining approach in such a case.

It may be questioned whether this method induces simultaneous equation bias. In fact the process builds up simultaneous equations models. In the usual regression model, y is the dependent variable and x's are the independent variables. An OLS regression requires that x's are independent of the error term, u. Therefore a crucial assumption is that they are exogenous. But in simultaneous equation models variables are classified as both endogenous and exogenous. The following is an example:

$$y_1 = \alpha_1 y_2 + \beta_1 X_1 + \varepsilon_1 \qquad (6.15)$$

$$y_2 = \alpha_2 y_1 + \beta_2 X_2 + \varepsilon_2 \qquad (6.16)$$

However our model contains a group of multivariable regressions, that is:

$$y_i = \alpha_i X + \varepsilon_i \qquad (6.17)$$

which has the same X in each equation, and X is assumed to be exogenous in order to explain different y's. A possible problem is whether the introduction of the disequilibrium supply side variable (government borrowing and overdrawing from the banks) correlates with ε_i or not in our multivariable regression model – $\Delta M = \beta_i \Delta X + \tau_i \Delta GB + \varepsilon_i$. The reasons for us to assume that this variable is exogenous are as follows.

First, it is likely that ΔGB will reflect political and industrial forces rather than monetary forces. Second, the bias might not be large. If ΔGB is endogenous, then the τ of $\tau \Delta GB$ will be a biased estimate. τ_i in the dynamic Model 5 are quite small, which suggests a low correlation. Third, it is likely to be difficult to find valid instruments that (1) explain ΔGB very well and (2) are not correlated with monetary shocks. Finally, endogeneity problems may be larger for ΔY, π and r, but this is generally ignored in Western literature.

OLS regressions

Model 1

As discussed, some Chinese demand for money literature suggests a model for China similar to the Western traditional demand for money equation. By replacing P_t with π_t and adding three seasonal dummies into Equation 6.2 for necessary seasonal adjustments, we get

$$\log MD_t = \alpha_i + \beta_i \log Y_t + \delta_i R_t + \eta_i \pi_t + \vartheta_i D1_t + \xi_i D2_t + \nu_i D3_t + \varepsilon_t \qquad (6.2a)$$

where the quarterly Y is not available and therefore is replaced by industrial output (IG), which is the major component of China's GDP, and where the coefficient is expected to be positive. Both the nominal interest rate (R) and inflation (π) are expected to be negatively related to MD. The results of the OLS regressions in logarithms are shown in Table 6.1.

Although the R^2 for each regression is above 96 per cent, the standard errors of the regressions, ranging from 0.07 to 0.147, are relatively high.[14] Despite the small sample, cointegration is not rejected in three of six equations. Since the augmented Dickey–Fuller test has low power and fails to reject the null of a unit root in the residuals, this is quite reassuring. (Review the section on discussion of the data.) As one would expect with a cointegrating regression, four of the six equations show serial correlation of the residuals. Although they are reported, standard errors and t statistics are unreliable in a cointegrating regression.

Although these equations might be interpreted as cointegrating relations in econometric terms, it is difficult to interpret them in traditional terms. The output elasticities are very large and the interest rate and inflation effects have the wrong signs, according to traditional theory. Since these coefficients are implausible as long-run functions, first-difference versions that deal with non-stationarity shall be examined and will provide estimates of the short-run demand for money function.

Model 2

The problems of Model 1, especially those of cointegration, serial correlation and the difficulty of interpreting the coefficients, encourage us to try Model 2, which takes first differences of the variables in Model 1. Appendix 6.3 shows that all the variables should be stationary after first differencing, and that π is $I(0)$. The model becomes a short-run dynamic regression (see also Hafer and Hein, 1980).

$$\Delta\log MD_t = \alpha_i + \beta_i\Delta\log Y_t + \delta_i\Delta R_t + \eta_i\pi_t + \vartheta_i D1_t + \xi_i D2_t + \nu_i D3_t \tag{6.2b}$$

At least two dummies remain significant in most of the regressions, except that of UD, which justifies adding dummies for seasonal adjustments (see Table 6.2).

Although the ratios of R^2 are all relatively lower, especially those on the regressions of demand for M0, M1 and M2, the standard errors, the Durbin–Watson statistics and the serial correlation ratios are significantly improved after the differencing in Model 2. The normality ratios of the regressions of demand for UD and M2 are also much below the critical

Table 6.1   OLS estimation of traditional demand for money equations, levels plus seasonals

MD	RD (43)[1]	UD (46)[1]	ED (46)[1]	MO (43)[1]	M1 (43)[1]	M2 (43)[1]
α_i	−20.33	−14.66	−11.95	−9.75	−10.5	−11.7
SE	(1.33)	(1.11)	(0.94)	(0.59)	(0.78)	(0.88)
t	−15.30	−13.20	−12.70	−16.40	−13.40	−13.40
$\log Y_t$	3.45	2.70	2.50	2.09	2.35	2.55
SE	(0.19)	(0.15)	(0.13)	(0.08)	(0.11)	(0.12)
t	18.20*	17.00*	18.60*	24.80*	21.20*	20.50*
R_t	0.12	0.19	0.07	0.12	0.09	0.12
SE	(0.01)	(0.01)	(0.01)	(0.01)	(0.01)	(0.01)
t	7.90*	14.90*	6.70*	17.90*	10.10*	12.50*
π_t	0.31	0.76	0.79	1.14	0.84	0.73
SE	(0.70)	(0.58)	(0.49)	(0.31)	(0.41)	(0.46)
t	0.40	1.30	1.60	3.60*	2.00*	1.60
D_1	0.24	0.24	0.16	0.11	0.13	0.17
SE	(0.07)	(0.06)	(0.05)	(0.03)	(0.04)	(0.05)
t	3.40*	4.00*	3.00*	3.50*	3.10*	3.60*
D_2	−0.29	−0.16	−0.24	−0.29	−0.27	−0.24
SE	(0.69)	(0.06)	(0.05)	(0.03)	(0.05)	(0.05)
t	−4.30*	−2.80*	−4.90*	−9.50*	−6.50*	−5.30*
D_3	0.05	0.07	−0.05	-0.12	−0.07	−0.02
SE	(0.08)	(0.06)	(0.05)	(0.04)	(0.05)	(0.05)
t	0.67	1.10	−0.90	−3.40*	−1.50	−0.30
R^2	0.96	0.97	0.96	0.98	0.97	0.97
CR ADF(1)	−2.35	−1.72	−3.10	−4.08	−3.33	−2.46
s	0.147	0.127	0.11	0.07	0.09	0.097
DW	0.57	0.67	0.85	1.28	0.98	0.83
SC^2 $\kappa_2(4)$	25.40	21.92	16.19	7.58	12.08	16.62
FF $\kappa_2(1)$	10.86	0.32	1.42	0.02	1.79	0.006
Norm^3. $\kappa_2(2)$	6.24	26.07	1.90	0.72	0.45	8.22
Het.^{4} $\kappa_2(1)$	3.99	1.61	0.87	0.60	0.001	0.23

Notes:
1. Observations numbers.
2. LM chi-squared test for autocorrelation of the residuals; chi-sq (4.5%/1%) = 9.49/13.28.
3. LM chi-squared test for normality of the residuals; chi-sq (2.5%/1%) = 5.99/9.21.
4. LM chi-squared test for homoskedasticity of the residuals; chi-sq (1.5%/1%) = 3.84/6.63.
* significant values.

Table 6.2 OLS estimation of traditional demand for money equations, first differences plus seasonals

MD	RD (42)[1]	UD (45)[1]	ED (45)[1]	MO (42)[1]	M1 (42)[1]	M2 (42)[1]
α_i	0.12	0.08	0.15	0.15	0.15	0.13
SE	(0.015)	(0.007)	(0.03)	(0.02)	(0.02)	(0.02)
t	8.40	10.60	5.00	7.50	6.10	7.90
$\Delta \log Y_t$	−0.05	−0.06	0.07	0.42	0.19	0.10
SE	(0.19)	(0.09)	(0.38)	(0.25)	(0.31)	(0.21)
t	−0.30	−0.70	0.20	1.70	0.60	0.50
ΔR_t	−0.12	0.02	−0.26	−0.05	−0.19	−0.12
SE	(0.07)	(0.04)	(0.15)	(0.10)	(0.12)	(0.08)
t	−1.60	0.60	−1.70	−0.50	−1.60	−1.60
π_t	−1.02	−1.10	−1.12	−0.26	−0.77	−0.91
SE	(0.20)	(0.10)	(0.41)	(0.27)	(0.32)	(0.22)
t	−5.10*	−11.10*	−2.70*	−1.00	−2.40*	−4.20*
D_1	−0.03	−0.002	−0.16	−0.15	−0.15	−0.09
SE	(0.03)	(0.003)	(0.06)	(0.04)	(0.04)	(0.03)
t	−3.90*	0.30*	−2.60*	−7.10*	−4.00*	−4.00*
D_2	−0.10	−0.003	−0.13	−0.23	−0.16	−0.11
SE	(0.02)	(0.01)	(0.05)	(0.03)	(0.04)	(0.03)
t	−2.30*	−0.40	−1.50	−1.30	−1.50	−1.60
D_3	−0.07	−0.005	−0.08	−0.05	−0.07	−0.05
SE	(0.03)	(0.01)	(0.05)	(0.04)	(0.05)	(0.03)
t	−1.00	−0.10	−2.90*	−4.10*	−3.40*	−3.20*
R^2	0.827	0.918	0.50	0.74	0.59	0.70
s	0.03	0.016	0.07	0.04	0.05	0.035
DW	1.90	1.01	2.25	1.78	1.99	1.95
SC[2] κ_2 (4)	11.58	11.13	6.65	1.62	6.12	8.32
FF κ_2 (1)	0.84	0.06	3.00	2.74	4.53	1.61
Norm.[3] κ_2 (2)	0.80	0.81	27.07	4.53	10.0	1.75
Het.[4] κ_2 (1)	1.18	10.33	4.41	6.11	9.95	9.25

Notes: See notes to Table 6.1.

values, in spite of the fact that the same ratios of the regressions of demand for *ED* and M1 are worsened to 27 and 10 respectively, and that the heteroscedasticity ratios of the regressions of demand for *UD*, M1 and M2 are also worsened. Thus the model improves the misspecification of Model 1 in general, leaving some problems unresolved, which is not surprising for such a small sample from a transitional economy. The specifications of the regressions of demand for *RD* and M0 are obviously better than the others according to these tests, though the regression for *UD* gets the lowest standard error (0.016). This analysis shows that Model 2 is generally better than Model 1, though the heteroscedasticity levels in the regressions of *UD*, M1 and M2 are between 9.25 and 10.33.

Another significant change in Model 2 is that all the coefficients on π, and most of those on ΔR (except that of the regression of demand for *UD*) have become negative. A possible explanation is that Model 1 is a long-run model where elasticities with respect to prices and the interest rate are positive due to their original low levels (review the section on theory above), while Model 2 is a dynamic model that picks up short-term effects. Alternatively Model 1 could be misspecified. The positive deposit-rate elasticity of the changes of demand for *UD* is reasonable though low, while the same negative elasticity of the changes of demand for *RD* could be caused by some short-term effects. The interest elasticities are insignificant in most of the regressions. The same elasticity in the regression of demand for real enterprise deposits is almost significant (–1.7), and the negative interest elasticity in this regression remains the highest absolute value (–0.26), which may indicate that enterprises in China are becoming sensitive to changes in interest rates, at least in the short run. As discussed above, the interest elasticities of demand for cash (M0) and for broader money (M1 and M2) are all reasonably negative and broad money is more sensitive than cash to the interest rate. Even where the coefficients are not significantly different from zero, their sign, size and, in particular, the pattern of coefficients across the different measures of money is informative.

The coefficients on R are negative in most of the regressions except that of *UD*. That for enterprise deposits should be negative since it signifies the costs of *ED*, while it should be positive for urban household deposits since it is an income of the depositors. The negative signs of the coefficients on R in the regression of *RD* imply the unimportance of R in rural areas in the short run in this model.

With the restricted interest rate, inflation could become the opportunity cost of holding money. Although π in the regression for M0 is not significant in the short-run model ($t = -1.0$), which differs from the long-run model ($t = 3.6$), the inflation terms are very significant in the others and the price elasticities of demand for other components of real money are around minus one in those regressions. This indicates that demand for household money (*RD*, *UD*) and enterprise money (*ED*), and therefore M2, is very sensitive to inflation in the short run, being approximately unit proportional.

Unfortunately, output ($\Delta \log Y$) turns out to be insignificant in most of the regressions except that of M0 ($t = 1.7$; coefficient $= 0.42$), and its coefficients on the regressions of demand for RD and UD become negative. This could be because the short-run transactions demand has a low value, but it is more likely to be the result of the fact that the measure of Y (industrial output) is a relatively poor measure of income, particularly for rural and urban households. Therefore an experiment with another transaction measure (using I and C) is useful, allowing for supply shocks.

Model 3

This leads us to try another model specified in Equation 6.13.

$$\Delta \log MD_t = \alpha_i + \beta_i \Delta \log I_t + \phi \Delta \log C_t + \delta_i \Delta R_t + \eta_i \pi_t +$$
$$\tau_i \Delta \log GB_t + \vartheta_i \varepsilon_t \qquad (6.13)$$

First of all, can the disaggregated parts of Y and the disequilibrium-supply-side GB be added into Model 2?

The variable addition tests (see Appendix 6.4) show that only in the regression for M0 has $\Delta \log GB$ a significant F statistic. $\Delta \log NFI$ is significant in the regressions except those of ED, M0 and M1. But the other disaggregated regressors, such as $\Delta \log RC$ and $\Delta \log UC$, have not passed the tests. Adding one of them instead of the complete replacement of Y by all three ($\Delta \log NFI$, $\Delta \log RC$ and $\Delta \log UC$) is theoretically disprovable. However we may see whether Model 2 can be improved by adding the disequilibrium-supply-side variable $\Delta \log GB$.

$$\Delta \log MD_t = \alpha_i + \beta_i \Delta \log Y_t + \delta_i \Delta R_t + \eta_i \pi_t + \lambda_i \Delta \log GB_t +$$
$$\vartheta_i D1_t + \xi_i D2_t + \nu_i D3_t \qquad (6.13a)$$

By adding $\Delta \log GB$ into the regressions (Table 6.3), the situation of the originally improved specifications of each regression and the signs and the significant levels of the regressors ΔR and π in Model 2 remain basically unchanged. This indicates that the introduction of this disequilibrium-supply-side variable is reasonable, at least from the specification's point of view. It certainly improves the regression for M0, where the additionally significant $\Delta \log GB$ (its t statistic is 2.0) helps the regressor $\Delta \log Y$ to be more significant, the t statistic of which is increased from 1.7 to 1.9. If we were following a traditional specification search we could ignore the other variables, impose a zero coefficient in inflation and try to remedy the marginal failures on normality and functional form with dummy variables. Then we could present a 'good' equation. But this would be misleading, as

Table 6.3   OLS estimation of expanded traditional demand for money equations with an additional disequilibrium-supply-side variable (*GB*), first differences plus seasonals

MD	RD (42)[1]	UD (42)[1]	ED (42)[1]	MO (42)[1]	M1 (42)[1]	M2 (42)[1]
α_i	0.12	0.07	0.14	0.14	0.14	0.12
SE	(0.02)	(0.008)	(0.03)	(0.02)	(0.02)	(0.02)
t	7.80	9.40	4.30	7.00	5.60	7.40
$\Delta \log Y_t$	−0.07	0.03	0.06	0.46	0.21	0.12
SE	(0.19)	(0.10)	(0.41)	(0.24)	(0.31)	(0.20)
t	0.40	−0.30	0.10	1.90*	0.70	0.60
ΔR_t	−0.11	0.03	−0.26	−0.03	−0.17	−0.11
SE	(0.07)	(0.04)	(0.16)	(0.09)	(0.11)	(0.08)
t	−1.40	0.70	−1.60	−0.30	−1.40	−1.30
π_t	−0.88	−1.02	−0.92	0.04	−0.56	−0.73
SE	(0.23)	(0.03)	(0.49)	(0.29)	(0.37)	(0.25)
t	−3.80*	−8.60*	−1.90*	0.10	−1.50	−3.00*
$\Delta \log GB_t$	0.07	0.03	0.07	0.15	0.10	0.08
SE	(0.06)	(0.01)	(0.12)	(0.07)	(0.09)	(0.06)
t	1.20	1.10	0.60	2.00*	1.10	1.40
D_1	−0.02	0.003	−0.14	−0.14	−0.14	−0.09
SE	(0.03)	(0.01)	(0.06)	(0.07)	(0.04)	(0.03)
t	−0.80	0.20	−2.40*	−3.90*	−3.10*	−3.00*
D_2	−0.10	0.001	−0.11	−0.23	−0.16	−0.11
SE	(0.02)	(0.01)	(0.05)	(0.03)	(0.04)	(0.03)
t	−3.90*	−0.10	−2.20*	−7.50*	−4.00*	−4.10*
D_3	−0.07	−0.004	−0.08	−0.06	−0.08	−0.06
SE	(0.03)	(0.015)	(0.06)	(0.04)	(0.05)	(0.03)
t	−2.50*	−0.20	−1.40	−1.70	−1.60	−1.90*
R^2	0.83	0.92	0.45	0.76	0.60	0.71
s	0.033	0.02	0.07	0.04	0.05	0.03
DW	1.96	1.03	2.06	1.99	2.08	2.06
SC² κ_2 (4)	10.72	10.67	6.08	0.97	5.87	7.56
FF κ_2 (1)	0.49	0.01	3.32	4.94	5.06	2.09
Norm.[3] κ_2 (2)	0.02	0.26	49.18	8.38	19.81	6.57
Het.[4] κ_2 (1)	1.69	9.49	3.32	5.35	7.56	6.43

Notes: See note to Table 6.1.

comparison across the measures indicates. The coefficients of the $\Delta \log Y$ in most of the regressions are increased, except those for *RD* and *ED* which remain almost unchanged. Only the coefficient of this variable in the regression for *RD* remains negative. This indicates that Model 3 has generally been improved by adding the disequilibrium-supply-side $\Delta \log GB$. Government borrowing and overdrawing from the banking system has a certain positive effect in the money function. In this system, the regressions of demand for *RD* are relatively better specified than the others, according to the misspecification test results. It is again the regression of *UD* that gets the lowest standard error (0.02) among the group.

It is interesting to see that the signs of the interest rate in the regressions are the same as those in Model 2, and even the *t* ratios are about the same. The interest elasticity of demand for *UD* is positive, while the same elasticities for the rest are all negative. The reasons for this could be the same as in Model 2. In terms of the level of *t* statistics, whenever the interest elasticity is insignificant or very insignificant, the level of inflation is significant or very significant, for example in the regressions of *RD*, *UD*, *ED* and M2. This again agrees with the results of Model 2.

The price elasticities of demand for different forms of money remains negative, except that in the regression of M0. The same elasticities of demand for household deposits and enterprise deposits (not for M0) remain around unity, similar to Model 2. This again indicates that the demand for money in these two sectors is sensitive to inflation in the short run. In the regression of M0, $\log Y$ ($t = 1.9$; coefficient $= 0.46$) and $\Delta \log GB$ ($t = 2.0$; coefficient $= 0.15$) are more important than ΔR and π.

Model 4

Model 3 encourages us to use Equation 6.3 as a theoretical model and try Equation 6.3a in logarithmic levels, which disaggregates output into *I* and *C* and introduces *GB* from the disequilibrium supply side.

$$\log MD_t = \alpha_i + \theta_i \log NFI_t + \gamma_i \log RC_t + \upsilon_i \log UC_t + \delta_i R_t + \tau_i \log GB_t + \vartheta_i D1_t + \xi_i D2_t + \nu_i D3_t \tag{6.3a}$$

After OLS estimation, it was found that π and the seasonal dummies are insignificant in all the regressions of different components of money, which may imply that the interest rate in this model compensates for inflation. Dropping π helps us to concentrate on investigating the remaining variables (Table 6.4). There is no seasonal pattern in this long-run equation. By dropping π and D_i, we get Equation 6.3b.

$$\log MD_t = \alpha_i + \theta_i \log NFI_t + \gamma_i \log RC_t + \upsilon_i \log UC_t + \delta_i R_t + \tau_i \log GB_t \tag{6.3b}$$

Augmented Dickey–Fuller(1) statistics show that almost all the regressions are cointegrating ones except that of *UD*, which has also a normality problem (47.36). R^2 ratios of the regressions are all above 0.95. The regression of *RD* has high values of serial correlation (15.11) and functional form (13.69). The regressions have relatively low Durbin–Watson statistics, except those of M0 (1.59) and M1 (1.53), and relatively high standard errors (0.08–0.10).

Table 6.4   OLS estimation of the demand for money with the disaggregated output and disequilibrium-supply-side variables in logarithmic levels plus seasonal dummies

MD	RD (39)[1]	UD (39)[1]	ED (39)[1]	MO (39)[1]	M1 (39)[1]	M2 (39)[1]
α_i	−6.65	−5.13	−2.73	−1.38	−1.57	−2.31
SE	(0.81)	(0.70)	(0.74)	(0.64)	(0.62)	(0.60)
t	−9.18	−7.34	−3.69	−2.12	−2.52	−3.84
$\log NFI_t$	0.05	0.04	0.07	0.07	0.07	0.06
SE	(0.03)	(0.02)	(0.03)	(0.02)	(0.02)	(0.02)
t	1.77*	1.57	2.63*	3.25*	3.24*	2.72*
$\log RC_t$	1.35	0.82	1.27	1.34	1.31	1.10
SE	(0.38)	(0.32)	(0.34)	(0.30)	(0.29)	(0.28)
t	3.57*	2.52*	3.68*	4.45*	4.51*	3.91*
$\log UC_t$	0.28	0.19	0.46	0.11	0.33	0.30
SE	(0.27)	(0.23)	(0.25)	(0.22)	(0.21)	(0.20)
t	1.04	0.79	1.85*	0.50	1.57	1.46
R_t	0.02	0.10	−0.01	0.05	0.01	0.04
SE	(0.14)	(0.01)	(0.01)	(0.01)	(0.01)	(0.01)
t	1.48	8.63*	−0.70	4.75*	1.37	4.36*
$\log GB_t$	1.00	1.20	0.43	0.27	0.36	0.72
SE	(0.24)	(0.21)	(0.22)	(0.19)	(0.18)	(0.18)
t	4.19*	5.83*	1.96*	1.40	1.98*	4.04*
R^2	0.97	0.98	0.95	0.97	0.97	0.98
s	0.10	0.09	0.09	0.08	0.08	0.08
CR ADF (1)	−2.96	−2.23	−3.82	−4.96	−4.75	−3.72
DW	0.86	0.96	1.21	1.59	1.53	1.30
SC[2] κ_2 (4)	15.08	8.72	10.10	13.76	12.50	7.80
FF κ_2 (1)	13.66	0.007	3.02	0.11	1.15	0.01
Norm.[3] κ_2 (2)	0.46	48.60	0.08	0.95	0.87	7.40
Het.[4] κ_2 (1)	0.07	3.40	0.01	0.30	0.35	0.97

Notes: See notes to Table 6.1.

All the output signs, including those of *NFI*, *RC* and *UC*, and the signs of *GB*, are positive in all the regressions, which is as expected. The most consistently significant regressor is the per capita rural consumption level, the elasticities of which are greater than unity. This again indicates the significant effect of the reforms in the rural sector in the period. Compared with this, per capita urban household consumption levels do not look as important, but they are positively related to money and their coefficients are relatively low. This implies that *UC* has not changed as radically as *RC*, although it has changed. In the regression of enterprise deposits, this term is significant at the 10 per cent level ($t = 1.85$; coefficient = 0.46). Reasonably, the coefficients on *RC* and *UC* in the regressions of *RD* and *ED* are the highest among the group – higher than those of the other components of money.

Government borrowing and overdrawing from the banking system, *GB*, is significant in most regressions except that for M0. *GB*'s coefficients in the regressions of *RD* and *UD* are above unity. This again indicates the role of the disequilibrium supply side in the household sector. This is an effect of the reform policies of the Chinese government, which often uses subsidies – such as price subsidies in price reforms – to stabilise prices in order to secure the reforms.

Investments in the fixed assets of the SOEs (*NFI*) are significant in almost all the regressions, which is to be expected, but the coefficients are very low (0.04 to 0.07). The model seems to indicate that demand for money in that period was motivated mainly by consumption and government behaviour,[15] rather than by investments in this long-run regression. The policy implication could be related to consumption control and the control of government borrowing and overdrawing for the equilibrium.

The most unstable variable, in terms of its effects upon different components of money, is the interest rate. It is positive and significant (in terms of *t* ratios) in the regressions of urban household deposits ($t = 8.68$), M0 and M2, but it is negative and insignificant in the regression of enterprise deposits ($t = -0.7$; coefficient = -0.01). Similar to Model 1, the higher the interest rate, the higher the income of households, though at the same time the higher the cost of borrowing from banks. The insignificant interest rate in the regression of *ED* again indicates that Chinese SOEs might not be as sensitive as urban households to the interest rate in the long run. The coefficient in the regression of *UD* is 0.10, the highest among the regressions, which shows that urban households are most sensitive to the deposit rate. The same coefficient in the regression of *RD* is insignificantly different from zero, but it shows a positive level, which indicates the lesser sensitivity of the interest elasticity of demand for *RD*. The corresponding elasticity of demand for M0 is 0.05, and significant. These effects have certainly contributed to the interest elasticities of demand for M2. Bearing in mind that Equation 6.3b is a long-run equilibrium model, and that the interest rate started to rise from a very low level, the interest rate of a CPE may not necessarily follow inflation dynamics closely and may present positive signs for the coefficients in the whole period of research.

Model 5

We can treat Equation 6.13, which is in log first differences, as an independent model based on the theoretical model of Equation 6.3, despite the variable addition tests, in order to see how this model works. As it was insignificant in Model 4, π is omitted from in Model 5 also.

$$\Delta \log MD_t = \alpha_i + \theta_i \Delta \log NFI_t + \gamma_i \Delta \log RC_t + v_i \Delta \log UC_t + \delta_i \Delta R_t + \tau_i \Delta \log GB_t + \vartheta_i D1_t + \xi_i D2_t + \nu_i D3_t \qquad (6.13b)$$

Most of the dummies in Equation 6.13b are significant, which justifies their addition. The results of the misspecification tests are not bad, comparatively speaking (Table 6.5). The levels of R^2, the standard errors and the Durbin–Watson statistics are about the same as each regression in Model 2. The Durbin–Watson statistics and serial correlation are good, while R^2 is relatively lower throughout. The main problem in diagnostic tests are the high levels of normality for the regressions of ED (105.07), M1 (24.33) and M2 (7.52).

Investment in fixed assets is negative and relatively insignificant in the regressions of RD and ED, which affects those of M1 and M2. This could be caused by further differencing the already stationary $\log NFI$. The coefficient of per capita rural household consumption is positive and significant (which is understandable for a country with such a huge rural population) while per capita urban household consumption is consistently insignificant and is negative in two cases (UD and M1).

However there are two properties that are interesting compared with Model 4. First, $\Delta \log GB$ is significant in three cases except UD, M0 and M1, and it is positively related to different components of money, especially UD, RD and M2. This again indicates that government borrowing and overdrawing from the banking system seems to have a positive impact on money demand, especially in the household sector. Relating this to the most influential rural consumption level, RC, it seems to indicate that demand for money could be consumption motivated rather than investment motivated in this short-term model.

Table 6.5 OLS estimation of the demand for money with the disaggregated output and disequilibrium supply-side variables in logarithmic first differences plus seasonal dummies

MD	RD (38)[1]	UD (38)[1]	ED (38)[1]	MO (38)[1]	M1 (38)[1]	M2 (38)[1]
α_i	0.12	0.05	0.19	0.12	0.16	0.14
SE	(0.04)	(0.03)	(0.07)	(0.04)	(0.05)	(0.04)
t	2.89	1.48	2.72	2.95	3.03	3.50
$\log NFI_t$	−0.03	0.0001	−0.11	0.03	−0.05	−0.05
SE	(0.05)	(0.04)	(0.09)	(0.06)	(0.07)	(0.05)
t	0.61	0.002	−1.12	0.46	−0.70	−0.93
$\Delta \log RC_t$	0.36	0.29	0.77	0.63	0.72	0.53
SE	(0.22)	(0.18)	(0.39)	(0.23)	(0.30)	(0.22)
t	1.60	1.60	1.97*	2.68*	2.40*	2.46*
$\Delta \log UC_t$	0.06	0.08	−0.07	0.02	−0.04	0.01
SE	(0.12)	(0.10)	(0.22)	(0.13)	(0.16)	(0.12)
t	0.52	0.79	−0.32	0.17	−0.23	0.10
ΔR_t	−0.25	−0.003	−0.68	0.002	−0.41	−0.28
SE	(0.13)	(0.11)	(0.23)	(0.14)	(0.18)	(0.13)
t	−1.90*	−0.03	−2.90*	0.10	−2.30*	−2.16*
$\Delta \log GB_t$	0.29	0.31	0.20	0.18	0.20	0.25
SE	(0.11)	(0.09)	(0.20)	(0.12)	(0.15)	(0.11)
t	2.50*	3.36*	0.97	1.47	1.30	2.29*
D_1	−0.09	0.02	−0.38	−0.15	−0.28	−0.20
SE	(0.12)	(0.10)	(0.22)	(0.13)	(0.16)	(0.12)
t	−0.69	0.24	−1.76*	−1.14	−1.70	−1.70
D_2	−0.07	0.004	−0.07	−0.18	−0.11	−0.07
SE	(0.02)	(0.02)	(0.04)	(0.025)	(0.03)	(0.02)
t	−2.80*	0.19	−1.60	−7.29*	−3.50*	−3.20*
D_3	−0.13	−0.04	−0.19	−0.08	−0.15	−0.12
SE	(0.04)	(0.035)	(0.08)	(0.05)	(0.06)	(0.04)
t	−2.89*	−1.09	−2.49*	−1.77*	−2.50*	−2.96*
R^2	0.76	0.741	0.50	0.745	0.61	0.68
s	0.039	0.031	0.07	0.04	0.05	0.037
DW	1.26	1.644	2.29	1.88	2.28	2.20
SC[2] κ_2 (4)	10.14	2.99	3.98	2.85	5.33	3.14
FF κ_2 (1)	4.497	9.24	1.37	7.45	3.90	0.02
Norm.[3] κ_2 (2)	0.81	1.32	105.07	0.33	24.33	7.52
Het.[4] κ_2 (1)	1.52	2.23	0.90	4.02	3.04	1.46

Notes: See notes to Table 6.1.

Second, the coefficients of the interest rate are very significant in most cases except for *UD* and M0, and the signs are negative except for the correlation with M0. But it is insignificant, the coefficient being 0.002, in the regression of M0, demand for which is not significant but is sensitive to interest rates and inflation in all these short-term regressions. It is not clear whether this is actually the case, or whether it is caused by the small sample size.

What we can conclude for Model 5 is as follows. Investment (*NFI*) has no influence and a tiny coefficient, as does urban consumption (*UC*), in the short run. But rural consumption (*RC*) seems quite a good proxy for transactions. The interest rate effect tends to be negative and the supply shocks (*GB*) have a positive effect of about 0.25 on all measures.

CONCLUSIONS AND POLICY RECOMMENDATIONS

The approach adopted above provides a very severe test. To be successful a theoretical model must provide a coherent and plausible model of all six monetary measures. Given that there is a short span of noisy data and the absence of certain explanatory variables, it is not surprising that none of the specifications have passed this stringent test. Some individual equations perform quite well, but reporting them alone (as is often done) would give a misleading impression. In particular, M0 in our system fits the models relatively well, no matter whether it is in levels (Model 1), in first differences (Model 2) or in the OLS estimation by disaggregating the components of output and adding disequilibrium-supply-side *GB* (Models 4 and 5). But if this measure only is provided we may fail to examine the whole picture of the demand for money in China.

Interpretation of the above five models is highly constrained by the small sample size. The non-existence of lags also prevents the model from presenting more dynamic information. However the system does provide useful information through the OLS estimations. By using quarterly data with seasonal dummies, these thirty regressions model the demand for and supply of money in China from different points of view. The plots of actual and fitted values of the regressions contained in Tables 6.2 to 6.4 show that the regressions fit the actual values reasonably well and there is no obvious 'missing money' phenomenon in any of them (see Figures 6.5 to 6.7). Most of the regressions in the five models have passed CUSUM stability tests, except that on *ED* in Model 4. Most of the regressions in Models 2 and 3 have also passed CUSUMSQ stability tests, except that on *RD*. The CUSUM tests are particularly useful for detecting systematic

Figure 6.5   Plot of actual and fitted values, M0

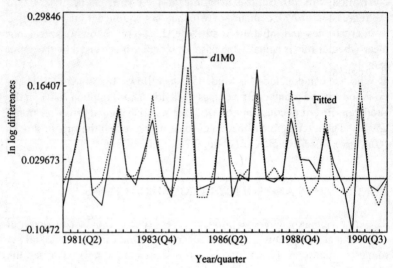

Figure 6.6   Plot of actual and fitted values, M1

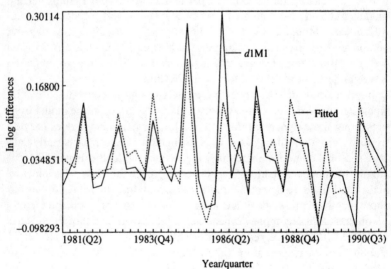

Figure 6.7 Plot of actual and fitted values, M2

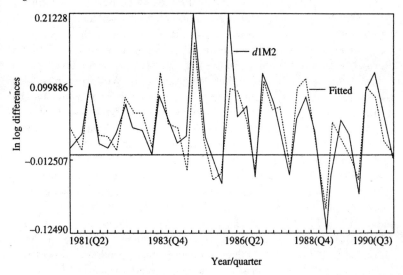

Figure 6.8 Plot of cumulative sum of recursive residuals, M0

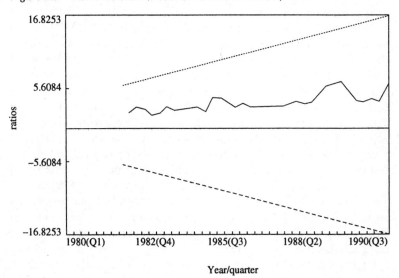

Note: The straight lines represent critical bounds at 5 per cent significance level

changes in regression coefficients. Accordingly the models are generally stable (for an example of M0, see Figure 6.8). In such a short and uncertain period of transition, some regressions can hardly avoid the situation in which departure from the constancy of the regression coefficients is haphazard and sudden, according to the CUSUMSQ tests, such as those on *RD* and *UD*, each with three failures respectively (see Appendix 6.5).

The Chinese literature implies that traditional Western demand for money functions that originate from the quantity theory of money can be applied to the Chinese case. The money function for M0 in Table 6.1 seems to confirm this, though those for the other components of money can be improved through modelling. According to the diagnostic tests, the money functions for *RD* in Tables 6.2 and 6.3, for M1 in Table 6.4 and for *UD* in Table 6.5 seem to be well specified, though we have not made our judgements simply according to the specification test results. All are based on the traditional Western demand for money function. It may be a little naive to use this kind of model in some free market economies because investment and consumption are largely endogenous and uncontrollable, and this can also actively influence government expenditure. However it should cause no surprise that the traditional Western demand for money model upon which our regressions are based may be applied to RCPEs such as China, because the original, powerful foundation for government intervention may be utilised to control investment and consumption, at least in the important state sector.

The difficulty of estimating demand for broad money may be caused by the estimation difficulties of the narrow components of money. It seems that it is demand for varied deposits, especially enterprise and household deposits, that becomes difficult to model. As we know, *RD* and *UD* should be stable in a CPE. After reforms, deposits become more flexible not only because of money income deregulation, but also because of inflation expectations and uncertainty. The increase in the proportion of household deposits in total deposits certainly increases risks from at least the bankers' point of view. The difficulty of estimating *ED* and *UD* implies that the demand for money functions in urban areas are more unstable than in rural areas, which is likely to affect the regressions for M1 and M2. Therefore it has been more appropriate for the Chinese literature to stress research that matches the different definitions of money to the control of money supply. A well-modelled narrow money function does not necessarily tell the whole story of money.

Interest effects in the money regression cannot be easily generalised. Demand for money may not be sensitive to the interest rate in the short run, but it could become sensitive over the whole period 1979–90 (Models

1 and 4). This may imply that it takes time for the interest rate to become sensitive. Sensitivity cannot be judged by simply looking at the negative signs and the significance of the variable coefficients in different regressions. For example the reason for the positive interest elasticity of demand for urban household deposits in Models 1, 2, 3 and 4 are that the high deposit rate attracts more household depositors, who are creditors of banks. The reason for the lowest (in Model 1) or even negative interest elasticities in the regressions for enterprise deposits in Models 2, 3, 4 and 5 could be that the high rate means firms incurring high costs as debtors of banks. Tight monetary policies, in the form of high interest rates, leads to a reduction in enterprise borrowing. This brings to mind the issue of inter-enterprise debt discussed in Chapters 2 and 4. The relative insensitivity of SOEs to changes in R could be a reflection of the relatively low, positive or negative coefficients of R in the long-run regressions for the period of the sample. Although it remains insignificant in all regressions in short-run Model 2, the interest elasticity in the regression of demand for real enterprise deposits is nearly significant (-1.7), and the negative interest elasticity in this regression is the highest absolute value (-0.26). Similar results are found in Model 3. In Model 5 it is even clearer ($t = -2.4$, coefficient = 0.68). These results indicate the increasing sensitivity of *ED* to changes in interest rates in China, at least in the short run.

In the long run, inflation seems insignificant and the effects of the interest rate are significant. In the short run, inflation becomes significant in some regressions (Model 3) and it can even relate to the demand for money unit, proportionally, in most regressions of Model 2. In Models 2 and 3 the interest elasticities are less significant or the short-run effects of the interest rate are small. This suggests that inflation could become the opportunity cost of holding money if the interest rate is relatively restricted by monetary policy in the short run. Both inflation elasticity and the interest elasticity of demand for *ED* and *UD* are higher than those of demand for *RD* in Models 1, 2 and 3. This indicates that the relatively monetised urban areas could be more sensitive to both inflation and the interest rate.

Whenever the interest rate is insignificant or less significant, inflation remains significant or very significant in Model 2 and Model 3. It is difficult to judge whether there may have been a crowding-out effect of the interest rate in respect of inflation. But the interest rate should be fully utilised as an instrument to cope with inflation. Meanwhile inflation should be controlled by the help of other means if the interest rate cannot clear the market.

It is reasonable that demand for cash, M1 and M2 have negative interest elasticities, at least in the short-run models (see Model 3). In the long run it is difficult to say. In the Chinese case, the original levels of interest rates were meaninglessly low. Even if inflation goes down, this does not mean that the interest rate will necessarily follow closely. Therefore the long-run equilibrium interest elasticities of demand for money could be positive (see Models 1 and 4). The small sample size can also cause sign problems.

In the long run, output is significant and positive in Model 1. The significant regressor among the disaggregated output variables and the other positive variables in Models 4 and 5 is often per capita rural consumption, which is more significant than urban consumption. This may indicate the radical changes of rural consumption in the reforms.

By adding the disequilibrium supply side (GB), the coefficients of output (Y) of many regressions in Model 3 are improved and the GB term is significant, at least in the regression for M0 in Model 3. Its coefficients have the above unity proportional changes in the regressions of RD and UD in Model 4. Linking this with the significance of the consumption variable RC, the low values of the investment coefficients in Model 4 and the insignificant investment variable in Model 5, demand for money in the period seems to be consumption motivated in the short run. This supports the argument of Guo (1990) discussed in Chapter 5, although it needs further research. Many of the regressions in Models 4 and 5 not only justify the necessity of adding the disequilibrium-supply-side variable into money holding function, but also highlight the importance of government expenditure and its behaviour in relation to the demand for money.

The above results seem to suggest, either directly or indirectly, that it may be necessary for the reforming economy to regulate investment, consumption and government expenditure in order to realise monetary equilibrium. Investment control could be direct, through credit planning or rationing (see chapter 3), or indirect, through the opportunity costs effect. Control of consumption could be conducted through certain wage and bank cash controls (Hellwig, 1977). This may require the control of firms and banks, which could be effected through the contingent control system suggested by Dewatripont and Tirole (1993). By increasing central bank power and/or independence (see Roll, 1993), government borrowing behaviour may also be disciplined. This links with budget deficit control of the government, since GB reflects the budget situation indirectly.

The approach of an econometric framework that takes account of practical, theoretical and econometric considerations under the criteria of relevance, consistency and adequacy is superior to a single equation estimation, although these estimations have not provided any fresh theoretical model for the demand for money.

FUTURE RESEARCH – MONEY BASED ON THE DIVISIA INDEX

This econometric exercise does not recommend a new model for the demand for and supply of money function. Rather, it explores a new way of understanding monetary control during transition and a new approach to dealing with a small sample size when insufficient data is available. In an economy in transition such as China, time-series analysis is often based on a short period, with possible data deficiencies and structural changes over time. The modelling in this chapter is not perfect, but it could be a starting point. With the development of market mechanisms and the increased availability of data, it will be possible to modify and improve the regressions. When precise quarterly or even monthly data on exact investment, consumption and government expenditure are available, the disaggregated money model specified by Equation 6.13 may be more successful. An increase in the number of observations may also allow the use of more lagged dependent variables, which are more likely to be exogenous and could promote understanding of the important dynamics that have had to be ignored here. Then it may be possible to see more clearly whether consumption or investment, or both, significantly influence the demand for money.

It is argued that simply adding components of the money supply, for example, cash and deposits, is misleading because they have different liquidity characteristics. When the money components are aggregated, the Divisia index approach may be used to see how sensitive the measures are to this problem (see Appendix 6.1). This approach weights the components by their user costs. Unfortunately no such data is available. The rates of alternative or non-monetary assets (government bonds) are published annually. These do not have the same effect as the gilts rate because bonds were often sold for political reasons before the end of the 1980s and could not be traded. To compare the simple money aggregate approach, we assume that there was an alternative asset that paid 1 per cent above the deposit rate, to provide an estimate for R_t. This is inaccurate, but it provides a figure that allows us to gauge the effects using a Divisia index.

When obtained by this approach, M1 does seem to deviate less in its growth pattern than the simple unweighted average (see Figure 6.9), which suggests that the unweighted average exaggerates the volatility of the money supply. This is interesting. The findings may be generalised with the application of more components. The problem is that there is not a different interest rate for each of them. Therefore the components of money (*PD, UD, ED* and M0) can only be modelled as a system and the pattern across the series commented on, with M1 and M2 as the extra experi-

Figure 6.9   Comparison between simple aggregate and Divisia aggregate, M1

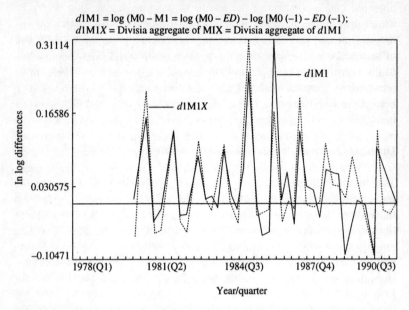

$d1M1 = \log (M0 - M1 = \log (M0 - ED) - \log [M0 (-1) - ED (-1);$
$d1M1X = \text{Divisia aggregate of MIX} = \text{Divisia aggregate of } d1M1$

Year/quarter

ments. However the identification problems may have to be discussed and resolved when applying simultaneous equations.

APPENDIX 6.1   WESTERN STUDIES ON THE DEMAND FOR MONEY

Literature on the demand for money comprises a major part of the development of the theory of monetary economics in the West. The size of the interest elasticity and stability of demand for (narrow) money may influence the efficacy of fiscal and monetary policy, such as in the simple fixed-price IS-LM model. Money supply can either depress or stimulate inflation via excess demand and (often long-run vertical) price expectations. The trade-off between the speed at which inflation is reduced and temporary loss in real output are often topics of discussion in macroeconometric modelling. The following theories are relevant to the work in this chapter.

The simple-sum index should be abandoned

Barnett *et al.* (1992) indicate that studies of the demand for money are based on official monetary aggregates (M1, M2, M3) constructed by a method (simple-sum aggregation over arbitrary financial components) that does not take advantage of the results of existing aggregation theory or recent developments in the application of demand theory to the study of financial institutions. An alternative to the simple-sum approach is the use of microeconomic aggregation theory to define money. One branch leads to the construction of index numbers using methods derived from economic theory. Barnett *et al.* explain the underlying microeconomic theory behind the Divisia index. The non-linearity produced by economic theory is important.

Demand for money models are questionable

The 'quantity theory' approach posits a positive (and possibly proportionate) relationship between transactions and money, a unit price level elasticity (homogeneity) and a positive 'own yield', and leaves the signs on the other variables to be determined by the data. In Keynesian theory, volatile expectations might cause parameter instability. Expectations formation may be such as to cause a highly elastic response of money holdings to a small change in the interest rate (the 'liquidity trap'). In Friedman's view, the quantity (and quantitative) relationship between these variables and the demand for money should be determined by empirical work.

By applying the ADL–ECM approach to the demand for money for both the UK and the US, Hendry's long-run model of demand for M1 in the UK gives a positive unit income elasticity, negative interest rate and annual inflation semi-elasticities. His dynamic model has the same signs for these variables (Hendry 1979, 1985). Hendry and Ericsson (1991) examine demand for broad money in the UK and yield a preferred ECM equation with negative price and interest elasticities. For the US, Rose (1985) finds a stable demand function for the missing money period that has positive income elasticity and negative interest and inflation elasticities. The signs of the variables in the dynamic long-run equilibrium are the same. Baba *et al.* (1988) find that, in the long run, the demand for real money balances in the US has a real income elasticity of 0.5 and an inflation elasticity of –1.3, and exhibits a negative relationship with the yield on alternative M2 instruments. The bond volatility measure has a direct positive effect on demand for M1 and additionally raises the (positive) bond–bill spread. The dynamic model has similar signs for the same variables. Overall the error feedback approach has yielded reasonable results for demand for M2 in European countries (see Cuthbertson, 1991). Hendry and Mizon (1978) present an ECM of demand for M3 by the UK personal sector that has a positive yield on long-term government debt. In

Taylor's (1987) conventional ECM demand for sterling M3 equation, the coefficients for bill rate, bonds rate and total final expenditure are negative.

Cooley and LeRoy (1981) question the demand for money studies on two independent counts. The first is that the negative interest elasticity of money demand reported in the literature represents prior beliefs much more than sample information. The second is that the treatment of simultaneity in the literature is totally inadequate.

They argue that many empirical studies of money demand are based on selective reporting of the results of a specification search. Researchers have acted as advocates of consensus theory by conducting specification searches and reporting only evidence that is consistent with their belief in the theory. For Keynesians, a negative estimated interest elasticity is an absolute necessity for IS-LM models. But the issue of interest elasticity is not of primary importance to monetarists. Monetarist doctrine stresses the dependence of nominal interest rates on expected inflation, though monetarists are much more willing than Keynesians to reverse their stand on the question of interest elasticity if the data indicates it.

In rational-expectations macroeconomic models, interest rates are not directly involved in the link between monetary shocks and changes in real activity, because participants are, by assumption, unable to distinguish between nominal and real shocks. Researchers associated with the rational-expectations' tradition would not be required to find a negative relationship between monetary changes and interest changes. The proposition that increases in money stock are correlated with declines in short rates may not be supported by empirical tests (Mishkin, 1988). The problem is that a demand equation is applied to data other than those used to fit the equation. Overinterpreting the data has caused money stock to be overpredicted by a large margin.

What is required is a more formal and explicit means of representing prior information about model specification. Leamer's analytical procedure and reporting style (Chamberlain and Leamer, 1976; Leamer, 1978) is one way of fulfilling this requirement. The approach obviates the need for specification of the prior covariance matrix. According to the theorem, specification of the prior location and the sample covariance matrix is sufficient to constrain the posterior means to lie within a particular ellipsoid, the 'locus of constrained estimates.'

A strong prior presumption for the existence of correlation between the explanatory variables and the error implies that the estimate of the coefficient of the focus variables will be inconsistent. However the overwhelming majority of studies of money demand rely on OLS estimators, and most studies do not even mention the simultaneity problem. Cooley and LeRoy (1981) see no reason for supposing that the lagged money stock may serve as an instrument in estimating demand any more than that of supply. They distinguish the definition of exogeneity that is relevant to statistical estimates (observed variables are independent, in the probability sense, of the unobserved explanatory variable) from the definition that is relevant to macroeconomic theory (observed variables are not determined within the model). The important questions are whether explanatory variables for the money stock are predetermined, and whether they are statistically exogenous. It is possible that the money stock may be taken as statistically exogenous in that interest rates adjust to it in economics (Laidler), while interest rates are exogenous in that the money stock adjusts to them in econometrics. If there is uncertainty about which normalisation direction is more likely to eliminate simultaneity problems, it would appear to be reasonable to try both and then ascertain how much difference the direction of normalisation makes to the parameter estimates of interest.

After criticising the empirical literature on money demand for minimising the seriousness of simultaneity problems, and for representing obviously inadequate corrections as adequate, Cooley and LeRoy (1981) consider several apparently reasonable approaches to the problem, but conclude that they are in fact no more plausible than the remedies analysed and rejected.

Some Western modelling approaches to demand for money functions

Having concentrated on the interaction between theory and applied work based on Western theories and applied studies, Cuthbertson (1991) generally puts Western modern literature on the demand for money into three main categories: the 'motives' approach ('transactions models'), the 'consumer demand' approach ('precautionary models') and buffer stock models.

Transactions models

Even in traditional CPEs money was regarded as a universally accepted means of exchange. Therefore Western 'transactions models' based on this characteristic of money, and which divide into sub-approaches, may be theoretically worth testing in an RCPE case. The well-known quantity theory identity $MV = PY$ (Fisher, 1930) shows that velocity is determined by the payment mechanism. Pigou (1917) reduced this model to $M^d = kPY$, which emphasises the desired demand for money by consumers, and that the level of transactions, k, may depend on other variables in the consumer allocation problem, such as interest rates and wealth.

Keynes (1936) accepted the transactions demand from the Cambridge view, but emphasised other motives: precautionary and speculative. It is his pessimistic view on interest rates that in some way justifies the less meaningful interest rate in the RCPEs. For the side effects of the prompt increase of interest rates discussed in Chapter 3, the effectiveness of interest rates in an RCPE may take time to be realised even when they become sensitive. The significance of this is that the monetary authorities have to find other means to restrict the investment motive of agents. This is why the factors on the supply side – such as reserves, total bank loans and investment – remain the most important targets of the monetary authorities.

Risk aversion models address the problem of choice in a set of assets or a diversified portfolio that has uncertain capital (Markowitz, 1952, 1959; Borch, 1969; Feldstein, 1969). These models have the same feasibility problem in a CPE, where most individuals have no intention of maximising utility by trading off risk and return, subject to a wealth constraint. This does not mean that it will not be interesting to research risk aversion issues in the future. Monetisation and financial deepening will surely lead to diversification of assets.

The consumer demand approach

Friedman (1956) argues that demand for assets should be based on axioms of consumer choice. He approaches the theory of demand for assets by considering explicit motives for holding money, but he does not present an explicit model.

Money can be defined narrowly or broadly. Asset demand equations may be separated accordingly, if the agents undertake some form of multi-stage budgeting. Decisions about consumption and saving may be independent of variables affecting the choice between real and financial assets. Demand for money may be determined by many variables, such as yields on assets that could be held as alternatives to money (bonds and equities), inflation, human wealth, total wealth and even changes in tastes and preferences (Harris, 1981).

When deposit rates that are compared with inflation cannot attract money held by households, and there are few alternative assets to be invested, consumption in an RCPE is easily boosted. On the demand side, household consumption and money income are among the important factors. CPE planners always stressed the importance of macroeconomic equilibrium because the effects of excess demand were so clearly dysfunctional. A balance between the money income and expenditure of the population was a key element in the planning process, and planners disposed of powerful policy instruments to achieve their targets. The influence of consumption upon the demand for money became even greater. So-called 'overdistribution of the national income' frequently occurred in the 1980s in China.

The buffer stock approach

Laidler (1984) finds that the interest rate and the exchange rate often overshoot monetary targets, and it is hard to understand why people hold 'money' when it is dominated by other assets. To solve the problems encountered when trying to estimate stable 'conventional' demand for money functions, and to understand the 'long and variable lags' of monetary policy, recent literature has increasingly regarded money as a buffer stock, that is, as an asset that acts as a 'stock absorber' enabling agents temporarily to postpone otherwise costly adjustments to alternative economic variables such as employment, investment and output, and to economise on 'information'. Buffer holdings of money are voluntarily held in the short run and then dissipated in a slow, real balance effect. This notion explains 'temporal instability' in demand for money functions and the 'long and variable lags' of monetary policy.

The buffer stock approach considers disequilibria originating in either demand or supply, because the costs of marginal adjustments to prices, wages, production and real stock levels may be more substantial than the interest forgone by holding excess money balances. Shocks can be caused to firms' production and employment plans or to the money supply. Shocks to money supply are often caused by an increase in the supply of bank advances, which may lead to unexpected changes in money holdings by other agents when the advances are spent. A variety of factors affect the speed with which firms adjust their excess holdings of money (Goodhart, 1984). Generally, the higher the efficiency of the money-transaction technology and the lower the cost of transferring between 'money' and 'near money', the wider the set of assets of which buffer assets are likely to consist relative to transaction balances. For large firms it may be liquidity rather than simply 'money' that acts as the buffer stock. But in a CPE case such as China, money in the form of cash was strictly controlled by banks, while other financial assets were not available. Since the reforms, transferring cost is still out of the question because of the underdeveloped financial markets. Buffer assets may consist of money, government subsidies or bank 'policy credits',[16] commercial bills and even interenterprise debt. 'Buffer stock money' models can be classified as follows (Cuthbertson and Taylor, 1987; Milbourne, 1988).

First, *single-equation disequilibrium money models* have a sizeable autoregressive component, which has frequently been interpreted as reflecting slow adjustment of short-run to long-run desired money holdings, but the market clearing level of interest rate obtained when such equations are inverted will grossly overshoot its long-run equilibrium value in response to an exogenous change in the current-period money supply. Various authors interpret these estimated demand for money parameters as representing a slow real balance effect, and advocate inverting the demand for money function prior to estimation. Agents are temporarily forced to drop away from their long-run function because of slow adjustment of interest rates, output or the price level if the supply of money is independent of demand factors.

Under the assumption of slow adjustment of interest rates or nominal income, a number of inverted long-run demand for money functions are estimated with different conclusions (Artis and Lewis, 1976; Hendry, 1985, for UK M1; Milbourne, 1988, for US narrow money). The single-equation disequilibrium money approach has a major problem, that is, it chooses only one argument as the dependent variable, whereas on a priori grounds one might expect all the arguments of the demand for money function to adjust simultaneously.

Portes and Winter (1980) apply this approach to test the macroeconomic relationships in CPEs systemically against aggregate time-series data. They deal with aggregate measures of consumer goods and services, c, and suppose that prices or other potential equilibrating variables do not adjust sufficiently to equate demand for and supply of consumption goods and services in period t, assuming that the quantity sold is given by the minimum of supply and demand (the 'min condition'). The disequilibrium econometric model is as follows:

$$C_t^d = C_t^d(X_t^d) + \varepsilon_t \qquad (6.14)$$
$$C_t^s = C_t^s(X_t^s) + \eta_t \qquad (6.15)$$
$$C_t = \min(C_t^d, C_t^s) \qquad (6.16)$$

X_t are vectors of exogenous variables, ε_t and η_t are error terms (customarily assumed to be jointly normal with mean vector zero, covariance matrix Σ, and serially uncorrelated) and C_t^d and C_t^s are unobserved by the econometrician but C_t is observed. The econometric evidence justifies rejecting the hypothesis of sustained repressed inflation.

Second, *complete disequilibrium monetary models* remedy the above model and disequilibrium money holdings are allowed to influence a wide range of real and nominal variables of the following type:

$$\Delta X_t = f(Z_t) + \gamma(L)(M_t^s - M_t^d) \qquad (6.17)$$
$$M_t^d = d_0 P_t + \alpha_1 R_t + \alpha_2 Y_t \qquad (6.18)$$

where X_t may be a set of real and nominal variables (for example, output, prices, exchange rate), Z_t is a set of predetermined equilibrium variables, M_t^d is the long-run demand for money and $\gamma(L)$ is a lag polynomial. The model yields cross-equation restrictions on the parameters of the long-run demand for money function (as the money disequilibrium term appears in more than one equation) with reasonably good performances. By using cointegration techniques the residuals, with additional variables in some expenditure equations are viewed as disequilibrium money.

The drawback of the full systems approach is that any estimates are conditional on the correct specification of the whole model if the coefficients of long-run money demand are the investigator's parameters of interest. However the complete model approach has the considerable advantage of showing the various routes whereby monetary disequilibrium affects the economy.

There are other kinds of approaches, such as '*shock absorber approaches*', which estimate the demand for money function by assuming that shocks to the money supply are initially voluntarily held in transactions balances (Carr and Darby, 1981; Cuthbertson and Taylor, 1988); and '*forward-looking buffer stock models*', which recognise possible deficiencies in conventional backward-looking formulations of the demand for money function that ignore potentially important variables, that is, future values of the demand for money (Sargent, 1979).

Dynamic modelling

The error correction model (ECM) has become a very popular specification for dynamic equations in applied economics, especially its application to the demand for money, because it encompasses both levels and differences of variables and is compatible with long-run equilibrium behaviour (Engle and Granger, 1987). An ECM model is derived by Domowitz and Hakkio (1990) from a stochastic dynamic programming problem incorporating rational expectations. A parametric restriction entails the failure asymptotically to close the gap between the choice variable and the growing target. This is accomplished by testing a partial adjustment model with forward-looking expectations within the error correction paradigm. The counterintuitive behaviour embodied in the error correction model is not supported by the data in the context of a cross-country comparison of cash balances.

Having started from a single-period loss function of a typical partial adjustment form, Domowitz and Hakkio (1990) abstract the first order conditions from the intertemporal loss function at time t. Some tedious algebraic manipulation yields the optimal policy at time t in terms of conditional expectations of m_{t+j}^*. By substituting an expectation formula, they arrive at the final ECM rule, which is rewritten in unrestricted form as

$$\Delta m_t^* = \alpha_0 + \alpha_1 \Delta m_t^* + \alpha_2(m^* - m)_{t-1} \qquad (6.19)$$

The desired balances relationship is given by

$$m_t^* = \gamma_0 + \gamma_1 y_t + \gamma_2 i_t + \gamma_3 e_t^e + \gamma_4 \pi_t \qquad (6.20)$$

where y is the logarithm of a measure of real income. Substituting (6.17) to (6.16) yields

$$\Delta m_t = a_0 + a_1 \Delta y_t + a_2 \Delta i_t + a_3 \Delta e_t^e + a_4 \Delta \pi_t + b_1(m - \gamma_1 y)_{t-1} + \\ b_2 i_{t-1} + b_3 e_{t-1}^e + b_4 \pi_{t-1} \qquad (6.21)$$

where $a_i = a_1 \gamma_i$ ($i = 1, ..., 4$), $b_i = a_2 \gamma_i$ ($i = 2, 3, 4$), $a_0 = \alpha_0 + \alpha_2 \gamma_0$, $b_1 = -\alpha_2$. The term $(m - \gamma_1 y)_{t-1}$ is the hallmark of unconstrained ECMs for money demand. If the long-run income elasticity of money demand is unity ($\gamma_1 = 1$), the term in Equation 6.21 is inverse velocity. Their statistical tests indicate that, once forward-looking behaviour is introduced via a standard expectations mechanism, the partial adjustment model is indeed appropriate, and the extra structure underlying the ECM appears to be superfluous. By incorporating fixed adjustment costs in a dynamic setting, in which expectations play a non-trivial role, they believe that data can be fitted well, without explicitly relying on a lagged dependent variable.

APPENDIX 6.2   CHINESE STUDIES ON THE DEMAND FOR MONEY

Many studies have estimated demand for money functions for the Chinese economy, based mainly on Western economic theories and methodologies. There is little differentiation of the demand for money models for China between the prereform period and the post-reform period, most probably because econometrics is constrained by minimum observations. The approaches to applying the theory and econometrics are diversified, and therefore the results and conclusions are different. Assessment of these studies helps in developing the demand for money model. The literature is classified roughly into that measuring the demand for money for the prereform period up until the 1980s, including papers published afterwards, and that modelling the demand for money for the post-reform period, starting at the end of the 1970s. The prereform period literature can be thought of as measuring the demand for money because the approach is characterised by measuring purchasing power to investigate excess demand. The post-reform literature benefits from econometrics and various newly developed techniques to model the demand for money directly, though some economists still use the simple ratio comparison or base themselves on the 'purchasing power approach'.

The demand for money literature highlights two basic approaches to analysing the demand for money in China: the 'purchasing power approach', pioneered by Perkins (1966), and the 'quantity theory' approach, which deals with the demand for money from a theoretical point of view, though it is difficult to generalise these different approaches. From a methodological point of view, the econometric models can be classified as those based on pooled data without periodical distinction and those that distinguish between the prereform period and the post-reform period. It is important to understand the differences between their theoretical assumptions. Causality is an important issue, but it seems more important to look at the behaviour of the SOEs and the household sector, the functions of money and the roles of banks in the transitional period. The changes include not only the institutional framework, but also mechanism changes after reform of the planning, budgetary and banking systems. With the development of the Chinese economy, variables may have to be added, adjusted or changed. Two recent papers on the demand for money in China are of interest in this respect.

Econometric studies on the subject appear mainly to estimate China's money demand equations based directly on the stylised quantity theory of money (for example, Zhang, 1986; Chow, 1987; Yi, 1990; Li, 1990). There is the issue of how to model China's money demand mechanism as well as the issue of constancy. Qin *et al.* (1992) seek to determine whether there exists an economically meaningful money demand equation with relatively constant coefficients. 'For many Chinese economists, the non-constancy of the money demand relation seems a self-evident fact, and they have concentrated their discussions on the role of monetary policies in the excess expansion of the aggregate demand' (Qin *et al.*, 1992, p. 1). More specifically, their discussions centre on the causality between money and inflation, and their views are roughly divided between those who regard the increase of money supply in excess of economic growth as the main cause (for example, Zhang, 1988; Chen, 1991), and those who disapprove of the existence of independent monetary policy and ascribe the cause to government credit policy, mainly the wage and investment plans (for example, Song, 1988; Kang, 1988; Dai, 1992).

Qin *et al.* try to settle the disputes over China's aggregate money demand relation with supporting econometric evidence. They follow Hendry's general simple reduction approach (1991), starting from a general linear dynamic equation:

$$a(L) \, lnM_t = c + b(L)X_t' + \text{seasonals} + \varepsilon_t$$

where $X_t = (LnY_t R_t IM_t RSL_t)$, in which Y is income or wealth; R is the real interest rate; IM is a monetisation index taking the average of two ratios: the price ratio of the industrial output deflator to the agricultural output deflator, and the output ratio of state-owned industries to the whole of industry; $a(L)$ is the autoregressive polynomial; and $b(L)$ the distributed polynomial (initially six lags).

They present the following arguments. First, 'China's economic reform did not seem to have discontinued the relatively constant relation of aggregate money demand, provided all the main relevant factors have been taken into consideration ... it would be pointless to discuss effective monetary policies if there were no relative stable money demand relations for it to be based upon' (Qin *et al.*, 1992, p. 19). Second, 'Inflation appeared to have exerted a significant effect on money, since there have been far fewer changes in the nominal interest rate over the past years ... the postulate of inflation causing money is observed to hold more constant than that of money causing inflation' (ibid., p. 20), confirming that inflation was not fundamentally caused by money expansion during the reform (see Dai, 1992). Third, 'The significance of both the long-run and short-run coefficient of the interest rate indicated that the cost of holding money did not matter in the general savings behaviour despite the rigidity of the government control over the interest rate in the past'. Therefore no chronic excess money with respect to demand was observed. Fourth, the 'softening of government budget constraint has been pinned down by the long-run disequilibrium force here in a CPE. This poses an interesting question of whether softening of budget has overriding power in CPE, or what is the exact binding force of the softening' (Qin *et al.*, p. 22). Fifth, there is 'a disequilibrium tendency in the enterprises' behaviour under the CPE environment (that is, a long-run soften-budget characteristic). Sixth, government investment behaviour and its income policy, 'are more fundamental than money' (ibid., p. 22).

Huang (1993) seeks to correct two 'principal problems' in considering money demand in China during the reform period (1979–90). One problem was the lack of separate consideration of China's prereform period and the reform period. In their empirical work, most studies have used data from the 1950s to the early or mid-1980s. The reform period

(1979 until the present) has essentially been neglected as one that merits separate consideration. The stability of money demand in China became problematic in the midst of market-oriented transition, rapid monetisation and the changes in China's economic structure. Another problem concerned the specifications and performance of the models. The previous models applied the partial adjustment (PA) model directly without studying the properties of the data. It is unknown whether the models were specified correctly. In addition there was no evidence that these models and the explanatory power of the variables remained stable, since the possible effects of economic reform were ignored. Finally, in most cases common diagnostic tests, forecasting tests and recursive regression tests were not performed. His model is a simple ECM regression:

$$(M2 - P)_t = f[(M2 - P)_{t-2}, Y_{t-2}, Pt, ECM_{t-1}]$$

His model suggests that the dynamic mechanism of money demand in China maintained overall stability during the reform period, and that the explanatory power of most variables also remained stable, which indicates that despite the dramatic changes in China's economy, money supply control is still one of the viable instruments for the Chinese monetary authorities.

APPENDIX 6.3   UNIT ROOT TEST

Variables	DF	ADF (1)	Variables	DF	ADF (1)
logPD	−2.14	−1.44	logPD	−5.16*	−5.54*
logDS	−0.61	−3.22	logDS	−6.10*	−6.04*
logED	−1.11	−2.01	logED	−7.43*	−7.45*
logRC	−2.17	−1.86	logRC	−6.72*	−6.90*
logUC	−1.75	−2.54	logUC	−7.11*	−7.06*
logMO	−2.67	−2.67	logMO	−7.19*	−8.47*
logMI	−1.88	−1.67	logMI	−7.20*	−6.46*
logM2	−1.97	−1.98	logM2	−6.65*	−6.53*
logIG	−2.38	−4.57*	logIG	−15.65*	−15.53*
logGB	−4.60*	−7.74*	logGB	−5.71*	−7.90*
logNFI	−9.43*	−6.12*	logNFI	−13.95*	−6.60*
IR	−1.40	−2.49	DIR	−6.59*	−4.81*
logSI	−0.31	−0.54	logSI	−4.61*	−4.61*
logSC	−3.16*	−2.03	logSC	−9.40*	−5.38*
CPI	0.64	0.50	CPI (or)	−6.27*	−9.72*

* Larger than the critical value in absolute term. All variables are in log real terms.

APPENDIX 6.4   VARIABLE ADDITION TESTS

(OLS case with regressors: logY, IR, + three dummies)

Variables	F-statistics	Variable added	F-statistics
Dependent variable: logRD			
logGB F (1, 34) =	1.48 [0.23]	logNFI F (1, 34) =	4.92 [0.03]*
logRC F (1, 34) =	0.12 [0.73]	logUC F (1, 30) =	0.07 [0.796]
Dependent variable: logUD			
logGB F (1, 34) =	1.21 [0.28]	logFI F (1, 34) =	4.24 [0.05]*
logRC F (1, 37) =	0.44 [0.51]	logUC F (1, 30) =	0.001 [0.97]
Dependent variable: logED			
logGB F (1, 34) =	0.33 [0.57]	logNFI F (1, 34) =	1.56 [0.22]
logRC F (1, 37) =	0.02 [0.88]	logUC F (1, 30) =	0.33 [0.72]
Dependent variable: logMO			
logGB F (1, 34) =	0.04 [0.05]	logNFI F (1, 34) =	0.47 [0.50]
logRC F (1, 34) =	0.16 [0.69]	logUC F (1, 30) =	0.43 [0.52]
Dependent variable: logM1			
logGB F (1, 34) =	0.47 [0.50]	logNFI F (1, 34) =	1.33 [0.26]
logRC F(1, 34) =	0.14 [0.71]	logUC F (1, 30) =	0.18 [0.67]
Dependent variable: logM2			
logGB F (1, 34) =	1.89 [0.18]	logNFI F (1, 34) =	3.49 [0.07]*
logRC F (1, 34) =	0.48 [0.49]	logUC F (1, 30) =	0.20 [0.65]

* Variable has successfully passed the F test.

APPENDIX 6.5 STABILITY TESTS

Variables:	RD	UD	ED	MO	M1	M2
Model 1						
CUSUM:	accept	accept	accept	accept	accept	accept
CUSUMSQ:	accept	NOT	accept	accept	NOT	NOT
Model 2						
CUSUM:	accept	accept	accept	accept	accept	accept
CUSUMSQ:	NOT	accept	accept	accept	accept	accept
Model 3						
CUSUM:	accept	accept	accept	accept	accept	accept
CUSUMSQ:	NOT	accept	accept	accept	accept	accept
Model 4						
CUSUM:	accept	accept	NOT	accept	accept	accept
CUSUMSQ:	NOT	NOT	accept	NOT	accept	NOT
Model 5						
CUSUM:	accept	accept	accept	accept	accept	accept
CUSUMSQ:	NOT	NOT	accept	accept	accept	accept

Notes: Accept – the null hypothesis that the regression equation is correctly specified is accepted at the 5 per cent level of significance. NOT – the same hypothesis must be rejected at the same level of significance.

7 Conclusions and Suggestions

A 'planned economy' is not only a feature of socialism. Capitalism also has plans. A 'market economy' is not only a feature of capitalism. Socialism also has markets. Both planning and markets are economic mechanisms.... The objective of systemic reform is to establish a socialist market economy in order to liberalise and develop productive forces (translated from report by Jiang Zeming in the *People's Daily*, 20 October 1992).

INTRODUCTION

This book has examined the advantages and disadvantages, especially the costs, of decentralising the banking system in a reforming centrally planned economy.

Once a centrally planned system is replaced by a kind of market system, financial institutions, including banks and other financial intermediaries, become important. This may not be immediately obvious. Conventionally, if a production system is liberalised it may be thought that the banking system must undergo similar change. When I first argued for the need to control banks and impose banking control, the Eastern European socialist economies and the former Soviet Union were collapsing. These collapses have not brought about universally improved economic conditions, and in some countries have been followed by worsening crises. Some have argued that China will sooner or later share the fate of the Soviet Union and some Eastern European countries by falling into intractable crisis.

This study argues that the absence of a similar threat in the West, where ruling parties are not as powerful as those in CPEs and China, cannot be wholly explained by the existence of effective market mechanisms, since in fact the mechanisms are not always effective. Rather it is the different control mechanisms *inside* the systems that really matter. As money and banks become much more important in an emerging market economy compared with a CPE, control functions may largely be shifted from planners to bankers.

Controversial arguments have been developed step by step in the six preceding chapters. Having pointed out the control functions of the banking systems in CPEs in Chapter 1, in Chapter 2 there followed an analysis of the problems and financial effects of decentralising the banking system after economic reforms have been launched. Western financial development literature, modern banking literature and the experience of the successful economies were analysed in Chapter 3, and supported the hypothesis that it is necessary to lay emphasis on the control of banks and banking control during the transitional period. The financial disorders experienced by China, explained in detail in Chapter 4, further confirm the necessity for control. Chapter 5 argued that disorder costs cannot be overlooked while administrative costs are being dealt with. With the arguments against some established theories and literature, for example, McKinnon and Shaw's model (McKinnon, 1973) and Peebles' books (1991a, 1991b), and with systematic econometric modelling, the possibility of control seems to be upheld.

The following conclusion of the study begins with a macroeconomic analysis of the problems brought about by the fundamental changes in RCPEs, then goes on to summarise the findings of the research. Some other issues are stressed, and finally some ideas for a suggested banking model during the period of transition are offered.

ANALYSIS OF THE PROBLEMS OF CPE REFORMS

The most influential systemic difference between a market economy and a CPE was that the latter, such as China under the leadership of Mao Zedong, basically rejected market mechanisms. Mao's completely new system might have been less economically incentive-generating and competitive than some successful economies based on markets, but there was no open or long-term inflation. Economic fluctuations did exist, but they were created mainly for political motives. The central planning mechanism imposed a rough balance between supply and demand in each product category without requiring help from the financial system. Rapid economic growth was even sustained in the period of the Cultural Revolution (1966–76).[1]

Deng Xiaoping has challenged the traditional CPE model by introducing market mechanisms and foreign investment into China. Great achievements have been brought about by the economic reforms. No one can deny that the current Chinese economy is more modern and prosperous than Mao's model. However, serious inflation, economic fluctuation and financial disorders have also come about, and time and again these have undermined the attempts to decentralise decision making.

Various questions can be raised. For example, how could central planning in Mao's model stabilise economic development through fiscal and monetary policies? Why should Deng's decentralisation strategy lead to inflation while weakening direct physical planning? What are the optimal arrangements for China's banking system to secure a market-oriented transition without price disturbances?

The answer to the first question is linked to the features of a CPE, such as Mao's model, with its characteristics of direct enterprise profit extraction and passive money. State ownership of all industrial and agricultural properties enabled the government to withdraw surpluses from enterprises, control wages through enterprises and control the retail cost of consumer goods, including luxuries, through a system of price controls. Thus no explicit system of taxation, such as income tax and sales tax, was necessary.

Deposit money for transactions between enterprises and cash for transactions between enterprises and households and within the household sector were entirely separated as two types of money. Excess demand for goods could be dealt with by direct control over supply without affecting the demand for labour. The quantity of money was automatically adjusted by the monetary authorities to planned physical flows (given planned prices) and to the degree of their actual implementation without any need for monetary policy. Actual monetary control was exercised on the flow of incomes, and wages determined the supply of money to the household sector.

On the loan side, the state bank functioned as a cashier, not a decision maker, although the banks did supervise and control the production system (see Chapter 1). Plans entitled enterprises to borrow from the state banks as required for fulfilment of the targets without being restrained by interest rates and credit ceilings. On the deposit side, the cash balances of enterprises were extremely small because any cash that was not quasi-blocked (by the government) was immediately spent by enterprises worried about the possibility of reregulation of these funds. The demand for money by enterprises was indeterminate, and the government cut off the cash of SOEs deposited in banks whenever necessary or allocated it for certain other purposes. All these factors helped the government to minimise the extra-liquid cash balances in the hands of households in order to prevent inflation.

With regard to the second question on the causes of inflation, since decentralisation operational rights have been separated from ownership. In some places they have been privatised. Autonomy has been given to enterprises, although property is still generally owned by the state. Meanwhile the formal apparatus of central planning has been weakened. Enterprises can now determine a certain proportion of wage rates, a large amount of 'available' money income (bonuses), the number of employees, the price of many products and their capital investment. These are the preconditions for both cash and credit increases. Granting discretion to enterprises over investment and wages has resulted in an investment and consumption boom, but paradoxically also a fall in profits (see Chapter 2). The drastic decline of financial surpluses in modern industry seems to be 'entirely' attributable to the impact of changing relative prices. These prices were initiated by increased agricultural procurement prices and intensified by the downward pressure on relative manufacturing prices created by lowered barriers to entry, as well as increases in depreciation charges and interest rates (Naughton, 1990). The decline may also be attributable to the fundamental problems of inefficiency in the current economic system. Much of this is due to a continuation of price distortions, which cannot be corrected in the short run.

Enterprise surpluses were easily taxed by the authorities, but now this extraction has been significantly reduced by firms' retention autonomy. 'Cash cows' have been liberalised, while vehicles for indirectly taxing households have been abandoned (McKinnon, 1991). The absence of a formal internal revenue service as a result of poor codification in formal tax law has helped firms and the new 'duchesses and princesses' (local governments) to bargain with central government and even to escape taxes. The lack of a modernised tax system means that changes in relative prices introduced in the wake of the reforms have caused a substantial erosion of government fiscal revenues.

As a result the revenue of the consolidated government has declined sharply during decentralisation (see Chapter 2). Interest rates below market clearing levels have discouraged the non-banking public from buying government bonds. Budget deficits had to be financed through borrowing from the state banking system, which also injected money into the economy more energetically than ever before, either to stimulate high economic growth or to subsidise loss-making companies. Thus supplies of unrestricted cash owned by households and the overhang of quasi-blocked deposit money owned by enterprises have increased. Increased household savings, on the other hand, have made it possible to finance large public sector deficits under certain conditions.

Inflation seems inevitable and is enhanced by two factors besides the monetisation factor caused by the pricing system reform. One is the anxious spending of enterprise quasi-blocked balances that are subject to seizure. The other is enterprise overbidding for storable material inputs, foreign exchange, capital goods and so on due to the absence of attractive monetary assets bearing a positive real rate of interest. Without effective aggregate control through credit markets, high inflation is logically accompanied by financial disorder, with the banking system out of control (see Chapter 4).

In answer to the third question on how to secure the reform without price disturbances, the market should be treated carefully, an issue that is repeatedly debated by modern financial development theories. As far as the financial market is concerned, a key issue is the reliability of the interest rate in clearing financial markets. If interest rates could clear markets, radical CPEs would not have been created; the cyclic economic recessions once sharply criticised by Marx and Lenin would not have continued; Keynes (1936) would not have discussed the 'liquidity trap' problem; Gesell (1929) would not have suggested stamp tax on money; the neo-structuralists would not have argued that raising interest rates increases inflation in the short run through a cost-push effect and lowers the rate of economic growth; and McKinnon (1991) would not have altered his original views (see Chapter 3).

A high rate of interest may not necessarily be the key determinant of economic growth when market immaturity coexists with firm monopoly and economic imbalances between areas and sectors. Therefore the once popular remedy of financial liberalisation may not be appropriate for RCPEs. Something further is needed. One key factor is financial control. Yang (1988) argues that when the production system is decentralised during transition, the banking system should not simply be decentralised in a similar fashion. The issue lies in utilising the advantages of the existing banking systems while shedding their drawbacks; the main concern is how to bring the banking system fully into play in implementing stabilisation policy.

A successful reform, a transition with minimal turmoil, relies on a series of effective arrangements in order to shift the scarce resources of the economy, overbid by households and enterprises, back to government revenue and to the banks for investment. Both fiscal mechanisms and monetary mechanisms are crucial to the process. An internal revenue service should be established in order to collect broadly based value added taxes, personal income tax and specific producer and consumer excises. A banking system tightly controlled by the state is still necessary to finance both government expenditure and SOEs.

The Chinese monetary authorities have, in recent months, been conducting a set of financial redisciplinary policies. Chapter 4 of this book argues that this is justified. But is this arrangement a temporary tactic or a strategic decision?

Whether capital structure matters to a firm is a classical question. The answer is different according to different theorems. Banks are necessary in any economy. Even in the West, justification of the continued existence of financial intermediation is still subject to debate. There must be some essential role for banks to play; they should be distinguished from other financial institutions. Banks are the most important investors in market economies, and information asymmetries and the possibility of bank runs have led Western monetary authorities to control banks by various means. This may shed light on the marketisation path taken by RCPEs.

THE FINDINGS

This study has investigated how well a market competitive banking system can serve as a model for CPEs, how far it is possible for the banking system to decentralise itself and how banks can help the authorities to stabilise a reforming economy. The main argument is that *liberalisation of the banking system should not be attempted as long as the industrial system is not subject to proper financial discipline.* The following findings support this hypothesis.

First, one of the essential functions of a banking system, no matter whether it is in a market economy or in a planned economy, is financial control (see Chapters 1, 3 and 4). Banks in CPEs strictly followed government policy and helped planners and the authorities to supervise and regulate investment projects, through which the production system was controlled (see Chapter 1). The inevitability of banking system reforms lies essentially in the need to change the method rather than the nature of control. It is the weakness of monetary policy rather than a need to reduce the power of the monetary system that makes them necessary. Actually, application of the following propositions of Western banking literature to an RCPE is important.

The essential role of banks, besides the well-known conventional functions, is to *control*. In market economies, banks have a net cost advantage in *monitoring*. Banks are able to *impose penalties* upon their borrowers via contracts. Their *reputation* helps banks to act as monitors. These market banking properties are so crucial that without them reform in the socialist economies cannot be successful, because the market system is not mature during transition and SOEs do not easily adhere to financial discipline. The distinguishing feature of banks is their ability to exert control. Bankers therefore should largely replace planners in fulfilling the momentous tasks of transition. Banking system reforms inevitably relate to the method of control. Even in market economies, debtors' cash expenditures need to be controlled by their creditors. Without this control the consequences of decentralisation can be disastrous.

Second, there is no positive link between radical banking reforms and economic effects. In fact radical decentralisation of banking systems has resulted in quite a number of financial disorders and inflation problems. Often, the more radical the decentralisation of the banking system, the worse the economic disorder. In contrast with the production system, which suffers from insufficient discipline, the banking system in transition suffers from an insufficiency of ability and methods to exercise discipline. The main task of economic reform for the production system is to release rigid administrative control over firms in order to let them work more efficiently and more profitably than before. The main task of the financial system reform is somewhat different – it is to let the production system work properly under its supervision and regulation. The widespread problem of interenterprise debt indicates that the banking system should play a greater role in stabilising the immature markets with the help of an effective legal framework (see Chapter 4). Therefore a good banking system is not judged by its superficial structure but by whether it can keep inflation low and stabilise the economy through controls, as well as financing it properly. What really matters is a kind of banking system that the monetary authorities can control easily and can itself conduct financial control efficiently.

Here the specialised financial institutions may still be necessary during transition. Universal banking lowered financing costs in Germany from 1870 to 1914 thanks to its specialities being suited to the German economy (Calomiris, 1993). In the RCPEs at the beginning of transition, a group of banks owned by the state and specialised to a certain extent in some businesses may be easier to discipline than a private commercial banking group. In turn they may be better able to discipline their partners in compliance with government policies during transition. Radical transformation of this banking framework will rely on the attitude of the production system towards market discipline. Commercialisation of the banks in the RCPEs needs to take a gradual route that allows market discipline to be effective. Banking in China may have to be separated from security investment services until regulations are able to secure universal banking.

Third, the economy lays the foundation of a banking system, which may in turn determine its nature. It is the control nature of the economic system that determines the importance of the banking system. The corporate governance structure in a planning regime (CPE) was supported by the joint and/or contingent control mechanisms of the political party system and the planning system (see Chapter 1). Once the systems are changed or removed, a new corporate governance structure should be designed with the support of the newly established control mechanisms. Debt-holders and equity-holders need to control the production system contingently

(Dewatripont and Tirole, 1993). It is necessary for RCPEs to experiment with the contingent control of borrowers by banks and their shareholders (the authorities being the major participants). Chapter 3 suggested a new governance structure within which financiers and shareholders could control the production and banking systems (contingently based on market mechanisms under the legal framework) with the help of administrative regulations. China has so far benefited from the gradual reform approach, which has meant that the traditional joint and contingent control systems have not been suddenly abolished, but instead are still being used effectively until other mechanisms are able to replace them.

The radical reform approaches adopted in many Eastern European countries and the former Soviet Union have left a control vacuum, which has generated enormous problems (see Chapter 5). Reformers and (foreign) investors should closely cooperate in narrowing this vacuum and minimising the disorder costs under a new corporate governance structure. Meanwhile banks should be encouraged to help borrowers in financial distress to restructure or renegotiate (see Chapter 3). Restructuring should be emphasised because sympathetic renegotiation could lead to inter enterprice dept accumulation.

Credit markets are an important channel for the effects of monetary policy, and the ability of banks to screen and monitor the production system is the fundamental justification for their existence. The reforming banking system in the East can learn from the West in terms of systematic banking supervision arranged by specific departments and in terms of strict, well-organised banking legal frameworks to regulate, direct and secure banks, and especially to avoid bank runs. Credit planning should not simply be abandoned, and it may be superior to conventional credit rationing in reconciling macro interests with micro interests.

Fourth, closer involvement of banks and production systems and the time span of loans to fund projects are extremely important banking issues. Market-type banking systems can hardly be generalised. However, in comparatively successful Germany and Japan there are close relations between the banking system and industry. They involve control by 'insiders', which appears to be a more effective system of corporate control, providing both commitment to long-term policies and a mechanism for penalising poor management (see Chapters 3 and 4). Subservient to production systems, banks transform short-term savings into long-term loans. Longer-term loans increase project viability by reducing the initial cost to company cash flows and repaying loan charges out of project earnings (Edwards, 1987). In this respect the specialised banks in China after reform and those in Hungary before reform did not necessarily perform badly (see Chapter 2).

But in RCPEs during transition, where substantial asymmetric information exists and where the number of poor projects can outweigh the number of good ones, venture capital markets may also fail to emerge. The nascent commercial banks in some Eastern bloc countries have not really been successful with respect to economic restructuring. Once specialised banks are put in a competitive position after commercialisation, they can also be biased towards short-term investments. In the interest of maturity transformation, banks should be encouraged to set up long-term credit projects. Bank financing has prepared the necessary rather than the sufficient conditions for a better investment mechanism. The funding of long-term investments requires a power balance under the contracts (see Chapter 3). A banking system guided by correct monetary policies and linked closely to the production system without too much competition may be a necessary remedy for restructuring the economy during transition.

Fifth, it is not difficult to replace planning idealism with market idealism, but the market does not always function well. The mechanisms functioning in the stylised market framework may not be effective in solving the problems of either a recessional RCPE (Hungary) or an overheating RCPE (China) during transition (see Chapter 5). It has also been argued in this book that there are not only administrative costs, but also disorder costs. The latter could be enormously high if proper financial control does not exist (see Chapter 4), and disorder costs may accelerate faster than the former though they may relate with each other negatively. From the macroeconomic point of view a combination of market mechanisms, such as the IS curve, and planning mechanisms such as credit rationing and planning under a well-designed legal framework are in the third-best alternative (see Chapter 5). Both 'invisible hands' and 'visible hands' are needed. A long-term view of investment will be more helpful than a short-term one to foreign investors because they will respect local regulations and policies and contribute their efforts to the establishment of a good corporate governance structure, under which disorder costs can be minimised. Western experiences will be useful when establishing the the legal system.

This book has tried to distinguish between RCPEs, mature market economies, traditional CPEs and other developing countries. Some scholars, such as those of the Liberal Financial School (see Chapter 3) and the Shortage School (see Chapter 5), fail to understand the importance of this distinction and mislead reformers by offering inadequate explanations of the CPE model and incorrect suggestions for policy making. The distinction is fairly important, as it highlights the special characteristics and mechanisms within the systems in transition (see Chapter 5).

Sixth, in the face of structural changes and data that are restricted to relatively short periods, econometric models can hardly explain reforms. An econometric framework that takes account of practical, theoretical and econometric considerations under the criteria of relevance, consistency and adequacy may be better than a single equation estimation. The estimations in this book model the demand for and supply of money in China from different points of view. The regressions fit the actual values reasonably well and the stability tests indicate that the models are generally stable.

The Chinese literature implies that traditional Western demand for money models that originated from the quantity theory of money are usable. But well-modelled narrow money cannot tell the whole story. The difficulty in estimating broad money may be caused by the estimation difficulties of the narrow components of money – the demand for varied deposits, especially for enterprise and household deposits. The money function in urban areas is less stable than in rural areas.

Interest effects in money regression cannot be easily generalised and sensitivity cannot be judged simply. Demand for money may not be sensitive to interest rates in the short run, but it seems to become sensitive in the overall period 1979–90 (Models 1 and 4). The relative insensitivity of SOEs to changes in the interest rate in the long run could be accompanied by an increasing sensitivity of *ED* to interest rate changes in the short run.

Inflation could become the opportunity cost of holding money if the interest rate is relatively restricted by monetary policy in the short run. More monetised urban areas could be more sensitive to both inflation and the interest rate. The long-run equilibrium interest elasticity of demand for money could be positive in the early, more certain period of transition.

The per capita rural consumption level is more significant than the urban one for the radical changes in rural consumption in the reforms. Models 4 and 5 indicate that demand for money during the period was consumption rather than investment motivated. This needs further investigation.

Some regressions not only justify the necessity of adding the disequilibrium-supply-side variable into the demand for money function, but also imply the importance of government expenditure and its behaviour in relation to the demand for money.

All this seems to suggest, either directly or indirectly, that it may be necessary for the reforming economy to regulate investment, consumption and government expenditure in order to realise monetary equilibrium. Control could be implemented through credit planning or rationing (see Chapter 3), through banks' cash control (Hellwig, 1977), through the contingent control system suggested by Dewatripont and Tirole (1993), and through increasing central bank power and/or independence (see Volcker, 1990; Roll, 1993).

In conclusion, the banking system should not necessarily be decentralised at the same time as the production system, and just as 'financial deregulation' is demanded in the West, 'financial regulation' is badly needed in the East. Reform can bring about relative prosperity and reduce the suffering of the people if the dialectic relationships between market mechanisms and planning, and between reform and stabilisation is clearly understood and well handled. As systematic policy direction and institutional management are unavoidable, the banking system will share important historic responsibilities of reforming and stabilising the economy. Foreign investors have an active role to play in the establishment of a healthy economic environment with a good corporate governance structure.

ADVICE FOR FOREIGN INVESTORS IN THE REFORMING ECONOMIES

The previous chapters have concentrated on issues of domestic banking in RCPEs. The discussions are illuminating and supply some clear guidance to foreign investors that can be called the 'three-W' approach – where, what and who.[3]

First, where are the markets? A conventional approach when dealing with recession or demand constraints in market economies is supply depression, cutting off employees and reducing output, waiting for the economic cycle to be over. Strategic changes are reluctantly made. Actually identification of real markets, especially emerging markets, can be a good remedy, in spite of the fact that systemic reforms or adjustments are still unavoidable.

Foreign investors often confront this identification question in the first instance. A potential market can be identified according to different standards: stable political environment, healthy economic growth, reasonable legal framework and so on. Outside politicians and the media are often unhelpful, in which case investors must investigate markets themselves or through well-established investment banks or financial companies.

Most of the economies in East Asia have been growing rapidly for a decade or more. Southern China has the best opportunity for growth in the 1990s (Lehman Brothers, 1993), and China will become one of the three or four largest economies in the world by 2000 according to World Bank experts. Company managers see China as the powerful engine of Asian NICs, a less risky and more profitable investment than areas we may be relatively more familiar with. I myself predicted such a development trend in 1989 (see also Yang, 1994a).[2]

Macroeconomic and political stability during transition is certainly most important because fundamental social and economic changes are taking place. The authorities, no matter which political party rules, must be able to control the situation in the host economy for a considerable time. This is understandable. Another important question is whether the corporate governance structure in the economy is well designed and in the process of being established. The control vacuum left by removing central planning must be filled by placing control, especially financial control, in the hands of other capable agents, such as the banking and legal systems. This microeconomic issue is often ignored. In these two respects China performs relatively well, although it has other problems. China's gradual reform approach has more advantages than the radical approaches adopted by the Eastern European countries in respect of reducing the control vacuum at both macroeconomic and microeconomic levels.

Second, what should be used to open the door? Western investors have experienced difficulty in doing business in the East for either cultural, social or historic reasons. Possibly some money-oriented and short-term-biased Hong Kong businessmen are limited in their understanding of Chinese affairs, though they could have a better knowledge of marketing. An increase in the number of mainland Chinese staff is absolutely necessary. Investors often ask what type of person is more useful when doing business – political dissidents or patriots. Some investors have tried to recruit local people in order to make progress. Whether a job applicant has access to sources of information and influential officers (so-called 'connections') has become a priority question in interviews. A bank in the City of London recently hired a graduate who belonged to the young generation of 'high-rank cadres' ('*gao gan zi di*' in Chinese). This was believed to be the best way of gaining access to the RCPEs, at least during the transitional period.[3] However 'going through the back door' ('*zou hou men*' in Chinese) encourages corruption and damages the newly established legal systems of the host economies. It reflects short-termism. In the past, for example during the Chinese turmoil of 1989, quite a few *gao gan zi di*, and some political dissidents as well, have passed incorrect information to the outside world. Mistakes have been made by relying on the mechanisms of the old systems (the man-ruled systems, or '*ren zhi*' in Chinese) rather than on research and the legal systems (the law-ruled systems, or '*fa zhi*'). This short-termism will eventually damage business.

Actually the doors of the RCPEs have already been opened and it would be wise to go through the front door rather than looking around for a back door. Meanwhile foreign advice and consultancy should be welcomed by local authorities and businessmen in order to improve efficiency and the legal framework, subject to local regulations. As far as personnel are concerned, those who know something of macroeconomics, besides their professional subjects, and who base their knowledge of the host economies on hard studies and honest research at home and/or abroad, are more credible than those who are short-term biased or politically narrow minded. If the latter are appointed to positions of strategic decision making, business can be delayed or even ruined.

Third, who should be trusted to do business? This question relates to two very strategic issues: how to deal with the local authorities (the state) and how to treat the SOEs.

Bankers ought to be prudent and selective simply because capital is largely borrowed and has to be returned. Foreign bankers are concerned with making profits through correct lending. In China there were only 3800 stock companies by the end of 1993. A mere 7 per cent of these were publicly held, the great majority being owned by either employees (47 per cent) or companies (46 per cent) (Bank of Tokyo, 1994). This indicates that most Chinese companies, especially large and medium-sized ones, may not have been taken seriously as a market for foreign investors. SOEs are often considered by Westerners to be insufficiently reliable. If this attitude were to be extended to Chinese SOEs, the market size will be small. The majority of large and medium-sized companies and almost all the banks in such a fast growing economy could become irrelevant for a significant length of time.

The RCPEs cannot develop well without strong authorities. According to Corbett and Mayer (1991) and Nolan (1993), the key changes are not in ownership. The lessons from the Four Little Dragons are 'that free markets are rarely the best way to grow. On the contrary, they show that the state is at the heart of the explanation for their rapid growth. The key to their growth lies in the non-ideological way in which the state interfered in different ways at different times to try to correct for market failure' (Nolan, 1993). Jeffrey Sachs (Harvard University) argues that the IMF's approach to stabilisation in Eastern Europe and the former Soviet Union has been inappropriate because it fails to understand the economic consequences of the state's political bankruptcy. As for the debates on the fundamental task of the World Bank and the IMF, the sharper focus is on the 'disease' that lies almost always in the functioning of the state.[4] Of course the state should take seriously what it thought and said (or implement its plans and promises seriously) in the initial circumstances (see the East Asian examples in Rodrik, 1994a, 1994b).

Public ownership is likely to dominate the Chinese economy so long as the socialist system remains unchanged. It would be wise for foreign investors to concentrate less on equity market profitability and expand their business beyond equity investments. This could also help to withdraw some inflationary currency from circulation. Helping indigenous entrepreneurs to modify the ownership system may be more pragmatic than changing it radically. One way of improving the system, suggested by Nuti (1990), is through a share-holding system under public ownership. Ownership diversification has been going on in China and the other RCPEs. In fact most of the SOEs, especially the large and medium-sized 'key' projects supported by the authorities, are profit makers so there is no reason why foreign businessmen cannot do business with them.

Generally speaking, investment strategies on a long-term basis are better than short-termism. If it remains in Western economies, short-termism is more likely to be adopted by the foreign managers of foreign investment projects due to the influences of narrow-minded nationalism (indigenous people may call this 'new colonialism'). Here it is worth mentioning the lessons of the Latin American debt crisis in the 1980s. Before foreign investors put money into the region, healthy economic mechanisms supported by good institutional systems and legal frameworks had been ignored. Short-termism dominated the investment tide. The financial crises in Turkey and Mexico in 1994–95 offered the same message. The consequences were painful and memorable. Investors and bankers are strongly recommended to set up their businesses on a long-term basis.[5] Great effort should be dedicated to constructing a well-designed corporate governance structure at least within investment projects. Joint effort by the local authorities and foreign investors is also needed to establish a healthy national environment.

A long-term strategy implies positive, active and prudent attitudes. With a positive attitude, problems can be overcome by the joint effort of local and foreign investors. With an active attitude, economies in recession can benefit from helpful investments, while an overheated economy can be cooled by following tight monetary policies. With a prudent attitude, correct investment directions are chosen with care. No business can be sucessful without macroeconomic stability. This stability can be established by the businessmen of both sides. The markets are emerging, and the profits are there.

SOME IDEAS FOR A NEW BANKING MODEL[6]

It is vital for RCPEs to choose the right direction before radical steps are taken, since misunderstanding the situation can create inadequate models.

It is well known that the freedom of banks to create credit can generate an over-supply of money. This is because banks individually ignore the effects of credit upon the rest of their banking activities and upon the economy as a whole, which may lead to overheating of the economy. Meanwhile, the greater the extension of credit, the higher the risk of default, and so on.

However there must be an optimal level of credit creation by banks. The task is to discover what that level is. To do this, we not only need techniques such as statistical methods and econometrics, but also, and probably more importantly, a better system to link macro- with microeconomic interests in order to match financial supply with demand, and to link bank lenders with corporate borrowers. This was thought to be easy by classical, Keynesian and Marxist theorists, but it is problematic in reality. Conflict between the two sides frequently occurs, causing the economy either to overheat or to slide into recession.

Different countries have different systems. There is a great variety across different banking systems, partly as a result of historic evolution. Financial systems can be organised in different ways, but they may perform equally well. Mayer (1988) indicates that in financing practice there does not appear to be a close correspondence between the 'development' of a financial system and its performance in funding industry. On the contrary, what might be deemed to be rather primitive bank-dominated systems in France, Germany and Japan have supported substantially higher funding activity than those in either the UK or the US. The distinctive feature of successful financial systems is their close involvement with industry. A primary characteristic of market-based systems is an arm's-length relationship between investor and firm.

If an RCPE is stable and the production system is subject to market discipline, it would be reasonable to give the banking system more freedom than before. Different banking frameworks could be attempted, including a system based on commercial banks. But gradual transformation of the system is preferred, not only for its stability but also because of the capital strength of the system. Some experiences of Asian NICs are worth mentioning here. For example the transformation of the Development Bank of Singapore from a specialised bank completely owned by the state to a shared bank operating commercial banking businesses was begun only after the economy had taken off. Meanwhile control of and by banks should never be underrated, and long-term financing remains essential during transformation. For these reasons a certain number of specialised banks will remain necessary.

Generally there are three criteria that an improved system should satisfy. One is that development of the banking system should match development of the production system. The second is that the system should limit competition between banks without loss of efficiency. The third is that the system should serve as a close intermediary between micro- and macroeconomic interests.

As economies develop, firms merge with each other in competition and large company groups emerge as a result of economies of scale. Relatively stable relationships between banks and companies, banks and economic sectors, and banks and regions have proved less costly than anticipated. It is possible for banks to base themselves on certain large groups of firms and to compete with banks based on other company groups. Then bankers too can be grouped. In this way, efficiency remains subject to certain competition. Bank supervision of company groups – from the head offices of banking syndicates and company groups down through their branches – becomes easier to organise. Further, the freedom of banks is limited by the large scale of the organisation. It also becomes easier for central banks to look after and regulate banks, because the number of grouped banks is smaller than that of ungrouped ones, and the banking syndicates can also share certain responsibilities of supervision themselves.[7] Of course certain legal frameworks should be established to secure competition and guarantee regulation.

SOME FINAL THOUGHTS

When Eastern and Western economists got together during a conference held by the Centre for Economic Policy Performance at the London School of Economics in 1990, enthusiastically discussing the on-going radical changes in CPEs, I called for emergency policies for financial control possibly through a banking system. At the Annual Conference of the Chinese Economic Association (UK) in 1991 I argued that liberalisation of the banking system should not be attempted as long as the industrial system is not subject to proper financial discipline. Given that the production system of a CPE is decentralised, the banking system should be correspondingly controlled in terms of banking regulation, credit control and investment assessment. Indeed, without proper control of banks, banking control and a well-designed corporate governance structure, the economic and social costs of reform, such as inflation and/or financial disorder, will be increased. This study was completed when the Chinese government was deciding on a radical financial reform programme. No matter what form it eventually takes, I must again stress the essential control function of the banking system. It is to be hoped that the new programme will be designed carefully and implemented steadily.

To sum up, in a planned economy people are 'forced' (or more accurately, 'planned') to be free, while in a market economy people are free to be forced (or to be put under market discipline). In either of these situations certain control mechanisms are necessary, simply because there always exists a relationship of contradictory unification between principals and agents. Tragically many people in RCPEs dream that once planning is abandoned, free markets can easily bring about a higher level of welfare than hitherto. This idea has led to many real tragedies. Although it was wrong for the central planners to ignore the importance of market mechanisms, it is also wrong to ignore the importance of state roles. 'Money talks', but money can also introduce evils.

The gradual reform strategy adopted by the Chinese government has generally been effective. I supported this approach even in 1989, when China experienced turmoil and faced Western sanctions. My paper *China Steps Forward* (1989) argued that the 'Eastern Lion' had awakened and was stepping forward successfully and irrevocably. No newspapers or magazines cared to publish it at the time. An American banker in Hong Kong had a similar experience, but recently published a book entitled *China: The Next Economic Superpower* (Overholt, 1993).

The centre of world development has changed from time to time and has never been permanently associated with any particular area. China too was once a centre of development, and if the Chinese people become more disciplined and continue to work hard there is nothing to prevent it from recapturing that position. It is necessary to learn from the lessons of the former Soviet Union in its decline from superpower status.

Although I call for control of the banking system and an active role for government, I am mindful of the problems of bureaucracy and corruption. Supervisory functions, which could be assumed by more actively organised trade unions and a more independent judiciary, need to be strengthened in order to improve the authorities' management efficiency and prevent corruption. However these issues are beyond the parameters of this study.

Finally, it is my honour to conclude by quoting the final words of a reappraisal of the planning literature by the late S. Chakravarty (1991, p. 19), former chairman of the State Planning Commission of India:

The leap from a 'command' system to a market-based economic regime cannot be equated with the leap from the 'realm of necessity' into the 'realm of freedom'. A deeper understanding of the interface between market and planning may prove to be of strategic significance in ensuring a humane existence for vast masses of people, whether they are living in the so called 'third world' or in what used to be called the 'second world'. It is important to note, however, that failures are due as much to political factors as to the inability of the planners to adapt to changing circumstances. What the present conjuncture strongly suggests is the need to introduce an evolutionary perspective on the planning process itself and make corresponding changes, rather than to seek salvation in the market system, whose self-regulating properties were questioned very effectively by Keynes more than half a century ago.

Notes and References

Introduction

1. Schumpeter (1934) defined the kernel of the credit phenomenon and regarded credit function as the 'keystone' of modern economic structure.
2. Products are distributed mainly through plans in the former, and sold to customers according to prices in the latter, though money is not prevented from playing a certain active role in the centralised model, as Brus (1972) admitted.

1 Socialist banking systems and their reforms

1. Pawnshops give loans to members of the population against pledged items and charge interest on them.
2. See *The Soviet Financial System* (1969), pp. 44–9.
3. Zloty data estimated from the figure for cash in circulation shown in Table V-27 of the *The Financial & Fiscal System of Poland*, prepared for the US Arms Control & Disarmament Agency, Washington, DC, by Columbia University, New York, Contract WALDA/E-45, vol. III, May 1968.
4. *The Soviet Financial System, structure, operation, and statistics*, US Department of Commerce Bureau of the Census, International Population Statistics Report Series, P-90, no.30, June 1986, p. 233.
5. See *Ekonomicheskaya gazeta*, no. 47 (18 November 1964), p. 38; *Finansy SSSR*, no. 2 (February 1965), pp. 91–3. The regulations of October 1965 on financing construction projects and activities provided a wealth of detail on the functions and responsibilities of Stroybank in all construction operations. See also *Ekonomicheskaya gazeta*, no. 45 (November 1964), pp. 25–8.
6. According to 'Sample Balance of Revenues & Expenditures of a Polish Khozraschet Unit' in *The Financial & Fiscal System of Poland* (op. cit., pp. 718–24), the planned and executed investments allocated from the budget were 189 000 and 232 000 zlotys respectively, while those obtained by other means were only 30 000 and 45 000 zlotys respectively.
7. See *The Soviet Financial System*, op. cit., pp. 226–40.
8. *Financial and Fiscal System of Poland*, op. cit., p. 277.
9. Wang (1987, pp. 413–15) indicates that the state bank constantly failed to control the quantity of money. Whenever there was a budget deficit, the state bank was always asked to increase the money supply. Whenever the financial plans for circulation were ready, the banks had to supply money; whenever the plans were changed, the credit plans also had to be changed, and there was no room for bargaining.
10. *The Soviet Financial System*, op. cit., p. 228.
11. The importance of the SPC has been modified since 1992 as a part of the policy of marketisation.
12. See *People's Daily* (the overseas version) (2 January 1989) (in Chinese).
13. According to *Zhongguo Jinrong Nianjian*, 1988, pp. 170–2, these policies were late changed as tight fiscal and monetary policies.

14. See *Jingrong Shibao* (*Financial Times*), Beijing, 6 April, 1989 (in Chinese).
15. The decline in 1989 could have been caused by the tight monetary and fiscal policies. The growth trend was recovered from the second half of 1990.
16. *China Statistical Yearbook*, (China Statistical Publishing House, 1990), p. 241.
17. *Jinrong Shibao* (The Financial Times), 6 April 1989 (in Chinese).
18. *People's Daily*, 18 December 1990 (in Chinese).
19. Jing Jiandong, chief of the Bureau of Financial Management of the PBC was interviewed in *The Economic Report of Hong Kong* in August 1990. He pointed out five areas that required a developed financial market in China: (1) budget deficits and priority construction projects; (2) enterprise's long-term investments; (3) the reduction of bank credits and risks; (4) uses of foreign investment; and (5) adjustments to the economic structure.
20. See *People's Daily*, 21 January 1993 (in Chinese).
21. The base rate in 1968 was 8 per cent.
22. Overall credit policy in 1968 was intended to increase the flow of consumer and producer goods by stressing 'productive' credit to restrict unprofitable investments and the accumulation of surplus stock, and to give priority to the financing of the production of export goods.
22. See Zwass (1979). See also order no. 37/1967 (x.12) KORM of the Council of Ministers and its executive order no. 34/1967 (XII.24) PM of the Minister of Finance. Various other promulgated bank regulations were published in *Pensugi Kozlony*. These detailed and lengthy statutes covered bookkeeping and reporting procedures, money circulation, general regulations for payments, foreign exchange management, and so on.
24. See *VWD*, Osteuropa, Eschborn, 14 July 1992.

2 Problems of selected RCPEs

1. See *The Report of the Third Plenary Session of the Eleventh Congress of the CPC Central Committee*, 1978.
2. These have been confirmed by both the Chinese and the Western media. See also *Financial Times*, 18 November 1993; and *People's Daily* (overseas edition), 25 September, 28 December and 29 December, 1993 (in Chinese).
3. IMF, *International Financial Statistics Yearbook*, 1990.
4. Actually the distinguishing of the three big economics sectors by Marx (1887) and the analysis of the relationship between consumption and accumulation by Mao (1976) lay sufficient emphasis upon investment.
5. NMP (net material product) growth rates followed a similar trend to GDP.
6. ECE secretariat *Common Data Base*, derived from national statistics.
7. Economic Research Institute (1990).
8. Institute of the MoF, Hungary, 1990.
9. The explanation of 'equity' here is mine. This is because there were no 'ordinary shares' in the issued capital of any company that, as in market economies, were held on terms that made the holder a 'member' of the company and thus entitled to vote at annual meetings, elect directors and share, through dividends, in the profits of the company.
10. Institute of the MoF, Hungary, 1990.

11. NBH *Monthly Report*, March 1992, p. 28, and July 1992, p. 29.
12. Veszteseges Gazdalkodo Egysegek, Industrial Department, Budapest Bank, 1990.
13. *Economic Trends in Hungary*, 1990, Economic Research Institute.
14. This is a system of sharing the responsibilities for the budget revenues and expenditures by central government and the local administrations respectively.
15. This is an economic responsibility system that aims to clarify the responsibilities, rights and interests of the state, enterprises and employees so as to encourage people to improve economic development by linking economic results with income distribution (see Wang and Zhu, 1987, p. 970).
16. Extra budgetary funds are not centrally budgeted, but are collected and disposed of by local governments, administrative units, enterprises and other public utilities, according to the scope granted by state policies (*China Statistical Yearbook*, p. 246). Although not part of the central government budget, they had to be reported to the state for supervision. In order to finance projects that were extra to the plans, the users of the budget expenditure often tried to expand the collection of the funds. The state then had to supervise the funds more carefully than before by incorporating these items into plans from 1987, although their collectors had the autonomy to use them.
17. Here and below, 'mimeo' after a source indicates that the information was collected in my field studies.
18. Differing from state pricing control and the market pricing system, the state directive pricing system allows the state to control the price of certain commodities indirectly or by setting up price ceilings according to the market situation in a specific period.
19. A recent survey of 30 provinces and municipalities shows that the average per capita income of farmers in 1994 reached 1220 yuan, 32 per cent more than in 1993, or an inflation-adjusted increase of 5 per cent (*Xinhua News Bulletin*, 27 March 1995).
20. The reasons for this will be explained in the following chapters.
21. Interview note in the Debt Clearing Office, Beijing, October 1990.
22. 'Appropriations' refer to the fact that local administrations and the community asked for money contributions from enterprises for all kinds of reasons, such as road maintenance, tree planting, infant care, education and so on.
23. The so-called independent accounting system covers most of the state economic entities that hold an separate account with the financial system.
24. NBH, *Market Letter*, June 1991, pp. 5–6.
25. Interview notes of the author, Beijing, October 1990.
26. Western banks suffered greatly from the events in 'Black October' 1987, but several banks made large profits on speculation in 1992.
27. Which means that specific funds borrowed or being allocated have to be spent for specific projects without any misappropriation. This policy is designed to regulate the use of funds in the SOEs in China.

3 Financial development and Banking Control

1. According to Burkett and Lotspeich (1992, pp. 72–3), the capital overvaluation problem may be smaller in the liberalising LDC due to the prior repression of long-term finance and the channelling of cheap credits, mostly

towards narrow fiscal deficits and political rents (including capital flight) rather than long-term capital investment (Vogel, 1979). This differs from the RCPEs, where the state enforced the allocation of high aggregate savings towards fixed capital.

2. SOEs and local governments in China often exaggerate projects' positive qualities while underestimating investment costs.

3. An interesting implication of the delegated monitoring model is that intermediary assets will be illiquid. This is because the intermediary is delegated the task of observing information about each loan which no one but the entrepreneur/borrower observes. In one sense, such assets are totally illiquid, as the intermediary contracts to hold them and enforce the contract, rather than sell them. The centralisation of monitoring each loan by a single intermediary will mean that there are no active markets for these assets (again illiquid).

4. In a one-asset optimal saving model, an agent maximises the expected present value of the utility of consumption over an infinite time horizon:

$$E\int_0^\infty e^{-\delta t} u\,(c[t])dt$$

subject to the constraint $k(t) = R(k[t]) = y(t)\text{-}c(t)$,

$$k(t) \geq \text{-}A, k(0) = k_0, c(t) \geq 0.$$

The agent can borrow by letting his capital holdings become negative. However there is a credit limit, A, above which his interest obligation out of his current non-interest income is negative ($R[\text{-}A]+ y < 0$). As a result he defaults and goes bankrupt. Until he reaches the credit limit, he obtains additional credit without difficulty.

5. An example of the latter is an influential slogan in China that dates from the mid-1980s: 'high consumption leads to high production', which had been the theoretical reason for the third period of national financial disorder in this economy (See also Chapter 4).

6. That is, outside claim holders and the manager can contract *ex ante* on 'hard information', compared with non-verifiable soft information.

7. The Availability Doctrine at the end of The Second World War relied on three steps: (1) Federal open market sales of Treasury securities would cause banks to reallocate their portfolios from loans to Treasury securities (Lindbeck, 1963); (2) banks would tend to reduce the quantity of loans through credit rationing, not by raising loan interest rates; (3) as credit rationing rose, rationed firms would face a rising shadow price for credit, causing their investment activity to fall, even though market interest rates were quite stable according to F. Modigliani.

8. Credit rationing takes the form of refinancing credits in Hungary, as Chapter 2 demonstrated.

9. I personally visited a branch of the People's Construction Bank in Beijing in October 1990, where credits are rationed to technical innovation projects according to systematic policies and regulations. Credit rationing was also used by the planners in the Hungarian Credit Bank, where I conducted a field study in Budapest in December 1989. Each item in the balance sheets of the bank had an internally planned target.

10. According to Arndt (1982), the adverse selection effect refers to the fact that those who are willing to pay higher interest rates are likely to be higher-risk

borrowers, so that as interest rates rise, the average riskiness of those who borrow increases, possibly reducing the bank's profits. The incentive effect refers to the fact that higher interest rates, which reduce the return on projects that succeed, are likely to induce firms to undertake projects with lower probability of success but a higher payoff when successful.

4 Financial disorder and banking control

1. This differs from the accumulation rate of the West, which is the ratio of domestic investment divided by GNP. Depreciation is included in both the denominator and domestic investment in the Western definition, but not in the Chinese definition. Furthermore the output of the non-productive sector, such as services, is included in GNP while it is not in the Chinese definition. Because of the latter, the result of the Western ratio could be relatively smaller than the Chinese one.
2. Defined in Chapter 6.
3. Moral hazard and adverse selection may affect the likelihood of loan repayment.
4. For example, in a closed triangular relationship, if the link is A–B–C–A and primary interenterprise debtors are at the same time final creditors, given that the linkages between them are all working well – that is, the products are good and are able to attract buyers – there is no need for banks to invest additional credit to clear the debts. After a few business cycles the debts will be repaid. In an open linear relationship the link is A–B–C, and debtors may not be creditors. Debtor A owes Debtor B who owes Debtor C, but C does not owe A. Thus there is a linear relationship between them.
5. Begg (1992) reports an early attempt by the Commercial Bank of Czechoslovakia to clear interenterprise credit and debt in 1991 that reduced estimates of the stock by over 20 per cent.
6. The planned projects become legal economic entities right after they had been planned by the state.
7. *People's Daily*, 26 December, 1992 (in Chinese).
8. Soft budget constraint (Kornai, 1980) has become a significant problem in CPEs only since regulation and control have been removed by some reforms (see Portes, 1983, 1993).
9. According to the flow of fund accounts (Jaffee and Stiglitz, 1990).
10. Late payment of bills endangered companies' survival in the UK during the recent recession, which forced the chancellor to announce measures to tackle the problem, according to a survey quoted by the *Financial Times* on 5 November 1992.
11. It was quite the opposite: it was the planners who worried about unhealthy and growth in China (see Zhu, 1986).
12. That is, stock.
13. The reason for using household annual deposit rates here is that they were adjusted by the monetary authority almost simultaneously with enterprise annual deposit rates and lending rates during the period.
14. According to Wang, 1990, there was one financial institution for every 3500 people in Hainan Province (a newly established special economic zone in

China), while in much more monetised Hong Kong there was one for every 3000 people. By the end of 1988 there were about 10 000 varied financial institutions in China. In a large booming economy this number is typically just one for 100 000 head of population. However their speed of establishment may imply that the ability to bear the costs of setting them up was ignored.

15. Competition had turned into a perpetual 'civil war', especially in the fourth quarter of 1988. Branches of the People's Bank and the People's Construction Bank in Ningxia Province wrote reports to certain administrative bodies and news agencies complaining about each other's alleged illegal accounting, clearing, postponing, blocking, payment rejection, bill misappropriation and forcible account opening.

16. According to one investigation, out of all the enterprises in China, the proportion with more than one clearing account was 10–15 per cent, and in some places it was 30 per cent. Among these enterprises, collectively owned enterprises accounted for 70 per cent, commercial companies 20 per cent and state firms 10 per cent (Wang, 1990).

17. In Shengyang City in north-east China, 'cross deposits' (deposits put into a greater number of financial institutions than was permitted under the banking regulations) amounted to 1290 million yuan, which was 11.1 per cent of total deposits; and 'cross credit' (loans to a greater number of customers than was permitted) amounted to 1070 million yuan, which was 5.7 per cent of total credit by the end of June 1989. This increased the difficulties for the central bank in its efforts to maintain an efficient system of control.

18. Nationally, the proportion of interbank lending within 30 days to total interbank lending was 11 per cent, 10 per cent and 20.3 per cent from the first quarter to the third quarter respectively in 1988; while the proportion of interbank lending within one to four months to total interbank lending was 53.8 per cent, 60.7 per cent and 45.7 per cent in the same period respectively.

19. The highest rates of monthly interbank lending in China in 1988 were 0.768 per cent, 0.84 per cent and 1.2 per cent in quarters one, two and three respectively.

20. A company in Beijing lent 10 million yuan (about one million pounds sterling) to a customer of another bank without submitting anything in the way of a report to its regulator (Wang, 1990).

21. According to regulations, foreign investment needs 90 per cent of domestic currency to back up expenditure on project construction.

22. *BBC Summary of World Broadcasts*, issued by BBC Monitoring, Reading, UK.

23. Ibid.

24. Of the increase in bank loans, 9.8 per cent could have been caused by reform of the pricing system in the agricultural sector (see Chapter 2).

25. This means that this kind of deposit gets an extra interest rate in addition to their original interest rate when they mature.

26. The meaning of these terms as used by economists differ from the usage adopted in other disciplines. Measuring and comparing the degrees of decentralisation of various decision-making structures is a very difficult problem (Lynch 1988).

27. Such as the queue for washing powder in Minsk when I visited there in the summer of 1989, and the queue for cigarettes and even food in Moscow in the summer of 1992.
28. Here I acknowledge the help of S. J. Choi of the Korean Long-Term Credit Bank and D. M. Su of the Taiwan monetary authority.

5 Monetary equilibrium and disequilibrium

1. Stalin's formulation of the basic economic law of socialism is 'the securing of the maximum satisfaction of the constantly rising material and cultural requirements of the whole society through the continuous expansion and perfection of socialist production on the basis of higher techniques' (see Ellman, 1971, p. 188). This was the theoretical basis of planning.
2. This could be questioned since intensifying administration may also lead to information distortion, bureaucracy and corruption. But we assume that the political discipline of the ruling party and legalisation of economic activities and the administration minimise the problems. The Chinese battle against the fourth nationwide disorder discussed in Chapter 4 supports this assumption.
3. The second stream, reviewed by Charemza (1989), has, in a similar way to the Portes school, been developed from Borro–Grossman foundations, but unlike Portes it claims non-testability of the excess demand hypothesis. Permanent excess demand is maintained.
4. Kornai argues that 'aggregate excess demand is not an operational category' (1980, p. 477).
5. Jao compares the increases of transactions demand with the growth rate of national income to establish the extent of 'a sizable monetary excess demand held in check only by complete controls in the commodity and factor markets' (p. 110).
6. 'pd' describes Δ, the growth rate. The 'pdL' further on describes Δ log.
7. The services industry.
8. NI excludes *B*. *B* was estimated as 0.05 per cent before 1980 (Zhang, 1988) and 0.20 per cent during 1980–9 (Liu, 1991).
9. Even Cassel (1990, pp. 32–3) argues that his 'cash-balance inflation' did have 'system-specific effects on allocation, growth, and distribution', though these effects are negative in the long term.
10. Definitions of hidden inflation, repressed inflation and forced saving can be found in Nuti (1988). The main opposing arguments are quoted by Portes (1989).
11. A similar error can also be found in the work of other authors, such as Feltenstein and Farhadian (1987), whose discussion often includes the post-reform period in a model of 'an economy where controls are strictly enforced' with rigid price and capital controls (p. 138).
12. Xin Hua News Agency, 9 August 1993.
13. Xin Hua News Agency, 9 May 1993.
14. Peebles supports 'the simplest of techniques with unadjusted annual data' and believes that 'introducing arbitrary dummy variables' would make it 'very difficult to put the explanation into simple straightforward English' (Peebles 1991a, p. 4).

15. I wonder whether Peeble was correct to use the term 'commodity *hueilong*' (ibid., pp. 9, 107, 219) as '*hueilong*' means withdrawal of something, for example money, from circulation. Commodities are sold to consumers rather than '*hueilong*', that is commodity '*liutong*' (circulation) or sales.

16. See Xien Chen, *Terminology of the Plan of National Economy and Social Development*, The Institute of Planned Economy, The SPC, September 1984 (in Chinese, p. 291).

17. Quantity theorists concede that monetary expansion has an immediate short-run effect on output, that this can last from three to ten years, and that the effect will begin to show up on prices with a time lag of twelve to eighteen months (Friedman and Sichel, 1987, p. 17). Peebles considers that 'this is true of capitalist economies where there is very little or no government price control' (1991a, p. 57). But Goodhart (1989a, pp. 82–103) indicates that during the years of international economic disruption (1973–6), especially during the period after 1979, previous single-equation estimates of the DFM have not been able to take adequate account of these supply shocks, policy regime changes or more fundamental structural changes.

18. Goldman, another predictor, based his prediction of crisis in the Soviet Union on the more rapid growth of savings deposits rather than retail sales, attributing it to frustrated purchasing power over the period 1975–80 (Goldman 1983, pp. 55–6). Such measures of excess demand as the ratio of wealth to retail sales (consumption flow) have been criticised by Portes as 'theoretically unjustifiable' (Portes 1989, pp. 39–40). If Goldman's assumptions on the shortage of certain consumption goods are removed or changed, his theory of excess demand for money would no longer stand, or at least it would be deflationary. In fact many shortages have been partially removed by price mechanisms in China and some other RCPEs.

6 Modelling money demand and supply in China

1. There is an enormous array of literature discussing DFM modelling, besides those quoted in the Appendices.

2. From the central bank's point of view, this is *primary financing credit*, but from its banks' point of view, it is *refinancing credit*.

3. This book is a very important source of information on Chinese monetary economics not only because it was written by a group of top-level Chinese intellectuals, but also because it reflects the views of the monetary authorities.

4. See 'The Decision on the Outline of the Current Industrial Policies', State Council, 15 March, 1989.

5. In 1989 the amount of 'economic construction fees' allocated from the state budget was still more than the sum of the other budget expenditures, although only 8 per cent of national fixed assets investments came from the budget, compared with 17.3 per cent from bank credits and 56.9 per cent from 'self-collecting funds'.

6. Wei Guo (in Ma *et al.*, 1990, p. 611) defines *budget overdrawing* from the banking system as the interest free loans of the PBC to the MoF for making up a deficit, while *budget borrowing* is defined as the interest bearing loans

of the PBC to the MoF for other uses approved by the State Council. Here *GB* does not separate the two.

7. Diewert (1974) discusses the demand for durables. Portes (1979) and Sargent (1982) also discuss some issues on inflation.

8. Once the budget ran into deficit, the normal way for the Chinese Treasury (MoF) was to borrow and overdraw money (*GB*) from the banks. Then the PBC had to print money to finance the budget because there was no guarantee that the government would pay this *GB*.

9. Actually, $r = R_t - (P_t - P_{t-1})/P_{t-1}$; $1 + r = (1 + R_t)/(1+)$ and is inflation. $R_t - \pi_t$ is an approximation of the real interest rate.

10. In the unit root tests we allow only 4 lags for each variable and check 95 per cent critical values by $ADF(1)$, in spite of the fact that more lags should be added, according to Engle and Yoo (1987) and the information criterion of Akaike (*AIC*) (1973). $AIC = ln(SSR/T) + 2q$, where T is the number of observations to which the model is fitted, SSR is the sum of squared residuals and q is the number of parameters being estimated. The lag structure is chosen to minimise *AIC*.

11. Perron (1988) demonstrates that if a series is stationary about a linear trend but no allowance for this is made in implementing the unit root test, the probability of a type II error (failure to reject the unit root hypothesis) is high.

12. There are a number of other ways to count the maximum lag length. A variety of such criteria as $FPE = [(T + K)/ (T - K)]^*(RSS/T)$ is used to calculate the length of the lag. T is the number of observations, K is the number of parameters used and RSS is the residual sum of the squares. Our sample size seems not to allow us to apply these criteria.

13. Such as those of the consumption function, the function of house prices and the *demand for money* function written by Hendry. Hendry and Ericsson (1991), criticised by Friedman (ibid), is an example, in spite of the fact that Hendry's approach has its own advantages.

14. These standard errors of regression are still much lower than those of the *PPI* regressions run by Peebles (see Chapter 5).

15. Of course it is unlikely to be the government's investment policy; it could rather be the incomes policy or subsidies.

16. In China, 'policy credits' are granted to firms and rural production units in the form of working capital according to government policies in different periods.

7 Conclusions and suggestions

1. The annual average growth rate in the ten-year period was about 8 per cent, according to the *China Statistical Yearbook*.

2. By the way, the novel *Wild Swans* (by Chang, Jung, Harper Collins, 1993) is the type of writing regarded as 'scar literature' by the Chinese at the beginning of the 1980s. By following its logic we cannot explain why China has been developing so successfully and why radical changes may lead to turmoil. The novel fails to understand political economics.

3. In fact bankers in the West are highly disciplined. For example in some banks even the names of important creditors are confidential to the borrowers.

4. See Martin Wolf: 'Bretton twins at an awkward age', *Financial Times*, 7 October 1994, p. 19.
5. Philips China Hong Kong Group provides a good example. Before 1991 the turnover of the company was stagnant. Since then they have adopted a clear strategy of building for the long term, after some personnel and management improvements. Their turnover has increased significantly and they are one of the largest foreign investors in China's industrial sector.
6. This section has benefited from a discussion with Professor C. Mayer.
7. According to Diamond (1984, p. 410), to the extent that members of subsidiary divisions can monitor each others' actions at low cost, conglomerate firms can allow the managers of the division to share the risks that they as a group must bear for incentive purposes. If the cost of conglomerate monitoring is fixed, firms with high firm-specific risk will be most likely to join together into conglomerates.

Bibliography

Aghion, P. and P. Bolton (1987) 'An "Incomplete Contract" Approach to Bankruptcy and the Financial Structure of the Firm', *Review of Economic Studies*, vol. 59.

Aghion, P., P. Bolton and M. Dewatripont (1988) 'Interbank Lending and Contagious Bank Runs', mimeo (London: CEPR).

Akaike, H. A. (1973) 'Information theory and the extension of the maximum likelihood principle' in B. N. Petrov and F. Csaki (eds), *Proceedings of the Second International Symposium on Information Theory* (Budapest: Akedemiai Kiado), pp. 267–81.

Akerlof, G. A. (1984) *An Economic Theorist's Book of Tales* (Cambridge University Press).

Alton, T. *et al.* (1981) 'Official and alternative consumer price indices in Eastern Europe', research project on National Income in East Central Europe, OP-68 (London: CEPR).

Anderson, S. P. (1993) 'Economic Credits and Financial Markets: The Experience of Four Asian Countries', in O'Brian, R. (ed.), *Finance and Economy*, 7 (Oxford University Press).

Arndt, H. W. (1982) 'Two Kinds of Credit Rationing', *Banca Nazionale del Lavoro Quarterly Review*, vol. 143 (December), pp. 417–25.

Artis, M. J. and M. K. Lewis (1976) 'Demand for Money in the UK 1963–73', *Manchester School*, 44, pp. 147–81.

Asquith, P., R. Gertner and D. Scharfstein (1991) 'Anatomy of financial distress: an examination of junk bond issuers', working paper (University of Chicago, October).

Asselain, J. C. (1981) 'Mythe ou realité de l'épargne forcée dans les pays socialistes', in M. Lavigne (ed.), *Travail et Monnaie en Systeme Socialiste* (Paris: Economica).

Baba, Y., D. F. Hendry and R. M. Starr (1988) 'US money demand 1960–84', discussion paper no. 27 (Nuffield College, Oxford).

Balassa, A. (1992) 'The transformation and development of the Hungarian banking system', in D. Kemme and A. Rudka (eds), *Monetary and Banking Reform in Postcommunist Economist* (New York: Westview Press), pp. 6–42.

Ball, Sir James (1991) Short Termism – Myth or Reality?, *National Westminster Bank Quarterly Review* (August).

Banco de Portugal (1963) *Report of the Board of Directors for the Year 1962* (Lisbon: Banco de Portugal).

Bank of Japan (BoJ) (1982) *Banking System in Japan* (Tokyo: Bank of Japan).

Bank of Tokyo (BoT) (1994) *Tokyo Financial Review*, vol. 19, no. 7 (July).

Baran, Paul A. (1957) *The political economy of growth* (New York: Monthly Review Press).

Barnett, William, A. Douglas Fisher and Apostolos Serletis (1992) 'Consumer Theory and the Demand for Money', *Journal of Economic Literature*, vol. 2086 (December).

Bauer, O. (1919) 'Der Weg zum Sozialismus,' *Voemma*, vol. 26, quoted from L. von Mises (1920), 'Economic Calculations in the Socialist Commonwealth', *Socialist Economics*, vol. 85.

Begg, D. (1992) 'Economic reform in Czechoslovakia: should we believe in Santa Klaus?', *Economic Policy,* vol. 14.

Begg, D. and R. Portes (1993) 'Enterprise Debt and Economic Transformation: Financial Restructuring of the State Sector in Central and Eastern Europe', CEPR discussion paper no. 695 (1992).

Bhattacharya, Sudipto (1992) 'Financial Intermediation with Proprietary Information', Working Paper Series of the Network in Financial Markets, CEPR working paper, (London: CEPR, October).

Birman, Igor (1980a) 'The financial crisis in the USSR', *Soviet Studies,* vol. 32, no. 1 (January), pp. 84–105.

Birman, Igor (1980b) 'A reply to Professor Pickersgill', *Soviet Studies,* vol. 32, no. 4 (October), pp. 586–91.

Birman, Igor (1983) *The Economy of Shortages* (New York: Chalidze Publications).

Birman, Igor (1988) 'Rosefielde and my cumulative disequilibrium hypothesis: a comment', *Soviet Studies,* vol. 41, no. 1 (January), pp. 141–8.

Birman, Igor and Roger A. Clark (1985) 'Inflation and the money supply in the Soviet Economy', *Soviet Studies,* vol. 37, no. 4 (October), pp. 494–504.

Bochkov, V. (1987) Economist's remarks 'Banking Boom?', *Sotsialisticheskaya Indentiva* (20 Jan) in FBIS, Daily Report: Soviet Union, 79–80 (Feb).

Boot, A. W. A. and S. I. Greenbaum (1993) 'Bank regulation, reputation and rents: theory and policy implications', in Colin Mayer and Xavier Vives (eds), *Capital Markets and Financial Intermediation* (Cambridge University Press).

Borch, K. (1969) A note of uncertainty and indifference curves, *Review of Economic Studies,* vol. 36, pp. 1–4.

Borodin, S. V. (1963) *Financy; Kredit SSSR* (Moskva: Ministertro Finansor SSSR).

Brabant, Jozef M. van (1990) 'Socialist economics: the disequilibrium school and the shortage economy', *Journal of Economic Perspectives,* vol. 4, no. 2 (Spring), pp. 157–75.

Bray, M. (1986) 'Seminar on Long-term Finance', mimeo (London School of Economics).

BRJGP (1990) Beijing People's General Machine Plant, *Annual Report* (Beijing).

Brown, Alan A. and Egon Neuberger (1989) 'Basic features of a centrally planned economy', in Morris, Bornstein (ed.), *Comparative Economic System,* 5th edn (Homewood, IL: Irwin).

Brus, W and K. Laski (1989) *From Marx to the Market* (Oxford University Press).

Brus, W. (1972) *The Market in a Socialist Economy,* translated from Polish by Angus Walker (London: Routledge and Kegan Paul).

Bunich, P. G. (1988) 'The new economic mechanism and credit reform' (Ekonomika i organizatsiia promyshlennogo proizvodstva 3), *Problems of Economics,* vol. 31, no. 12, pp. 80–94.

Burkett, Paul and Richard Lotspeich (1992) 'Financial Liberalization, Development, and Marketization: A Review of McKinnon's The Order of Economic Liberalization: Financial Control in the Transition to a Market Economy (1991)', review article, mimeo (London: CEPR).

Burkett, John, P. (1993) 'Disequilibrium Markets: Comment', *Comparative Economic Studies,* vol. xxxv, no. 3 (Fall).

Burkett, John, P. (1988) 'Slack, Shortage, and Discouraged Consumers in Eastern Europe: Estimates Based on Smoothing by Aggregation', *Review of Economic Studies,* vol. lv, pp. 493–506.

Byrd, William (1983) *China's Financial System: The Changing Role of Banks* (Boulder, CO: Westview Press).

Byung-Nak, Song (1990) *The Rise of the Korean Economy* (Hong Kong and Oxford: Oxford University Press).

Caincross, A. (1988) 'Bank of England Relationships with the Government, the Civil Service and Parliament' in Gianni Tonido (ed.), pp. 39–72.

Calomiris, Charles (1993) 'Corporate Finance Benefits from Universal Banking: Germany and the United States, 1870–1914', NBER working paper no. 4408 (New York: NBER).

Calvo, G. and J. Frenkel (1991a) 'Obstacles to transforming centrally-planned economies: the role of the capital markets', working papers series no. 3776 (New York: NBER).

Calvo, G. and J. Frenkel (1991b) 'Credit markets, credibility and economic transformation', *Journal of Economic Perspective*, vol. 5.

Campbell, T. (1979) 'Optimal Investment Decisions and the Value of Confidentiality', *Journal of Financial and Quantitative Analysis,* vol. 14, pp. 913–24.

Cao, Yajun (1994) 'The Introduction to Foreign Investment and Inflation', *Zhongguo Wuja (China Prices)*, vol. 12 (Beijing: the Price Research Institute, the State Planning Commission of the PRC), pp. 13–18.

Cargill, Thomas F. (1988) 'Competition and the Transition of Finance in Japan and the United States', *Journal of Comparative Economics,* vol. 12, no. 3 (September).

Carr, J. and M. J. Darby (1981) 'The role of money supply shocks in the short-run demand for money', *Journal of Monetary Economics*, vol. 8, no. 2, pp. 183–200.

Cassel, Dieter (1990) 'Phenomenon and effects of inflation in centrally planned socialist economies', *Comparative Economic Studies*, vol. 32, no. 1 (Spring), pp. 1–41.

Chai, C. H. (1981) 'Money and Banking Reforms in China', *Hong Kong Economic Papers*, no. 14, pp. 37–52.

Chai, Jin (1990) 'A primary discussion on the rationalization of the relationship between the budget and banks', mimeo (in Chinese) (July).

Chai, Joseph C. H. (1987) 'Introduction: China's Economic Reforms: an interim assessment', in Joseph C. H. Chai and Chi-keong Leung (eds), *China's Economic Reforms* (Hong Kong: Centre of Asian Studies, University of Hong Kong), pp. viii–xviii.

Chakravarty, S. (1991) 'Development planning: a reappraisal', *Cambridge Journal of Economics*, vol. 15, pp. 5–20.

Chamberlain, G. and E. Leamer (1976) 'Matrix Weighted Averages and Posterior Bounds', *Journal of the Royal Statistical Society*, series B, no. 1, pp. 36, 73–84.

Charemza, Wojciech (1989) 'Disequilibrium and Shortage Modelling of Centrally Planned Economies', *Journal of Economic Surveys*, vol. 3, no. 4, pp. 305–24.

Chang, Gene Hsin (1992) 'Asymmetric "Min" Condition and Estimation for Disequilibrium Markets in Centrally Planned Economies', *Comparative Economic Studies*, vol. xxxiv, nos 3–4 (Fall–Winter).

Chen, Shiqian (1991) 'Assessment of current macroeconomy and some policy suggestions', *Zhongguo Jinrong (China Finance)*, no. 1 (in Chinese) pp. 21–3.

Chen, Yuan (1992) 'China's Monetary Policy and Its Prospects', *Caizheng Yanjiu (Financial Research)*, vol. 1.2–7 (in Chinese).

Chen, Yuan (1993) *The Times Higher Education Supplement* (9 July).

China Investment Bank (CIB) (1989) *Annual Report* (Beijing: CIB).

China Statistical Yearbook (various issues) (Beijing: State Statistical Bureau of the PRC*).*

Cho, Yoon Je (1984) 'On the Liberalization of the Financial System and Efficiency of Capital Accumulation under Uncertainty', PhD thesis (Stanford University).

Chow, G. C. (1966) 'On the long-run and short-run demand for money', *Journal of Political Economy*, vol. 74 (April), pp. 111–31.

Chow, G. C. (1987) 'Money and Price Level Determination in China', *Journal of Comparative Economics*, pp. 219–333.

Chow, Wensai (1990) 'Thinking of the Problems of the "Triangular Debts" and Their Solutions' (the Party School of Zhejiang Provincial Committee of the CCP, March) (in Chinese), pp. 15–21.

Cooley, Thomas. F. and Stephen F. LeRoy (1981) 'Identification and Estimation of Money Demand', *American Economic Review*, vol. 71, pp. 825–44.

Corbett, J. (1989) 'Patterns of Finance and Government Lending to Industry in Japan', mimeo (Oxford).

Corbett, J. (1990a) 'International Perspectives on Financing: Evidence From Japan', *Oxford Review of Economic Policy*, vol. 3. no. 4.

Corbett, J. (1990b) 'Policy issues in the design of banking and financial systems for industrial finance', *European Economy*, vol. 43.

Corbett, J. and C. Mayer (1990) 'Banks and Corporate Investment: Institutional Reform in Socialist Economies', paper commissioned by the New York Stock Exchange as part of a project on financial reform in the Soviet Union.

Corbett, J. and C. Mayer (1991) 'Financial Reform in Eastern Europe: Progress with the Wrong Model', CEPR discussion paper no. 603 (London: CEPR, September).

Cottarelli, Carlo and Mario I. Blejer (1992) 'Forced Saving and Repressed Inflation in the Soviet Union, 1986–1990, *IMF Staff Papers*, vol. 39, no. 2 (June).

Crawford, V. P. (1979) 'Optimal Investment Decisions and the Value of Confidentiality', *Journal of Financial and Quantitative Analysis*, vol. 14, pp. 913–24.

Cuthbertson, Keith (1991) 'Modelling the Demand for Money', in Christopher J. Green and David T. Llewellyn (eds), *Surveys in Monetary Economics*, vol. 1 (Oxford and Cambridge: Blackwell), pp. 1–55.

Cuthbertson, K. and H. Taylor (1987) 'Buffer stock money: an appraisal', in C. Goodhart, D. Currie and D. T. Llewellyn (eds), *The Operation and Regulation of Financial Markets*, (London: Macmillan).

Cuthbertson, K. and H. Taylor (1988) 'Monetary anticipations and the demand for money: some evidence for the UK', *Weltwirtschaftliches Archiv*, vol. 183, pp. 509–20.

Cuthbertson, K. and H. Taylor (1992) *Applied Econometric Technique* (Brighton: Harvester Wheatsheaf).

Dai, Yuanchen (1992) *Not A Free Choice: Inflation and Strategy During the Reform* (Beijing) (in Chinese).

Davis, Christopher and Wojciech Charemza (eds) (1989) *Models of Disequilibrium and Shortage in Centrally Planned Economies* (London: Chapman & Hall).

Davis, P. and C. Mayer (1992) 'Corporate finance in the euromarkets and the economics of intermediation', CEPR working paper (London: CEPR).

Delfs, R. (1986) 'The Long March Back', *Far Eastern Economic Review*, vol. 11 (December), pp. 82–5.

Dewatripont, M. and E. Maskin (1990) 'Credit and Efficiency in Centralized versus Decentralized Markets', Harvard University working paper (December).

Dewatripont, Mathias and Jean Tirole (1993) 'Efficient governance structure: implications for banking regulation' in Colin Mayer and Xavier Vives (eds), *Capital Markets and Financial Intermediation* (Cambridge University Press).

Diamond, D. W. (1984) 'Financial Intermediation and Delegated Monitoring', *Review of Economic Studies*, vol. 51, pp. 393–414.

Diamond, D. W. (1988) 'Monitoring and Reputations: The Choice between Bank Loans and Directly Placed Debt', mimeo. (London: LSE).

Diamond, D. W. (1989) 'Reputation Acquisition in Debt Markets', *Journal of Political Economy*, vol. 97, pp. 828–62.

Diamond, D. W. (1992) 'Seniority and Maturity of Debt Contracts', *Journal of Financial Economics*, vol. 32.

Diamond, D. W. (1993) 'Bank Loan Maturity and Priority When Borrowers Can Refinance', in Colin Mayer and Xavier Vives (eds), *Capital Markets and Financial Intermediation* (Cambridge University Press).

Diamond, D. and P. Dybvig (1983) 'Bank runs, deposit insurance, and liquidity', *Journal of Political Economy*, vol. 91, pp. 401–19.

Diao, Shouyan (1990) 'The current reforms of making the specialized banks into companies', mimeo (Beijing: State Planning Commission of the PRC, February) (in Chinese).

Diewert, W. E. (1974) 'Intertemporal consumer theory and the demand for durables', *Econometrica*, vol. 42, no. 3, pp. 497–516.

Dimitrijevic, Dimitrije and George Macesich (1973) *Money and Finance in Contemporary Yugoslavia* (New York: Praeger).

Dobb, M. H. (1928) *Russian Economic Development since the Revolution* (London: G. Routledge & Sons).

Dobb, M. H. (1970) *Welfare Economics and the Economics of Socialism* (Cambridge University Press).

Domowitz, I. and G. S. Hakkio (1990) 'Interpreting an error correction model: partial adjustment, forward looking behaviour, and dynamic international money demand', *Journal of Applied Econometrics*, vol. 5, pp. 29–46.

Dornbusch R. and S. Fischer (1987) *Macroeconomics*, 4th edn (New York: Mcgraw-Hill).

Drabek, Zdenek, Kamil Janacek and Zdenek Tuma (1992) 'Inflation in Czechoslovakia, 1985–1991', mimeo (London: CEPR).

Duca, J. (1986) 'Trade credit and credit rationing: A theoretical model', Research Papers in Banking and Financial Economics, Board of Governors of the Federal Reserve System (Washington DC).

Economic Research Institute (1990) *Economic Trends in Hungary* (Budapest: National Statistical Office of Hungary).

Edgeworth, F. V. (1988) 'The Mathematical Theory of Banking', *Journal of the Royal Statistical Society*, vol. 51, pp. 113–12.

Edwards, G. T. (1987) *The Role of Banks in Economic Development: The Economics of Industrial Resurgence* (London: Macmillan).

Ekonomicheskaya gazeta (1964, 1965), mimeo from Hungarian Finance Ministry.

Ellman, M. (1971) *Soviet Planning Today: Proposals for an Optimally Functioning Economic System* (Cambridge University Press).

Emmanuel, O. Kumah (1989) 'Monetary Concepts and Definitions', IMF Working Paper, WP/89/92 (Washington DC: IMF, November).

Engle, R. F. and C. W. J. Granger (1987) 'Cointegration and Error Correction: Representation, Estimation and Testing', *Econometrica*, vol. 55, pp. 251–77.

Engle, R. F. and B. S. Yoo (1987) 'Forecasting and Testing in Cointegrated Systems', *Journal of Econometrics*, vol. 35, pp. 143–59.

Estrin, S., Hare, P. and Suranyi, M. (1992) 'Banking in Transition', Centre for Economic Performance discussion paper no. 68 (London: Centre for Economic Performance).

Fama, E. F. (1985) 'What's Different about Banks?', *Journal of Monetary Economics*, vol. 15, pp. 29–39.

Fama, E. F. and M. R. Gibbons (1982) 'Inflation, Real Returns and Capital Investment', *Journal of Monetary Economics*, vol. 9, pp. 297–323.

Fan, Gang and Thye Woo (1993) 'Decentralized Socialism and Macroeconomic Stability: Lessons from China', working paper series no. 411 (Department of Economics, University of California, Davis).

Fan, Gang, Shuguang Zhang and Zhungwei Yang (1990) *Macroeconomics of Public Ownership* (Beijing: People's Press).

Fang, Shangpu and Yishuei Li (1993) 'The Transmission Mechanisms of the Financial Indirect Control and their Realization Methods', *Jingji Tizhi Gaige (Economic System Reforms)* (May) (in Chinese).

Farrell. John P. (1989) 'Financial "crisis" in the CPEs or "vsyo normalno"?', *Comparative Economic Studies*, vol. 31, no. 4 (Winter), pp. 1–9.

Fazzari, Steven, M. Hubbard, R. Glenn and B. C. Petersen (1988) 'Financing Constraints and Corporate Investment', mimeo (London School of Economics).

Feldstein, M. S. (1969) 'Mean-variance analysis in the theory of liquidity preference and portfolio selection', *Review of Economic Studies*, vol. 36, pp. 5–12.

Feltenstein, A. D. and Z. Farhadian (1987) 'Fiscal policy, monetary targets and the price level in a centrally planned economy: an application to the case of China', *Journal of Money, Credit and Banking*, vol. 19, pp. 137–56.

Finansy SSSR (1965) no. 2 (February) (Moskva: Ministerstvo Finansov SSSR, issued monthly).

Fisher, I. (1930) *The Theory of Interest* (New York: Macmillan).

Franks, J. and C. Mayer (1990) 'Capital Markets and Corporate Control: A Study of France, Germany and the UK', *Economic Policy*, vol. 10, pp. 189–31 (Cambridge University Press).

Friedman, B. M. (1981) 'The roles of money and credit in macroeconomic analysis', working paper 831 (New York: National Bureau of Economic Research).

Friedman, M. (1956) 'The quantity theory of money: a restatement', in M. Friedman (ed.), *Studies in the Quantity Theory of Money* (Chicago; University of Chicago Press).

Fry, Maxwell J. (1971) 'Turkey's First Five-Year Development Plan: An Assessment', *Economic Journal*, vol. 81 no. 322 (June), pp. 306–26.

Fry, Maxwell (1973) 'Manipulating Demand for Money', in Michael Parkin (ed.), *Essays in Modern Economics* (London: Longman), pp. 371–85.

Fry, M. J. (1988) *Money, Interest and Banking in Economic Development* (Baltimore, MD: The Johns Hopkins University Press).

Fry, M. J. (1993) 'Peebles: Socialist Money', book review, *Economic Journal* (July), pp. 1059–61.

Gale, D. and M. Hellwig (1985) 'Incentive-Compatible Debt Contracts: The One-Period Problem', *Review of Economic Studies*, vol. 171, pp. 647–63.

Garvy, George (1964) 'The role of the state bank in soviet planning', in Alec Nove and Jane Degras (eds) *Soviet Planning* (Oxford: Basil Blackwell), pp. 46–76.

Gesell, Silvio (1929) *The Natural Economic Order*, translated from the 6th German edn by Philip Pye (Berlin: Neo-Verlag).

Gibson, C. H. (1989) *Financial Statement Analysis: using financial accounting information*, 4th edn (London: PWS-Kent).

Gilson, S. C., K. John and L. Lang (1990) 'Troubled Debt Restructurings: An Empirical Study of Private Reorganization of Firms in Default', *Journal of Financial Economics*, vol. 27 (October), pp. 315–54.

Goldberger, A. (1991) *A Course in Econometrics* (Cambridge, Mass.: Harvard University Press).

Goldfeld, S. M. (1976) 'The case of the missing money', *Brookings Papers on Economic Activity*, vol. 3, pp. 683–730.

Goldfeld, Stephen M. and D. E. Sichel (1987) 'Money Demand: The Effects of Inflation and Alternative Adjustment Mechanisms', *The Review of Economics and Statistics*, vol. 69. pp. 511–15.

Goldman, Marshall I. (1983) *USSR in Crisis: the Failure of an Economic System* (New York and London: W. W. Norton).

Goldman, Marshall I. (1984) 'Reply to Frank Durgin', *ACES Bulletin*, vol. 26, nos 2–3 (Summer–Fall), pp. 111–16.

Goldsmith, R. W. (1969) *Financial Structure and Development: Studies in Comparative Economics* (New Haven, Conn. and London: Yale University Press).

Goldsmith, R. W. (1983) *The Financial Development of India, Japan, and the United States: a trilateral institutional, statistical, and analytical comparison* (New Haven, Conn.: Yale University Press).

Goldsmith, R. W. (1987) *Premodern Financial System: a historical comparative study* (Cambridge University Press).

Gonzalo, Jesus (1994) 'Five alternative methods of estimating long-run equilibrium relationships', *Journal of Econometrics*, vol. 60, pp. 203–33.

Goodhart, C. A. E. (1984) *Monetary Theory and Practice: The UK Experience* (London: Macmillan).

Goodhart, C. A. E. (1989a) *Money, Information and Uncertainty*, 2nd edn (London: Macmillan).

Goodhart, C. A. E. (1989b) 'The conduct of monetary policy', *Economic Journal* (June).

Granger, C. W. J. (1969) 'Investigating Causal Relations by Econometric Models and Cross-Spectral Methods', *Econometrica*, vol. 37 (January), pp. 24–36.

Grossman, G. (ed.) (1968) *Money and Plan* (Berkeley and Los Angeles: University of California Press).

Grout, P. (1984) 'Investment and Wages in the Absence of Binding Contracts: A Nash Bargaining Approach', *Econometrica*, vol. 52, pp. 449–61.

Grunewald, A. E. and A. J. Pollock (1985) 'Money managers and bank liquidity', *Proceedings of a Conference on Bank Structure and Competition* (Federal Reserve Bank of Chicago).

Guo, Jianying (1995) 'The Proportional Comparison Between the Three Different Price Forms in 1993', *Zhongguo Wuja (China Prices)*, vol. 69 (Beijing: The Price Research Institute, the State Planning Commission of the PRC) (in Chinese), pp. 26–30.

Guo, Shuqing (1990) 'Consumption, Investment and Saving', Jingji Yanjiu (*Economic Research*), no. 4 (in Chinese).

Gurley, J. G. and E. S. Shaw (1960) *Money in a theory of finance* (Washington, DC: The Brookings Institution).

Hafer, R. W. and S. E. Hein (1980) 'The Dynamics and Estimation of Short-run Money Demand', *Federal Reserve Bank of St. Louis Review*, vol. 62, no. 3, pp. 25–35.

Hafer, R. W. and A. M. Kutan (1994) 'Economic Reforms and Long-Run Money Demand in China: Implications for Monetary Policy', *Southern Economic Journal*, vol. 60, no. 4, pp. 936–44.

Hagelmayer, I. (ed.) (1987) *Inflacio es Penzugyek Magyarorszagon* (Inflation and Monetary Policy in Hungary) (Budapest: Kozgazdasagi es Jogi Konyvkiado).

Han, Keryung (1992) 'An Investigation and Analysis of the Efficiency Decrease in Banks', *Jingji Wenti (Economic Issues)* (Taiyuan, China, September) (in Chinese), pp. 42–7.

Harm, C. (1992a) *The Financing of Small Firms in Germany,* policy research working papers: Financial Policy and Systems, WPS 899 (Washington DC: Country Economics Department, the World Bank).

Harm, C. (1992b) *The Relationship between German Banks and Large German Firms,* policy research working papers: Financial Policy and Systems, WPS 900 (Washington DC: Country Economics Department, the World Bank).

Harris, L. (1981) *Monetary Theory* (New York: McGraw-Hill).

Harris, L. (1988) 'Financial Reform and Economic Growth: A New Interpretation of South Korea's Experience', in Harris *et al.* (eds) *New Perspectives on the Financial System* (London: Croom Helm).

Harris, L. (1993) 'Financial Fragility in the Transition to Market Economies', mimeo (Department of Economics, SOAS, University of London).

Hart, D. and J. H. Moore (1989b) 'Defaut and Renegotiation: A Dynamic Model of Debt', discussion paper, 57 (London School of Economics, June).

Hart, O. and J. H. Moore (1989a) 'Incomplete Contracts and Renegotiation', *Econometrica*, vol. 56, pp. 755–86.

Harvey, A. C. (1981) *The Econometric Analysis of Time Series* (Oxford: Philip Allan).

Hawtrey, R. (1919) *Currency and Credit* (New York: Longmans, Green & Co).

Hayek, F. A. (1935) in F. A. Hayek and N. G. Pierson (1975) *Collectivist Economic Planning: critical studies on the possibilities of socialism* (Clifton, NJ: A. M. Kelly).

Hellwig, M. F. (1977) 'A Model of Borrowing and Lending with Bankruptcy', *Econometrica*, vol. 45, pp. 1879–906.

Hellwig, M. F. (1991) 'Banking, financial intermediation and corporate finance', in A. Giovannini and C. Mayer (eds), *European Financial Integration* (Cambridge University Press).

Hendry, D. F. (1979) 'Predictive failure and econometric modelling in macroeconomics: the transaction demand for money', in P. Omerod (ed.), *Econometric Modelling* (London: Heinemann).

Hendry, D. F. (1982) 'Comment: Whither Disequilibrium Econometrics?', in R. E. Quandt, *Econometric Disequilibrium Models*, core reprint no. 491 (Center for Operations Research & Econometric, Université Catholique de Louvain).

Hendry, D. F. (1985) 'Monetary economic myth and the econometric reality', *Oxford Review of Economic Policy* (Oxford University Press).

Hendry, D. F. (1988) 'The encompassing implications of feedforward versus feedback mechanisms in econometrics', *Oxford Economic Papers,* vol. 40, pp. 132–9.

Hendry, D. F. (1991) 'Lectures on Econometric Methodology', mimeo (Oxford University), also in Qin *et al.* (1992).

Hendry, D. F. and N. R. Ericsson (1991) 'An Econometric analysis of U.K. money demand in monetary trends in the United States and the United Kingdom by Milton Friedman and Anna J. Schwartz', *American Economic Review*, vol. 81, pp. 8–39.

Hendry, D. F. and G. E. Mizon (1978) 'Serial correlation as a convenient simplification, not a nuisance: a comment on a study of the demand for money by the Bank of England', *Economic Journal*, vol. 88, pp. 549–63.

Hilferding, Rodolf (1910) *Finance Capital – a study of the latest phase of capitalist development*, translated by Morris Watnick and Sam Gordon in 1981, edited with an Introduction by Tom Bottomore (London, Boston and Henley: Routledge & Kegan Paul).

Hrncir, Miroslav (1993) 'Financial Intermediation (Progress Evaluation and Lessons from the Former Czechoslovakia)', mimeo (Institute of Economics, Czech National Bank, January).

Hua, Ercheng (1995) 'China's Macroeconomic Situation Analysis', *People's Daily* (in Chinese) (2 March), p. 9.

Huang, Guobo (1993) 'Money Demand for China in the Reform Period: An Error Correction Model', paper no. 49, Department of Economics and Finance, City Polytechnic of Hong Kong.

Huang, Jupo (1989) 'The Causes and Solutions of the Intensified Shortage of Enterprise Working Capital', *Monthly Bulletin of Economics* (3 April) (in Chinese).

Hungarian Credit Bank (HCB) (1987–90) *Annual Report* (Budapest: HCB).

Hussain, A. and N. Stern (1991) 'Effective Demand, Enterprise Reforms and Public Finance', CP no. 10, The Development Economics Research Programme, *STCERD*, London School of Economics; and *American Economic Review* (April).

IMF (1989, 1990) *International Financial Statistics Yearbook* (Washington DC: IMF).

IMF (1991) The International Monetary Fund, The World Bank, Organization for Economic Co-operation and Development, and European Bank for Reconstruction and Development, *A Study of the Soviet Economy,* vol. 1 (Washington DC: IMF, February).

Jaffee, D. (1971) *Credit Rationing and the Commercial Loan Market* (New York: Wiley).

Jaffee, D. and J. Stiglitz (1990) 'Credit Rationing', in B. Friedman and F. H. Hahn (eds), *Handbook of Monetary Economics,* vol. 2 (Amsterdam: North-Holland).

Jao, Y. C. (1967–8) 'Some notes on repressed inflation: a suggested interpretation of money and prices in Communist China, 1950–57, *Union College Journal,* vol. 6, pp. 99–114.

Jao, Y. C. (1989) 'Financial Reform in China and Hong Kong, 1978–88: A Comparative Overview', paper presented to the Inaugural International Conference on Asian-Pacific Financial Markets (Singapore, 16–18 November).

Jao, Y. C. (1990) 'Financial Reform in China 1978–89: Retrospect and Reappraisal', *Journal of Economics and International Relations,* vol. 3, no. 4 (Winter).

Jensen, Michael C. and William H. Meckling (1976) 'Theory of the Firm: Managerial Behavior, Agency Costs and Ownership Structure', *Journal of Financial Economics,* vol. 3, no. 4 (October), pp. 305–60.

Johansen, S. (1988) 'Statistical Analysis of Cointegration: Theory and Applications', lecture notes for a course on cointegration held at the Seminario Estivo di Econometrica, Centro Studi sorelle Clarke, Bagni di Lucca, Italy.

Johansen, S. and K. Juselius (1990) 'Some Structural Hypotheses in a Multivariate Cointegration Analysis of the Purchasing Power Parity and the Uncovered Interest for the U.K.', Institute of Mathematical Statistics, University of Copenhagen, unpublished preprint.

Kaldor, Nicholas (1985) *Economics without Equilibrium* (Armonk, NY: M. E. Sharpe).

Kang, Jia (1988) 'Tight money, or reduce investment scale', *Jingji Yanjiu (Economic Research)*, no. 5 (in Chinese), pp. 10–14.

Kareken, J. H. (1986) 'Federal Bank Regulatory Policy: A Description and Some Observations', *Journal of Business*, vol. 59, pp. 3–40.

Kaser, M. C. and H. Radice (eds) (1985) *Economic History of Eastern Europe* (Oxford University Press).

Keeton, W. (1979) *Equilibrium Credit Rationing* (New York: Garland)

Keynes, J. M. (1936) *The General Theory of Employment, Interest and Money* (London: Macmillan).

Klaus, V. and V. Rudlovcek (1982) 'Savings function as an inverse problem of disequilibrium consumption modelling: a case study of Czechoslovakia', paper presented to the International Conference of Applied Econometrics, Budapest.

Kornai, J. (1980) *Economics of Shortage*, 2 vols (Amsterdam: North-Holland).

Kornai, J. (1982) *Growth, Shortage and Efficiency* (Oxford: Blackwell).

Kornai, J. (1986) 'The Hungarian Reform Process', *Journal of Economic Literature*, vol. xxiv (December), p. 1719.

Kueh, Y. Y. (1989) 'The Maoist legacy and China's new industrialization strategy', *China Quarterly*, no. 119 (September), pp. 420–47.

Kueh, Y. Y. (1990) 'Growth imperatives, economic recentralization and China's open door policy', *Australian Journal of Chinese Affairs*, no. 24 (July), pp. 93–119.

Kuschpeta, O. (1978) *The Banking and Credit System of USSR* (Leiden and Boston: Martinus Nijhoff).

Kuti, Anna and Maria Mora (1989) 'Crisis Management in the Late 1980s', mimeo (Budapest: Economic Research Institute).

Laidler, D. (1977) *The Demand for Money: Theories and Evidence,* 2nd edn (New York: Dun-Donnelley).

Laidler, D. (1984) 'The buffer stock notion in monetary economics', *Economic Journal*, vol. 94 (supplement), pp. 17–34.

Leamer, Edward F. (1978) *Specification Searcher: Ad Hoc Inference with Non-Experimental Data* (New York: Wiley).

Lehman Brothers Bulletin (1993) (New York: Lehman Brothers).

Leipziger, D. M. (ed.) (1988) *Korea: transition to maturity* (Oxford: Pergamon).

Leland, H. and D. Pyle (1977) 'Information asymmetries, financial structure and financial intermediation', *Journal of Finance*, vol. 32, pp. 371–87.

Lenin, V. I. (1917) *Imperialism, the Highest Stage of Capitalism – a popular outline*, first published in pamphlet form in Petragrad, April 1917 (London: Lawrence & Wishart, 1948).

Levchuk, I. (1989) 'Share holding banks linked to tighter credit policy', *Pravitelstvennyy Vestnik*, vol. 22, no. 11, p. 8.

Lewis, M. K. (1989) 'Theory and Practice of the Banking Firm', mimeo (Oxford).

Lewis, M. K., K. Mervyn and K. T. Davis (1987) *Domestic and International Banking* (Oxford: Philip Allan).

Li, Bo-xi (ed.) (1990) 'Economic Development and Model of China', mimeo (in Chinese).

Li, Jingxi and Guangzu Lin (1990) 'On the Solutions of Clearing the "Triangular Debts"', *Xia Men University Bulletin*, vols 53–9 (March) (in Chinese).

Li, Maosheng (1987) *A Study of China's Financial Structure* (Shanxi: People's Press and China Social Science Publishing House) (in Chinese).

Li, Zhenzhong (1983) *Planning Economics* (Beijing: People's University Press of China), pp. 599–607 (in Chinese).

Lin, Zhiyuan (1993) 'On the Analysis of the Current Payment Ability of the Chinese Banking System', *Jingji Yanjiu* (*Economic Research*), no. 6 (Research Institute of the China Academy of Social Sciences).

Lindbeck, E. (1963) *A Study in Monetary Analysis* (Stockholm: Almqvist & Wiksell).

Liu, Hongru (1986) *Caizheng Jinrong Yanjiu* (*Research on Budget and Finance*), vol. 60 (August) (in Chinese).

Liu, Hongru, Yuan Chen, Chengming Wang and Jiandong Jin (1991) *China's Banking System* (Beijing: China Banking Publisher) (in Chinese).

Liu, Hongru and Zhiping Zhang (1987) 'China's Expanding Capital Market', *Jingji Yanjiu* (*Economic Research*) (20 January 1987) (in Chinese), pp. 47–52.

Liu, Yingqio (1991) 'On the Estimation of China's Aggregate Demand', PhD thesis, Economic Research Institute, Nakai University, Tianjin (in Chinese).

Lubrano, Michel, Richard G. Pierse and Richard Jean-Francois (1986) 'Stability of a U.K. Money Demand Equation: A Bayesian Approach to Testing Exogeneity', *Review of Economic Studies*, vol. 53 (August), pp. 603–34.

Lundberg, Erik (1964) *The Financial System of Portugal* (Washington, DC: International Monetary Fund and World Bank, October).

Lynch, Robert G. (1988) 'Modelling centralization and decentralization', *Journal of Comparative Economics*, vol. 13.

Ma, Guonan (1993) 'Macroeconomic disequilibrium, structural changes, household savings and money demand in China', *Journal of Development Economics*, vol. 41, pp. 115–36.

Ma, Hong *et al.* (eds) (1990) *Jinrong Dachuan* (*Encyclopedia of Financial Knowledge*), vol. 1 (Beijing: China Finance Press) (in Chinese).

Macdonald, R. and P. D. Murphy (1989) 'Testing for the Long Run Relationship between Nominal Interest Rates and Inflation Using Cointegration Techniques', *Applied Economics*, vol. 21, pp. 439–77.

Maegd, Hugo De (1972) 'De rei van de Staatsbank in de Sowjet-Unie' (The Role of the State Bank in the Soviet Union), *Tijdschrift voor Sociale Wetenschappen*, no. 2, pp. 171–97.

Mandel, E. (1968) *Marxist Economic Theory (Vols I and II)* (London: Monthly Review Press).

Mao, Zedong (1976) 'On the Ten Big Relationships', speech at the Political Bureau of the Communist Party Central Committee meeting on 25 April 1956. First published 26 December 1976, contained in *The Selected Works of Mao Tse-tung*, vol. v (in Chinese).

Marer, P. and G. Pall (1971) *Recent Development in the Hungarian Financial System*, edited by P. A. Thad, prepared for the United States Arms Control and Disarmament Agency, Washington DC (May).

Markowitz, H. (1952) 'Portfolio selection', *Journal of Finance*, vol. 7, pp. 77–91.

Markowitz, H. (1959) *Portfolio Selection: Efficient Diversification of Investment* (New York: Wiley).

Marx, K. (1887) *Capital* (London: Lawrence & Wishart, 1956), German edn: Berlin, 1887, 1893 and 1894.

Matutes, C. and X. Vives (1992) 'Competition for Deposits, Risk of Failure, and Regulation in Banking', working paper no.18 (London: CEPR and ESF, the Network in Financial Markets).

Mayer, C. (1988) 'New issues in corporate finance', *European Economic Review*, vol. 32.

Mckinnon R. I. (1993a) 'Gradual versus Rapid Liberalisation in Social Economies: the Problem of Macroeconomic Control', Proceedings of the World Bank Annual Conference on Development Economics (Washington, DC: World Bank), pp. 63–94.

McKinnon, Ronald I. (1973) *Money and Capital in Economic Development* (Washington, DC: Brookings Institution).

McKinnon, Ronald I. (1989a) 'The order of liberalization for opening the Soviet economy', report prepared for the International Task Force on Foreign Economic Relations, New York, rev. (April).

McKinnon, Ronald I. (1989b) 'Stabilizing the rouble', paper prepared for the Atlanta meetings of the American Economic Association (28 December).

McKinnon, R. I. (1989c) 'Financial Liberalization and Economic Development. A Reassessment of Interest-Rate Policies in Asia and Latin America', mimeo (Department of Economics, Stanford University, California).

McKinnon, Ronald I. (1991) *The Order of Economic Liberalization: Financial Control in the Transition to Market Economy* (Baltimore and London: Johns Hopkins University Press).

McKinnon, Ronald I. (1993b) 'Macroeconomic control in liberalizing socialist economies: Asian and European parallels', in Alberto Giovannini (ed.), *Finance and Development: Issues and Experience* (Cambridge University Press).

Meyers, S. (1977) 'Determinants of corporate borrowing', *Journal of Financial Economics*, vol. 5, pp. 147.

Meyers, S. and N. Majluf (1984) 'Corporate financing decisions when firms have investment information that investors do not have', *Journal of Financial Economics*, vol. 13, pp. 187–220.

Milbourne, Ross D. (1988) 'A Theorem Regarding Elasticities of the Transactions Demand for Money', *Economics Letters*, vol. 27, no. 2, pp. 151–4.

Min, Byoung Kyun (1976) 'Financial Restriction in Korea, 1965–1974', PhD thesis (Honolulu: University of Hawaii).

Mishkin, F. S. (1988) *Understanding Real Interest Rates*, NBER Working Paper (Cambridge, MA).

Mitchell, Janet (1993) 'Creditor passivity and bankruptcy: implications for economic reform', in C. Mayer and X. Vives (eds), *Financial Intermediation in the Construction of Europe* (Cambridge University Press).

Mitelman, E. Pribyl (1967) 'Rentabelnost, prossenty za kredit' (Income, Profitability, Interest), *Dengi i kredit*, no. 2 (February).

Mizsei, Kalman (1993) *Hungary: gradualism needs a strategy. Hungary: An Economy in Transition,* edited by Istvan Szekely and David M G Newbery (Cambridge University Press).

Modigliani, F. and M. H. Miller (1958) 'The cost of capital, corporation finance and the theory of investment', *American Economic Review*, vol. 48, pp. 216–97.

National Bank of Hungary (NBH) (1990) *Market Letters* (April) (Budapest: NBH).

National Bank of Hungary (NBH) (1987–90) *Annual Report (Budapest: NBH)*.

Naughton, B. (1990) *Why has Economic Reform Led to Inflation?* (San Diego: Graduate School of International Relations and Pacific Studies, University of California, San Diego).

Nolan, Peter (1993) *State and Market in the Chinese Economy: Essays on Studies on the Chinese Economy* (London: MacMillan).

Nove, Alec (1988) 'Ortona on Stalinism: A Comment', *Economie Appliquee*, vol. 41, no. 3, pp. 649–51.

Nuti, D. M. (1988) 'Perestroika: The Economics of Transition between Central Planning and Market Socialism', *Economic Policy*, no. 7 (October).

Nuti, D. M. (1990) 'Feasible Financial Innovation under Market Socialism', in Kessides *et al.*, *European Economy*, no. 43 (March).

Oblath, G. (1993) 'Hungary's foreign debt controversies and macroeconomic problems', in I. P. Szekely and D. M. G. Newbery (eds), *Hungary: an economy in transition* (Cambridge University Press), pp. 193–223.

OECD (1988) *OECD Financial Statistics* (Geneva: Organisation for Economic Cooperation and Development).

Ofer, Gur (1991) *Macroeconomic Issues of Soviet Reforms* (Hebrew University of Jerusalem), pp. 297–339.

Ofer, G. and Pickersgill, J. (1980) 'Soviet household saving: a cross-section study of Soviet emigrant families', *Quarterly Journal of Economics*, vol. 94, pp. 121–44.

Overholt, William H. (1993) *China: The Next Economic Superpower* (London: Weidenfeld & Nicolson).

Pagano, M. and T. Japelli (1991) 'Information Sharing in the Consumer Credit Market', working paper, Universita Bocconi (July) (Milan).

Peebles, G. (1981) 'Money incomes and expenditures of the population of Soviet Union: an East European comparison', *Hong Kong Economic Papers*, vol. 14, pp. 53–78.

Peebles, G. (1991a) *Money in the People's Republic of China: A Comparative Perspective* (London: Allen & Unwin).

Peebles, G. (1991b) *A Short History of Socialist Money* (London: Allen & Unwin).

Peng, Sungjian (ed.) (1985) *Zhongguo Caizheng Yu Jinrong (China's Budget and Banking* in Chinese) (Beijing: Beijing University Press).

Penzgugy Adator (1990) Hungarian Credit Bank internal material (Budapest).

People's Construction Bank of China (PCBC) (1991) *Annual Report* (Beijing: PCBC*).

People's Daily (1988–93) including the overseas issues (in Chinese).

Perkins, Dwight H. (1966) *Market Control and Planning in Communist China* (Cambridge, Mass.: Harvard University Press).

Perron, P. (1988) 'Trends and random walks in macro-economic time series', *Journal of Economic Dynamics and Control*, vol. 12, pp. 297–332.

Persson, Torsten and Guido Tabellini (1991) *Macroeconomic Policy, Credibility and Politics: Fundamentals of Pure and Applied Economics* (Chur: Harwood Academic Publishers).

Pesaran, M. H. and R. P. Smith (1985) 'Evaluation of macroeconometric models', *Economic Modelling* (London: Butterworth, April).

Pflanze, Otto (1990) *Bismark and the Development of Germany* (Princeton, NJ: Princeton University Press).
Pickersgill, Joyce (1976) 'Soviet household saving behaviour', *Review of Economics and Statistics*, vol. 58 (May), pp. 139–47.
Pickersgill, Joyce (1980) 'Recent evidence on soviet household saving behaviour', *Review of Economics and Statistics*, November, pp. 628–33.
Pickersgill, Joyce (1983) 'Household saving in the USSR', in F. Modigliani and R. Hemming (eds), *The Determinants of National Saving and Wealth* (London: Macmillan).
Pigou, A. C. (1917) 'The value of money', *Quarterly Journal of Economics*, vol. 37, pp. 38–65.
Pindak, F. (1983) 'Inflation under central planning', *Jahrbuch der Wirtschaft Osteuropas*, vol. 10, no. 2, pp. 93–131.
Portes, R. (1979) 'The control of inflation: lessons from East European experience', *Economica*, vol. 44, no. 174 (May), pp. 9–29.
Portes, R. (1983) 'Central Planning and Monetarism: Fellow Travellers', in Padma Desai (ed.), *Marxism, Central Planning and the Soviet Economy* (Cambridge, Mass.: MIT Press).
Portes, R. (1989) 'The theory and measurement of macroeconomic disequilibrium in centrally planned economies', in Davis and Charemza.
Portes, R. (ed.) (1993) *Economic Transformation in Central Europe: a progress report* (London: Centre for Economic Policy Research).
Portes, R., R. Quandt, D. Winter and S. Yeo (1984a) 'Planning the consumption goods market: preliminary disequilibrium estimates for Poland 1955–80, in P. Malgrange and P. A. Muet (eds), *Contemporary Macroeconomic Modelling* (Oxford: Blackwell), pp. 254–71.
Portes, R., R. Quandt, D. Winter and S. Yeo (1984b) 'Estimating the size of plan errors', research memo no. 48 (Princeton University Financial Research Center).
Portes, Richard, Richard E. Quandt, David Winter and Stephen Yeo (1987) 'Macroeconomic planning and disequilibrium: estimates for Poland, 1955–1980', *Econometrica*, vol. 55, no. 1 (January), pp. 19–41.
Portes, R., Richard E. Quandt and Stephen Yeo (1988) 'Tests of the Chronic Shortage Hypothesis: The Case of Poland', *Review of Economics and Statistics*, vol. lxx, no. 2 (May).
Portes, R. and A. Santorum (1987) 'Money and the consumption goods market in China', *Journal of Comparative Economics*, vol. 11, pp. 354–71.
Portes, R. and D. Winter (1978) 'The demand for money and for consumption goods in CPEs', *Review of Economics and Statistics*, vol. 60, pp. 8–18.
Portes, Richard and David Winter (1980) 'Disequilibrium estimates for consumption goods markets in centrally planned economies', *Review of Economics and Statistics*, vol. 47, pp. 137–59.
Prais, S. J. (1979) *Productivity and Industrial Structure, a statistical study of manufacturing industry in Britain, Germany and the United States*, Economic and Social Studies (Cambridge University Press).
Prindl, A. R. (1981a) *Japanese Finance: a guide to banking in Japan* (London: Wiley).
Prindl, A. R. (1981b) *Money in the Far East* (London: Wiley).

Qin, D., T. Wang, M. Zhou and Q. Liu (1992) 'Money Demand in China: the Effect of Economic Reform', paper no. 281 (Department of Economics, Queen Mary and Westfield College, the University of London).

Radcliffe-Brown, A. R. (1979) *Structure and Function in Primitive Society: essays and addresses* (London: Routledge & Kegan Paul).

Rajan, R. G. (1991) 'Insiders and Outsiders: The Choice between Informed and Arm's-Length', Working Paper (University of Chicago, December).

Riecke, Werner and Laszlo Antal (1993) *Hungary: sound money, fiscal problems. Hungary: An Economy in Transition,* edited by Istvan Szekely and David M G Newbery (Cambridge University Press).

Rodrik, Dani (1994a) 'King Kong Meets Godzilla: The World Bank and the East Asian Miracle', CEPR discussion paper no. 944 (London: CEPR, April).

Rodrik, Dani (1994b) 'Getting Interventions Right: How South Korea and Taiwan Grew Rich', paper presented at the twentieth panel meeting of Economic Policy, hosted by the Deutsche Bundesbank (Frankfurt, 21–2 October).

Roll, Eric (1993) 'Independent and Accountable: A New Mandate for the Bank of England' (London: Centre for Economic Policy Research).

Romashkin, (1979) 'Zakonodatel'nyye' (1961), in Zwass (1979).

Roosa, R. (1951) 'Interest rates and the central bank', in *Money, Trade and Economic Growth: Essays in Honour of John H. Williams* (New York: Macmillan), pp. 270–95.

Rose, A. K. (1985) 'An alternative approach to the American demand for money', *Journal of Money, Credit and Banking,* vol. 17, no. 4, pp. 439–55.

Rosefielde, Steven (1988) 'The Soviet economy in crisis: Birman's cumulative disequilibrium hypothesis', *Soviet Studies,* vol. 40, no. 2 (April), pp. 222–44.

Rostowski, J. (1992) 'A proposal on how to introduce a currency board based monetary system in the Republic of Latvia', discussion paper no. 23 (London: LSE, Centre of Economic Performance).

Rostowski, J. (1993) 'The Inter-enterprise Debt Explosion in the Former Soviet Union: Causes, Consequences, Cures', discussion paper no. 142 (London: LSE, Centre for Economic Performance).

Rudcenko, S. (1978) 'Household money income, expenditure and monetary assets in Czechoslovakia, GDR, Hungary and Poland, 1956–1975', discussion paper in economics no. 46 (revised) (London: Birkbeck College); *Jahrbuch der Wirtschaft Osteuropas,* vol. 8, pp. 431–50.

Rudolph, Richard, L. (1976) *Banking and Internationalization in Austria-Hungary, The Role of Banks in the Industrialization of Czech Crownlands* (Cambridge University Press).

Sachs, Jeffrey D. and W. Woo (1994) 'Reform in China and Russia', *Economic Policy,* vol. 18, pp. 101–31.

Sargent, T. J. (1979) *Macroeconomic Theory* (New York: Academic Press).

Sargent, T. J. (1982) 'The Ends of Four Big Inflations', in R. Hall (ed.), *Inflation* (Chicago: Chicago University Press).

Schumpeter, J. A. (1934) *Theory of Economic Development* (Cambridge, Mass.: Harvard University Press).

Schwert, G. W. (1987) 'The Effects of Model Specification on Tests for Unit Roots in Macroeconomic Data', *Journal of Monetary Economics,* vol. 20, pp. 73–103.

Sharpe, S. (1990) 'Asymmetric information, bank lending and implicit contracts: a stylized model of customer relationships', *Journal of Finance*, vol. 45 (September).

Shaw, Edward S. (1973) *Financial Deepening in Economic Development* (New York: Oxford University Press).

Sheng, Mujia (1989) *The Theories of Central Banking* (Beijing: China Banking Press) (in Chinese).

Shi, Shuenhua and Cai Yeohua (1993) 'On Several Urgent Issues of Strengthening the Central Bank's Functions', *Jingji Tizhi Gaige (Economic System Reforms)* (April) (in Chinese).

Shleifer, A. and L. Summers (1988) 'Breach of Trust in Hostile Takeovers', in Alan J. Auerbach (ed.), *Corporate Takeovers: Causes and Consequences* (Chicago: National Bureau of Economic Research).

Shu, Xin (1992) 'On the puzzle over the triangles, lines, points and two dimensions of debts', *Zhongguo Jingji Tizhi Gaige (China Economic System Reform,* no. 1 (in Chinese) (Beijing: State Commission for Restructuring Economic Systems PRC).

Sik, Ota and Marian Sling (1976) *The Third Way: Marxist–Leninist theory and modern industrial society,* translated by Marian Sling (London: Wildwood House).

Smith, B. D. (1984) 'Private Information, Deposit Interest Rates, and the "Stability" of the Banking System', *Journal of Monetary Economics*, vol. 14, no. 3 (November).

Sokil, C. and T. King (1989) 'Financial Reform in Socialist Economies: Workshop Overview', EDI Seminar Series (Washington, DC: World Bank).

Song, Guoqing (1988) 'Monetary policy under the dual price system', *Jingji Yangjiu (Economic Research),* no. 5 (in Chinese) pp. 18–25.

Soviet Financial System, The (1966, 1969, 1971) written by a group of authors at the Moscow Financial Institute, directed by D. A. Allakhverdyan.

State Statistic Bureau of China (SSB) *State Statistical Yearbook*, various issues (Beijing: SSB Press).

Stiglitz, J. E. (1985) 'Credit Markets and the Control of Capital', *Journal of Money, Credit and Banking*, vol. 17, no. 2 (May).

Stiglitz, J. E. (1993) 'Overview', in Alberto Giovannini (ed.), *Finance and Development: Issues and Experience* (Cambridge University Press).

Stiglitz, J. E. and A. Weiss (1981) 'Credit rationing in markets with imperfect information', *American Economic Review*, vol. 71, no. 3 (June), pp. 393–401.

Stiglitz, J. and A. Weiss (1983) 'Incentive Effects of Terminations: Applications to the Credit and Labour Markets', *American Economic Review*, vol. 73 (December), pp. 912–27.

Stiglitz, J. and A. Weiss (1987) 'Credit rationing with many borrowers', *American Economic Review*, vol. 77, pp. 228–31.

Sung, Zhengdong (1991) 'On the "Triangular Debt" Crisis and the Implementation of the Bankruptcy System', *Zhongguo Jingji Tizhi Gaige (China Economic System Reform)* (Beijing: State Commission for Restructuring Economic Systems PRC, January) (in Chinese).

Suranyi, L. and Gy Antal (1987) 'The Prehistory of the Reform of Hungary's Banking System', *Acta Oeconomica*, vol. 38, nos 1–2, p. 46.

Suzuki, Y. (1980) *Money and Banking in Contemporary Japan: the theoretical setting and its application*, translated by John G. Greenwood (New Haven: Yale University Press).

Suzuki, Y. (1986) *Money, Finance, and Macroeconomic Performance in Japan*, translated by Robert Alan Feldman (New Haven: Yale University Press).

Suzuki, Y. (1987) *The Japanese Financial System* (Oxford: Clarendon Press).

Sylla, R. (1988) 'The Autonomy of Monetary Authorities: The Case of the US Federal Research System', in Gianni Tonido (ed.), pp. 17–38.

Szalkai, Istvan (1990) *A monetaris iranyitas, Elmelet es gyakorlat* (Budapest: Kozgadasagi es Jogi Konyvkiado).

Szekely, I. (1990) 'The Reform of the Hungarian Financial System', *European Economy*, vol. 49 (Belgium: Commission of European Communities).

Tam, On Kit (1992) 'A Private Bank in China: Hui Tong Urban Co-operative Bank', *China Quarterly*, vol. 131 (September), pp. 766–77.

Tang, Xiaoqing (1990) 'The Causes and the Solutions of the "Triangular Debts"', mimeo (in Chinese) (Beijing, July).

Taylor, Lance (1979) *Macro Models for Developing Countries* (New York: McGraw-Hill).

Taylor, Lance (1981) 'IS/LM in the Tropics: Diagrammatics of the New Structuralist Macro Critique', in William R. Cline and Sidney Weintraub (eds), *Economic Stabilization in Developing Countries* (Washington, DC: Brookings Institution), pp. 465–503.

Taylor, Lance (1983) *Structuralist Macroeconomics: Applicable Models for the Third World* (New York: Basic Books).

Taylor, Lance (1993) book review, *Journal of Economic Literature*, vol. xxxi (March), pp. 279–80.

Taylor, M. P. (1987) 'Financial innovation, inflation and the stability of the demand for broad money in the United Kingdom', *Bulletin of Economic Research*, vol. 39, no. 3, pp. 225–33.

Thorne, Alfredo (1989) 'Why a market solution to financial crisis might be infeasible: the case for the restructuring of financial systems through the analysis of twelve cases', 2 documents (Washington, DC: The World Bank, October).

Tobin, J. (1956) 'The Interest-Elasticity of Transaction Demand for Cash', *Review of Economic and Statistics*, vol. 38, pp 241–7.

Tobin, James (1965) 'Money and Economic Growth', *Econometrica*, vol. 33, no. 4 (October), pp. 671–84.

Tobin, J. (1984) 'On the efficiency of the financial system', *Lloyds Bank Review* (July).

Tobin, J. (1985) 'Financial Innovation and Deregulation in Perspective', *Bank of Japan Monetary and Economic Studies*, vol. 3.

Tobin, J. and D. Hester (1963) *Financial Intermediaries and Economic Activity*.

Tonido, Gianni (ed.) (1988) *Central Banks' Independence in Historical Perspective* (Berlin and New York: Walter de Gruyter).

Townsend, R. (1979) 'Optimal contracts and competitive markets with costly state verification', *Journal of Economic Theory*, vol. 13, pp. 137–51.

Tsutui, Yushiro (1990) 'Japan's Banking Industry: Collusion under Regulation', *Japanese Economic Studies* (Spring).

Van Wijnbergen, Sweder (1982) 'Stagflationary Effects of Monetary Stabilization Policies: A Quantitative Analysis of South Korea', *Journal of Development Economics*, vol. 10, no. 2 (April), pp. 133–69.

Van Wijnbergen, Sweder (1983a) 'Interest Rate Management in LDCs', *Journal of Monetary Economics*, vol. 12, no. 3 (September), pp. 433–52.

Van Wijnbergen, Sweder (1983b) 'Credit Policy, Inflation and Growth in a Financially Repressed Economy', *Journal of Development Economics*, vol. 13, no. 1–2 (August–October), pp. 45–65.

Van Wijnbergen, Sweder (1985) 'Macro-economic Effects of Changes in Bank Interest Rates: Simulation Results for South Korea', *Journal of Development Economics*, vol. 18, no.s 2–3 (August), pp. 541–54.

Varhegyi, E. (1993) 'The modernization of the Hungarian banking sector', in I. P. Szekely and D. M. G. Newbery (eds), *Hungary: an economy in transition* (Cambridge University Press), pp. 149–62.

Vives, X. (1991) 'Banking competition and European integration', in A. Giovannini and C. Mayer (eds), *European Financial Integration* (Cambridge University Press), pp. 9–31.

Vogel, Robert C. (1979) 'Barriers to Financial Reform', paper presented at the Second International Conference on Rural Finance (Calgary, Canada, 29 August–1 September).

Volcker, Paul (1990) 'The Role of Central Banks', paper presented at a symposium on Central Bank Issues in Emerging Market Oriented Economies', sponsored by the Federal Reserve Bank of Kansas City, pp. 2–3.

Von Thadden, E. L. (1991) 'The term-structure of investment and the limits to the banks' insurance function', WWZ discussion paper no. 9107.

Wadhwani, S. B. (1988) 'On the Inefficiency of Financial Markets', *LSE Quarterly*, vol. 2, no. 1 (Spring).

Wang, Chuende, Qichao Huang and Min Li (1991) 'From the accumulation of consumption goods to the solution for the problems of the "triangular debts": an investigation of the interenterprise debts of the light and textile industry in Shanshi', *Zhongguo Jinrong* (*China Finance*) (Beijing: People's Bank of China, September) (in Chinese).

Wang, Guangan (1987) *Caizheng Jinrong Yanjiu* (*Research on Budget and Finance*) (Beijing, February) (in Chinese).

Wang, Guangqian (1990) *The Experience and Lessons of the Financial Reforms in the Last Ten Years* (Beijing: The Central Financial University) (in Chinese).

Wang, Jiye (1990) 'On the proper speed of economic growth', mimeo (Beijing: The State Planning Commission, June) (in Chinese).

Wang, Jiye and Yuenzhen Zhu (1987) *Manual of Economic System Reform* (Beijing: Economic Daily Press).

Wang, Kerhua (1989) *Socialist Money and Banking* (Wuhan: Wuhan University Press) (in Chinese).

WIIW (1993) 'Transition from the Command to the Market System: what went wrong and what to do now?', mimeo (Vienna: WIIW (The Vienna Institute for Comparative Economic Studies, March).

Winiecki, Jan (1985) 'Portes ante portas: a critique of the revisionist interpretation of inflation under central planning', *Comparative Economic Studies*, vol. 27, no. 2 (Summer), pp. 25–51.

World Bank (1989) *Annual Report* (Washington, DC: World Bank).

Wu, Qingcheng (1990) 'How to Develop a Financial Market in China', *Zhongguo Jinrong (China Finance)*, no. 9 (in Chinese).

Yan, Kalin (1992) 'Emphasis Should Be Laid on Restraining New Arrears', *Economic Daily*, 22 January (in Chinese).

Yan, Ming (1990) 'Thinking of the Reduction of Interest Rates', mimeo (Beijing, July) (in Chinese).

Yanelle, M. O. (1991) 'On Endogenous Intermediation', mimeo; also in Matutes and Vives (1992).

Yang, Haiqun (1988) 'China's Banking System and Its Reform', M.Phil. thesis (Faculty of Applied Economics and Politics, Cambridge University, May).

Yang, Haiqun (1989) *China Steps Forward* (London: House of Commons Library and China–British Trade Group Library).

Yang, Haiqun (1994a) 'On the Control of Banks and Banking Control', *Jingji Yanjiu (Economic Research)*, no. 5 (in Chinese).

Yang, Haiqun (1994b) 'Costs and Benefits of Decentralising a Banking System in Transition', PhD thesis (Economics Department, Birkbeck College, University of London).

Yi, Gang (1993) 'Toward estimating the demand for money in China', *Economics of Planning*, vol. 26 (Netherlands), pp. 243–70.

Yin, Jingchang and Xienchang Zhang (1987) 'The Analysis, Prediction and Control of China's Social Aggregate Demand', *Tongji Yanjiu (Statistical Research)*, no. 3, pp. 13–15 (in Chinese).

Zhang, Fengbo (1988) *The Macroeconomic Structure and Policy of China* (Beijing: China Fiscal Economic Press) (in Chinese), p. 105.

Zhang, Jue (1986) 'Quantitative analysis of money in circulation', in J. P. Wu (ed.), *Applications of Econometric Methods in China* (Beijing) (in Chinese).

Zhang, Shuguang (1988) 'Preliminary analysis of China's inflation problem', *China: Development and Reform*, no. 3 (in Chinese) pp. 30–9.

Zhou, Xiaochuan and Li Zhu (1987) 'China's Banking System: Current Status, Perspective on Reform', *Journal of Comparative Economics*, vol. 11, pp. 399–409.

Zhou, Zhongqing (1995) 'Implementing an Appropriate Tight Monetary Policy and Further Strengthening Banking Supervision in Order to Cope With Inflation', *Zhongguo Jinrong (China Finance)*, vol. 2 (Beijing) (in Chinese), pp. 4–8.

Zhu, Xiangqin (1986) 'Why should it be planned low but in fact grow high?', mimeo (Institute of Planned Economy, Planning Commission of Zhejiang Province) (in Chinese).

Zhu, Yifeng (1985) *Socialist Theory of Industrial and Commercial Credits* (Beijing: People's University Press) (in Chinese).

Zoteyev, G. (1989) 'Ob otsenke valovogo natsional'nogo produkta', *Ekonomicheskaya gazeta*, vol. 42, p. 10; and 'Perestroika kak strategiya perkhodnogo perioda: Vzglyad iznutri', in Ofer (1991).

Zwass, A. (1979) *Money, Banking, and Credit in the Soviet Union and Eastern Europe*, translated by Michel C. Vale (London: Macmillan).

Index